Life After Privatization

Life After Privatization

Raj Chari

OXFORD
UNIVERSITY PRESS

OXFORD
UNIVERSITY PRESS

Great Clarendon Street, Oxford, OX2 6DP,
United Kingdom

Oxford University Press is a department of the University of Oxford.
It furthers the University's objective of excellence in research, scholarship,
and education by publishing worldwide. Oxford is a registered trade mark of
Oxford University Press in the UK and in certain other countries

First Edition published in 2015

Published in the United States of America by Oxford University Press
198 Madison Avenue, New York, NY 10016, United States of America

British Library Cataloguing in Publication Data
Data available

Library of Congress Control Number: 2014947491

ISBN 978-0-19-965831-2

Acknowledgements and Dedication

Even a single author book is a team effort. This project would not have been possible without the support of the Chief Editor of OUP, Dominic Byatt. As the coach, Dominic allowed it the necessary gestation period and, in the end, time for final delivery. OUP's three anonymous reviewers also offered wonderful insights from which the book has greatly benefited. A big thank you also goes to other members of the OUP team—particularly Olivia Wells and Ellen Carey—as well as Sarah Cheeseman, for her good eye in editing the final manuscript.

Financial assistance through the 'New Ideas' scheme from the Irish Research Council (IRC) is also gratefully acknowledged. Beyond the IRC, I am deeply indebted to Trinity's Acquisition Librarian, Arlene Healy, who came to bat for me more than once. Along with the Bureau van Dijk's Key Accounts Manager, Dan McGovern, Arlene was the playmaker who ensured long-term access to both the Zephyr and Amadeus databases. This was during times when money was probably too tight to mention for Irish universities suffering from the impact of the financial and economic crisis. Actors from firms studied (and their competitors) as well as government officials who were interviewed over the last several years, many times in anonymity, also added significant insights from which this book really became a discovery of knowledge.

I am indebted to fellow team-players who offered invaluable advice during the development of this project, and/or commented on earlier versions of the original book proposal and, later, chapters. This includes (alphabetically): Frank Baumgartner, Patrick Bernhagen, Ravi Bhargava, Sinéad Boyce, Louis Brennan, Francesco Cavatorta, David Coen, Robert Elgie, José Elguero, David Farrell, José Folgado, Michael Gallagher, Klaus Goetz, Herwig Hoffmann, Eddie Hyland, James Killick, Sylvia Kritzinger, Mik Laver, Tom Louwerse, Caroline Martin, Claire Michau, Mick Moran, Gary Murphy, Eoin O'Sullivan, Barry Rodger, Andrés Rodríguez-Pose, Rick Sandell, Michael Schütte, Jessie Smith, Peter Stone, Robert Thomson, Benigno Valdés, and Peter Wells. I am particularly indebted to the Research Assistants from TCD who have worked on the project over the past five years: Michele Crepaz, Svenja Dahlmann, Anna Gavigan, Diego Scarbelli, Laura Schwirz, Manuela Sola, Adrian Sonder, Laura Sudulich, and Matt Wall. Two of my PhD students beyond Crepaz—Kristin

Semancik and Mark Carpenter—offered their careful eye reading some of the chapters.

More personally, I am indebted to the game-changers, including: *mis chicas*, Isabel and Celia ('Have you not finished the book yet?'); my friend Jeremy ('Just tell me what the rules are, Raj'); and Stephen and Pascale ('Stay with us anytime you come to Brussels'). In Madrid, José Juan, Juana, Juan Carlos, Julio, Luis, and Santi were sources of perspective and laughs.

Stealing home, this book is dedicated to the memories of the late Duff Spafford (1936–2014) and the late Vincent Wright (1937–99). The memories, as Dick Johnston stated on Duff's recent passing, are acute and warm—and all the more painful for that. Mine are as follows.

After I switched from studying chemistry to political science in the early 1990s when pursuing my undergraduate degree at the University of Saskatchewan in Canada, Duff's wonderfully mathematical mind guided that transition. He did so by teaching in a way few professors do and offering no-nonsense guidance with a human touch. His methods courses, in particular, served as a necessary bridge to understand how social science investigation should be done, with or without numbers. After many years of visiting him and his wife Shirley when in Saskatoon with *mis chicas*, in our last conversation in the summer of 2012 I lamented that some recent scholarship has conflated 'methods' with 'quants'. The latter, I told Duff, was sometimes no more than simple statistical analysis which has become fashionable, a far cry from being methodologically rigorous. His smiling response was, 'You are trained in natural science—the only thing that's really saved you—why would you let this bother you?'

Vincent's scholarship equally set the tone for many of us whom he taught and generously mentored. Those of us fortunate to have worked with him realize that he also shaped many aspects of our lives. Perhaps more importantly, as Martha Peach would say, we all have our 'Vincent story'. Here is mine. In the late 1990s I was a PhD student from Queen's University (Canada) whom Vincent took under his wing when I was based out of the Juan March Institute in Madrid. Born and raised in Canada, I thought it important for my then young daughter, Celia, to celebrate Halloween. I thus wanted to bring her to the *Instituto* to 'trick or treat'. Earlier that morning, I asked Vincent, 'Celia is coming this afternoon, dressed as a witch—would you like to meet her?' His response was a swift, 'No, I hate children.' I left depressed, but determined she still show up. When she did, Celia eventually received candy and conversation from many, even the hypocritical intellectuals who denied that privatization took place under the Spanish Socialists. Yet, there was no sign of Vincent. Some days later he asked, 'So I am going back to Nuffield College. Anything I can send to you from Oxford?' Still offended that he did not want to see my child, I chanced, 'Well, as you know, Celia was born in Madrid. But, I am slightly concerned that she's only speaking in Spanish and it would be great if she could watch a movie in English.' I expected nothing to come out of his swearing as he was writing on his yellow pad. Within days, however, I received a 'Winnie the Pooh' VHS tape, which I later found out he sent through Stephanie Wright with whom he worked and whom Celia eventually met years later in the spring of 2012.

Nothing shocked Vincent about privatization, as nothing fazed Duff about politics. Notwithstanding, I am certain that both would be concerned about some aspects of the life of privatized firms in a Europe my now bilingual daughter inherits. I'm not sure of their advice, but neither would start by giving candy.

Dublin and Madrid,
July 2014

Table of Contents

List of Figures

List of Tables

1

Remembering Privatization and Conceptualizing Life Thereafter: Alphas and Betas

We know that European countries have privatized state-owned enterprises (SOEs) since the late 1970s. But, what happened to these firms after privatization? In order to help answer this question, this chapter's main objective is to offer a fresh conceptualization of life after privatization. This will serve as a basis to set up the main questions guiding the book.

The chapter has three main sections. In the first, I review two sets of literature that have yet to fully meet eye to eye: that on privatizations and that on mergers and acquisitions (M&A). I start with a brief review of the privatization literature, highlighting ideas raised by scholars regarding what motivated sales of state-owned firms. Specific attention is then paid to developments in five main countries that represent *the* EU's 'biggest privatizers': the UK, France, Italy, Germany, and Spain. This section continues by reviewing the multi-disciplinary nature of the M&A literature. Using data before and after the recent financial economic crisis, it then analyses trends over time regarding worldwide and European M&A, highlighting again the importance of these five states.

The second section then considers the inefficiencies in the extant literature in the context of some significant observations over the last fifteen years. These observations points to a significant trend in the evolution of privatized firms. The trend identified is rather simple, but neither fully reported nor theoretically conceptualized in the literature. On the one hand, some privatized firms have become today's European and global giants, merging with or acquiring other firms. I refer to these firms as 'Alphas'. On the other hand, some privatized firms have been taken over by Alphas or other leading companies in the sector. I refer to these as 'Betas'. The Alpha–Beta classification scheme is significant because it is based on robust empirical tests

I develop—referred to as the 'Global Movers' and 'Independence' tests—that can be applied by social scientists to any privatized firm that operates today, from any European country, from any sector.

Both of these sections serve as the basis for the third, concerned with setting up the central questions that guide the rest of the book: which privatized firms are Alphas and Betas? And *why* do firms become Alphas or Betas? I highlight three reasons why asking these questions are significant and close by highlighting the structure of the book.

1.1 Remembering Privatizations, Considering Mergers and Acquisitions (M&A), and the Need to Move Beyond

The Privatization Debate: What Motivated Privatizations?

Throughout the 1980s and 1990s there was a significant rise in social science scholarship examining privatizations in Western Europe. Led by the pioneering works of Vickers and Wright (1989) and Moran and Prosser (1994), scholars commented on at least four main, oftentimes overlapping, dimensions that helped motivate the sale of state-owned enterprises (SOEs).

First, authors considered the *ideological* and *partisan* dimension: in answering the question 'why did countries choose to privatize in the first place?', attention was especially paid to initial developments under Thatcher's UK (see Moore, 1983; Veljanovski and Bentley, 1987). Vickers and Wright (1989, 5) highlighted that right-wing (or centre–right) parties were ideologically motivated to shrink the state and 'free' the economy. In Feigenbaum et al.'s view, such sales would be representative of *systemic privatizations* that are 'the most ideological in their origins' and with goals 'to restructure the institutional arrangements of society . . . initially intended and ultimately likely to shrink the state . . .' (Feigenbaum et al., 1999, 51, 52). Analysing developments throughout the OECD, Boix's work (1997) contended that the empirical evidence does indeed demonstrate that right-wing governments privatized more than left-wing governments. Yet, data from Maudit (2002) and from Berne and Pogorel (2004) shows that gross privatization incomes in France, for example, were actually equally significant for the left (Jospin, 1997–2002 at 31 billion EUR) and the right (Chirac, 1986–8, 13 billion; Balladur, 1993–5, 17 billion; and Juppé, 1995–7, 9.4 billion). As we will discuss later, others have also contended that the left, especially in countries like Spain, engineered a good number of sales of state assets throughout the 1980s and 1990s (Heywood, 1995).

Second, on a *financial* dimension, authors such as Vickers and Wright (1989, 5) argued that selling the state could help, on the one hand, to raise revenue by floating profitable firms. On the other, privatization could also save the state cash by selling loss-making firms that represented a long-term drain on Treasuries. Feigenbaum et al. (1998, 44) conceptualized such sales as *pragmatic privatizations*, which are 'short term solutions to immediate problems such as the need for cash'. For states such as Spain and Italy, for example, this was crucial, particularly in the context of both EU competition policies which demanded that state aid be reduced and EMU convergence criteria that required limits to deficits and debts (Chari, 1998). Another financial reason for privatization is that 'it fosters the growth of domestic stock exchange' (Wright, 1994, 17). Both Wright (1998) and Thatcher (2006), for example, have demonstrated that sales of state assets helped enlarge the capital base of the Paris Bourse and the Madrid Stock Exchange.

Third, on an *economic* dimension, Vickers and Yarrow (1991), Majone (1994), and Wright (1994, 15–16) paid attention to the economic goals and impact of privatization. Based on the assumption that the public sector 'works' worse than the 'private sector', the argument here is that privatization was seen as a means to increase efficiency of the firms (although studies have demonstrated mixed results (Villalonga, 2000)). Further, selling state assets was seen as a tool to increase the liberalization in sectors with monopolies. In this regard, Clifton et al. (2006, 752) highlight the importance of EU liberalization initiatives which acted as a 'catalyst' for sales of telecom, transport, and electricity firms in the continent.

Finally, although not a motivator per se, privatization helped scholars understand, to put it simply, how government worked. This was seen in the works of Young (1986), Megginson and Netter (2003), and Graham (2003) that focused on the methods, techniques, types, and processes of privatization. While some governments pursued privatizations in a relatively open and transparent environment, others pursued the policy in more opaque settings. During the French privatization process, for example, 'coordination has been either centralised and focused or fragmented—depending on the size, sector, industrial significance and method of privatization, its political dimension, its linkage with other policies, and the internal dynamics of the government' (Wright, 1998, 8). Also, as demonstrated by Clift's work, the French case sees the state playing a 'strategic role' by 'handpicking *noyau dur* or hard core "friendly" institutional investors', as seen in the case of France Télécom (Clift, 2001, 174). In the case of Spain, economic elites (particularly the banks) were heavily involved in the sales and bought large tranches of the profitable companies being sold (Chari and Cavatorta, 2002). Like Italy, the coordination process in Spain was a tightly centralized one that revolved around key members of the core executive, including the Ministries of Economy and Finance as well as Industry (Chari and Heywood, 2009).

The Main Privatizers in the EU: Comparing the Big 5

These dimensions aside, a simple question worth reflecting on after thirty-five years when the main privatizations started in the late 1970s is: what are the main SOEs that EU countries sold? While it is impossible to consider the sales in all of the EU, it is noteworthy to consider the main privatizations in five major EU states—the UK, Spain, Italy, Germany, and France.

Why these countries? The reason that these states are particularly significant is not only because they are representative of leading European economies, but also because they rank amongst the top five of the EU-25 in terms of revenues generated since they started their own privatization programmes, as seen in Table 1.1.

To gain a better comparative understanding of the evolution of privatization revenues over time in each of the main five countries, Figure 1.1 shows the yearly revenue generated by privatizations between 1979 and 2011 in the UK, France, Italy, Germany, and Spain.

Four overall trends can be discerned from Figure 1.1. First, the UK attained its peak revenues throughout the 1980s and early 1990s, indicating that it

Table 1.1. EU-25, Total Privatization Revenues

Country	Total Privatization Revenues (current US$ billion, 2011)	Rank
France	217.20	1
Italy	173.37	2
UK	153.38	3
Germany	137.57	4
Spain	55.92	5
Netherlands	52.34	6
Sweden	49.86	7
Poland	42.81	8
Portugal	40.80	9
Greece	33.70	10
Finland	30.28	11
Czech Rep	19.74	12
Austria	18.80	13
Hungary	16.25	14
Ireland	15.76	15
Denmark	9.46	16
Belgium	9.16	17
Slovakia	8.22	18
Latvia	3.40	19
Slovenia	3.13	20
Lithuania	3.10	21
Estonia	1.28	22
Malta	0.84	23
Luxembourg	0.44	24
Cyprus	0.01	25

Source: Privatization Barometer database for privatization revenues, available at <www.privatizationbarometer.net> [accessed 26 February 2013]

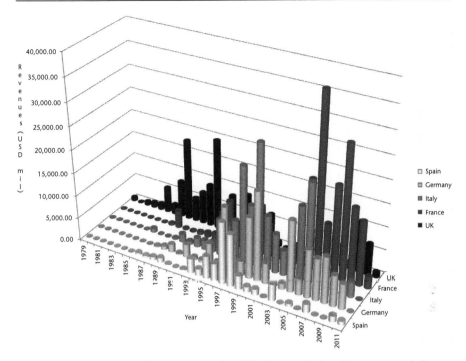

Figure 1.1. Privatization Revenues in the UK, France, Italy, Germany, and Spain, 1979–2011

Source: Author elaboration of data from Privatization Barometer, available at <www.privatization-barometer.net> [accessed 26 February 2013]

privatized first and more profoundly before any of the other four states. Second, although privatizing since the mid-1980s, France's revenues hardly attained UK levels in the 1980s but, rather, only attained their highest levels from the mid-2000s, particularly 2005. This year thus represents the highest levels in relative terms to the other four countries throughout the entire time period. This indicates that even though France pursued some of its most significant revenue-generating privatizations later than other states, such sales generated, comparatively, the highest incomes. Third, although relatively little was generated in the 1980s, Italy attained some of the highest revenues when compared to the others and peaked throughout the late 1990s. Similarly, while Germany did see some revenues generated in the second half of the 1980s in a similar vein to France, its maximum value was obtained throughout a time period between 1996 and 2000 in the same vein to Italy (even though absolute revenues were relatively lower). Finally, while Spain's revenues generally pale in comparison to the other four states throughout every year in the time series, the country's revenues tended to increase throughout the late 1990s and early 2000s.

5

To better understand these trends it is useful to review the main sales throughout these years. Indeed, several authors have provided in-depth analysis of privatizations in their countries over the last thirty years, including: on the UK, Parker (2004); on France, Berne and Pogorel (2004); on Italy, Goldstein (2004); on Germany, Benz and Goetz (1996); and on Spain, Chari and Heywood (2009). While it is beyond the objective of this section to analyse every sale, it is important to consider these authors' observations regarding each country's main privatizations in context of the observations found in Figure 1.1. We will discuss each country in turn, starting with *the* pioneers: the UK.

As is well known, the most significant privatizations in the UK took place under Conservative rule, particularly that of Margaret Thatcher between 1979 and 1990 but also that of John Major thereafter. With this in mind, it makes sense that revenues generated during the 1980s until the mid-1990s represent the highest levels for the UK in Figure 1.1. Parker (2004, 31–2) offers a full list of *all* the sales in the UK, and an initial, noteworthy, privatization by Thatcher was British Petroleum (first tranche 1979, second tranche 1983, and third tranche 1987). Following this was British Aerospace (1981 and 1985), as well as Cable and Wireless (1981, 1983, and 1985). Figure 1.1 indicates that 1984 represented one of the first years when revenues were around USD 5 billion with the flotation of the first tranche of British Telecom (BT, the second and third tranches were sold in 1991 and 1993), Enterprise Oil, and Jaguar. After the 1986 sale of British Gas, 1987 represented the second highest year of revenues generated, with the sale of British Airways (BA), the British Airports Authority, Rolls Royce, and the final tranche of BP. In 1989 the sales of several water companies were witnessed, while 1990 and 1991 (which represented the highest revenue-generating year in the UK of all years) saw significant privatizations in the electricity sector, including the sales of Scottish Hydro-Electric and Scottish Power. Even after the Labour Party was elected in 1997, there were some significant sales of remaining firms in the energy sector, including Magnox Electric (1998), Westinghouse Electric (2006), and the remaining shares of British Energy (2009). The UK privatization experience indicates that, today, the state generally has no remaining participation in the firms it has privatized and has generally favoured the 100 per cent sales of all its SOEs, something that is somewhat dissimilar to France, to which we now turn.

If the UK's main revenues can be seen in the beginning of the time period of Figure 1.1, then the French experience is somewhat different: it is characteristic of local maxima (or peaks) being attained at different times (particularly in 1987, the mid-late 1990s, and then the mid-2000s on), where such maxima have a greater relative value over time. The first small peak was seen around 1987 and this corresponded to the first major round of French privatizations (1986–8) during Chirac's Conservative administration (Alexandre and Charreaux,

2004, 473). This consisted of selling banks and insurance companies (including Paribas, Société Générale, and Sogenal), as well as firms working in industry and services (such as Compagnie Générale d'Electricité, Havas, and TF1). While shareholder capitalism was promoted in the UK, early French sales favoured the creation of what is referred to as a *noyaux dur*: a select nucleus of shareholders close to the Conservatives that held significant portions of capital and control. While Mitterand's election put a glitch in the privatization programme—resulting in the so-called 'ni-ni' (neither nationalization nor privatization) period between 1988 and 1993—a second round started in 1993 after the election of the right in the French legislative elections. As demonstrated by Berne and Pogorel (2004), major revenue-generating sales in 1993 and 1994 included the state-bank BNP, the insurance group UAP, around 40 per cent of the petroleum giant Elf-Aquitaine, and approximately 30 per cent of the car maker Renault. Other major sales in the decade included a third of France Télécom (FT, 1997–8), Thomson-CSF (now Thales, 1998), and the first tranche of Air France (1999), all deemed especially important in terms of helping attain Maastricht convergence criteria. Some of these sales, such as that of the electronics firm Bull in 1997 and the washed-up bank Crédit Lyonnais in 1999, saw 'handpicking of shareholders (that) was accompanied by pre-sale capital injections to restructure loss making companies on the selling block', particularly important to minimize long-term budgetary drains on the state (Chari and Cavatorta, 2002, 127). With revenues slowing down in the first few years of the start of the decade, one may argue that a major, third, round started in 2004 over a six-year period. This included partial sales of FT (2004, 2005, and 2007), Total (2004), SNET (2004), Air France (2004), Gaz de France (GDF) (2005 and 2008), and Électricité de France (EDF) (2005, 2007). The French state maintains shareholdings in some of its privatized firms even to this day, which contrasts to the UK's general policy of complete sell-offs. This includes, for example, AF, Renault, EDF, FT, GDF-Suez, and Thales. As will be conceptualized in Chapter 2, this factor may be of salience in understanding life after privatization.

Compared to especially the UK and even France, Italian large-scale privatizations did not occur fully until 1993 (Goldstein, 2004), where Figure 1.1 indicates that a peak in revenues was generated later in the decade between 1997 and 1999. During the 1980s reconstruction took place within the IRI (Istituto per la Ricostruzione Industriale), not dissimilar to events in Spain in the Instituto Nacional de Industria, where loss-making firms such as the car maker Alfa Romeo were sold. But it was only from 1993 that revenue-generating sales in banking and insurance companies took place over the next three years, including: Credito Italiano (1993), Banca Commerciale Italiana (1994), Istituto Mobiliare Italiano (IMI, tranches sold in 1994, 1995, and 1996), and the insurance company INA (tranches in 1994, 1995, and 1996). Thereafter, with Prodi's centre–left coalition in power, a peak was manifest starting in 1997 until 1999, a year that represents the highest level of revenue obtained by Italy in the time series. Goldstein (2004, 8) argues that 'activity over these three years represented roughly two-thirds (65.11%) of the 1992–2000 total'. Key sales in this period included: over 30 per cent of the electricity giant ENEL, representing one of the largest gross proceeds ever seen in an Italian privatization (Goldstein, 2004, Table 2); around 40 per cent of Telecom Italia (fully sold off by 2003); a further tranche of the airline Alitalia of around 20 per cent; the third and fourth tranches of the petroleum company ENI; and a majority sell-off of Banca Nazionale Lavoro. While revenues slowed over the next three years, in 2003 under Berlusconi one can see another wave starting, with peaks in 2004–5 in Figure 1.1 reflecting the large sales of Terna (the electricity grid, in 2004 and 2005) as well as approximately another 30 per cent of ENEL (2003–5). Similar to the UK, Italy has divested completely in state-owned enterprises in most sectors including the automobile, airline, and telecom sectors; but, similar to France, the state retains to this day partial ownership in firms such as ENEL and ENI in the electricity and petroleum sectors.

As a consequence of the 1983 privatization policy of Kohl's Christian Democratic coalition, Germany's privatization revenues started to peak slightly in the second half of the 1980s, not dissimilar to the smaller revenues generated in France during that time. This corresponded to the partial sale of VW, where 60 per cent was previously sold in Adenauer's Germany in 1961 (Clifton et al., 2006, 741). It also included a majority stake in the energy company VEBA. The period thereafter, until 1993, coincided with the restructuring of firms from East Germany, resulting in thousands of privatization transactions that were not profitable per se (Benz and Goetz, 1996). Throughout the 1990s, an increase in revenues would start again with the sales of the airline Lufthansa, the lignite producer Laubag, and the bank Bankgesellschaft Berlin. Although there were slight dips in revenues in 1997 and 1998 (where 1998 was the year when the SPD-Greens led by Schröder were elected), somewhat similar trends in terms of maximum revenues were seen in the second half of the 1990s, like in Italy: 1996, 1999, and 2000 witnessed some of the highest revenues obtained. This corresponded to the sale of Deutsche Telekom (three tranches in 1996, 1999, and 2000), the IPO of Deutsche Post, and the privatization of the water company Berliner Wasserbetriebe. Despite the slowdown in 2000–3, post 2004 saw a pick-up in revenues corresponding to the fourth tranche of DT in 2004, the sales by Merkel of the company operating Frankfurt Airport, Fraport, as well as the fourth tranche of Deutsche Post in the latter part of the decade. Interestingly, similar to France, the German state maintains shares in significant companies such as VW, Deutsche Telekom, and E.ON (which is a product of a merger between VEBA and VIAG as discussed later in the book).

Finally, turning to Spain, although revenues generated throughout the time period shown in Figure 1.1 were relatively much smaller than the other four states, its overall privatization revenue trend line is somewhat similar to Italy on two fronts. First, little was generated in the 1980s because the decade consisted not so much of large-scale privatizations of profitable enterprises, save the partial sales of both the electricity company Endesa and the petroleum giant Repsol. Rather, the 1980s largely consisted of restructuring and selling several loss-making firms belonging to the Institute Nacional de Industria (INI) in a similar vein to developments in Italy's IRI. Examples of these firms sold by the Felipe González's Socialists (PSOE) included the automobile maker SEAT as well as the truck maker ENASA (Chari, 1998). Second, similar to Italy, Spain's large-scale privatizations gained momentum starting in 1993, culminating in the highest revenues being obtained at the end of the 1990s, as seen in Figure 1.1. Between 1993 and 1996 the minority PSOE government floated the bank Argentaria (1993), a second and third tranche of Repsol (1993, 1995), a second tranche of Endesa (1994), a majority of the electronics firm ASDL (1994), as well as the tranches of both Telefónica and the leading European producer of eucalyptus pulp, ENCE (1995). This process was accelerated by Aznar's centre–right minority PP government which came to power in 1996, resulting in revenues that peaked in the mid–late 1990s. Such a peak can be explained because the PP had completed the sales of Telefónica, Endesa, Repsol, and ENCE, and also sold 52 per cent of the tobacco company Tabacalera (Chari and Heywood, 2009, 37). Although revenue slowed in 1999, this year the PP embarked on the important sale of Iberia airlines by way of selling 40 per cent of the firm by way of private sale in 1999 and 2000, and then floating the rest in 2001. Other major sales in the 2000s include that of the PP in 2003 of the highway construction firm ENA, as well as that of the PSOE in 2005 of the remaining shares in Altadis (which was a company founded in 1999 through the merger of Spain's Tabacalera and French tobacco giant SEITA). In terms of ownership structures of major firms that were privatized, and similar to the UK, the Spanish state divested completely and has little state participation in major privatized firms, something that contrasts to developments particularly in France, but also Germany and Italy.

The M&A Debate

In another set of literature, scholars have been concerned about mergers and acquisitions (M&A). Although there is much debate with regard to the precise definition of both, 'a merger typically refers to two companies joining together (usually through exchange of shares) as peers to become one' (Sherman and Hart, 2006, 11). Horizontal mergers are when rivals competing in the same market merge; vertical, is when two firms with an actual buyer–seller relationship merge; and conglomerate, is when there is a combining of firms who are neither sellers in the same market, nor stand in a buyer–seller relationship (Moeller and Brady, 2007, 7–8). An acquisition (or takeover) 'typically has one company—the buyer—that purchases the assets or shares of the seller' (Sherman and Hart, 2006, 11). The target (or acquired) company no longer exists from a legal vantage. One result of an acquisition is that the management of the target is often dispensed with.

Kumar's (2012) work highlights that M&A have taken place all over the world, in every major sector of the economy. He highlights that some of the big deals have occurred in several sectors, including airlines, automobiles, electricity, telecoms, pharmaceuticals, finance, and media and entertainment. Beyond potentially penetrating new geographic regions in the world, several reasons motivate firms to pursue M&A. Moeller and Brady emphasize that the most common ones 'are claims of market power, (cost) efficiency...pure diversification, information and signaling, agency problems, managerialism (offering managers better salaries and potential for career growth)...and (the reduction of) taxes' (Moeller and Brady, 2007, 18).

Scholars from economics and law examined issues in the M&A literature starting several decades ago, writing well before those analysing privatizations previously mentioned. Earlier works on M&A reflected on the danger of concentration of economic power in a few hands (Stigler, 1950; Flynn, 1988). As Brock's (2011, 724–32) and Julius' (1990) work highlights, some of the negative consequences of a concentration of economic power in the hands of the few include: decreased consumer choice and higher prices; limited competition which prevents new market entrants; and a disproportionate influence of large firms when lobbying government. Flynn (1988, 304) thus contended that anti-trust law (as it is known in the US), or competition law (as it is referred to in the EU), should have as its goals to enshrine 'the dispersion of economic power to protect legal, social and political processes from undue economic power...(and foster) the satisfaction of consumers'.

Even though economists and legal scholars spearheaded M&A research in the beginning, today scholars from a plethora of disciplines contribute to the debate. Recent volumes from Faulkner et al. (2012) as well as McCarthy and Dolfsma (2013) highlight the importance of understanding the various dimensions of M&A from multi-disciplinary perspectives, including not only economics and law, but also business studies, cultural studies, sociology, psychology, and political science. I consider at least three main dimensions to this scholarship that one finds at present, namely: the impact of M&A on the firm, the effect on workers, and issues of regulation.

On a first dimension, as indicated earlier, scholars have offered various findings with regard to the impact of M&A on firms. For example, Brozen's (1982, 57) evidence suggests that 'concentration results in cost savings', where one generally finds that there is cost efficiency and increased productivity of two firms joining together. Yet, other studies did find that after a merger the acquirers do 'not always maintain pre-merger efficiency' (Avkiran, 1999, 1010). While the global consultancy McKinsey has highlighted that acquisitions can fail because acquirers focus on cutting costs and lose focus on protecting revenue and generating growth (Bekier et al., 2001), other scholars point to increasing firm profits. Bjorvatn (2004), for example, argues that mergers in integrated markets can be profitable, and Zademach and Rodríguez-Pose (2009) explain that in order to understand European mergers and takeovers, attention must be paid to geographical proximity as well as the firms' desire to enter into new, key markets in the Community. Other researchers warn, however, that for mergers across borders to really work, firms must pay due attention to, and respect, cultural differences (Marks and Mirvis, 2011; Ulijn et al., 2010). Finally, direct economic benefits aside, the impact of M&A on the firms' ability to pursue new Research and Development as well as patents has also been the object of investigation, although Mcdougall's (1995) and Park and Sonenshine's (2012) studies suggests that there is no positive impact per se on innovation outcomes after a merger.

A second dimension of the M&A literature has specifically examined the impact of M&A on workers. Although the negative impact on both is most commonly feared by workers and the public alike, the literature offers no consensus on what really happens to employment and wages. For example, earlier studies in the 1980s on the theme gave mixed results: in Auerbach's (1988) edited book on corporate takeovers, Brown and Medoff (1988) argued that M&A do not result in massive layoffs and decreased wages, while Farber's (1988) contribution in this volume refuted this claim. More recent studies on the US have made several opposing claims, from the argument that M&A has resulted in an increase in employment (Doytch et al., 2011), to the contention that there are positive and negative impacts on employment and wages depending on when the deals take place (Nguyen and Ollinger, 2009), to the finding that the workers in the target company experience a drop in wages and employment after deals (Xiaoyang, 2012). Other studies outside the US show that while the number of employees drops after a merger, those who stay on as staff see their wages increase (Kubo and Saito, 2012).

Of particular importance to this study is a third dimension of the M&A literature that deals with its legal and regulatory aspects from global, single-country, and regional perspectives. Globally, Dabbah and Lasok (2012) have recently offered a comparative analysis of every merger control law in seventy jurisdictions from every continent in the world. Campbell (2011a and 2011b) has similarly examined selected legal issues surrounding major M&A in Europe, North America, Latin America, and Asia and the Pacific. Gerber (2010) has also focused on national regulations and how these relate to developments in international competition law. From a more domestic-level perspective, some scholars offer single-case studies of merger control regimes in selected countries throughout the world. This includes work from Botta (2011) on Brazil and Argentina; Rizzi et al. (2012) on China; and Parker and Majumdar (2011) on the UK. And from a more regional perspective, of specific interest to this book, several scholars have offered nuanced analyses of developments in the EU. This includes, from a more legal vantage, works by Vermeylen and Vande Velde (2012) and Van Gerven (2010); and, from a more political science perspective, Cini and McGowan (2008, 127–61), Shea and Chari (2006), and Chari and Kritzinger (2006, 93–102.)

Specifically examining the EU, its Merger Control Regulation of 1989 had as its objective to prevent concentrations which would create or strengthen dominant positions, empowering DG Competition of the European Commission to investigate mergers with a Community dimension (Motta, 2004, 37). With 2004 amendments, however, DG Competition officials investigating mergers are armed with tools to also consider the potential 'impact of the merger' on the European single market (Cini and McGowan, 2008, 142), where Article 2(3) of the revamped European Merger regulation thus states that:

> A concentration which would significantly impede effective competition in the common market, or in a substantial part of it, in particular as a result of the strengthening of a dominant position, shall be declared incompatible with the common market.

Despite the so-called 'competition criteria' to judge a merger, political scientists have lamented three main dynamics in Brussels-led investigations: its narrowness, opaqueness, and subjectivity. First, because the Commission is guided by 'competition-only' criteria, officials investigating a deal do not take into consideration the potentially negative impact of M&A on workers' employment or salaries. Second, the lack of transparency when decisions are made based on competition criteria makes it unclear what data and criteria are being used in each investigation (Neven et al., 1993). As we will see in the empirical chapters, while it is true that DG Competition does explain why it reached its decisions on every case that is investigated, even the simplest data such as 'the price of the deal' is not reported. A third criticism relates to the 'politics' that may guide some decisions. For example, some members of the Council of Ministers have leaned on 'their' Commissioner in order to attain outcomes which are of national interest or seek to protect national champions (Cini and McGowan, 2008, 159; Motta and Ruta, 2011, 91). Likewise, Competition Commissioners themselves may unilaterally block/approve a deal if they think it is preferred by a member state who may have spoken publically on the issue and have vested interests to see it fail/attain regulatory approval.

Trends in M&A

While the previous discussion has offered a glimpse of some of the main issues in the M&A literature, to help further justify the countries of study in this book it is useful to consider the M&A trends from a global, regional, and domestic point of view. This will be done using data from Bureau van Dijk's Zephyr database, one of the most exhaustive databases on M&A in the world.[1] After briefly considering global trends, I consider regional developments across the world and then close with examination of domestic-level developments in Europe.

In terms of global trends, Figure 1.2 considers the overall number of deals globally.

The figure indicates that the overall trend line between 2003 and 2012 has been generally positive over the time series. However, it has seen important fluctuations. Figure 1.2's trend line indicates that the number of deals peaked in 2007, almost doubling the number in 2003. But, since then, and despite a local maximum in 2009, the overall trend between 2007 and 2012 has been decreasing. The figure indicates the negative impact of the financial and economic crisis which started after 2007 on the number of deals. Despite the financial and economic crisis, however, 2012 deal numbers are still approximately the same as 2005. This means that while there has been a slowdown since 2007 it has not necessarily been as big as one might have otherwise expected.

In order to attain a more nuanced view of regional dynamics it is useful to examine Zephyr's data on target world regions, by considering the number of deals as seen in Figure 1.3. By so doing, we can gain comparative insights of

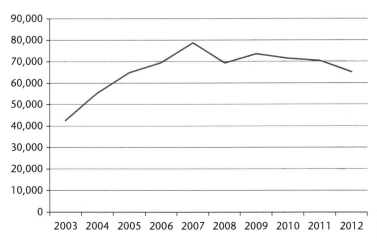

Figure 1.2. Global Number of Deals, 2003–12
Source: Zephyr

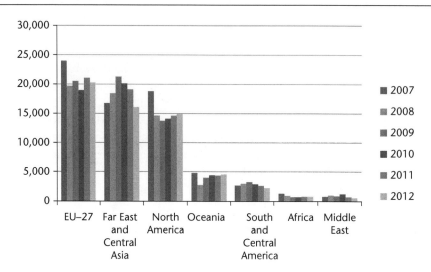

Figure 1.3. Target World Region: Number of Deals, 2007–12
Source: Zephyr

developments in the EU-27, North America, Oceania, South and Central America, and Africa between 2007 and 2012.

Data for 2012 reveals that the top three, most important target regions by the number of deals are the EU-27, followed by Far East and Central Asia, and then North America. Generally, one observes this trend in all years except 2009 (when the Far East and Central Asia had a higher value than the EU) and 2007 (when the US values were higher than the Far East and Central Asia).[2]

While Figure 1.3 considers regional dynamics—highlighting the significance of Europe in terms of overall M&A global deals—Figure 1.4 considers the main target countries in Europe by deal value.

Figure 1.4 shows the most significant targets in Europe, where the top five countries in 2012 are those studied in this book. As the Bureau van Dijk (2012, 15, 17) explains:

> [t]he UK was the most important target in Western European deal-making (followed by Spain, Germany, Italy and France), ranking highest by volume and value with 6.082 transactions, worth a combined 205,007 million (in 2012), which in monetary terms was a 21% increase on 2011. The result was impressive enough to put the UK second only to the US in terms of global M&A volume and value.

With these points in mind on both the literature on, and the trends found in, privatizations and M&A, the next section first considers why these two sets of literature need to meet eye to eye in order to move scholarship forward. It then turns to the central part of the chapter: defining the dependent variable of analysis.

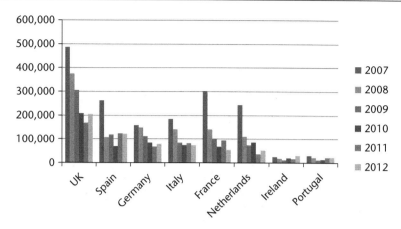

Figure 1.4. Most Important Targets in Europe by Deal Value (USD Mil), 2007–12
Source: Zephyr

1.2 The Need to Transcend the Privatization and M&A Debates: Conceptualizing Alphas and Betas

Despite the strengths of the two sets of literature discussed in the previous section—that on privatization and that on M&A—a major drawback is that they fail to meet each other. Neither examines nor explains the M&A activity of privatized firms in major European states over the last fifteen years.

This 'failure to meet' is significant precisely because of the nature of M&A activity of privatized firms which this section overviews. To be fair, some scholars in political science have analysed what subsequently happened to some firms after they were sold and what has happened to their regulatory relationships (Börsch, 2004; Thatcher, 2009). Yet, no study has offered a detailed comparative examination across various sectors analysing how and why some privatized firms might have become key global players and successfully merged and acquired, while others might have been taken over in the context of the increasing internationalization of the economy. In other words, there is a need for social scientists to focus on privatized firms as market actors in a business world where M&A is abundant.

This is a particularly significant omission considering that, writing in the mid-1990s, Jack Hayward, Vincent Wright, and their colleagues had already foreseen how 'national' champions were becoming 'European' champions that were increasingly seeking global expansion (Hayward, 1995). Yet, some twenty years on, there is no examination that fully addresses the important questions their work alludes to, namely:

- Is there evidence that privatized firms from major European countries have merged and acquired on a global scale? Of particular interest are those states examined in the previous section which have been the biggest privatizers and also witnessed a significant amount of M&A: the UK, France, Germany, Italy, and Spain.

- From a theoretical perspective, *how* can these privatized firms be characterized today (defining the dependent, or, outcome variable)?

Both of these questions are addressed in this section, setting up the main question for the book.

An initial answer to the first question is that there is strong evidence that privatized firms have merged and acquired throughout Europe and beyond over the last fifteen years.

For example, since its privatization in the 1990s, Lufthansa purchased Swiss International Airlines, BMI, Austrian Airlines, and a fifth of a stake in the US carrier jetBlue. Air France merged with KLM, later to purchase Belgium's VLM airlines and a 25 per cent controlling stake in Italy's privatized Alitalia. After a host of smaller acquisitions (such as TAT European Airlines and L'Avion) the once SOE, British Airways, has merged with Spain's Iberia Airlines forming IAG (International Airlines Group). IAG subsequently recently acquired BMI from Lufthansa. Iberia, too, had previously purchased companies such as Aerolíneas Argentinas, Vueling, and Clickair before its merger with BA.

The French automobile company Renault has formed a strategic alliance with Nissan, and has also acquired Dacia and a majority stake in Samsung Motors since its privatization. Volkswagen has added an impressive array of companies to its fleet—SEAT, Škoda, Bugatti, Lamborghini, Bentley Motors, Scania, MAN, Porsche, and, most recently, Ducati.

France's electricity company EDF has made significant purchases including London Electricity, British Energy, and US-based UniStar Nuclear Energy. Since its privatization, Spain's ex-SOE Endesa acquired a host of electric companies in South America in the 1990s through its purchase of Enersis. The Spanish company was in turn taken over by the privatized Italian company, ENEL, which also made several purchases since the 1990s.

When turning to privatized telecoms, one sees Deutsche Telekom's purchase of Max Mobile, MagyarCom, and Polska Telefonia; British Telecom's acquisitions of US-based Infonet, Radianz, and Ribbit Corporation; and France Télécom's acquisition of Orange, Spain's Amena, and Austria's One. Telefónica, with its large purchase of several carriers during the 2000s in Central and South America as well as O$_2$ and Český Telecom in Europe, now has its eye on expanding within the Brazilian market with its purchase of VIVO, as well as consolidating its position in Europe through its recent purchase of KPN's E-Plus.

One may argue that while these initial observations are important, it is necessary to try to theoretically conceptualize these developments and characterize the types of firms from any European country that have emerged after privatization. In other words, how can one better define the dependent variable of analysis for the study?

Alphas and Betas

In order to define the dependent variable, one must clearly differentiate between the terms 'mergers' and 'acquisitions'. In this regard, it is worth repeating from Sherman and Hart (2006, 11): 'a merger typically refers to two companies joining together (usually through exchange of shares) as peers to become one', while an acquisition (or takeover) 'typically has one company—the buyer—that purchases the assets or shares of the seller'. The target (or acquired) company ceases to exist legally and the management of the target is usually replaced.

With this differentiation in mind, a two-category ordinal dependent variable is constructed in order to better understand the two types of privatized firms that one sees today. I also refer to this as the 'outcome' variable: it is defined in terms of how the firm can be characterized now. I call the two types of firms one sees today 'Alphas' and 'Betas'.

On the one hand, *Alphas* are defined as today's European and global leaders in their sector that maintain their independence because they have never been taken over by another firm. After privatization, they have been expansionist and aggressive in terms of taking over other competitors around the world, or merging with them on an equal basis.

On the other hand, *Betas* are defined as those firms that are not global leaders and/or are not independent companies. The latter is because they have been acquired by an Alpha or another sectoral giant either at the point of privatization or years after privatization as a result of a friendly or hostile takeover. Some companies that are Betas today may have shown traits of being Alphas at some point in time after privatization. In fact, they may have represented leading global firms in terms of sales, assets, and profits years after their sale. They have, however, ultimately become targets of Alphas or other leading firms in the sector.

As explained more fully in the methodology section of Chapter 2, a firm must satisfy *two main empirical tests* I develop in order to be considered an Alpha. The first clearly indicates that the firm is a global giant—I refer to this as the Global Movers Test. There are two dimensions to this test and to be considered an Alpha, a privatized firm must meet these two dimensions; if a firm fails on even one, it is considered a Beta. First, in order to be considered an Alpha, a firm must appear in the most recent Forbes 2000 Index. This index is an invaluable tool referred to by international business and political leaders, as well as academics (Bernhagen and Mitchell, 2009). It measures the performance of the top 2000 global firms based on a mix of four metrics—sales, profit, assets, and market value. Second, to be considered an Alpha, a firm must appear today within the top 1 per cent of all companies in their sector in the EU-27 (hence, their peers) in terms of operating revenue/turnover, total assets, shareholder funds, and number of employees. Data from the Bureau van Dijk's (BvD) database, Amadeus, is analysed in the empirical chapters to demonstrate this second dimension to the Global Movers Test, as discussed more fully in the methodology section of Chapter 2.[3]

The second empirical test indicates that the ex-SOE has merged and acquired successfully and maintains its independence today, as it has never been successfully targeted by another firm. I refer to this as the 'independence test'. When turning to this test an Alpha must have demonstrated that, either during or after its privatization, it has not been acquired by another firm and maintains its independence, as no other company either directly, or indirectly, owns more than 25 per cent or more of the Alpha's shares. If a firm has been acquired by another firm it will be considered a Beta. To demonstrate whether or not a firm passes the 'independence test', I will rely on BvD's independence indicator, which is found in its Amadeus and Zephyr databases, as discussed more fully in the methodology section of Chapter 2. I will also argue that the two exceptions to these rules for the 'independence test' are if the state still owns more than 25 per cent of the firm after privatization, or a family with historical links to the privatized firm continues to own more than 25 per cent of it.

Taken together, the Alpha–Beta classification scheme is significant because it is based on robust empirical tests that can be applied by social scientists to any privatized firm that still operates today, from any sector, from any European country. It thus offers an objective classification scheme of *how* different privatized companies have evolved and can be characterized today.

1.3 Central Questions that Guide the Book

Considering that what has been discussed allows us to have an objective understanding of *how* privatized firms can be classified today, the main questions that therefore guide the rest of the book, which seeks to examine and explain life after privatization in the UK, France, Italy, Germany, and Spain, are:

- Which privatized firms became Alphas and Betas?
- And *why* do privatized firms become Alphas or Betas?

The first question is important because it allows us to see the development of European firms which were privatized, using a clear and rigorous analytical framework that can be used to classify privatized firms in any cross-sectoral and cross-national comparison, and thus trace the life after privatization in any comparative context.

The second question is important for at least three reasons. The *first reason* is because of the somewhat surprising variation between countries, as will be demonstrated in the empirical chapters of the book. *Prima facie*, before this study, one might have otherwise thought that firms from countries that privatized first—such as the UK under Thatcher, and even Spain, which started privatizing crown jewels such as Endesa in the 1980s under González's Socialists—would have initial competitive advantage in world markets. The reasoning here is that such firms had, theoretically, a 'head-start' independence to merge and acquire freely and robustly all over the world, being in a strong position that would make them immune from takeover. Similarly, one could have thought that the relatively late privatizers of crown jewels, such as France, might be in a position of relative disadvantage. However, as the findings will show, there seems to be no direct relationship between when states privatized their firms and whether or not their privatized firms become Alphas or Betas. Therefore, examining in detail *why* firms evolve as they do needs to be examined in order to address this seeming puzzle.

The *second reason* that answering this question is important is because it advances our understanding of M&A activity of privatized firms that will be of interest to scholars of privatizations and mergers. Equally important, answering the question allows us to build on the Varieties of Capitalism (VoC) and globalization literature.

Turning to the VoC literature, Hall and Soskice (2001, 4) state that a main contribution of their edited volume was 'to bring firms back into the center of comparative political economy'.[4] They distinguish between liberal market economies (LMEs), where firms' endeavours are coordinated primarily by markets, and coordinated market economies (CMEs), where firms 'depend more heavily on non-market relationships to coordinate their endeavours' (Hall and Soskice, 2001, 8). Examples of LMEs include the UK, US, Canada, and New Zealand, while CMEs include Germany, Japan, and Austria. Although Ingham (2008, 215) points out that 'France, Italy, Spain, Portugal, Greece and Turkey fall midway between the two polar types in ambiguous positions', authors such as Heywood have contended that Spain fits closer to a LME than a CME. Building on Shonfield's (1965) work, Schmidt (2003) points to a third variety found in France: 'state-enhanced' capitalism, 'in which the state still plays an active albeit much reduced role (compared to post-war dynamics), where CEOs exercise much greater autonomy, and labour relations have become much more market-reliant' (Schmidt, 2003, 533).

However, the VoC literature has not offered a systematic analysis of how a privatized firm's merging activity and global expansion may be better understood given the firm's relationship with the state. Therefore, asking this question seeks to discern if there is a difference in how firms from various LMEs, CMEs, and state-enhanced economies operate in both home and global markets, and if this can be explained based on the firms' (past and present) relationship with the state. By adding insights into the interaction between firms and states, the study also contributes to more general scholarship that cogently reflects on the relationship between politics and business power today (Moran, 2009). While some authors have argued that economic actors simply dictate their preferences to a compliant state, others have argued that firms adopt their demands 'to make them fit with government objectives' (Woll, 2008, 153).

Finally, the existing globalization literature offers insights in at least three main dimensions. First, it has questioned whether or not economic globalization is occurring, as seen in the work of Held and McGrew (2003) on the globalist versus the sceptic view. Second, others who have uncovered evidence of globalization have questioned whether it is a 'good or bad thing'. Examples of those that see globalization as a 'good' or 'positive' development include Bhagwati (2004), who claims that globalization can have a social 'good', and Shipman (2004), who highlights the positive impact of economic globalization in terms of creating more wealth for many. Those who are concerned about the effects of globalization include Ellwood (2001), who criticizes the globalization of the Western consumerist mentality given that it will result in a depletion of the world's natural resources, and Stiglitz (2002), who highlights that globalization is something that is mishandled by the Western world and threatens the future of nations in poverty. Third, some specific pieces devote attention to globalization as a constraint or challenge to public policy, as seen in Hay's (2006) work examining developments in trade, foreign direct investment, finance, and the environment.

However, the globalization literature lacks a cogent analysis of how and why privatized firms might have become global champions, including the geographic areas (including ex-colonial territories) such firms have gone to and why. Therefore, asking this question helps us to better understand the factors of importance in explaining the dynamics of firms expanding into the global economy. By linking itself to the VoC literature, this study will also add further to the political economy of globalization debate because it seeks a better understanding of the potential impact of state economic strategies in either fostering the global expansion of privatized national champions, or preventing other major global players from acquiring national champions.

A *third reason* that answering this question is significant is because by considering different factors that help explain why firms become Alphas and Betas, it helps business leaders and state officials predict future developments of firms operating in international markets.

The Chapter Ahead and Justifying Sectors Studied

With this in mind, Chapter 2 considers the explanatory variables (factors) that may help us to better understand *why* some privatized firms become either Alphas or Betas. I start with initial conditions during privatization. This includes the economic conditions of the firm when it was privatized as well as the role of the state during the privatization process. I then turn to factors that might have played a role after privatization, highlighting two broad categories. The first are those *internal* to the firm after privatization, including the firm's competitiveness and the goals of its managers, as well as the role of its shareholders (including, potentially, asset management firms and the state). The second set includes those factors *external* to the firm. These are: the impact of liberalization in the sector; the role of the state in terms of providing state aid after privatization as well as helping craft overseas M&A deals; the decisions of regulators in the EU and abroad when ruling on mergers and acquisitions; and the direct lobbying of the firm, including that of CEOs and M&A deal professionals.

These factors are then tested in the empirical chapters that examine developments in the airline (Chapter 3), automobile (Chapter 4), and electricity (Chapter 5) sectors in the UK, France, Spain, Germany, and Italy.

These sectors were chosen for two main reasons, beyond the idea that it would be impossible for a single study to analyse in detail all the major sectors of the economy.

First, it was ideal to attain a common denominator that served as a basis for comparative research across the five states: each country must have had a privatized firm in that sector. So, for example in the banking sector, while BNP and Paribas (France), Argentaria (Spain), and UniCredit (Italy) may be ideal cases to analyse, none of the major privatizations in the UK between 1979 and July 2001 involved a bank (cf. Parker, 2004, 31–2). Similarly, I considered analysing the petroleum sector. Yet, while BP (UK), Total (France), ENI (Italy), and Repsol (Spain) were significant petroleum entities that were privatized, there was difficulty in finding an equivalent company from Germany.[5]

Second, once a common denominator was obtained, I then had to determine which sectors to examine. It was decided to analyse those sectors where one found variation in the outcome variable, or, those sectors where one finds both Alphas and Betas today. While variation is found in the automobile, airline, and electricity sectors, this was not found in the telecommunication sector. After performing the Global Movers Test and the Independence Test, one sees that all firms—namely, Telefónica (Spain), BT (UK), Deutsche Telekom (Germany), France Télécom, and Telecom Italia—are Alphas, at least as of May 2014.[6]

With this in mind, the specific firms studied for each sector are:

- in the airline sector: Deutsche Lufthansa, Air France-KLM, IAG (the product of the merger between British Airways and Iberia), and Alitalia;

- in the automobile sector: Volkswagen, Renault, Jaguar, SEAT, and Alfa Romeo; and

- in the electricity sector: EDF, E.ON, SSE, ENEL and Endesa.

Each empirical chapter is similarly structured on three dimensions and will:

- briefly examine the history of the firm, its privatization, and life thereafter in terms of M&A that have been pursued (or not);

- clearly identify which firms are Alphas and Betas based on both the Global Movers Test and the Independence Test; and

- examine which of the explanatory variables outlined in Chapter 2 are of importance in understanding why some firms are Alphas and others Betas.

The concluding chapter summarizes the main findings. It also builds an innovative, more general, theory which will be of value to scholars, business leaders, and political actors. Such a theory also offers new insights to the debates on VoC, the relationship between business and politics, and globalization.

Endnotes

1. The Zephyr database from the Bureau van Dijk (BvD) is one of the world most authoritative sources on detailed information on M&A. For more information, please see: <http://www.amadeus.bvdinfo.com>. Access gained through Trinity College Dublin's Library subscription.

2. If we consider this in terms of deal value, 2012 data from Zephyr suggests that the order is slightly reversed with North America taking the lead, followed by the EU-27, and then the Far East and Central Asia. This is generally observed for all years except 2007 (when the EU had a higher value than the US). Oceania's number of deals is higher than those of Latin America, although the latter sees deal values that are higher throughout all years.

3. The Amadeus database of the Bureau van Dijk (BvD) is one of the most detailed and exhaustive in the world that offers full financial information on millions of companies in Europe. For more on Amadeus, please see: <http://www.bvdep.com/be-nl/AMADEUS.html>. Access gained through TCD's Library subscription.

4. Or, as Thatcher neatly notes, the VoC 'literature emphasises the importance of relationships for firms, and the development of institutions for coordination of

firms and other actors. The key relationship is between that of firms and government' (Thatcher, 2006, 3).

5. One relevant petroleum company from Germany was ARAL—it used to be owned by VEBA and, as long as that was (partly) state owned, it was also in state ownership. However, in terms of production and distribution its size paled in comparison to its counterparts from the other four European states.

6. When the final round of tests was performed between October 2013 and May 2014, one saw that all five telecom companies appeared on the latest Forbes 2000 List (of May 2014); all of them fared within the top 1 per cent of the firms in Europe in terms of turnover, total assets, shareholder funds, and number of employees (based on the latest available comparative data from 2012 on Amadeus); and all were independent companies which had not been taken over, attaining an A^+ BvD independence ranking, meaning that no one shareholder owned more than 25 per cent of each company's shares (please note that the method of analysis used to determine if a firm is Alpha or Beta is discussed in more detail in the methodology section of Chapter 2). However, telecom observers will note that Telecom Italia (TI) is showing signs of becoming a Beta being taken over by an Alpha because Telefónica has made aggressive moves in targeting the Italian company. Indeed, TI has a strong presence in Italy and the EU: it provides Internet and telephony services in Italy, Germany, France, and San Marino, and controls Telecom Italia Media, which has a strong presence in Brazil. However, particularly since 2007, Telefónica has taken an important stake in TI through Telco SpA (of which Telefónica is the largest shareholder). As of September 2013, Telco is the largest shareholder of TI (with 22.4 per cent) and a complete future takeover of TI by the Spanish giant was rumoured in October 2013. Interestingly, as examined in Chapter 5, Telefónica's controlling stake in TI can be understood in the context of ENEL's takeover of Endesa.

2

Explaining Why Firms May Become Alphas or Betas

The previous chapter had as its main objective to define Alphas and Betas (referred to as the dependent or outcome variable, Y). Alphas were defined as those privatized firms that have become today's European and global giants, merging with or acquiring other firms. Betas are those privatized firms that have been taken over by Alphas or other leaders in the sector.

This chapter's main objective is to outline the explanatory variables (factors) that may help us better understand why a firm becomes an Alpha or a Beta (Y). It conceptualizes that such factors can be seen in roughly two different time periods: those at play when the firm was privatized (X1) and those of potential salience after its privatization (X2). As this study is interdisciplinary in nature, it contends that several factors from particularly business studies and politics must be considered. As such, it invokes an array of factors rarely considered in the conventional business analysis literature—notably political settings and strategies—as well as factors not fully considered in political science investigation—namely, the role of managers as well as shareholders, including intermediary financial elites such as asset managers.

In more detail, the chapter starts by outlining the first set of explanatory variables (X1). They emphasize the initial conditions *when the firm was privatized*. Included here are whether or not the firm was a crown jewel and the role of the state during the privatization process. The second section of the chapter considers the second set of variables, which are representative of 'intervening variables' (X2) that may have played a role *after the firm was privatized*, eventually resulting in the firm becoming an Alpha or Beta (Y). I argue that there are two broad categories of intervening variables. The first are those internal to the firm, including the firm's competitiveness and the goals of its managers, as well as the role of its shareholders. The second set includes those factors external to the firm, representative of what one may argue are more 'political' factors. These are: the impact of liberalization in the sector; the role of the state in terms of helping craft M&A deals; the decisions of regulators in the EU and abroad when ruling on mergers and acquisitions; and the direct lobbying of the firm.

The chapter closes by outlining the method of analysis used throughout the empirical chapters to determine whether or not a firm is an Alpha or a Beta, and what methods are used to determine which of the explanatory factors are of salience.

2.1 Explanatory Variables: Initial Conditions (When a Firm was Privatized) and Intervening Variables (Post-Privatization)

Initial Conditions at Privatization (X1)

The first conditioning variable is whether or not a company was a crown jewel when it was privatized. The second is the role of the state during the privatization process. I consider both in turn.

CROWN JEWELS OR LOSS-MAKING ENTERPRISES

As indicated in Chapter 1, the literature highlights how two main types of firms were privatized by West European states (Wright, 1994; Chari and Cavatorta, 2002). On the one hand, were the profitable 'jewels of the crown', oftentimes enjoying monopoly power. Examples include, but are not limited to, those firms in the electricity, telecoms, petroleum, and natural gas sectors where there was little competition, if any, before privatization. Although historical recipients of state aid over time (depending on the country), national airlines were considered as flag carriers that historically functioned in largely protected sectors. As such, they too could be considered historical 'crown jewels'.

On the other hand, in contrast to the 'jewels', the literature highlights the sale of loss-making enterprises. These were historical recipients of state aid, represented a long-term drain on the state, and were firms that states wished to divest themselves of given the budgetary drain (Chari, 1998). Such companies were found in, but not limited to, the shipbuilding, mining, and automobile sectors.

With this in mind, one may reasonably hypothesize that firms that were crown jewels had a competitive advantage in their sector before privatization and are more likely to become Alphas today. Similarly, one may hypothesize that firms that were loss-making enterprises before their privatization, are more likely to have become Betas and been taken over by another firm, either at the point of privatization or shortly thereafter.

THE ROLE OF THE STATE DURING THE PRIVATIZATION PROCESS

The role of the state in the privatization process itself may be significant. As some companies may have suffered from long-term structural losses while in state hands, governments sought to divest themselves completely. However, when so doing, states may have desired that the companies be taken over by a profitable company, either from Europe or abroad, in order for the firm to survive and perhaps save jobs for thousands of workers (Chari, 1998).

As such, one may hypothesize that when privatizing companies, some states desired that the company's longevity would be guaranteed by privately selling to an international leader in the sector. Thus, the role of the state can explain why some companies (Betas) are taken over at the point of sale. Profitable companies, on the other hand, were generally sold by public flotation (and not to a single investor), raised revenue for the Treasury, and had the potential to become Alphas after privatization.

With this in mind, some firms may have become Betas based solely on initial conditions, as schematically represented in Figure 2.1.

I will argue that while initial conditions may explain why *some* firms become Betas, they do not necessarily explain why *all* firms that are Betas today fall into this category. This is precisely because some firms' initial conditions may have been such that they could have become Alphas—that is, they were profitable companies that were floated. We thus turn to discussion of potential intervening variables that may help explain why some firms became Alphas and others Betas post-privatization.

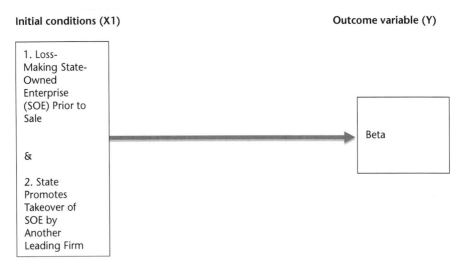

Figure 2.1. The First Model: How a Firm May Become a Beta (Y) Based on Initial Conditions at Privatization (X1)

Intervening Variables, Post-Privatization (X2)

Here I consider the intervening variables that may be at play after privatization. This helps us to better understand why firms that had the potential to become Alphas after privatization, given the initial conditions, eventually became Betas, and why some firms that had potential to become Alphas after privatization remain so today. I subdivide these intervening variables (X2), which may have played a role during a company's life at some point in time after privatization, into two main categories: those that are *internal* and those that are *external* to the firm.

With regard to those *internal* to the firm, the first variable considers the firm's competitiveness after its privatization and the desires of management who seek to expand and increase market share. The second underlines the role of shareholders, particularly the potential importance of the state as well as the major financial elite who may have bought a sizeable number of shares in the firm after it was privatized.

With regard to those variables that are *external* to the firm, I first consider the nature of liberalization in the sector. I then consider the potential influence of the state post-privatization in terms of its ability to help foster overseas deals.

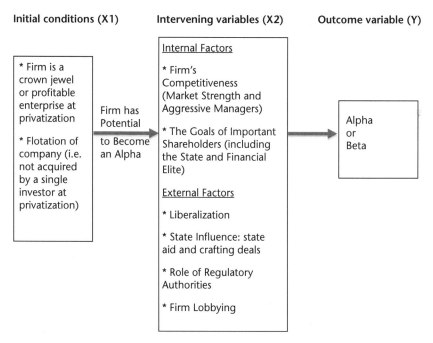

Figure 2.2. The Second Model: How a Firm May Become an Alpha or Beta (Y) Based on Initial Conditions at Privatization (X1) and Intervening Variables Post-Privatization (X2)

I then turn to the role of regulatory authorities. The lobbying role of the firm is then considered, particularly when regulatory authority is required.

It is important to note that each of these factors is not mutually exclusive and the empirical chapters seek to explore how they might interact in explaining why a firm has become an Alpha or a Beta today.

As a way of schematically representing how the initial conditions and intervening variables may be at play, and in order to clarify the structure of the second model in terms of the dependent and independent variables, Figure 2.2 offers the reader a summary of how all of the variables may influence whether or not a firm becomes an Alpha or a Beta, followed by fuller discussion.

Internal Factors

FIRMS' COMPETITIVENESS (MARKET STRENGTH AND AGGRESSIVE MANAGERS)

Here I consider two dimensions. The first is the firm's ability, post-privatization, to keep it in a strong and competitive market position and maintain production of solid goods and services (Moeller and Brady, 2007, 19). More importantly, as discussed in Chapter 1, the merger literature highlights that acquirers are oftentimes representative of strong companies that have managers that are skilled negotiators with long-term visions. Management teams also may be motivated to maintain intensive research and development in the firm, particularly important in high-technology sectors that require intensive research and development (Hall, 1988). Such leaders of the firm seek even more economic dominance in their sector given their own career growth and big bonuses that come with M&A (Auerbach and Reishus, 1988; Moeller and Brady, 2007, 19).

With these points in mind, one may reasonably hypothesize that the firms likely to become Alphas maintain a strong market position after privatization and are led by strong management teams that seek to merge and acquire globally in order to create an even more competitive, cost-efficient company. Managers, in particular, may be motivated by bonuses they receive for spearheading big deals and expanding globally. On the other hand, firms which had theoretical potential to become Alphas after privatization, but which ended up becoming Betas, may have a relatively weaker market position compared to Alphas after privatization (especially in terms of their size and influence in the EU market) and may have suffered from financial difficulties after their privatization: management knows that it cannot survive alone and the company eventually becomes a target. That said, CEOs and boards of directors of firms that end up Betas may also be able to sell shares they hold if acquired by a leader in the sector who is willing to pay a high price. By making such gains in acquisitions, managers of firms that become Betas may actively promote the acquisition of their firm.

SHAREHOLDERS

I consider the potential importance of two main shareholders within a firm post-privatization: the state and specific financial elites.

First, the state itself may still retain a strong vested interest in the firm by maintaining some form of ownership in the privatized companies. I argue that states that retain participation in firms do so for strategic reasons and want the firm to be an efficient, successful, and profitable enterprise, both at the European and global levels. One may expect differences between states that represent different 'varieties of capitalism'. For example, countries that fit within the CME (Germany) and state-led/enhanced model (France) may have retained some participation in some privatized firms, compared to LMEs (UK, Spain), which divested completely. Further, state ownership may also generate Treasury revenues as firms accumulate profits from domestic, supra-national, and international markets. In the case of France, one can extrapolate from Maclean et al. (2006) that this desire for partially state-owned enterprises to succeed is based on the close ties between business and politics: commonly referred to as *pantouflage*, elites move between high-level business and state posts. In other words, states that retain ownership in a company are more likely to resist the takeover of their firm.

As such, one may hypothesize that firms are likely to become Alphas if the state still owns part of the profitable company and wants to see the Alpha thrive; furthermore, Alphas are more likely to stay Alphas because the state has its own vested interest in not seeing the firm being taken over and becoming a Beta. One may hypothesize that Betas may not have any remaining (or only have a very insignificant) shareholding in the company and thus do not have this added 'protection' of the state.

Another dimension of shareholders relates to the significance of 'intermediary' financial elites (Davis, 2002; Folkman et al., 2007). The idea here is that asset management firms, insurance companies, and banks all manage money for individuals and various institutional investors. Examples of companies that manage funds on behalf of their various clients include: BlackRock, Invesco, Legal and General, the Capital Group, AXA, and La Caixa. For example, US-based BlackRock invests money for 'corporate, public, and union and industry pension plans . . . insurance companies, third party mutual funds, endowments, foundations, charities, banks, and individuals world-wide'.[1] Although not fully addressed in the political science literature, such firms have an important role in providing a solid financial base for firms when they seek to expand, merging and acquiring globally (Moeller and Brady, 2007, 78–9).

Table 2.1. Top Asset Managers Holding Shares in European Listed Firms

Asset Manager (country of origin)	Towers Watson Rank	Number of Listed Companies in Amadeus in which Asset Manager is a Shareholder	% of Listed Companies in which Asset Manager is a Shareholder
BlackRock (US)	1	1314	9.60
Vanguard Group (US)	5	1286	9.39
AXA (FR)	6	1151	8.41
JP Morgan Chase (US)	9	1006	7.35
BNP Paribas (FR)	7	997	7.28
Deutsche Bank (DE)	8	895	6.54
Allianz (DE)	3	849	6.20
State Street Global (US)	2	825	6.03
Capital Group (US)	10	362	2.64
Fidelity (US)	4	145	1.06

Source: Rankings (Column 2), Towers Watson, 2010 (24); shareholder data (Column 3), BvD's Amadeus Database, data as of July 2012; percentage (of 13,960 listed companies analysed in Amadeus, Column 4), author's calculation based on Column 3.

As little research is done on the role of these specific intermediary financial elites, it is useful to consider a global view of asset management firms' participation in listed European companies, before examining their shareholdings in the empirical chapters. This is necessary because it may foreshadow what we may see, or not see, while also offering significant insight into how asset managers act as shareholders in European firms today—something not fully considered in the literature.

Table 2.1 takes the top ten firms that Towers Watson (2010, 24) ranks in their analysis of what they conclude are the world's 500 largest asset managers (year end 2009), considering their ownership in the 13,690 publically listed firms found on the Amadeus database in July 2012.[2]

Table 2.1 highlights that BlackRock, the world's largest asset manager (Segal, 2011), tops the list, holding shares in close to 10 per cent of all 13,690 of Europe's listed firms in the Amadeus database. In terms of nationality, within the top five, there are three US firms—BlackRock, Vanguard, and JP Morgan Chase—and the two within the top five from Europe are from France—AXA and BNP Paribas. The German companies Allianz and Deutsche Bank are stronger than some others from the US such as Capital Group and Fidelity, but within the bottom five.

Beyond these shareholders of Alphas, attention will also be paid to the actions of shareholders of firms that are taken over by Alphas. Such shareholders may include CEOs and Directors (that may own shares and may gain significantly when taken over), asset management firms, as well as individual (small) shareholders of the target. The idea here is that such shareholders may not want to sell to Alphas if it is deemed that a low price per share is being paid. In such a scenario, shareholders of targets may demand a higher amount to be paid, or threaten to block a deal altogether.

Given the scale of investing in European firms by asset managers such as BlackRock, one may reasonably hypothesize that privatized firms are likely to become Alphas if they have the support of financial actors who seek to invest in the Alpha, provide shareholder stability to the firm, and potentially buy stocks in the company before and after major deals. Although such actors may not necessarily gain a controlling stake in the Alpha, they may be able to exercise some influence when important company decisions are made, including major M&A. Also, the capital that such companies may provide an Alpha allows it to easily pursue takeover activity on a global scale. During their life after privatization, firms that eventually become Betas, on the other hand, may not necessarily have the support of these institutional investors which may have refrained from being shareholders in the Beta throughout its life after privatization. Further, one may hypothesize that shareholders of firms that are taken over (potentially including Betas studied here) may demand that a higher price be paid, and may potentially hold out on the sale of their company until a better offer is made.

External Factors—Liberalization, State Influence, Regulatory Authorities, and Lobbying by Firms

While the internal conditions already mentioned may be of importance to a firm, it is necessary to consider in some detail the external factors that may be of importance in explaining why firms become Alphas and Betas, starting with liberalization initiatives. One may consider these factors more 'political', as they are concerned with the political environment at different levels of governance that firms find themselves having to deal with.

LIBERALIZATION

Significant contributions to the literature on the nature of liberalization initiatives in Europe (Coen and Thatcher, 2001; Eising, 2002; Geradin 2000; Thatcher, 2009) highlight their importance on three levels of governance. The first relates to initiatives at the member-state level. As is well documented, some EU states, such as the UK, pursued liberalization initiatives in various sectors—such as electricity—before other European states. The second relates to EU-wide liberalization measures. As will be seen in the empirical chapters, once the Single European Act was signed in 1986—with the goal to effectively create a free trade area within the EU by 1992—further EU liberalization initiatives were pursued in the airline, automobile, and electricity sectors. One may argue that the more liberalized the sector, the easier it is for a firm to pursue M&A deals and expand within the Union. The third factor relates to liberalization initiatives in countries outside the EU: firms from Europe may seek to expand in states abroad that are fully liberalized, or at least seeking international companies in their drive towards liberalization, as seen in some transition economies in Latin America (Conaghan and Malloy, 1995).

Given this, it would seem reasonable to hypothesize that having a strong position and potentially being protected in a home market, while still having the ability to expand into other EU and world markets, would form ideal conditions for a firm to become an Alpha. One may also hypothesize that a firm operating in a liberalized domestic market, but where liberalization has not occurred fully at the Community level and where there is limited opportunity to expand in states outside the EU, is more likely to become a Beta, given that Alphas can more easily take them over.

'STATE INFLUENCE': STATE AID AND CRAFTING DEALS

Even if the state is not a shareholder in the firm after its sale, it may still exert political influence which shapes a firm's development. In a first dimension, states may continue to subsidize firms after their privatization by giving state aid (Hancher et al., 2012). As noted, before their privatization, loss-making firms in certain sectors received public subsidies throughout the 1970s and 1980s. Yet, less attention has been paid to how states may continue to subsidize even profitable firms after privatization. Such subsidies which may include regional aid, are given towards helping fund large long-term investment projects, grants earmarked for research and development, and training aid. Depending on the case, these funds may come from either member states that the firm originates from, or other states wherein firms pursue large expansionary deals. In some cases, too, Alpha home states may attempt to earmark state funds received by firms through various public–private partnerships held and contracts received (Bovis, 2006; Sanchez Graells, 2012). With this in mind, one may reasonably hypothesize that firms are likely to become Alphas if they continue to receive state funds after their privatization. Such aid may not necessarily be essential for an Alpha's survival, but helps in its consolidation to be a leader in the sector, or for its expansion into other markets. If a firm which has potential to become an Alpha after its sale does not receive state funds, particularly when needed, then it may be more likely that the state prefers that it is taken over by a sectoral leader and becomes a Beta.

On a second dimension, successful firms oftentimes rely on their own states when 'crafting deals'. This has been raised in Thatcher's (2006, 12, 13, 18) work, which cogently demonstrates the state's role in helping the firm pursue overseas expansion while allowing the companies to be protected at home. One may conceptualize that one mechanism through which the state can help secure the deals when firms are expanding is through direct intervention when M&A is pursued at home, in Europe, and globally. Further, the state may have a more subdued influence on developments in a firm seeking to globally expand by way of having representatives with past links to the state (such as ex-Ministers or higher-level civil servants) who serve the firm's board of directors (BoD). This mechanism helps ensure that a tight link between business and the state is retained. In this regard, it is also noteworthy to consider the phenomenon of 'revolving doors', where political actors move from public offices to the private world (Chari et al., 2010). For the purposes of this study, this may see state actors previously involved in privatization, later crafting deals while potentially holding significant positions in the privatized firm's board.

Another added dimension to the role of the state of significance for international expansion, and extending on arguments by Guillén (2005), Chislett (2002), and Frynas and Paulo (2007), is that the state may have historical ties to parts of the world where firms seek to globalize. For example, Spain with Latin America; France with Africa, parts of the Caribbean, and French Indo-China; the UK with North America, Ireland, India, and Australia; and Germany and Italy with Central and Eastern Europe. Brennan and Garvey (2009) tell us that such areas may represent states with common historical ties, languages, and culture, which the firm can more easily expand into with the help of the state given the close 'psychic-distance'.

The influence of 'home states' aside, a related potentially significant factor is the role of states from 'abroad' in allowing for expansion of firms. The term 'abroad' simply refers to those states which are not home states from which firms are from. For example, the privatization literature has examined the role of the Spanish state, motivated by desires to liberalize and privatize its economy, in facilitating the sale of several of its companies to foreign competitors from states such as Germany and Italy (Chari, 1998). While the home states of Italy and Germany may have been important in driving the deals for their firms, the state from abroad—in this case, Spain—played even more of a crucial role in allowing for firm expansion.

With all of these points in mind, one may hypothesize that firms are likely to become Alphas if they have the help of state actors (which may also have representation on the firm's BoD) when expanding within the EU and globally, especially in those areas with which the state has a close 'psychic-distance'. State actors from non-Alpha states from 'abroad' (that is, states which are not those from which Alphas come, but which they may have to deal with) may have also facilitated Alpha expansion, especially if such states chose to sell to Alphas when they were privatizing themselves. If they took over companies at one stage, Betas too may have enjoyed benefits offered by their home states at one time. However, such a benefit would not last if the

Beta was then taken over by another international giant. Such a takeover, interestingly, may have also had the full support of their home state that potentially intervened in the deal.

THE ROLE OF REGULATORY AUTHORITIES

As seen in the previous chapter, there is a widespread literature on the import-ance of regulatory authorities, particularly DG Competition which is involved in approving state aid as well as M&A in European political space (Bishop and Kay, 1993; Chari and Kritzinger, 2006, 84–8, 93–7). As previously discussed, scholars have lamented that such decisions by the EU, particularly those approving M&A with a Community dimension, have lacked consistency, transparency, and objectivity. Additionally, there may also be a role for domestic regulatory authorities (Vickers, 2001). Rodger's (2009, 3) work, for example, discusses the importance of the UK's Monopolies and Mergers Commission (MMC, which was superseded by the Competition Commission) that 'was required to assess mergers referred to it according to the public interest'. Finally, it is also crucial to note that there may be a role for author-ities beyond Europe (where firms may have merged with, or taken over, companies) when expansion outside Europe is pursued. As such, the ability of such firms to merge with, or acquire, other firms significantly depends on the decision of regulators at potentially different levels of governance: national, EU, and, if merging outside European space, other national regula-tory authorities.

With this in mind, one may hypothesize that a firm is likely to become an Alpha if it gains regulatory approval to receive state aid or to merge with or takeover other firms. On one dimension, approval will ideally be characterized as having no, or few, conditions imposed by the regulator. On another dimen-sion, regulatory authorities may also make no decisions, for example by not investigating whether or not a state aid was compatible with the Common Market or by not investigating a merger or acquisition. In such a scenario, it is reasonable to argue that inaction by regulators indicates implicit approval—a non-decision on a deal would effectively signal that a green light has been given. This may take place when a deal flies under any 'regulatory radar' at any level of governance. From a Beta's perspective, one may also hypothesize that regulators must also have approved that their firm be taken over by an Alpha or other sectoral giant, or taken no decision on the takeover which effectively amounts to implicit approval.

FIRM LOBBYING

There is a significant body of literature on the firm as a political actor which discusses how firms directly lobby to either change policies at the domestic and supranational levels of governance (Bernhagen and Mitchell, 2009; Chari and Bernhagen, 2011; Coen, 1997, 1998, 2009), or maintain the status quo (Baumgartner et al., 2009). As Braithwaite and Drahos (2000) show, business has also become increasingly involved in participating in standard setting bodies. Beyond direct lobbying, some firms may work through their trade association (representing sectoral interests) such as ACEA that represents the common interests of the major European motor-vehicle manufacturers at EU level (Chari and O'Donovan, 2011).

In order to gain more transparency into the activity of all lobbyists, the European Union has set up a lobbying register, first at the European Parliament in 1996, then at the European Commission in 2008, and, finally, a 'Joint Transparency Register' (JTR) between both institutions since 2011. The downside of the Register is that it does not give specific details with regard to 'which lobbyist' met with 'which EU official' at any one time, comparing in contrast with the detail available in other highly regulated systems around the world such as Canada and the US (Chari et al., 2010, 99–115). Nevertheless, both the Commission's 2008 register and the JTR do offer some financial information regarding how much firms spend when they seek to influence policy decisions. This gives us useful data to better see how much in-house corporate and trade associations are spending on lobbying activity in Brussels.

With this in mind, it is reasonable to hypothesize that a firm is likely to become an Alpha if it has sophisticated, well-financed lobbying strategies, especially when seeking regulatory approval when merging with or taking over other firms. A firm that becomes a Beta may have lobbying strategies that eventually prove insufficient to prevent it from being taken over.

To summarize, these explanatory variables should not be seen as being mutually exclusive and that any combination of them may be intertwined, or linked together, to convincingly explain why firms become Alphas or Betas.

2.2 Methodology

As Bryman (2008, 379) writes, 'triangulation entails using more than one method or source of data in the study of social phenomenon', and with this in mind this study relies on quantitative analysis, qualitative examination of primary and secondary documents, as well as elite interviews. I consider these in an integrated discussion which is structured around measurement of the dependent and explanatory variables.

METHOD OF ANALYSIS WHEN DETERMINING WHICH FIRMS
ARE ALPHAS AND BETAS
The first method includes quantitative analysis of the data found on BvD's Amadeus and Zephyr's databases.[3] In terms of the dependent variable, Amadeus data will be analysed when performing the Global Movers Test and the

Independence Test (discussed in Chapter 1) and determining which of the firms are Alphas or Betas.

It is worth discussing the methodology employed when performing the tests. This is useful for scholars seeking to replicate the study, or examine developments in other sectors beyond those studied in this book. As discussed in Chapter 1, in order to be considered an Alpha, a firm must 'pass' all elements of the tests; if it fails even one, it will be considered a Beta. Let us consider each of the tests in turn.

First, with regard to the first part of the Global Movers Test which seeks to demonstrate whether or not the firm is a global giant, analysis is made of the latest available Forbes 2000 Index. This index measures the performance of the top 2,000 public companies in the world based on sales, profits, assets, and market value. The Forbes 2000 list examined in this study is the latest one available at the time of writing, which in this case was that released in May 2014.[4] The objective here is to see if the studied firm appears in this list of top 2,000 global companies. If a firm appears on the list, it has passed one of the elements to become an Alpha; if it does not, it will be considered a Beta. This analysis is relatively easy and only requires analysis of the complete Forbes list.

Second, with regard to part two of the Global Movers Test which seeks to understand whether or not the firm is a European giant, analysis will be made of BvD's Amadeus database which has data on over 19 million (listed and unlisted) European firms. Amadeus thus represents one of the most complete databases on European firms and represents a solid tool to perform cross-comparative sectoral analysis of European companies. Through analysis of this database, the study wishes to gauge whether or not the firm is one of the key European leaders in their sector in terms of metrics which include: operating revenue/turnover, total assets, shareholder funds, and number of employees. With reference to these metrics, I seek to demonstrate that Alpha firms will be representative of the leaders amongst their European peers, while Beta companies will not be comparatively well positioned. While the first part of the Global Movers Test (the Forbes test) is relatively easy because it simply involves analysing whether or not the firm is on the list of the 2,000 world's biggest firms, this test on whether or not a firm is an EU giant offers more methodological questions regarding how it should be performed: how can one convincingly demonstrate that a firm which may be considered an Alpha is a European leader on all of these dimensions and what is the cut-off point for when firms should be considered Betas?

One way of setting up this test is by stating, for example, that in order for a firm to be an Alpha, it must demonstrate that it is within the top ten (or even top twenty-five) of all firms in their sector in Europe regarding each of these metrics in the latest year for which complete data is available; if a firm is below this cut-off point of top ten (or top twenty-five) in their sector, it should be considered a Beta. A problem with this, however, is that the different sectors studied are not the same size and have a different number of competitors operating with them in the EU. As we will see in the empirical chapters, this ranges from a relatively smaller number of firms operating in vehicle manufacturing, compared to a relatively higher number in electricity and gas.

As such, an alternative approach which tackles this problem is to state that in order for a firm to be considered an Alpha, it must demonstrate that on all metrics it ranks within the top 1 per cent of all EU firms in their sector in the latest year for which complete data is available in Amadeus (in this study, 2012.) This represents the *crème de la crème* of European firms. To ascertain how many companies were in the respective sector, it is important to note that each firm in Amadeus is associated with a NACE Rev 2 code. NACE Rev 2 is a classification of European industrial activity approved by the European Commission. Thus, a first step is to perform a clean search on Amadeus, clicking on 'industry and activity' and then defining the relevant NACE codes. Doing a search using this code, and then refining it according to geographic area (the EU) and year for which latest accounts are available (2012), thus allows for a list (and a total number) of all listed and unlisted firms operating in the sector.[5] As will be explained in the respective empirical chapters, for the sectors studied in the book the corresponding industry classification codes were used: 51 (Air Transport), 291 (Manufacture of motor vehicles), and 351 and 352 (Electricity and Gas). The search thus gave the number of firms in the Union in the sector in 2012, plus data for all the firms in all metrics, such as operating revenue, total assets, etc., which could be analysed in more detail for comparative peer ranking.

So, for example, let us say that a search for all companies in Sector X in the Union, in 2012, resulted in 2,000 firms being found on the Amadeus database. We have set the test so that, on all metrics, a firm has to be in the top 1 per cent of all firms in the sector in order to be considered an Alpha. This means that being in the top 1 per cent in Sector X signifies that the firm has to be in the top twenty of all 2,000 firms. So, in this hypothetical example, if a firm is in the top twenty, then it can be considered an Alpha; otherwise, it would be considered a Beta. Being in the top twenty of all firms in Sector X would thus represent a cut-off point in this sector for being an Alpha or Beta. As will be shown in the empirical chapters, detailed analysis can then reveal how each firm ranks when compared to their peers.[6]

Finally, when turning to the 'independence test', an Alpha must have demonstrated that, either during or after its privatization, it has not been acquired by another firm and maintains its independence. To demonstrate this, I rely on BvD's 'independence indicator', which is found in its Amadeus database. Other scholars, such as Cuellar Fernández et al. (2011, 94), have similarly relied on this indicator, which empirically characterizes the degree of independence of a company with regard to its shareholders. A company with an independence indicator of 'A' is a fully independent one with a known number of recorded shareholders, with none having more than 25 per cent of direct or total ownership. This is further qualified by BvD as A[+], A, or A[−], as follows:

- A[+] is given to companies with six or more identified shareholders whose ownership percentage is known.
- A as above, but includes companies with four or five identified shareholders.
- A[−] as above, but includes companies with one to three identified shareholders.
- The qualifications of '+' or '−' do not refer to a higher or lower degree of independence, but to the degree of reliability of the indicator that is attributed.[7]

I argue that in order to be an Alpha, the firm will have to have attained a BvD independence indicator of A[+]: while the firm may have been aggressive in terms of pursuing M&A activity in European and world markets, it has never been taken over by another firm, it maintains its independence as a global actor today because it is not a subsidiary of any other firm, and we can be sure that the independence indicator that is attributed to it is a reliable one.

In other words, if a firm does not attain an independence indicator of A[+] it will be considered a Beta: BvD's independence indicators of 'A', 'A[−]', 'B', 'C', and 'D' companies thus serve as a basis for defining Betas and serve as *cut-off points* between Alphas and Betas. A 'B' company is where one or more shareholders have a direct, total, or calculated ownership percentage above 25 per cent, although none has over 50 per cent. The further qualification of B[+], B, or B[−] is assigned according to the same criteria as for the 'A' indicator. A company with a BvD Independence indicator of 'C' has no shareholder recorded with more than 50 per cent of *direct* ownership, but one shareholder with more than 50 per cent of *total calculated ownership* (i.e. the company is indirectly majority owned). A company that has a BvD Independence indicator of 'D' has one shareholder recorded with more than 50.01 per cent of *direct* ownership (i.e. the company is directly majority owned). As the empirical chapters will demonstrate, most Betas analysed in the book are reflective of 'D' companies, where a majority of the company has been taken over by another firm.

There are two, reasonable, exceptions to the 'independence test' rules. The first is referred to as 'Exception 1'. This is applicable to cases where the state still owns more than 25 per cent of the firm after privatization, resulting in a firm that does not attain an independence indicator A[+]. This is justified based on the idea that the state may still be in the process of fully privatizing the company. The high state ownership in some companies will be seen most notably in the case of EDF, as discussed in Chapter 5.

The second, referred to as 'Exception 2', is applicable to cases where a family which has historical ties to the privatized firm maintains more than 25 per cent ownership today, meaning that the firm may not have attained a BvD independence indicator of A^+. The justification behind this exception is based on arguments raised in the literature on corporate governance. Enriques and Volpin's work (2007, 118) highlights the importance of family ownership in firms throughout Germany, France, Italy, and the US, arguing that 'family control is quite common even amongst the largest corporations'. One example they point to is that of the family of Bernard Arnautt, which in 2005 had 47 per cent control of Louis Vuitton Moët Hennessy, while another is seen in the family of Marco Tronchetti Provera, which in 2005 controlled almost a fifth of Telecom Italia (Enriques and Volpin, 2007, 120–1). Other examples in the automobile sector in Europe include Peugeot (36.8 per cent owned by the Peugeot family), Fiat (30.1 per cent owned by the Agnelli family), and BMW (46.7 per cent owned by the Quandt family).[8] As will be seen in this study, I will invoke this exception to the independence test in the complicated case of Volkswagen, which has a history of cooperation and cross-ownership with the Porsche–Piëch family, which has been intimately involved in VW since Ferdinand Porsche designed the first Beetle.

METHODS USED TO DETERMINE WHICH EXPLANATORY VARIABLES ARE OF VALUE

Analysis of BvD's Zephyr, one of the most exhaustive and reliable databases in the world, will allow for examination of the various aspects of the M&A deals that will be essential when determining which of the factors outlined in this chapter are of salience. Qualitative information on Zephyr includes: an M&A deal value; when the deal was rumoured and finally completed; what other companies were interested in potentially offering a counter bid; financial information pre- and post-deal; notes on regulatory decisions; the names of the M&A deal professionals that advised the companies during deals; and comments by CEOs and other actors involved. Beyond specific M&A deal information, and as with Amadeus, the database offers a complete list of present and historical shareholders in the firm. Amadeus information can supplement these findings, such as offering a biography of each member of the board of directors of the firms including whether or not such actors once held state positions. Zephyr also allows the user to perform segmentation analyses of the areas in the world that each firm has made acquisitions since 1997.

Supplementing this information from Zephyr, qualitative analysis will be made of company reports, government documents, EU state aid and merger control decisions, major newspaper reports on the deals, and ministers' speeches. Again, this analysis will be essential when determining which explanatory variables are salient.

Finally, and adding a more nuanced view in understanding why firms become Alphas and Betas, I rely on elite interviews with high-level officials, some from the various companies studied as well as their competitors. Further, interviews were performed with actors in national governments (particularly core-executives based in the Ministries of Economy and Finance as well as Industry, or their equivalent), and European Commission officials in DG Competition. During the past ten years, over forty interviews have been performed in the countries of study and Brussels with state officials, in-house lobbyists, and European Commission officials.

In sum, using different methods will allow the study to gather evidence in order to better understand which of the explanatory factors are of more value as well as to explore the potential interaction between them.

PLAN AHEAD

With this in mind, each of the following empirical chapters on airlines (Chapter 3), automobiles (Chapter 4), and electricity companies (Chapter 5) is similarly structured and divided into three main sections. In the first, I briefly examine the history of the firms, their privatization, and (if applicable) M&A pursued thereafter. In the second, I then perform the tests to determine whether or not the firm can be characterized as an Alpha or a Beta. Finally, I analyse which of the explanatory variables (factors) discussed in this chapter can help us better understand why the firm is an Alpha or a Beta. As the empirical chapters are structured similarly, readers seeking to examine developments in only one sector can freely turn to the relevant chapter, keeping in mind the models developed thus far outlining the dependent and explanatory variables. Chapter 6 summarizes the main findings of the comparative study and develops a new grounded theory that emerges from the evidence uncovered in this study.

Endnotes

1. On BlackRock, please see <http://www2.blackrock.com/global/home/AboutUs/index.htm> (last accessed 2 January 2014). As stated in interview with an actor from an asset management firm, 'insurance companies (such as AXA and Allianz) buy consistent return on investments (pensions) in safe places, while firms such as BlackRock and JP Morgan will take more chances but still want safe returns . . . (and)

are likely to invest in shorter periods of time than insurance companies which have investments for a longer time.' Interview with author, in Brussels, November 2012.

2. Analysis was performed 20 July 2012.

3. Because Zephyr is one of the most comprehensive databases on mergers and acquisitions in the world, it is widely used by businesses as well as analysts. In April and May 2010, TCD's Acquisition librarian, Arlene Healy, negotiated access to Zehyr with the Key Accounts manager of Bureau van Dijk—Dan McGovern—for the course of my study, where my access was generously financed by the TCD Library, with some assistance from my own research funds through TCD's Arts and Social Science Benefactions Fund.

4. For a note on the Forbes methodology, see: <http://www.forbes.com/sites/an dreamurphy/2014/05/07/global-2000-how-we-crunch-the-numbers/>.

5. The reason why publicly listed and unlisted companies found in Amadeus were both included is because some significant peers may still be 100 per cent state owned and remain unlisted. This does not mean, however, that such firms are not strong competitors with a solid position in the single market. This is seen in the case of the fully state-owned company from Sweden, Vattenfall, in the electricity sector, which has core markets in Sweden, the Netherlands, and Germany, as well as presence in Denmark, Finland, and the UK. For more on Vattenfall and its ranking amongst European peers, see Chapter 5.

6. There are at least three sources of error in performing this test that should be noted by social scientists replicating this study. First, some of the firms may have to be manually included in the search because Amadeus may have classified a firm belonging to a specific sector with a different NACE Rev 2 code. For example, even though a firm may manufacture motor vehicles (291), it may be assigned a primary code of 6420 (activities of holding companies). Second, there may be a delay from when company data for the latest financial year is available, and when it is actually inputted by the BvD into the Amadeus database. This may result in a differing number of firms being counted (depending on whether or not the data from all the firms has been inputted) when determining the cut-off points. Third, while Amadeus is one of the most authoritative databases on European companies, there is always a possibility that some firms are missing from it.

7. This information is taken from Amadeus' user guide, under the title 'BvD Independence Indicator'.

8. This data is based on company reports outlining shareholders of the firms found in the Amadeus database, specifically: Peugeot (BvD Company ID number, FR 552100554, latest date of information for current shareholder March 2012); Fiat (BvD ID number, ITO0000118, date of information for shareholder September 2013); and BMW (BvD ID number, DE1870003036, date of information for shareholder September 2013.) In the case of BMW, the family shareholding is divided amongst Stefan Quandt (17.39 per cent), Johanna Quandt (16.70 per cent), and Susanne Hanna Ursula Klatten (12.60 per cent).

3

Airlines: Come Fly With Me

Introduction

Similarly structured to the two other empirical chapters, the first section analyses each of the five airlines—Air France, Lufthansa (Germany), British Airways, Iberia (Spain), and Alitalia—on three dimensions. First, a brief history of the airline is given. Then main points regarding its privatization are highlighted. Finally, the deals pursued by each airline before and after privatization—including those at home, within Europe, and globally—are considered. This broad overview of the main transactions offers the reader a glimpse of the consolidation of European airlines over the last fifteen years. It also serves as a foundation and reference point to understand which firms are Alphas and Betas—and why—as examined in the remainder of the chapter.

The second section thus performs a comparative analysis of the Global Movers Test and the Independence Test to determine which firms are Alphas and Betas today. It concludes that Air France, Lufthansa, and IAG (the product of the merger between BA and Iberia) represent ex-SOEs that are Alphas, while Alitalia is a Beta.

The third section considers which factors explain why some are Alphas and others Betas. By paying reference to the various deals outlined in the first section of the chapter, it is argued that factors internal to the firm are of importance to understand the life of Alphas. This includes the competitive market position of the firm before and after privatization, the goals of managers of the firms, and the significance of non-state shareholders, such as BlackRock. While these factors are important, however, they are not sufficient. In this regard, liberalization initiatives in the sector, state officials' role in influencing expansion, regulators' importance in approving deals, and firm lobbying are all significant. In order to understand why Alitalia is a Beta, it is argued that while its poor economic performance and the role of managers are important, the impact of liberalization, the role of the state, and the approval of regulators explains why it was eventually taken over by an Italian-based consortium, only to be partially sold off to Air France-KLM in 2009.

3.1 Brief History of the Firm, Privatization, and Life Thereafter

This section highlights each of the airlines' history, as well as the main aspects of privatization, including when sold, how sold, and what remains in state hands. It then considers life thereafter, focusing on M&A as well as Joint Ventures (JVs) embarked upon. Examination starts with Air France given its precedent-setting merger with KLM in 2004, and then turns to Lufthansa, which followed by consolidating its position with its purchase of Swiss International, Brussels Airlines, and Austrian Airlines, amongst others. Thereafter, attention is paid to British Airways and Iberia that both merged in 2011. The section closes by examining Alitalia. Relying on data from <www.privatizationbarometer.net> privatization proceeds are reported in US dollars in order to keep discussion consistent with overall values reported in Chapter 1. And relying on Bureau van Dijk's data found in the Zephyr database and other sources, deal values between 1997 and 2012 are reported in euros.

Air France

BRIEF HISTORY, PRIVATIZATION, AND LIFE THEREAFTER
Air France is a product of the merging of five French airlines in 1933: Air Union, Air Orient, Société Générale de Transport Aérien, CIDNA, and Aéropostale.[1] Similar to Renault, it was nationalized by the French government after the Second World War. During the late 1950s and 1960s the jet plane revolution meant the flag carrier would offer regular services not only on the Paris–New York route, but also North Africa and the Middle East. Air France was just like all other flag carriers studied in this chapter, where throughout the 1960s they 'held a monopoly over domestic flights and were the sole national airline for most international routes' (Thatcher, 2009, 220).

Before its privatization, Air France acquired two domestic carriers: with the purchase of UTA (Union de Transports Aériens) in 1990 it would eventually gain control of Air Inter (Kassim, 1996, 117), consolidating its position as France's national champion. Although the airline suffered losses after the 1990 Iraq War and faced strike action in response to cost-cutting measures pursued in 1993 (Thatcher, 2009, 227), by the end of the decade the company had become the '4th in the world in terms of total international passengers in 1997 ... and the 2nd in Europe in terms of long-haul traffic (revenue passenger–kilometers) in 1998'.[2]

Starting in February 1999 Jospin's centre–left government partially privatized Air France, although as Thatcher (2009, 228) notes, the term privatization was avoided, stating instead that 'Air France's capital was opened'. After its initial IPO, the state retained 63.4 per cent, employees 11.8 per cent, and 24.8

per cent was in private hands.[3] The price of the international offering was FRF 93.15 per share, 'which was 25%–40% higher than expected...(and was) oversubscribed by 1,000%'.[4] The sale-generated revenues of over USD 676 million[5] during a time of other lucrative privatizations in France seen in the last part of the 1990s as discussed in Chapter 1.

In its initial life after (partial) privatization, Air France, in its own words, 'further beefed up its structure by integrating, in 2000, Regional Airlines, Flandre Air, Proteus, Brit Air and CityJet to create its regional center'.[6] As an example of smaller deal values involved in these minor acquisitions, one sees the case of CityJet, the Irish-based airline that was acquired between 1999 and 2000, for an overall estimated consideration of €4.9 million.[7]

Within a few years, Air France sought alliances with European giants, seen in its 2004 merger with KLM.[8] This represented one of Air France's first notable transactions in its life after privatization and eventually witnessed the end to state-majority ownership. The precedent-setting merger between the French and Dutch carriers also represented one of *the* first and largest of its kind at the time in Europe where two complementary airlines with northern and southern routes joined forces (with AF's presence in southern Europe/ Africa and KLM's in northern Europe/the Far East).

Even before the merger, there were rumours that KLM sought alliances with another major European carrier, and vice versa. For example, KLM previously expressed interest in taking 40 per cent of Iberia during the first stage of its privatization in the late 1990s (discussed later in the chapter). However, Spanish state officials were against the offer because it meant that too much of Iberia would go to one competitor.[9] Then, in 2000 it was reported that BA sought a minority stake in KLM with future plans for a full merger, something eventually denied by BA.[10]

Initial rumours of the Dutch and French courtship surfaced in 2002.[11] After the ECJ's significant decision of 2002 (discussed in Section 3), and after the French government announced its predisposition to reduce its majority stake in August 2003, the deal was set. On 30 September both airlines announced their merger. There were two main dimensions to the AF–KLM deal, having a value of €1.72 billion that created the largest European airline at the time in terms of turnover, officially launched in April 2004.[12] First, Air France issued new shares to KLM investors, reducing the French state's stake in AF–KLM to around 44 per cent, while KLM shareholders attained a 19 per cent stake and Air France shareholders owned 37 per cent of the new entity.[13] Second, at the same time that the Netherlands' government reduced its stake to 6 per cent, over time there was a gradual reduction in the French state's ownership in AF–KLM, selling around 18 per cent in December 2004[14] and a further reduction of around 8 per cent in March 2005 (which was made available to staff in return for a salary cut).[15] The less than 20 per cent of the French state's stake in

AF–KLM in 2005 was reduced over time to the approximately 16 per cent it retains to this day, examined in more detail in Section 2.

Thereafter, a notable purchase by AF–KLM was VLM Airlines, based in Deurne Belgium and a market leader in transport between London City Airport and the continent. It was acquired in March 2008 for €180 million[16] and later absorbed under the CityJet brand in 2010.[17] For an undisclosed amount, AF–KLM also took over the Netherlands'-based cargo-airline Martinair in 2008, of which KLM already owned 50 per cent.[18] Another small deal included fully taking over France-based operator Airlinair in February 2013, in which it had a previous minority stake through its subsidiary Brit Air.[19] Finally, Alitalia is another acquisition where AF–KLM gained a controlling stake in 2009, discussed in Sections 1 and 3.

Outside of Europe, deals have also been pursued in Africa, the US, and China. Before its merger with KLM, in the early 2000s Air France made purchases in Africa when it gained a 34 per cent stake in Société Nouvelle Air Ivoire (formerly Air Ivory) as part of the Ivory Coast's privatization of the airline in 2000.[20] In the US, between 2005 and 2009 AF–KLM acquired the Miami-based Aero Maintenance Group which services and repairs aircraft components.[21] In China, in June 2008 AF–KLM announced a joint venture with China Southern Airlines to create a Sino-European air-freight company that came into effect in 2009.[22] In late 2010 both partners announced another JV, based on revenue sharing on the Paris–Guangzhou route.[23]

Lufthansa

BRIEF HISTORY, PRIVATIZATION, AND LIFE THEREAFTER
Founded in 1926, Deutsche Lufthansa is the product of the merger of Deutsche Aero Lloyd and Junkers Luftverkehr.[24] During the Second World War, the airline was obliged by the Nazis 'to provide services, transport flights and technical operations', followed by a momentary pause with the end of the War.[25] In 1953 it was re-established and during the decade operations recommenced with new hubs in Cologne, Hamburg, and Frankfurt. This was followed by massive restructuring of the firm which was over 80 per cent owned by the state in the 1960s (Sparaco, 1997), resulting in several long-haul routes carried by Boeing B707s.[26] The oil crises in the 1970s resulted in rationalization of the airline, which consequently allowed it to develop into a European leader by the 1980s.[27]

With the end of the Berlin Wall in sight, the government sold around 25 per cent of the airline in 1987 and 1989 through capital increases the state did not participate in.[28] In 1989 Lufthansa and Turkish Airlines pursued a joint venture, SunExpress, operating flights between Germany and the Turkish Riviera's Antalya.[29] Yet, by 1991 Lufthansa was experiencing losses of close to DM450 million (Bruch and Sattelberger 2001, 349). With the state still holding slightly more than 50 per cent of Lufthansa, a plan for further restructuring and privatization ensued once the state had agreed payment of DM1.55 billion to 'cover some of the airline's pension liabilities'.[30] As Macchiati and Siciliano (2007, 136) explain, '(i)n 1994, Lufthansa raised new equity capital through a rights issue and the state sold its stock rights through a public offering so that its stake reduced to roughly 35%'. After the government transferred its remaining shares to the state-owned *Kreditanstalt für Wiederaufbau* in 1996 (Sparaco, 1997), the final tranche was sold in October 1997. The total estimated value of the transactions in 1989, 1994, and 1997 was over USD 3.6 billion.[31]

In terms of its life after privatization, Lufthansa made acquisitions not only in its home market, but also significant European ones. The latter include attaining either full ownership of, or controlling stakes in, airlines from Italy, Switzerland, Austria, and Belgium. It has also pursued M&A as well as JVs in the US and Asia.

In more detail, focusing on the home market, Lufthansa consolidated its position by taking a minority stake in Eurowings—that at the time represented the third largest airline in Germany—where negotiations started in 2000. With a strategy to 'offer customers in North Rhine–Westphalia better connections to European business centers', this 24.9 per cent stake was bought in January 2001 from the Chairman of Eurowings' supervisory board, Albrecht Knauf, who previously owned 99.1 per cent of the company.[32] Lufthansa's ownership increased to 49 per cent in December 2005 and the remainder was acquired in December 2008.[33] A simultaneous transaction, which came into effect on 1 January 2009, also saw Lufthansa take full control of Eurowings' low-cost airline, Germanwings.[34] Other notable acquisitions in Germany include a close to 10 per cent control of Fraport AG, the Frankfurt airport operating company, which was attained between 2005 and 2006.[35]

In the first of acquisitions in other European states, at the same time Eurowings was unfolding, a 26 per cent stake was attained in the Trento-based airline Air-Dolomiti in 1999 for an undisclosed value. This left the main shareholders in the Italian carrier, the Leali family, with 45 per cent and the Friuli regional investment fund with 15 per cent.[36] Within four years, Lufthansa gained full control: in April 2003 its stake increased to 52 per cent for a purchase price of around €40 million, and in June it bought the remaining 48 per cent for an undisclosed consideration.[37]

Simultaneously the German airline initially looked north, seeking to increase its number of slots (i.e. the landing and take-off rights at specific times) held in Heathrow: in 2000 it acquired a fifth of British Midland (BMI) for €145 million.[38] This was bought from SAS (Scandinavian Airlines System) which is, still today, almost majority owned by the states of Sweden (21 per cent), Denmark (14.3 per cent), and Norway (14.3 per cent).[39] Similar to Air Dolomiti, Lufthansa gained 100 per cent control of BMI within the decade in different stages. First, it acquired 10 per cent of BMI held by Sir Michael Bishop in 2002. Then, despite rumours in 2007 of both Virgin Atlantic's and British Airway's desires to take over BMI, Lufthansa acquired Bishop's remaining shares (50 per cent) in July 2009, bought for an estimated €56 million.[40] Finally, after having gained 80 per cent control, Lufthansa bought the remaining 20 per cent of BMI from SAS in October 2009 for an estimated €41.5 million.[41] Three years later, however, Lufthansa eventually sold BMI to IAG (discussed in the section on Iberia).

In the wake of the precedent-setting Air France–KLM merger, starting in the mid-2000s Lufthansa made a host of acquisitions of flag carriers from neighbouring states. Certainly, there were previous signs of this development in December 1992 when it acquired a 13 per cent stake in Luxembourg's national airline, Luxair.[42] Yet, Lufthansa's acquisitions after privatization were much more impressive.

The first was Swiss International Airlines, a troubled carrier that was a successor to the bankrupt Swissair, that remained almost a third state-owned in 2004 (Doganis, 2006, 226). Despite rumours that BA was interested in purchasing Swiss, in May 2005 Lufthansa acquired a minority stake of 11 per cent for an undisclosed amount.[43] Between 2006 and 2007, Lufthansa acquired the remainder for €217 million.[44] Within a year Lufthansa increased its strength in Switzerland when Swiss acquired Edelweiss Air.[45]

A second, main acquisition was in Belgium. The context of this is the Belgian flag carrier Sabena, which filed bankruptcy in November 2001. Within weeks after bankruptcy was declared, a group of Belgian financiers (led by Etienne Davignon) operating as 'SN Airholding' gave 'a symbolic offer of €1 for former Sabena-controlled short-haul carrier Delta Air Transport (DAT)',[46] which was later renamed SN Brussels Airlines in early 2002.[47] In 2004 agreement was reached that SN Airholding would take over Richard Branson's low-cost carrier, Virgin Express,[48] and 'in March 2006, the two companies announced the merger which resulted in Brussels Airlines on the 25th March 2007'.[49] A year and a half later, in August 2008 Lufthansa made a bid for a controlling stake of 45 per cent of SN Airholding, the parent of Brussels Airlines, with a future option to purchase the remainder after 2011.[50] Via a capital increase, Lufthansa finally acquired this controlling stake in the major airline, flying out of Brussels Airport for an estimated value of €65 million in July 2009.[51]

Austrian Airlines was then targeted. In the late 1980s the Austrian flag carrier had been partially (37.9 per cent) privatized.[52] While the state reduced its shareholding over the years, in the early 2000s it still had more than 40 per cent ownership. The flag carrier had also been involved in some minor M&A,

having bought Tyrolean Airways in the late 1990s and Lauda Air in the early 2000s.[53] But, throughout the decade, it was suffering from declining operating revenues, as seen in 2007 when this was down by close to 5 per cent from the year before.[54] It was sold to Lufthansa in two main stages between 2008 and 2010. First, was the privatization of the 41.46 per cent held by the state (*Österreichische Industrieholding AG*, ÖIAG, Austria Industry Holding, which is the privatization agency of the Republic). This share was purchased by Lufthansa in December 2008 for an estimated €162 million.[55] This first stage also attracted the interest of others, including AF–KLM, which withdrew from the process in October 2008 given the high price of €1.4 billion that was reportedly being asked of it to purchase the Austrian flag carrier.[56] Second, in September 2009 Lufthansa increased its stake to 95.4 per cent by purchasing a majority of the shares of Austrian on the market for an estimated value of €213 million,[57] followed by the remainder in February 2010 for €2 million.[58]

Europe aside, Lufthansa has also embarked on deals in the US. In 2008 it acquired a 19.11 per cent stake in New York-based low-cost carrier JetBlue Airways for an estimated value of €213 million.[59] This represented one of the first major ownership investments by an EU carrier in the US. Although it was rumoured in 2011 that Lufthansa sought to sell this stake, today Lufthansa retains approximately 17 per cent of the US carrier and has two representatives on JetBlue's board of directors (BoD).[60] In another deal, in 2008 Lufthansa Cargo (a subsidiary of Lufthansa) and US-based DHL Worldwide Express (a subsidiary of Deutsche Post World Net) announced a 50:50 joint venture called Aerologic, based in Leipzig.[61]

China's Shenzhen Airlines, Lufthansa Cargo, and the German government previously announced a cargo joint venture in 2004, Jade Cargo International, representing the first Chinese-based cargo airline with foreign ownership.[62] In terms of structure, Shenzhen Airlines (now part of Air China) owned 51 per cent, Lufthansa Cargo 25 per cent, and the German government's development fund DEG (*Deutsche Investitions und Entwicklungsgesellschaft*) 24 per cent. Although the company served China, Malaysia, India, Singapore, and Thailand, it suspended operations in 2012 given the low demand.[63]

Where more success has been seen in Asia is through Lufthansa's subsidiary LSG Sky Chefs, the global airline caterer which consists of '151 companies with 211 customer service centers in 52 countries (which was) . . . formed after the takeover of Sky Chefs, American Airlines' former catering subsidiary, by Lufthansa's catering division Lufthansa Service GmbH'.[64] Notable deals with Asian firms throughout the 2000s include: acquiring Korean-based Asiana Airlines' catering business in 2003; a joint venture with HNA Air Catering Holding (part of China's Hainan Airlines Group) in 2007; that same year, a JV with the catering unit of the China Eastern Airline Group; and buying part of Hong Kong-based Cathay Pacific's catering service in 2008.[65]

British Airways

BRIEF HISTORY, PRIVATIZATION, AND LIFE THEREAFTER

Similar to Air France, the history of BA is based on an initial merger of smaller airlines and then nationalization. Somewhat dissimilar, post-nationalization witnessed dividing the entity, only to see merging of some of the parts again some years later. Kassim (1996, 111) succinctly describes events between 1924 and the mid-1970s:

> In the UK, the government formed Imperial Airways out of a merger of four existing carriers in 1924, nationalized the company in 1939, dismantled it in 1946 to form three new public corporations—British Overseas Airways Corporation (BOAC), British European Airways (BEA) and British South American Airways (BSAA)—and merged BOAC and BEA in 1974 to form British Airways (BA).

Although plans to privatize were announced in 1979, the sale was delayed because the early 1980s witnessed a deterioration of profits due to increases in fuel prices, where losses in 1981–2 amounted to over £500 million.[66] The airline's productivity nevertheless improved in the following years because unprofitable routes were eliminated, staff reduced, and reorganization of operations pursued.[67] Its 100 per cent sale eventually took place in February 1987. In an offer which was eleven times oversubscribed, the estimated proceeds amounted to approximately USD 1.34 billion.[68]

During its first two decades as a privatized firm, BA started with acquisitions in the UK, consolidating its position as national leader. For example, within months of its privatization BA expanded its production capacity by acquiring BA's long-time competitor and Gatwick-based carrier British Caledonian, in July 1987. Another operation at home included the 1992 takeover of UK-based Dan-Air (Davies and Newman Air), which flew within the domestic market.

BA also embarked on smaller deals outside the UK. In 1992 it attained 49.9 per cent of the airline TAT, which principally operated French domestic flights, for an estimated value of £15 million (Doganis, 2006, 76). BA exercised its option for the remainder within five years. Complementing this was the 2008 purchase for €68 million of the French operator Elysair, which traded under the name L'Avion and had flights between Paris Orly and New York.[69] And in 2000 BA acquired a minor 18.3 per cent stake in the South African regional airline operator Comair for slightly more than €27 million.[70]

Yet, beyond acquisitions, BA also sold some airlines that it had either bought, or started, in the 1990s. For example, Air Liberté was taken over by

BA in 1997 when the French airline went into receivership, eventually merging it along with TAT under the banner of Air Liberté.[71] However, because it was unable to compete against the market power of Air France (Doganis, 2006, 76–7), Air Liberté was eventually sold in 2001 to a venture capital provider, Taitbout Antibes, which later merged it with France's number three carrier at the time, AOM, that was jointly controlled by the Swissair Group.[72] Similarly, Go Fly Limited (or, Go) was also founded in 1998 by BA as a low-cost airline based out of London Stansted. But it was later sold to private equity firm 3i and management in 2000 (for approximately €180 million), only to be later bought by easyJet in 2002 for over thrice the value.[73] Finally, in 2007 BA sold its subsidiary BA Connect to the UK's FlyBe. Although no consideration was disclosed, in exchange BA received a 15 per cent stake of FlyBe,[74] a stake it still owns as of October 2013.

Beyond these relatively smaller transactions, early on as a privatized firm BA flirted with some of the industry's giants: it took a 25 per cent stake in Australia's Qantas Airways in 1993, which was diluted to 18.25 per cent by 2004 due to capital increases.[75] BA sold this minority stake in September 2004, just months after the KLM deal, with net proceeds of an estimated €631 million.[76] Given losses that had piled up in the wake of 9/11, the Iraq War, and outbreak of diseases such as Foot and Mouth and SARS—which had impacted the industry as a whole—proceeds were used towards repaying its existing debt, strengthening balance sheets, and allowing the carrier to be in a credible position to seek alliances with other major European carriers over the next decade.[77] Swiss International and BMI were partners that BA initially considered, both eventually acquired by Lufthansa. As the decade continued to witness its falling share prices in 2008, there were rumours that BA itself could be a takeover target of another airline, such as Cathay Pacific.[78] This was followed with renewed speculation that BA sought to merge with its old ally, Qantas, which too was officially withdrawn in December 2008.[79]

BA finally settled on merging with Iberia in 2011. Not dissimilar to Qantas, Iberia was an 'old friend' with which BA had previous dealings—in Iberia's case it was, interestingly, during the first stage of Spanish airline's privatization, to which I now turn.

Iberia

BRIEF HISTORY, PRIVATIZATION, AND LIFE THEREAFTER

Iberia Airlines of Spain (*Iberia Líneas Aéreas de España*) has its roots in *Iberia Compañía Aérea de Transporte* that was founded in 1927, where its first flights linked Madrid and Barcelona.[80] After the Civil War, Iberia was nationalized by Franco in 1944 and housed within the National Industry Institute (INI.) Over the next twenty years flight service extended beyond Spain to include

London, the US, Africa, and Central and South America, the latter of which represented an area where Spain traditionally served as the hub to/from Europe. The importance of the area to Iberia is reflected in its 1990 takeover of Aerolíneas Argentinas, which eventually proved a debt-ridden burden throughout the next few years.

Despite the magnitude of Iberia's routes, throughout the 1990s it suffered from low profits, high debt to equity ratios, and an aging fleet that justified two large capital injections of PTS120 billion in 1992 and PTS87 billion in 1995 (Cini and McGowan, 2008, 151). The aid helped improve Iberia's financial structure, pay redundancies to around three thousand workers, and renew fleets (Chari, 2004). Thereafter, Iberia saw a slight turnaround: before-tax profits reached over PTS20 billion by 1997 and increased to over PTS65 billion by 1998 (*El País*, 3 October 1999). The SEPI (*Sociedad Estatal de Participaciones Industriales*, which was the new post-1995 name for the former INI) transferred its other domestic carrier—Aviaco—to Iberia in 1998. This was done in a similar vein to when Air France and BA took over other domestic competitors, thereby promoting consolidation of the national champion. To ease the burden on Iberia's road to privatization the SEPI assumed full control of the loss-making Aerolíneas Argentinas in 1996.[81]

Led by Josep Piqué, the Minister of Industry where the SEPI was housed, as well as the Ministry of Economy and Finance, Rodrigo Rato, the Partido Popular subsequently privatized Iberia in two stages. First, in contrast to other airlines examined, in 1999 the state chose industrial and institutional partners to take over 40 per cent of Iberia, as opposed to immediate flotation.[82] Industrial partners with a proven track record ensured Iberia's growth in the sector, while institutional partners largely from Spanish banks represented a solid financial base.[83] Regarding industrial partners, the SEPI informally negotiated with EU-based carriers—BA, Alitalia, KLM, Air France—as well as those from the US—AA, United, Northwest, and Delta. Given the price offered, their pre-existing relationship as part of the Oneworld alliance, and their complementary markets, the state eventually chose to sell 9 per cent to BA and 1 per cent to AA.[84] Chari and Cavatorta (2002) outline that the financial partners chosen included key players in the Spanish economy: Caja Madrid (10 per cent), BBVA (7.3 per cent), Logista (6.7 per cent), Ahorro Corporacion (3 per cent), and El Corte Ingles (3 per cent). The total price paid was over USD 1.5 billion, which Chari and Cavatorta (2002, 127) argue represented a 20 per cent discount. In the second stage of its privatization, an IPO of around 50 per cent belonging to the state was completed in early April 2001. The price was lowered by 'nearly 40% in an effort to avoid a weak showing when shares start(ed) trading',[85] resulting in approximately USD 435 million in total revenue.[86] At the end of the transaction, the SEPI retained a minority shareholding of a little more than 5 per cent of Iberia.

After unsuccessful attempts to make potential acquisitions in Latin America in the early part of the 2000s, as seen in its failed bid for Mexicana,[87] the first deal in Iberia's life after privatization was to form new low-cost airline based out of Barcelona, Clickair. In this 2006 joint venture with four other partners each took a 20 per cent stake.[88] After months of negotiation, in 2009 Clickair merged with the other main budget airline also based out of Barcelona-El Prat, Vueling. The new entity represented the second largest carrier in Spain. The Vueling brand was retained for the newly merged airline and Iberia would have a controlling 45.85 per cent stake.[89]

Iberia's major deal—and the most significant one for its partner, BA—was the 2011 merger of the Spanish and British flag carriers, forming the International Airlines Group (IAG).[90] In terms of BA's history with Iberia, it initially gained a small stake in Iberia during the first stage of its privatization. After the second stage when Iberia was floated, there were immediate rumours that the two would merge. With the AF–KLM announcement in 2003, both BA and Iberia were keen to monitor how it unfolded, prudently using it as a litmus test to see if merging two giant carriers that were run as separate entities, but owned by the same shareholders, was possible. After the sale of Qantas in 2004, a debt-ridden BA stated that it feared rushing in and increasing its ownership in Iberia. But, it did exactly that in July 2005 by slightly increasing its stake to 10.32 per cent for €7.35 million as well as increasing joint flights between Madrid Barajas and London Heathrow. Still, no concrete moves to tie the knot.

Two years passed, when somewhat surprisingly Lufthansa announced in February 2007 desires to take 'all or part' of Iberia, something it bowed out of months later when focusing its energies on both Austrian and Brussels Airlines. A month later, US-based private equity firm Texas Pacific Group (TPG) made a non-binding offer to purchase all of Iberia. But with its 10 per cent stake, BA 'held the right of first refusal over offers for approximately 30% of Iberia', and could potentially act as a veto player.[91] Further, because TPG was restricted in holding 49 per cent of Iberia given foreign ownership rules (discussed in Section 3), it had to later find Spanish investment companies with whom to form a consortium.[92] By May 2007, BA joined the TPG consortium, only to leave it in November 2007. Different consortiums targeting Iberia later sprang up, including that led by private equity group Apax Partners that was in reported talks with Air France to make a joint rival bid.[93] By the end of 2007, however, all potential bids were either never tabled, or withdrawn.

Talk was finally put into action between BA and Iberia in 2008: the last part of the decade witnessed both suffering badly from the consequences of the financial and economic crisis, and an alliance was a considered a necessity by the two to help cut costs and ensure their strong survival. After Iberia intimated that 'you could leave me now or love me forever' when BA was flirting (again) with Qantas in late 2008, BA and Iberia negotiated over the next few months. They presented a memorandum of understanding in November 2009, finally signing the agreement in April 2010 in a deal whose value is estimated at €2.3 billion. The merger was implemented through a newly created holding company called International Airlines Group (IAG), officially formed in January 2011 with the view to save €500 million over five years.[94] In this 'merger of equals', BA shareholders held 55 per cent of IAG, Iberia shareholders 45 per cent. Vueling Airlines was subsequently absorbed into the parent IAG. In terms of the SEPI's shareholding, its minority stake since Iberia's IPO meant that it owned 2.71 per cent of IAG when it was formed. The Spanish Cabinet under Zapatero officially approved the sale of this stake in April 2011,[95] although the evidence from both the SEPI and Zephyr databases suggests that the process of sale is still ongoing at the time of writing, as discussed in Section 2 when the independence test is performed.

A year later, after launching low-cost Iberia Express in March 2012, IAG purchased BMI from Lufthansa. On the one hand, IAG was keen to strengthen its presence in Heathrow and, on the other, Lufthansa was eager to dump out of its loss-making acquisition. In a sale which also received a bid from Virgin Atlantic, Lufthansa eventually sold BMI to IAG for an estimated €211 million in April 2012.[96] Lufthansa would thus make a slight loss considering that between 2000 and 2009 it purchased BMI for an estimated €242.5 million, as seen earlier. IAG's interest was to integrate the BMI mainline business, and not to maintain the subsidiaries BMI Regional and the budget airline BMI-Baby. Aberdeen-based BMI Regional was thus eventually sold to Sector Aviation Holdings in June 2012 for close to €10 million;[97] BMIBaby was shut down in September 2012, taking with it 450 jobs based out of East Midlands Airport.[98]

Alitalia

BRIEF HISTORY, PRIVATIZATION, AND LIFE THEREAFTER

Later than the other airlines previously examined, Alitalia–Aerolinee Italiane Internazionali was founded after the Second World War in September 1946 with British financial assistance of around 900 million lira.[99] In 1957 the IRI coordinated its merger and LAI (Linee Aeree Italiane), which was also founded in 1946 and owned by the IRI and Trans World Airlines. The resultant company, Alitalia–Linee Aeree Italiane SpA (henceforth Alitalia), had 3,000 employees and 37 airplanes.[100] In 1960, 'the first jets entered service and the new Leonardo da Vinci airport in Fiumicino was opened',[101] expanding flights within Europe and globally. Although the 1970s and 1980s witnessed technological improvements which led to competitive positions among international airlines, Thatcher (2009, 227) notes that 'Alitalia made large losses, especially after oil price rises and subsequent recessions in 1973, 1979–80, and 1990'.

Opposite to Iberia's sale that can be characterized as first being partially sold to private investors with the remainder being floated later, Alitalia was first partially floated and later sold to private investors. In 1985, 22 per cent was sold by way of public offering, where the transaction value was approximately USD 328 million. This was followed by 18.4 per cent in 1998 (USD 448 million) and 12.1 per cent in November 2005 (USD 16 million), after which point the state held less than half of Alitalia.[102] Throughout the 2000s, as discussed later in the chapter, the firm continued to suffer from serious financial difficulty.

In its life after partial privatization, there are two noteworthy developments in the 2000s relating to acquisitions and making ties with the French Alpha which would prove essential as the decade continued. With regard to its acquisitions, Volare Airlines was a small airline based out of Milan-Malpensa. It filed for bankruptcy in 2004, to be later sold by auction in 2005.[103] Making a bid of €38 million, Alitalia was chosen as the winning bid ahead of the other main Italian carrier, Air One. However, this was appealed by Air One in 2006, which took the case to the regional court in Lazio. In the end, the court decided to invalidate the ranking of the auction (Alitalia, Air One, Meridiana), but did not invalidate the deal per se, leaving Alitalia in control of Volare.[104]

With regard to making ties that would prove essential throughout the decade, in 2001 Air France and Alitalia 'entered into a cooperation agreement aimed at creating a European multi-hub system based on their main airports of Paris Charles de Gaulle (CDG), Rome Fiumicino and Milan Malpensa around which they interconnect their world-wide networks'.[105] This was followed by increased ties between both firms, with a 2 per cent share swap in 2003.[106] These events served as a basis for events at the end of the decade: as discussed in more detail in Section 3 when I consider why firms become Alphas or Betas, AF–KLM eventually took a controlling stake in Alitalia in 2009 which it obtained shortly after a deal orchestrated by Silvio Berlosconi when Alitalia was sold to Compagnia Aerea Italiana (CAI) in 2008. However, after AF–KLM refused to participate in a €300 million capital injection in December 2013, this set the stage for Alitalia to enter into talks with Etihad Airways, which is owned by the Government of Abu-Dhabi. At the close of writing the book, in August 2014 a deal valued at €1.76 billion was signed between the two parties where Etihad will acquire 49 per cent of Alitalia, a deal which gained Brussels regulatory approval months later in November 2014 (European Commission, 2014).[107]

Table 3.1 summarizes the main deals pursued by the privatized firms.

Table 3.1. Air France, Lufthansa, BA, Iberia, and Alitalia M&A

Company	When Sold	Main Mergers and Acquisitions (Chronological)
Air France	1999, 2004 (remaining state stake, 15.9%)	AF Acquires Aer Inter and UTA (1989); acquires 34% stake in Société Nouvelle Air Ivoire (2000); purchases CityJet (amongst other smaller carriers, 2000); merger of AF–KLM (2004); purchase of VLM Airlines (2008, Belgium; subsequently forms part of Group's Dublin-based CityJet operations); pursues a joint venture with China Southern Airlines to create a Sino-European air-freight company as well as revenue-sharing agreements (Gungzhou, China, 2008, 2010); acquires Aero Maintenance Group (US, 2009); AF–KLM Group purchases 25% of Alitalia (2009)
Lufthansa	Various offers in 1989, 1994, and 1997	50:50 joint venture with Turkish Airlines, SunExpress (1989). Takeover of Eurowings and Germanwings (2000–9). Purchased Air Dolomiti (1999–2003). Acquired BMI (2000–9, later to sell it to IAG in 2012). Acquired Swiss International Airlines (2005–7). Stake of 25% of Jade Cargo International 2004 (first cargo airline based in China with foreign ownership, co-owned with Shenzen Airlines, abandoned in 2012). 19% purchase of JetBlue (US, 2007; first major ownership investment by EU carrier in the US). Edelweiss Air (through Swiss, 2008). 45% stake in Brussels Airlines (formerly Sabena, 2009; option for full buyout). Purchased Austrian Airlines (2009). Sold BMI to IAG (2012, see BA and Iberia, 2012)
BA	1987	Acquisition of British Caledonian (1988); acquisition of Gatwick-based carrier Dan-Air (1992); purchased TAT European Airlines (France domestic carrier, 1996) and Air Liberté (France, 1997), both of which are later sold. Sale of its 18.25% stake in Qantas (2004). BA takes a stake of 15% in Flybe (2007); purchases L'Avion (France, 2008); BA calls off merger talks with Qantas (2008); merger with Iberia, where BA shareholders retain 55% of merged airline, and Iberia 45%, forming International Airlines Group (IAG, 2011). IAG absorbs Vueling, launches Iberia Express (2012), acquires BMI from Lufthansa (2012)
Iberia	1999, 2000, 2001	Purchase of Aerolíneas Argentinas (1990, later sold to Grupo Marsans, 2001). In a joint venture with four other companies, Iberia forms low-cost airline Clickair (2006). Clickair and Vueling merge (2009), giving Iberia control of Vueling. Merger with BA (IAG, 2011). IAG absorbs Vueling, launches Iberia Express (2012), acquires BMI from Lufthansa (2012)
Alitalia	Various 1985, 1998, 2005, 2008	Acquires Volare Airlines (2006). Alitalia acquired by Compagnia Aerea Italiana (CAI; Italy, 2008); CAI also bought Air One (2008); CAI then sold 25% of Alitalia to the AF–KLM Group (2009)

3.2 Determining Alphas and Betas

This section determines which of the privatized airlines can be considered Alphas and Betas today. It starts by considering the results of the first part of the Global Movers Test, which examines Forbes data, and then turns to the second part analysing how the firms rank against their Europe peers using BvD's Amadeus database. Thereafter, examining the shareholder structure of the firm, the Independence Test is performed.

Table 3.2. Privatized Airlines Studied on Forbes 2000 List, 2014

Company	Country	Ranking of the Company in the Forbes 2000 List	Sectoral Ranking
Lufthansa	Germany	580/2000	4/21
IAG	UK/Spain	773/2000	6/21
AF–KLM	France	1036/2000	10/21
Alitalia	Italy	Not Ranked	Not Ranked

Sources for classification: Forbes 2000 Index, May 2014 <http://www.forbes.com/global2000/list/> [accessed 6 June 2014]

Global Movers Test

In the first part of this test, I consider whether or not the airline appears on the latest Forbes 2000 list of 2014. Table 3.2 summarizes which companies are found on the list and, if so, what is their overall ranking compared to the 2,000 companies (Column 3), and how they rank in their sector amongst the twenty-one international airlines which appear on the list.

All the airlines studied, except for Alitalia, are ranked in the Forbes list in 2014, thereby relegating Alitalia to being a Beta already in the first dimension of the Global Movers Test. Of all global airlines on the Forbes list, Lufthansa leads all European carriers and is ranked only below Delta Airlines, United Continental, and Southwest Airlines. The second leading Europe carrier is International Airlines Group (the product of the BA/Iberia merger, and which also includes the low-cost carrier based out of Barcelona, Vueling), which is followed by Ryanair (which has an overall rank of 936). Air France–KLM's ranking in 2014 remains roughly the same from its position in 2013, ahead of international giants such as Latam Airlines (Chile), China Eastern Airlines, Qantas, and Turkish Airlines. Given the results, Lufthansa, BA/Iberia, and AF–KLM can be deemed to have attained one of the thresholds to be considered an Alpha.

The second part of the Global Movers Test considers how the privatized airlines fare against their European peers with regard to operating revenue, total assets, shareholder funds, and number of employees. The objective is to see if the firms fall within the top 1 per cent of European firms in the sector and, if so, if they can be considered to have attained one of the thresholds to be considered an Alpha. To ascertain the number of firms that constitutes the top 1 per cent, a search was done on the Amadeus database of all active companies in the EU-27, with a primary NACE Rev. 2 code of 51 (Air transport) and which all had accounts available in the latest year, which in this case was 2012. The number of companies that were found in the database was 3,526.[108] As such, to be in the top 1 per cent of all firms according to the various metrics the firm had to fall within the top thirty-five. Comparative analysis and

Table 3.3. The Airline Sector: The European Giants, 2012

Company name	Country	Operating revenue (Turnover) mil EUR	Rank (amongst top 100 firms in EU-27)	Total assets mil EUR	Rank	Shareholders funds mil EUR	Rank	Number of employees	Rank
2012									
LUFTHANSA	Germany	33,033	1	28,419	1	8,298	1	116,839	1
AIR FRANCE–KLM	France/ Netherlands	25,865	2	27,474	2	4,924	3	100,744	2
IAG	UK/Spain	18,117	3	19,837	3	5,055	2	59,574	3
SAS AB	Sweden	5,082	4	4,274	6	1,297	5	14,897	4
RYANAIR	Ireland	4,884	5	8,943	4	3,273	4	9,059	7
EASYJET	UK	4,871	6	4,959	5	497	12	7,524	9
AIR BERLIN	Germany	4,439	7	2,151	9	126	32	9,315	6
ALITALIA–CAI	Italy	3,925	8	2,634	7	201	23	14,259	5
VIRGIN ATLANTIC	UK	2,905	9	1,491	16	53	57	8,480	8
FINNAIR	Finland	2,494	10	2,242	8	786	9	6,784	11

Source: Amadeus

ranking of the top 100 (of the 3,526) companies in the sector was performed, and Table 3.3 summarizes the findings.

The main conclusion to be drawn in the second part of the Global Movers Test is that Lufthansa, IAG (BA and Iberia), and Air France–KLM represent some of the leading firms in the sector in Europe: all have clearly passed the cut-off point and attained the thresholds outlined in the second part of the test. However, it is important to note the strength of the low-cost airlines which have a significantly lower number of workers, particularly Ryanair as well as easyJet, which both made the Forbes 2000 list as well. Alitalia–CAI (the product of Alitalia's takeover) also appears (although not in the top ten of all firms on all dimensions) and would have, theoretically, passed the second part of the test; however, not appearing on the Forbes list as being one of the leading international airlines in the world means that it remains a Beta.

The Independence Test

With regard to the Independence Test,[109] the only airline where the state owns a significant amount of the privatized company is Air France–KLM, in which the French state holds close to 16 per cent, as seen in Figure 3.1.

While the German state owns no shares in Lufthansa, the evidence as of December 2013 suggests that the Spanish state through its holding company SEPI maintains a 2.71 per cent stake in IAG. This is the case even though the Spanish Cabinet approved the sale of this stake after IAG's formation in January 2011. How can this be explained? The evidence starts with a letter

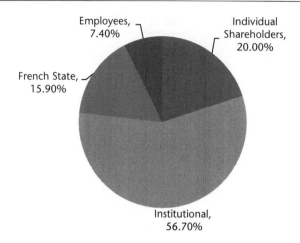

Figure 3.1. Breakdown of AF–KLM Shareholding as of 30 September 2013

Source: <http://www.airfranceklm-finance.com/en/Shares/Capital-structure-and-equity-threshold-declarations> [last accessed 25 November 2013]

dated 8 April 2011, written by SEPI's Director of Administration and Resources (Juan Gurbindo Gutiérrez) to the Spanish regulators (CNMV), where there was confirmation that the Spanish Council of Ministers (i.e. Cabinet) agreed to allow SEPI to sell its 2.71 per cent stake in IAG.[110] The letter goes on to state, however, that the sale will not necessarily take place immediately, but when there are favourable market conditions.[111] Analysis of the shareholder structure of the firm in December 2013 reveals that the state has yet to sell this stake, as verified by three sources. First, information on shareholdings of IAG, compiled by the BvD and found in their Amadeus and Zephyr databases, verifies that the state maintains this 2.71 per cent. Second, the SEPI's webpage highlights that the state maintains this stake in IAG.[112] Third, and considering that the webpage may have been outdated, this information was verified in phone interviews between the author and SEPI officials that confirmed that it is still in the process of selling this non-strategic 2.71 per cent stake.[113] One explanation for SEPI not selling may be based on the evolution of IAG's stock price over time: this dropped more than 40 per cent between early 2011 and the middle of 2012, only to recover by early 2013. As SEPI is clearly guided to sell at a profit when there are favourable market conditions, it is apparently in the process of waiting for the appropriate moment.

Regardless of the state's ownership in both AF–KLM and IAG, no one shareholder of either firm owns more than 25 per cent. As a result, both firms are assigned a BvD Independence ranking of A⁺. This is also the case for Lufthansa. As such, all three pass the Independence Test. In the case of Alitalia, 25 per cent owned by AF–KLM since 2009, the BvD gives the firm an

Table 3.4. Summary of Independence Test Findings for Airlines

Privatized Company	BvD Independence Ranking	Exception 1: Does the state still own more than 25% of the firm?	Exception 2: Does a family with historical relations own more than 25%?	Has the firm been taken over by another firm during/after privatization? If so, which firm is the Global Ultimate Owner?	Given exceptions (if applicable), did the firm pass the Independence Test?
Air France–KLM	A$^+$	No (but French state still owns ~ 16%)	No	No	Yes
Lufthansa	A$^+$	No	No	No	Yes
IAG (BA Iberia)	A$^+$	No	No	No	Yes
Alitalia	A$^-$ (under AF–KLM ownership since 2009) B (under Etihad's scheduled 49% ownership)	No	No	From 2009, AF-KLM have controlling stake; from late 2014, Etihad scheduled to have controlling stake	No

independence ranking of A$^-$ and has therefore not passed the criteria of the Independence Test as outlined in Chapter 2. Etihad's scheduled takeover of 49 per cent of Alitalia, which recently gained European Commission approval in November 2014 (European Commission, 2014), would result in a BvD independence indicator of B, equally meaning that it would not pass the Independence Test. Table 3.4 summarizes the test's main findings.

Taking all of the test results together, AF–KLM, IAG, and Lufthansa can all be considered Alphas, while Alitalia is a Beta. The next section explains why the firms are either Alphas or Betas.

3.3 Explaining Why Firms Become Alphas and Betas

This section considers which factors are of salience in explaining why firms become Alphas and Betas. It starts with a comparative analysis of all Alphas (AF–KLM, Lufthansa, and IAG), examining both the internal and external (more political) factors of salience. It then concentrates on the only Beta, Alitalia.

As none of the firms was taken over at the point of privatization, the theoretical conceptualization in Figure 2.2 of Chapter 2 serves as a framework for this section's discussion. To remind the reader of the framework, a slightly modified version is presented in Figure 3.2, which shows which airlines can be considered Alphas and Betas today based on the tests performed in the previous section (Y, outcome variable).

| Initial conditions (X1) | Intervening variables (X2) | Outcome variable (Y) |

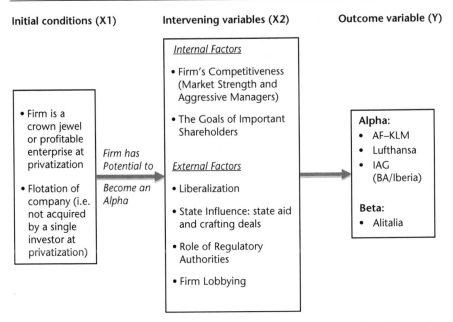

Figure 3.2. The Second Model: How an Airline May Become an Alpha or Beta (Y) Based on Initial Conditions at Privatization (X1) and Intervening Variables Post-Privatization (X2)

Explaining the Alphas—AF–KLM, Lufthansa, IAG

In terms of initial conditions (X1), and as explained in Section 1, all of the Alphas were crown jewels or successfully floated when privatized (with the exception of Iberia, which saw a combination of flotation and private sale). I thus turn to a discussion of the intervening factors at play post-privatization (X2), focusing first on the internal factors, followed by analysis of the external, more political ones.

Internal Factors

COMPETITIVENESS (MARKET STRENGTH AND MANAGERS)
There are roughly three general conjunctures of Alphas' privileged market positions. First, as noted before, all virtually held monopoly positions on domestic and international routes, with full liberalization only taking place after the 1986 Single European Act (as later discussed in the section on liberalization). Before and after privatization, when they enjoyed a privileged position in their home markets, deals were pursued in the 1980s, 1990s, and early 2000s to help consolidate their position as *the* national leaders: they took over other airlines in their country or smaller airlines from bordering ones. In the case of Air France, for example, before its partial privatization it acquired

UTA and Aer Inter, in a similar vein to Iberia taking over Aviaco before the first stage of its privatization. After its partial sale, Air France later acquired a host of smaller airlines, including CityJet. In a similar vein, after its sale Lufthansa started with the process of consolidating its position in the German market by acquiring a minority stake in the third largest carrier in the country, Eurowings. It also bought Air Dolomiti and a small stake in BMI. Likewise, within months of its sale BA scooped up its main competitor—Gatwick-based British Caledonian—later purchasing smaller French airlines such as TAT and Air Liberté.

In a second conjuncture, cross-border deals within European space were pursued and Alphas' market share as European giants grew. This started with the 2004 AF–KLM merger, where the group later acquired Belgium's VLM. Shortly after AF–KLM, Lufthansa's pursued a string of acquisitions of bordering countries' airlines (Swiss, Brussels, and Austrian). This was followed by the eventual merger between British Airways and Iberia.

Ringbeck and Schneiderbauer's work (2007), reproduced in Figure 3.3, offers a neat conceptualization of the market position of the traditional flag carriers shortly after the AF–KLM merger, but before Lufthansa's, Iberia's, and BA's deals from 2005 onwards.

Figure 3.3 highlights that even in the mid-2000s AF–KLM, Lufthansa, BA, and Iberia were the leaders amongst the traditional flag carriers in terms of number of passengers carried as well as revenue passenger kilometres (RPKs). The Figure helps us see, in hindsight, that some of the acquisitions pursued post-2005 were of Alphas acquiring other leading flag carriers from other EU

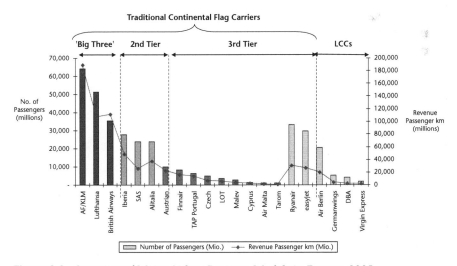

Figure 3.3. Overview of Major Airline Business Models in Europe, 2005

Source: Graph fully reproduced with permission from Strategy& (formerly Booz & Company), from Ringbeck and Schneiderbauer (2007, page 3, Exhibit 2). LCCs refer to Low Cost Carriers.

member states (such as Lufthansa's acquisition of Austrian), Alphas merging with each other (British Airways–Iberia), or Alphas taking a controlling stake in a Beta (AF–KLM's partial acquisition of Alitalia).

Alphas also pursued deals internationally during the latter part of the 2000s (such as AF–KLMs and Lufthansa transactions in Africa, the US, and Asia), which ultimately paved the way for arguably a third conjuncture where Alphas now represent some of the world leaders in the sector. Although this is captured in the Forbes data previously presented, more industry-specific data also demonstrates that the 'home-bases' of the Alphas, significant in terms of generating jobs, all rank within the top of the world's largest airports. As Table 3.5 demonstrates with ACI data, the Alpha home-bases are within the top fifteen of the world in terms of passenger traffic in 2011. These include Heathrow and Barajas (IAG), Charles De Gaulle and Schiphol (AF–KLM), and Frankfurt (Lufthansa). Of all Alpha airports, Heathrow ranks the highest in terms of passenger traffic, followed by Charles De Gaulle, Frankfurt, and then Madrid Barajas, all of which outrank New York's JFK. With the exception of Barajas, all Alpha home-bases saw an increase in total passengers from the year before.

When turning to the management of the firm, Woll (2008, 113) has argued that leading airlines have been led by teams seeking to consolidate and

Table 3.5. Passenger Traffic: Top Twenty Airports Worldwide, 2011

Rank	City (Airport)	Total Passengers	% Change (from year before)
1	ATLANTA GA, US (ATL)	92,389,023	3.5
2	BEIJING, CN (PEK)	78,675,058	6.4
3	LONDON, GB (LHR)	69,433,565	5.4
4	CHICAGO IL, US (ORD)	66,701,241	(.1)
5	TOKYO, JP (HND)	62,584,826	(2.5)
6	LOS ANGELES CA, US (LAX)	61,862,052	4.7
7	PARIS, FR (CDG)	60,970,551	4.8
8	DALLAS/FORT WORTH TX, US (DFW)	57,832,495	1.6
9	FRANKFURT, DE (FRA)	56,436,255	6.5
10	HONG KONG, HK (HKG)	53,328,613	5.9
11	DENVER CO, US (DEN)	52,849,132	1.7
12	JAKARTA, ID (CGK)	51,533,187	16.2
13	DUBAI, AE (DXB)	50,977,960	8.0
14	AMSTERDAM, NL (AMS)	49,755,252	10.0
15	MADRID, ES (MAD)	49,653,055	(.4)
16	BANGKOK, TH (BKK)	47,910,904	12.0
17	NEW YORK, NY, US (JFK)	47,644,060	2.4
18	SINGAPORE, SG (SIN)	46,543,845	10.7
19	GUANGZHOU, CN (CAN)	45,040,340	9.9
20	SHANGHAI, CN (PVG)	41,447,730	2.1

Source: Airports Council International (ACI), Passenger Traffic (Annual Traffic Data, 2011), reproduced in full with permission. Passenger traffic is measured by the ACI as 'total passengers enplaned and deplaned, passengers in transit counted once'. This data (and that for all top thirty airports in 2011) can be found on <http://www.aci.aero/Data-Centre/Annual-Traffic-Data/Passengers/2011-final> [accessed 12 January 2014]

expand globally. There are at least two main dimensions of the importance of company directors.

First, they can offer long-term visions of Alpha's expansion, well before the deals are completed.[114] For example, during the 1994 privatization process, Jürgen Weber, the Chairman of Lufthansa, intimated that privatization could help increase the profitability of the firm and gain access to new markets, highlighting the importance of alliances and foreshadowing deals that would manifest over the next ten years. As reported by the *New York Times* in 1994, 'Mr. Weber said Lufthansa had also discussed a "triangle relation" with Swissair and Austrian Airlines, but said "all three have to love one another", which isn't yet the case.'[115]

Second, company directors can play a key role in driving deals that allow Alphas to grow, where there is evidence for at least three different scenarios. One scenario sees managers leaning on governments that have companies on the selling block. This is seen in the case of Lufthansa's eventual acquisition of Austrian airlines: some fourteen years after Weber's comments in 1994, in March 2008 the chief executive of Lufthansa, Wolfgang Mayrhuber, stated that the Austrian state should seriously consider the possible future privatization of Austrian Airlines. This 'leaning' on the state took place well before the official privatization process of Austrian started on 12 August 2008. Interestingly, the full sale of the company was something that the then Austrian Transport Minister was not fully in favour of, given that he stated on 5 August 2008 that the state should retain a 25 per cent stake in its national carrier.[116]

In another scenario, CEOs are simply talented operators who take the necessary time to patiently and skilfully lead negotiation of the deals. This is particularly seen in the case of Willie Walsh—a trained pilot who worked up to the top position in Aer Lingus, turned the Irish carrier around after its disastrous performance after 9/11, before moving to become BA's CEO in October 2005. He carefully negotiated with Iberia at a time when others were targeting the Spanish airline. After the formation of IAG, Walsh was also quick to strengthen the merged airline's position in Heathrow with the BMI acquisition.[117]

In a final scenario, directors can spearhead strategic investments that are not necessarily directly related to acquiring other airlines. This is done with the view to leverage influence and strengthen their firms' competitive advantage in Europe and abroad. This is seen in comments by Lufthansa's Chairman and CEO Mayrhuber on the airline's minority stake in Fraport, as well as an AF official's comments on the purchase of Miami-based Aero Group.[118]

In all of these scenarios, while management teams are driven to pursue M&A to see their Alphas grow, they also reap the benefits: talented CEOs can be highly rewarded, as seen with Willie Walsh after BA's merger with Iberia. As *The Guardian* reported, Willie Walsh's move from chief executive of BA to IAG corresponded to a pay increase of 12 per cent (from £735,000 to

£825,000 a year), where he could also 'pick up a potential cash-and-shares annual bonus of up to £1.65m if he exceeds performance targets, capped at 200% of base salary'.[119]

SHAREHOLDERS

When turning to shareholders, none of the Alphas has one shareholder that owns more than 25 per cent of the firm, as seen in Section 2. But, the state maintains slightly more than 15 per cent ownership in AF–KLM, with potential to result in important Treasury revenues as well as representation on the board of directors, as will be examined later when we consider the importance of the role of the state in helping understand the Alpha's ability to have become world leaders.

With regard to the importance of non-state shareholders in the firms, particular attention must be paid to the asset management firms discussed in Chapter 2. Considering the ideas raised earlier in the book—that it is more likely that main asset managers will invest in Alphas than they will in Betas— one main question is whether or not asset managers have been shareholders in Alphas, potentially shying away from investing in Betas. To answer this question, analysis was made of ownership data between 2007 and 2011 in each of the privatized firms—AF–KLM, Lufthansa, Alitalia, BA, and Iberia. In a first instance, I simply seek which of the main asset managers have consistently held shares in Alphas or Betas. Later, I seek to better understand what are the relative percentages over time held by the asset management companies in the privatized firms.

In order to perform this analysis, the Amadeus database was examined. Amadeus not only allows us to see the various shareholders of the Alphas and Betas, but also the percentage that the main asset management firms held at the end of each fiscal year between 2007 and 2011.[120] Keeping discussion consistent with previous findings in other chapters, I consider principal global asset management firms discussed in Chapter 2—BlackRock, State Street, Allianz, Fidelity, Vanguard, AXA, BNP–Paribas, Deutsche Bank, JP Morgan, and Capital Group. Further analysis was performed to see whether or not other asset management companies which have more strength at the national level—such as Legal and General (UK), Natixis (France), Commerzbank (Germany), Santander (Spain), and Generali (Italy)—may also appear as shareholders in our privatized companies.

Table 3.6 highlights which of the top global asset management companies invested in the Alphas and Betas during 2007–11.

A general observation from Table 3.6 is that most of the top ten global asset management firms are found to have been shareholders in AF–KLM, Lufthansa, BA, and Iberia, but not Alitalia. Some exceptions are found: Deutsche Bank and Capital Group were shareholders in all Alphas during the time period, except Iberia, and Fidelity is the only one which did not hold shares

Table 3.6. Main Asset Management Firms Holding Shares in Airline Alphas and Betas, 2007–11

	Shareholder in *All* Alphas (AF–KLM, Lufthansa, BA, Iberia)	Shareholder in *Some* Alphas (AF–KLM, Lufthansa, BA, Iberia)	Shareholder In *No* Alphas (AF–KLM, Lufthansa, BA, Iberia)
Not a Shareholder in a Beta (Alitalia)	BlackRock; State Street; Allianz; Vanguard; AXA; BNP–Paribas	Deutsche Bank (held shares in all except Iberia); Capital Group (all except Iberia)	Fidelity
Shareholder in a Beta (Alitalia)	JP Morgan, in 2007 only	None	None

Source: Amadeus

in any airline. From a different perspective, with the one exception being JP Morgan which held shares in Alitalia for one year in 2007 (the same as BNY Mellon), none of the top ten asset managers was found to have been a shareholder in the Betas. As such, the world's top asset management companies are, generally, more likely to have invested in Alphas than Betas.

Closer inspection of other asset management firms beyond the top ten similarly reveals that several have also invested in Alphas, but not Betas. This includes UBS, the DekaBank Group, UniCredit, Credit Suisse, ING, and KBC. Only two other major US-based players—BNY Mellon and Morgan Stanley—have invested in some of the Alphas (such as BA and Lufthansa) and Alitalia (but only in 2007). Others from Europe have concentrated in privatized firms from their countries/or a selected group of Alphas, but never Alitalia:

- In Spain, such shareholders include BBVA, Sabadell, and Caja Madrid (all only in Iberia), as well as Santander (Lufthansa/BA/Iberia) and La Caixa (Iberia/Lufthansa).

- In France, Natixis (only AF–KLM); Covea Group (only AF–KLM); Crédit Mutuel (with main stakes in AF–KLM, but also BA and Lufthansa).

- In Germany, Commerzbank (Lufthansa and Iberia).

- In the UK, Lloyds Banking Group (BA); Legal and General (BA and Air France); HSBC (BA, AF–KLM, Lufthansa); Standard Life (BA, Lufthansa, Iberia); and Schroders, as well as Aberdeen Asset Management (BA/ Lufthansa);

- In the case of Italy, we see that Generali held shares in AF, Lufthansa, and Iberia throughout the time period, but not in Alitalia.

The second main set of results shows the fluctuation of global asset managers' shareholdings in Alphas over time. While it is of interest to see how those such as AXA, Deutsche Bank, and Capital Group have invested in Lufthansa and BA over time, of particular interest is BlackRock's participation in BA, before and after the approval of the BA–Iberia merger (Figure 3.4), compared to its shareholdings in Lufthansa between 2007 and 2011 (Figure 3.5).

Figure 3.4 highlights the overall increase of BlackRock's shares in BA. Its stake in BA increased from owning 4.35 per cent earlier in 2009 to 9.09 per cent by the end of September—a month before the BA–Iberia merger was

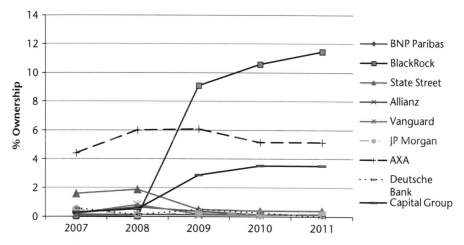

Figure 3.4. Global Asset Management Firms' Shareholdings in BA, 2007–11

Source: Shareholder data for the firm based on reported BvD's Amadeus and Zephyr, representing the percentage held as of 31 December of any year. 2011 values correspond to those held on 20 January 2011 (BA's last day of trading before shares of IAG were listed in London and Madrid on Monday, 24 January)

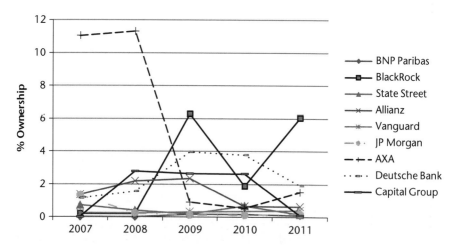

Figure 3.5. Global Asset Management Firms' Shareholdings in Lufthansa, 2007–11

Source: Shareholder data for the firm found in BvD's Amadeus, representing the percentage held as of 31 December of any year. 2011 values correspond to those held on 20 January 2011 (BA's last day of trading before shares of IAG were listed in London and Madrid on Monday, 24 January)

officially announced—in a transaction where the shares had an estimated value of over GBP 108 million.[121] This positively increased to slightly over 10.5 per cent by September 2010. Figure 3.5 shows that BlackRock owned around 6 per cent of Lufthansa at the end of 2009. After successive sales of Lufthansa stocks, by September 2010 BlackRock's shareholdings in Lufthansa were down to slightly less than 2 per cent, closing the year holding a 1.88 per cent stake, only to increase to 6.27 per cent by the end of 2011. Comparing both Alphas suggests that BlackRock's stakes were not static, increasing shares in one Alpha (BA), while buying, selling, and then buying again in another (Lufthansa). BlackRock's concentrating on attaining a stake over 10 per cent in the British airline by September 2010 may be explained because it was clear that the European Commission had granted regulatory approval for the BA–Iberia merger in July 2010 (discussed later). It also represented a time period before BA shareholders officially approved the takeover (which occurred in late November 2010), thereby giving BlackRock some extra sway as one of BA's largest shareholders after taking an over one-tenth stake. This participation in BA would eventually increase to close to 11.5 per cent before BA was delisted, meaning that the US-based firm would be one of the most significant shareholders in the newly formed IAG, of which it would own slightly less than 7 per cent by March 2011.

As seen in Figure 3.6, however, BlackRock's shareholdings in IAG have experienced local maxima and minima since, highlighting that the stakes

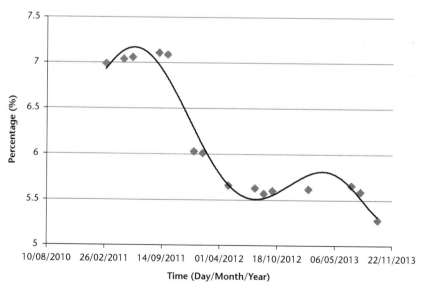

Figure 3.6. Percentage of IAG Owned by BlackRock, 2011–13
Source: Data from BvD's Amadeus

held by asset management firms in Alphas may fluctuate over time, which generally differentiates such shareholders from states that may maintain constant percentage ownership in firms over years even after their privatization.

Figure 3.6 highlights that BlackRock's stakes in IAG ebbed and flowed, but overall fell from a high of well over 7 per cent in September 2011, to around 6 per cent by January 2012, and then to 5 per cent in October 2013. Part of this explanation may lie in the poor performance of the IAG stock since August 2011, which only recovered by spring 2013.[122] This, along with the case of BlackRock and Lufthansa, suggests that shares may be bought and sold according to market value with the goals to maximize profits/minimize losses, and that there is no allegiance of the asset management firms to the Alphas per se.

An added dimension, which links the previous discussion on managers as well as that with shareholders, is the evidence of the links—likened to revolving doors—between the managerial bosses of Alphas and asset management companies. For example, the CEO of Lufthansa between June 2003 and December 2010, Wolfgang Mayrhuber, joined the board of directors of the global financial services firm UBS in 2010.[123] The Amadeus database provides evidence that UBS owned shares in Lufthansa between 2007 and 2013, from a high of around a 1.3 per cent stake in June 2008, shortly before Lufthansa's purchase of over 40 per cent of Austrian Airlines in December 2008.[124] Despite objection amongst some, institutional investors eventually approved Mayrhuber's bid in May 2013 to become Chairman of Lufthansa, supplementing his supervisory board positions in UBS, BMW, and Infineon.[125]

As a final note, while shareholders of Alphas may be significant, other large shareholders of firms that are acquired are also noteworthy. In some cases, for example, they can delay deals pursued by Alphas: well before Lufthansa purchased Swiss International in 2005, Swiss's directors were in talks with Lufthansa for its full takeover in August 2003. By September 2003 it was reported that 'Swiss International shareholders would be offered a combination of Lufthansa shares and dividend payments. In return, Lufthansa would expect Swiss International shareholders to inject fresh capital to the value of CHF500 into Swiss', something which the troubled carrier later stated was unacceptable to shareholders.[126] Almost immediately, Swiss joined BA's Oneworld alliance, with rumours abound that BA was ultimately keen on Swiss's takeover and its fourteen slots in Heathrow. Unfazed by this, within weeks Lufthansa reiterated its interest in Swiss and continued negotiation over the next two years. By March 2005 a better offer was made to Swiss, which eventually had the support of major shareholders including the Swiss Confederation, the Canton of Zurich, and others, with minority shareholders soon following.[127]

Similarly, minor shareholders from acquired firms ultimately agree to being taken over by Alphas given the financial benefits they receive. For example, after the state's stake of 41.56 per cent of Austrian Airlines was sold to Lufthansa, in the second stage of its acquisition Lufthansa needed to acquire the remaining shares of Austrian held by shareholders. Analysis of the second stage reveals that, in an offer readily accepted by shareholders, on 27 February 2009 Lufthansa offered €4.49 per share. Based on Austrian Airlines' closing price the day before of €3.46, 'the offer represents a premium of 29.77%'.[128]

External Factors

As much as the previous section highlights that the strong market position of Alphas before and after privatization is important, as are the goals of managers and shareholders, such factors are not sufficient in explaining why firms could pursue different deals and become Alphas today. Rather, external factors are of significance. The main argument to be developed is threefold. First, EU liberalization initiatives in the sector set the stage for Alpha expansion through cross-border M&A. Second, state actors (from Alphas' member states as well as other states) who supported consolidation in the sector facilitated some of the deals and (in some cases) played a role in the Alphas' boards of directors. Third, domestic-level and especially supra-national regulatory decisions ensured that the deals were approved for Alphas, which, compared to their peers in the sector, have a significantly larger lobbying presence in Brussels.

LIBERALIZATION

Although there was historically little liberalization in the sector, ultimately allowing flag carriers a privileged position, this changed in the wake of the Single European Act of 1986. As a broad objective, the SEA promoted the free movement of goods, services, and capital within the European Single Market. Its adoption gave both DG Competition and DG Transport the needed justification for liberalization of air transport, something they had tried to convince the Council of Ministers of since the 1970s (Doganis, 2006, 45). Three important liberalization initiatives proved to be game-changers, as discussed by Doganis (2006, 45–6): the 'December 1987 Package' which 'introduced a more liberal fares regime'; the 'Second Package' of 1990 which 'loosened constraints on pricing, on capacity restrictions and on market access'; and, most significantly, the 'Third Package' of aviation measures of 1993, a key variable in explaining life after privatization.[129]

The reason that the 'Third Package' had a significant impact, as discussed in examinations of European air transport policy (Kassim and Stevens, 2010), is because three main areas of EU legislation were developed, setting the stage for cross-border alliances and M&A. First, airlines with an operating base in one member state were allowed to fly on any route within the EU from 1992 and, from 1997, to fly on the domestic routes of other member states (Thatcher, 2009, 223). Second, there was the abolition of price controls. Third, the regulations allowed 'EU nationals or companies from any member state to set up and operate an airline in any other member state or to buy such an airline' (Doganis, 2006, 47). However, 'ownership of an EU airline by non-EU nationals or companies is limited to 49%', a feature also seen in the US where foreign ownership cannot exceed 25 per cent (Doganis, 2006, 55, 56). In this context, one can better understand some of the relatively smaller transactions (as well as partial stakes in some airlines) taking place during the 1990s, such as BA's acquisition of TAT, AF's purchase of CityJet, and Lufthansa's minority stake in Eurowings.

However, even though the sector witnessed liberalization in the internal market, this was not met with a common external policy: despite the Third Package, throughout the 1990s there were still several bilateral agreements between member states and third countries, such as the US, which favoured nationally owned flag carriers. Doganis (2006, 53) illustrates this with a clear example:

> [A] British owned airline, Virgin Express, could be based in Brussels and operate flights from Brussels to other points in the EU, or between points within the Union but outside of Belgium, as it did in 2004, flying from Amsterdam to Rome. But, it could not fly from Belgium, to say Moscow or Tunis. This is because bilaterals between these two countries and Belgium specifically require that the Belgian-designated airlines should be substantially owned and effectively controlled by Belgian nationals.

In the words of the Commission, such bilateral agreements meant that 'European carriers must keep over fifty per cent of their shares in the hands of the nationals in their home country, or risk losing their traffic rights',[130] thereby effectively preventing cross-border mergers between major airlines and consolidation. As such, in 1998 the Commission took several countries— including Austria, Belgium, Denmark, Finland, Germany, Luxembourg, and Sweden—to the European Court of Justice (ECJ) for signing bilateral agreements with the US, known as Open Skies deals, on the grounds that such pacts distorted competition within the single market. In the ECJ's November 2002 judgment, the Court sided with the Commission and ruled that such bilateral agreements were illegal, highlighting that nationality clauses were contrary to the Treaty and had to go.[131] This led to a series of further liberalization initiatives approved by the Council of Ministers in 2003, including giving the Commission the right to renegotiate existing bilaterals (Doganis, 2006, 64, 65).

The impact of EU liberalization initiatives was twofold. First, beyond some minor M&A, initial liberalization initiatives in the 1990s fostered conditions for the emergence of different alliances between airlines (Van Houtte, 2000, 84). Such alliances took on different forms and included route-specific, regional, strategic and marketing, and global (Doganis, 2006, 79–84). The global alliances resulted in three main groups, of which the Alphas were co-founders.[132] The first was the Star Alliance of 1997, co-founded by Lufthansa, Air Canada, SAS, Thai Airways International, and United Airlines, and would later include others such as Austrian Airlines and British Midlands. Oneworld was established in September 1998 and its co-founders included BA, AA, Cathay Pacific, and Qantas, later to include those such as Iberia. Finally, Skyteam was founded in June 2000 by Air France, Delta Airlines, Korean Air, and AeroMexico, where KLM and Alitalia later joined the alliance.

Second, the ECJ's decision of 2002 effectively served as a catalyst for major cross-border deals to take place. This started with AF–KLM, which was announced within a year of the ECJ's ruling. Establishing a counter-factual argument, the importance of the ECJ's ruling is also demonstrated by the fact that its absence saw previous potential cross-border deals involving large EU carriers falling flat. For example, one BA official stated with reference to BA's failed bid to take over KLM in 2000 that it 'was really blocked by these ownership and control arrangements'.[133] Like many, the DG Commissioner for Transport, Loyola de Palacio, believed that the ECJ's decision would thus lead to consolidation in the sector, which she openly favoured. The *New York Times* reported that 'she even held out the prospect of a handful of European carriers flying a European flag'.[134] Indeed, the impact of the Court's decision was clearly referred to by the bosses of Air France and KLM when they announced the merger in September 2003: the chief executive of Air France, Jean-Cyril Spinetta, stated that '(i)t's time for the airline industry to accept this European dimension', while Leo van Wijk (KLM chief executive) stated that '(a)ll airlines know that the (national) structure of our industry cannot be maintained'.[135]

Given this dual impact of liberalization, one witnessed a string of cross-border M&A between members within alliances, where many of such deals were led by the Alphas. In other words, with alliances having been formed, the ECJ's decision paved the way for Alpha airlines leading the alliances to merge with, or acquire, others within their group over the next ten years. This was logical considering that liberalization initiatives co-existing with ownership rules in the US meant that EU airlines could not easily merge with/acquire US-based global players outside the EU. Nor could businesses from the US take over European airlines given EU ownership rules.[136] Table 3.7 summarizes some of the transactions discussed in Section 1 between members of the various alliances.

Table 3.7. M&A within Airline Alliances

Alliance Member (date of entry)	Deal(s)	When Deal Finalized	Observation
Star Alliance			
BMI (July 2000)	SAS sale of BMI stakes to Lufthansa (LHA, original co-founding member of Star Alliance)	December 2000 (20%) and October 2009 (20%)	Deals between members of alliance (where vendor, SAS, is also founding member of Alliance)
SWISS (April 2006)	LHA purchase of Swiss	May 2005 (11%) January 2006 (100%)	Swiss joins Alliance after LHA purchase
Brussels Airlines (December 2009)	LHA purchase of Brussels	July 2009, 45%	Brussels joins Alliance after LHA purchase
Austrian Airlines (March 2000)	LHA purchases Austrian, 2008–9	December 2008, 45%; September 2009–February 2010, 100%	Deals between members of Alliance
ASIANA Airlines (March 2003)	LSG SkyChefs purchase of catering company	April 2003	Deal between members of Alliance
Oneworld Alliance			
Iberia (September 1999)	BA (alliance co-founder, September 1998) purchase of small stake in Iberia, and later merger	9% stake, December 1999; merger, January 2011	Deal between members of Alliance
Qantas (alliance co-founder, September 1998)	Sale of BA 18.25% stake in Qantas	September 2004	Deal between members of Alliance
Skyteam			
KLM (application to join Alliance, 30 September 2003)	Merger between AF (alliance co-founder in June 2000) and KLM	Deal announced 30 September 2003; official merger September 2004	Deal between members of Alliance
Alitalia (July 2001)	AF–KLM purchases 25% Alitalia	2003; 25% stake, March 2009	Deal between members of Alliance
China Southern Airlines (November 2007)	JV with AF–KLM pursue a joint venture to create a Sino-European air-freight company; revenue-sharing agreement on Paris–Guangzhou route	2009 and 2010	Deal between members of Alliance

Sources: Date of alliance entry (Column 1) is based on following links from the alliances: Star Alliance, <http://www.staralliance.com/assets/doc/en/about/member-airlines/pdf/Star_Alliance_Chronological_May2012.pdf>; Oneworld, <http://www.oneworld.com/general/about-oneworld>; Skyteam, <http://www.skyteam.com/en/About-us/Organization/History/> [all URLs last accessed 22 December 2013]. The second and third columns are based on information presented in Section 1 of this chapter.

A main observation is that several of the M&A occurred between alliance members, highlighting that previous association in the alliance matters in terms of which firms Alphas targeted.[137] Not all deals can be explained based on alliance structure, however. Table 3.7 shows that in some of Lufthansa's acquisitions, such as Swiss and Brussels, these firms did not join the alliance until after the deal was completed. Further, other purchases happen outside of the alliances, such as BA's (Oneworld) purchase of BMI (Star Alliance) from Lufthansa in 2012.

STATE INFLUENCE: STATE AID AND CRAFTING DEALS

With the exception of BA, it is well documented that the other Alphas received a significant amount of state aid from their home states throughout the 1990s, ultimately approved by the European Commission. This includes aid worth over FRF 20 billion to Air France in 1994, a DM 1.55 billion contribution by the German government to Lufthansa's pension fund in 1995, and two aid packages towards Iberia totalling over Pts 200 billion in 1992 and 1996.[138] Both Air France and Iberia effectively used this aid to restructure and increase competitiveness before privatization (Doganis, 2006, 252; Chari, 2004, 10–11).

Starting in the early 2000s, and consistent with EU liberalization initiatives, the European Commission explicitly clamped down on the use of aid in the sector, arguing that it distorted competition (Chari, 2004, 38). This was in spite of the difficult time many European carriers faced in the wake of 9/11. Although this basically crippled member states from making big cash injections, Brussels did allow for 'short term government or government guaranteed loans to help airlines on the verge of collapse to keep going long enough to be "rescued"' (Doganis, 2006, 247). By approving such aid, the Commission effectively promoted consolidation in the sector and indirectly aided the Alphas because they would eventually acquire the 'rescued' airlines. There are two key examples.

First is the case of a loan of USD 113 million given in October 2001 by the Belgian government to Sabena, which 'did not save Sabena, but it helped in the launch of SN Brussels as a replacement airline' (Doganis, 2006, 247). As seen earlier, Sabena declared bankruptcy in November 2001 and from it emerged SN Brussels, headed by a group of financiers led by Etienne Davignon (a once vice-president of the European Commission) that eventually sold a controlling stake to Lufthansa.

A second example is Austrian Airlines, where aid was given towards its restructuring before being acquired by Lufthansa. Not dissimilar to Volkswagen's purchase of SEAT as seen in the next chapter, the case of Austrian represents the purchase of a privatized company that was financially restructured before its sale to an Alpha. This is seen in developments in December 2008: after the ÖIAG-approved the sale of 41.56 per cent of Austrian to

Lufthansa, it also announced that part of the deal included the Austrian government giving restructuring aid of €500 million to Austrian Airlines.[139] This aid was eventually approved by the European Commission in late August 2009.[140]

Aid elements aside, the case of Austrian doubly shows how states from other parts of the EU are instrumental in crafting Alpha's deals: state officials from Austria helped facilitate the sale, thinking their own national interests would be served by selling to an Alpha from a reliable neighbouring country. In the words of Peter Michaelis, Chief Executive Officer of ÖIAG:

> The sale we have concluded today is the right decision both for Austrian Airlines and for the business location surrounding Vienna International Airport in general. Partnership with Lufthansa consolidates the status of Austrian Airlines as a leading carrier in Central and Eastern Europe. In addition to this, the Lufthansa concept provides for the preservation of the long-haul connections that are so important for the location. The affiliation between Lufthansa and Austrian Airlines therefore offers stability and opportunities for the Vienna hub and for the location as a whole ... (and) safeguard[s] Austrian interests. ÖIAG has therefore fulfilled the privatization mandate issued by the Federal Government, and the bidding process, while in turbulent circumstances, has served to produce a desirable result.[141]

In the sale of BMI to Lufthansa here, too, one sees the importance of states that are not the home of Alphas in driving Alpha expansion. In June 2007 the CEO of the SAS Group, Mats Jansson, developed its 'Strategy 2011' (S-11) to sell non-core assets (such as its shareholdings in BMI, Air Baltic, and the now defunct Spanair) in order to focus on its core market and to buy new aircraft. By the first quarter of 2009, through their board member representatives, the governments of Sweden, Denmark, and Norway instructed the sale of the remaining 20 per cent of BMI to Lufthansa. This instruction was based on losses of SAS throughout the decade and the states' desire not to give more subsidies.[142] A similar dynamic was previously seen when major shareholders from the Swiss state were also keen to sell Lufthansa once the price was right.

Alpha 'home' states are also important in life after privatization, just as they were before privatization, cognizant of the thousands employed by airlines, as seen in Table 3.3. Related to this is the indirect employment generated: Table 3.5 highlights the most important airports in the world are in Alphas home states, where Ringbeck and Schneiderbauer's (2007, 4) work highlights the concentration of traffic around European hubs and emerging multi-hubs: Frankfurt–Munich–Zurich–Vienna (Star Alliance), Paris–Amsterdam–Rome (Skyteam), and Madrid–London (Oneworld).

When turning to the importance of the state in France, Kassim (1996) neatly shows that, along with the state aid given by the French government before

AF's privatization, the state helped orchestrate deals to create national champions, as seen when AF acquired UTA and Air Inter. After its partial privatization, French state actors with vested interests in AF–KLM championed the creation of European giants to rival the large American airlines. In fact, the AF–KLM 2004 deal could not have taken place without the state giving the go-ahead in August 2003 to reduce its stake. Further, the revenue generated (when its stake was taken to less than 20 per cent) would be used for debt reduction. As stated by the then French Finance Minister Hervé Gaymard, 'proceeds from the sale will be used for the State's debt and not to finance new expenditure'.[143] Overseas deals where the French state has historical relations is also seen in the case of AF's 34 per cent stake in Société Nouvelle Air Ivoire in 2000.

Wright's (1994, 38) work similarly shows that Alpha home states are essential in driving deals after their privatization, even when such states retain no ownership, where he argues that the Thatcher government:

> ...continued to protect the company (BA) after privatization. When the partly state-owned SAS made its bid during November–December 1987 to buy a controlling stake in British Caledonian in an attempt to form the first major cross-border airline in Europe, it was blocked by the Thatcher government, which allowed a counter-bid by BA to succeed, thus consolidating BA's hold on the market. The Conservative government also allowed BA to swallow another private sector company (Dan-Air) in 1992. It was clearly more concerned with protecting a national champion (even if privatized) than furthering competition.

In terms of impact on the firm, the state's facilitating BA's takeover of British Caledonian was significant because 'RPK grew by roughly 20% between 1986 and 1988 and the number of (BA) employees came back to (1980) levels' (Macchiati and Siciliano, 2007, 134).

When turning to Germany, even though there are cases where it has acquired abroad (such as jetBlu), performing a segmentation analysis (to see a breakdown of the countries where Lufthansa has made acquisitions) shows that a plurality between 1997 and 2012 are with bordering countries with which Germany has historical ties.[144]

Figure 3.7 highlights that while many of its transactions have taken place at home (which includes the purchase of Eurowings and Germanwings), it has also focused its energy on neighbouring states with which Germany has historical ties: Switzerland (Swiss International and Edelweiss Air), Northern Italy (Air Dolomiti), Austria (Austrian Airlines), and Belgium (Brussels Airlines).[145] Similar analysis for Air France reveals that a plurality of its transactions have taken place in France, supplemented with those in Europe, Africa, the US, and China. BA sees a majority of its completed deals taking place in the

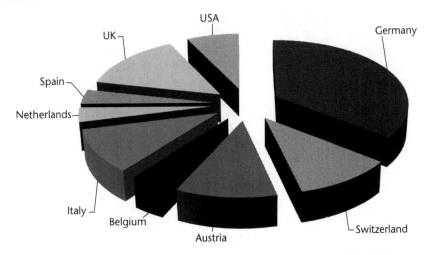

Figure 3.7. Geographic Breakdown of Lufthansa's Deals, 1997–2012
Source: Zephyr

UK, Spain, and France, while Iberia similarly has a majority completed in Spain and the UK.

When looking at specific transactions related to Lufthansa, the German state has helped craft deals both abroad and at home. For example, part of the state apparatus (DEG) actively participated in the Joint Venture between Lufthansa and Shenzen Airlines to create Jade Cargo in 2004. National interests were also served with Lufthansa Cargo's 2008 joint venture with DHL Worldwide Express, Aerologic. DHL is owned by Deutsche Post World Net, which is a subsidiary of Deutsche Post AG that is still over 20 per cent owned by the German state bank *Kreditanstalt für Wiederaufbau* (KfW).[146] The importance of the deal for national interests was summarized as follows:

> With the new cargo carrier, Lufthansa and Deutsche Post World Net are building consistently on years of highly successful business relations. The new company will not only strengthen Germany as an economic base, but will also create additional, highly qualified jobs in the Leipzig region.[147]

In the case of Iberia, the Spanish state's historical ties with Argentina resulted in the state actively spearheading Iberia's acquisition of Aerolíneas Argentinas, well before Iberia was privatized. Such ties proved less successful, however, when Iberia sought acquisitions in Mexico in the mid-2000s, given ownership rules preventing non-nationals from leading takeover: in 2003 Iberia had expressed interest in purchasing Mexicana, but the Mexican government later announced in 2005 that any takeover would have to be done by a consortium controlled by Mexicans.[148]

Later developments in Iberia demonstrate the even more interesting phenomenon that Bauby and Vorone's (2007) work highlights, of political and administrative leaders still exercising important influence in the firms, not just in those companies that retain some state ownership but also in those companies with none. Another way of conceptualizing this is 'revolving doors': state officials involved in the privatization are later involved in crafting deals after privatization and occupying significant positions in the Alphas' boards of directors (BoDs).

In order to contextualize the phenomenon of revolving doors in the case of Iberia, it is useful to offer a more general examination of the make-up of BoDs of all the Alphas: of all those serving on the Alphas' boards, what percentage have held state positions at one time in their career? To answer this, information on the Amadeus database on the biographies of those serving on Alphas' BoDs in 2011 was analysed. The BoDs' composition was verified by examination of the companies' annual reports of that year. The summary of the findings for the Alphas is as follows:

- *Air France-KLM*: In 2011 there were a total of fourteen members of the BoD.[149] This includes eleven directors who were appointed by shareholders (including two representing employee shareholders) and three French state representatives. Beyond the three state representatives, a further three of the directors had at one time worked in the French state or the Dutch state as ministers or high-level civil servants.[150] As such, six out of the fourteen (over 42 per cent) have had association with the state at some point in their career.

- *IAG*: There are a total of fourteen members of the BoD in 2011.[151] Of these fourteen, three had at one time worked for the Spanish state (as either ministers or MPs), one from the US (holding senior positions under various presidents), and one from the British state, Baroness Kingsmill, who was the former Deputy Chairman of the Competition Commission and presently serves as a member of the House of Lords.[152] As such, five of the fourteen (over 35 per cent) had some form of past state association.

- *Lufthansa*: In 2011 its supervisory board had twenty-one members.[153] Of these twenty-one members, there are only two (close to 10 per cent) with past state association (one from Germany, the other from the US).[154]

The overall evidence shows that the French state has a larger presence compared to the others. Yet, the analysis reveals that state links are maintained in all Alphas, regardless of ownership structures. That is, those firms that still see some state ownership (AF–KLM), or those that do not (Lufthansa), have directors that have worked closely with the state at one time in their career, as either ministers, or high-level civil servants, or even regulators. As seen in the case of IAG, Baroness Kingsmill—someone who will appear on another firm's board later in the book—not only has past links to the state, but also has been a member of the House of Lords since 2006. Revolving doors is not a phenomenon limited to specific countries, and privatization did not mean that links between firms, governments, and civil servants were severed. An added dimension in both IAG and Lufthansa's BoDs is that it is not just a matter of having former state officials from the Alpha's home. But, given the global M&A that is being pursued, such as the stake that Lufthansa has in New York-based jetBlue, the 'multi-statal' dimension of having past state officials from key countries such as the US is also important.

Turning back to Iberia, it offers a clear illustration of how public officials key in the privatization process later gained key board positions in the firm's life thereafter, involved in important deals. Two key figures in this regard are Josep Piqué and Rodrigo Rato, both of whom were ministers under Jose Maria Aznar's *Partido Popular* (PP) administrations. Piqué was the Minister of Industry between 1996 and 2000. This ministry controlled the SEPI where Iberia was housed. Rodrigo Rato was the Minister of Economy and Finance between 1996 and 2004. During the first stage of Iberia's privatization, both Piqué and Rato played key roles, especially in choosing the partners—including BA—that took over 40 per cent of the airline (Chari and Cavatorta, 2002).

After heading Industry and then Foreign Affairs in the early 2000s, Piqué returned to regional politics in Catalonia. In 2007 he became President of Catalan-based Vueling Airlines. In this position he ultimately helped lead the merger talks between Vueling and Clickair, which ended with Iberia controlling the newly merged airline. For his part, after leaving Spanish politics, Rato was named the Managing Director of the IMF between 2004 and 2007. He was later appointed President of the Spanish savings bank Caja Madrid in 2010 (later renamed Bankia after its merger with several smaller banks). Caja Madrid was controlled by the regional government of the Community of Madrid, of which the PP was in power. As President of Caja Madrid, which owned 23.4 per cent of Iberia, Rato was named the Vice-President of Iberia in February 2010. He ultimately played an essential role in ensuring that the BA–Iberia deal would 'go through'.[155] When it finally did, Piqué continued to direct Vueling, which was absorbed in IAG, while Rato was named to IAG's board of directors.

Perhaps surprisingly, the 'revolving door' argument may be extended to former European Commission officials involved in crafting deals after they left public office and then took on significant board positions, as seen in the case of Etienne Davignion. He served as a European Commissioner (1977–85), having acted as a Vice-President of the Commission and holding portfolios in the Internal Market as well as Industry and Energy. Cini (1996, 65) explains that 'Davignon was usually able to get his way with his fellow Commissioners, even in the policy areas not directly under his control. And in some ways, he seemed to hold the reins of Commission more tightly than the President himself'. In 1985 he went into private practice and joined the Société Générale de Belgique, where he served as Chairman (1988–2001). As discussed before, after the European Commission approved state aid to be given to Sabena in October 2001, the airline declared bankruptcy in November. But the aid gave Sabena's short-haul carrier a lifeline, and it was eventually acquired by Davignon and other investors (Banque Bruxelles Lambert, Dexia, Fortis Banque, KBC, Electrabel, and Solvay) for a symbolic amount of €1.

Some may argue that Davignon was instrumental in the survival of SN Brussels. The aid, along with the funds the investors raised, allowed the airline to keep flying and eventually grow into Brussels Airlines, in which Lufthansa gained a controlling stake years later. Others may point out, however, that for his efforts he continued to be the Chairman of the board of directors of Brussels Airlines even after the sale to Lufthansa, a position still held at the time of writing.[156]

REGULATORY AUTHORITIES

The evidence shows that all Alpha deals ultimately had to be approved by regulators at one of two levels of governance: domestic or supranational. Generally, domestic regulators were involved in the relatively earlier smaller deals, while the European Commission played a role in approving larger cross-border ones. Dissimilar to the automobile and electricity sectors (seen later in the book), there is little evidence of deals going under any regulatory radar. Yet, similarly, all Alpha M&A investigated were readily approved by domestic or supranational regulators, either with or without conditions.

At the domestic level, Lufthansa's first stakes in BMI and Eurowings, as well as its JV to form Aerologic, were approved by Germany's Federal Competition Authority, the Bundeskartellamt, without conditions.[157] The sale of Aerolíneas Argentinas to Air Comet similarly received the green light from Spain's CNMV, while the sale of BA Connect to FlyBe was approved by the UK's Office of Fair Trading.[158] Overseas, China's Civil Aviation of China approved Lufthansa's Joint Venture to form Jade Cargo, as it also did on AF–KLM's transactions with China Southern.[159] And, as in AF–KLM, which was investigated by the Commission as discussed later, the US Department of Justice approved the merger.

While a majority of cases adjudicated by national regulators went through unscathed, in some instances domestic-level approval was conditional. As also seen in some of the European Commission decisions described here, one key condition oftentimes placed relates to surrendering slots in order to ensure competition. A national-level example of this is when BA had to surrender slots in Gatwick when purchasing British Caledonian, a deal which the MMC intimated served national interests.[160] Another example was in the OFT's approval of AF–KLM's purchase of VLM, which prescribed a slot divestment remedy for the London City to Amsterdam route.[161]

Turning to the European Commission, in the 1990s it approved BA's acquisitions of Dan-Air, TAT, and Air Liberté.[162] In fact, BA's acquisition of TAT is a consequence of conditions stipulated by the Commission in another deal: when Air France acquired UTA and Air Inter, the Commission forced AF to sell its 35 per cent stake in TAT, the third largest domestic airline at the time (Doganis, 2006, 112; Thatcher, 2009, 231).

The more significant Commission decisions on major cross-border M&A took place during the 2000s, starting with AF–KLM. In its investigations, the Commission has been driven (or divided) by two poles. One pole sees the Commission as a staunch defender of airline consolidation in Europe. In its view, M&A increases efficiency in the sector, while doubly creating global players that can compete against others such as American Airlines (which purchased TWA in 2001), Delta–Northwest (which merged in 2008), and United (which merged with Continental in 2010). Early evidence of this is seen not only in previous comments by De Palacio after ECJ's 2002 decision, but also before AF–KLM had formally notified the Commission of its intention to merge: within two weeks of AF–KLM's announcement, but before official notification had been given to the Commission, on 13 October 2003 Competition Commissioner Monti announced he was in favour of European airline consolidation and supported the first takeover between major European airlines.[163]

The other pole sees the Commission ensuring that consolidation is not done to the detriment of consumers. As such, when there is concern that the merger/acquisition will eliminate (or significantly reduce) competition on routes (resulting in higher fares and limited choice for consumers), a main remedy is to seek surrender of slots, where 'such remedies must lead to actual, sufficient and timely entry of new competitors'[164] to operate flights. In AF–KLM, for example, the Commission argued that even though the companies' networks were largely complementary, its investigation revealed that the merger would reduce competition on fourteen continental and long-haul routes, such as that between Paris and Amsterdam. Thus, the remedy pursued was that the merged airline would have to surrender forty-seven pairs of slots, allowing competitors to enter the market, thereby ensuring a choice of services and competitive prices for consumers.

Starting with AF–KLM, Table 3.8 summarizes the outcomes of the Commission's investigations of all of the main Alpha deals between 2004 and 2012. Table 3.8 shows that *every* main cross-border merger or acquisition pursued by Alphas was ultimately approved by the Commission, a majority with

Table 3.8. Summary of European Commission Decisions on Airline Alphas' Main Deals, 2004–12

Deal	Outcome	Commission Decision/Conditions (if any)
Air France/KLM (2004)	Approved	Commission found that the merger will eliminate or significantly reduce competition on fourteen routes. As a remedy, AF–KLM committed itself to surrender forty-seven pairs of slots on the routes.
Lufthansa/Swiss (2005)	Approved	Commission found that acquisition would eliminate competition on several intra-European routes. Lufthansa agreed to surrender slots at Zurich, Frankfurt, Munich, Düsseldorf, Berlin, Vienna, Stockholm, and Copenhagen in order to allow competing airlines to emerge on affected routes.
Lufthansa/Eurowings/ Germanwings (2005)	Approved	Commission found that the acquisition would eliminate competition on three routes: Cologne/Bonn–Vienna, Stuttgart–Vienna, and Stuttgart–Dresden. Lufthansa agreed to surrender slots at Stuttgart and Vienna.
KLM/Martinair (2008)	Approved	Commission found that deal would not significantly impede competition in the single market. No conditions placed.
Lufthansa/SN Brussels (2009)	Approved	Commission found that acquisition would raise competition concerns on routes from Brussels to Hamburg, Munich, Frankfurt, and Zurich. Lufthansa made commitment to offer slots that would allow new entrants to operate flights on these routes.
Lufthansa/Austrian Airlines (2009)	Approved	Commission identified various concerns and Lufthansa mades commitments to offer slots on the routes from Vienna to Frankfurt, Munich, Stuttgart, Cologne, and Brussels.
Iberia/Vueling/Clickair (2009)	Approved	Commission found that deal would restrict competition or even lead to a monopoly on nineteen routes. Remedy agreed was to offer slots at several airports, in particular Barcelona and Madrid.
Lufthansa/BMI (2009)	Approved	Commission found that deal would not significantly impede competition. No conditions placed.
BA/Iberia (2010)	Approved	Commission found that deal would not significantly impede competition. No conditions placed.
IAG/BMI (2012)	Approved	Commission found that transaction would lead to high market shares/monopoly on flights out of London Heathrow. IAG agreed to release twelve daily slot pairs in Heathrow.

Sources: European Commission, Case No. COMP/M.3280 Air France/KLM; Case No. COMP/M.3770—Lufthansa/Swiss; Case COMP/M.3940—Lufthansa/Eurowings; Case No. COMP/M.5141—KLM/Martinair; Case No. COMP/M.5335—Lufthansa/SN Airholding; Case No. COMP/M.5440—Lufthansa/Austrian Airlines; Case No. COMP/M.5364—Iberia/Vueling/Clickair; Case No. COMP/M.5403—Lufthansa/BMI; Case No. Comp/M.5747—Iberia/British Airways; Case No. COMP/M6447—IAG/BMI

conditions. A majority of the investigations were sealed in Phase 1 and did not go into deeper Phase 2 investigation (which is only seen with Austrian Airlines, SN Brussels, and Martinair).

The relative ease to obtain the green light from regulatory authorities begs the question: are Alphas with roots as flag carriers favoured by the Commission? One way to demonstrate this is to ask if the Commission has blocked M&A proposed by others in the sector. Two deals blocked have been Olympic

Air/Aegean and Ryanair/Aer Lingus. Turning to the Greek carriers, in 2011 it prohibited the deal between Olympic Air and Aegean Airlines,[165] reasoning it was a transaction involving two airlines with the same home-base. Yet, in the wake of the 2012 IAG/BMI deal, which was approved by Competition Commissioner Joaqiun Almunia from Spain—also responsible for approving the BA–Iberia merger—it seemed clear that the argument to not allow M&A of carriers from the same home markets was ditched. The Commission eventually cleared the Greek deal in October 2013, but justified it on Olympic's inevitable demise in the context of Greece's financial and economic crisis. The Commission reasoned that 'with or without the merger, Olympic would soon disappear as a competitor to Aegean. . . . The merger causes no harm to competition that would have not occurred anyway'.[166]

Less lucky has been the low-fares airline Ryanair, which, like easyJet, could also be classified as an Alpha.[167] The Irish-based airline is led by outspoken CEO Michael O'Leary, who characterized the BA–Iberia merger 'as two drunks . . . holding each other up on the way home'.[168] After its privatization in 2006, the state retained a stake of roughly 25 per cent in Aer Lingus, while Ryanair itself purchased Aer Lingus stocks totalling close to 30 per cent. Seeking full control, Ryanair's first attempt to fully acquire its fellow Dublin Airport-based airline was formally notified to the Commission in late 2006. It was eventually prohibited in June 2007 by Competition Commission Neelie Kroes from the Netherlands on several grounds: the combined airline would account for 80 per cent of Dublin traffic, having a monopoly on twenty-two routes, and the limited number of slots offered would not stimulate entry of competitors.[169] In its judgment the Commission told Ryanair it could make a fresh bid if it offered more slots to rivals at Dublin Airport. After withdrawing another bid in 2009, Ryanair made a third try a few years later, only to be blocked again by the Commission in February 2013.[170] In Ryanair/Aer Lingus (III), there were similar grounds of reasoning as in 2007: the merged airline would now have a combined market share of over 87 per cent, a monopoly or dominant position on forty-six routes, and, again, it was deemed that Ryanair offered insufficient remedies. This was despite the fact that competitors such as IAG and Flybe were committed to operate routes between Dublin and London, Shannon and London, and Cork and London. Commissioner Almunia stated that '(t)he Commission's decision protects more than 11 million Irish and European passengers who travel each year to and from Dublin, Cork, Knock and Shannon. For them, the acquisition of Aer Lingus by Ryanair would have most likely led to higher fares'.[171]

To be fair to the Commission, the potentially combined Irish airline's market share (into and out of a small island country) would have been extremely high, where nothing comparable has been seen in any of the other Alpha acquisitions. However, Almunia's indication that the acquisition 'would have most likely led to higher fares' seems to outline a lack of trust in O'Leary's offer, particularly the remedies, or to want to take Ryanair seriously. Why?

Beyond the outspoken nature of O'Leary and aggressive practices by Ryanair which have driven others out of Dublin Airport, an explanation for this lack of trust is the continued importance of the state. As a main shareholder in Aer Lingus that held blocking minority power over key firm decisions even after privatization, the Irish government did not want the 2007 O'Leary-led deal to go through. The reasoning was based on maintenance of transatlantic services out of Dublin and the island's global connectivity through its twenty-three slot pairs in Heathrow, the third largest at the time. In this regard, Department of Transport officials in Dublin interviewed during this study[172] confirmed that the state fed into the process of Commission's Phase 1 and Phase 2 investigations in 2006/7 through submissions and presentations. In the latest takeover attempt in 2013, Transport Minister Leo Varadkar hardly hid the state's views, openly stating during the Commission's investigation that he did not want the Commission to approve it and warmly welcoming its negative decision.[173]

The reason this 'trust' element is important for the Commission is because once a merger is approved by the Commission, there really is no going back. While a Monitoring Trustee must be named by the firms involved to ensure that conditions placed on deals are followed through (as seen in the AF–KLM case), the Commission itself does not independently investigate if the remedies outlined, once approved, work later on. In other words, it trusts the firms to self-regulate themselves once approval is made and therefore needs trustworthy partners. As one Case Officer involved in different airline cases stated in interview, 'in one case we tried to reinforce these remedies, but we don't investigate if the remedies work'.[174] Related to this, the interviewee also stated that in the EU 'you can't unwind a merger ex-post'.[175] Alphas with their close ties to the state still make good partners and, as seen in the next section, sometimes have their state even lobby Brussels on the firms' behalf.

LOBBYING

While Commission decisions on M&A are publically available, the documents exchanged between the Commission and firms in the process are not, making it difficult for outsiders to know specific lobbying tactics used to gain regulatory approval. Yet, extending on ideas raised by Kassim (1996, 124), Woll (2008), and Kassim and Stevens (2010) on firm lobbying, and supplementing this with interviews held with Commission officials in November 2012, one sees different stages to the lobbying process. First, are informal negotiations between the firm and the Commission even before official notification. The firm ensures that its lawyers that will act on its behalf are assembled, while the Commission puts together its case team. At this stage, the burden is heavy for lawyers that have to prepare answers to forms of over one hundred pages and collect documentation, including internal reports. Formal notification is then made, if it appears that the chances for approval are good. At this time the Commission's official investigation starts. Throughout the first three weeks, the merging/acquiring parties may have to submit commitments if there are competition concerns. Such concerns may be a consequence of passenger surveys the Commission has performed or third party concerns. As this Phase 1 investigation continues (or if it goes into a deeper Phase 2 investigation), company CEOs may get involved. In exceptional cases, member states' governments may also get involved. With these points in mind, there are two noteworthy dimensions to an airline's lobbying strategy: money spent and getting the right lobbyists at the right time, to make sure deals are approved by regulatory authorities.

With regard to the money spent on lobbying (including that for lawyers hired by firms as well as in-house corporates having permanent offices in Brussels), Table 3.9 considers the lobbying costs declared by the trade association representing the main European airlines—the Association of European Airlines (AEA)—and all of its members, except Cargolux, DHL, and TNT which are principally preoccupied with cargo. The Table demonstrates that all of the Alphas are not only registered and have offices in Brussels, but also have declared more than the trade association. AEA's lobbying costs are relatively low because it primarily seeks to influence legislation in the sector impacting all members. When it comes to M&A lobbying that requires teams of lawyers, the firms go it alone: AEA is not involved because DG Competition would be looking at the impact of the merger/acquisition on all of its members, and if AEA defends a merging/acquiring firm ahead of its other members it would be considered a conflict of interest. Thus, AEA's funds are eclipsed by those earmarked by Alphas, the highest of which at over €1.25 million is BA–Iberia in 2012. These high costs can be explained given the political activity of BA related to its purchase of BMI during the first half of 2012. With the exception of Air Berlin and SAS (both of which appear within the top ten in the sector as seen in the second part of the Global Movers Test), none of AEA's members—including Alitalia—has declared any costs related to EU lobbying.

Second, in terms of getting the right lobbyists, firms need to place a strong team of advisors together. For example, lawyers from Freshfields represented Lufthansa in the Austrian Airline acquisition.[176] Other Alphas may work with the same law firms over multiple deals. For example, in the BMI deal of 2012, IAG was advised by Clifford Chance LLP, and Slaughter and May.[177] The Slaughter and May team, led by Mr David Whitman, had also previously advised BA when it merged with Iberia and, some ten years earlier, when it sold its no-frills airline Go.[178]

Table 3.9. Airline Lobbying Costs in Brussels

Trade Association/Airline	Registered in EU's Joint Transparency Register (Financial Year 2012)	Lobbying Costs Declared in Transparency Register
Association of European Airlines	Yes	€100,000–150,000
Air France–KLM*	Yes	€150,000–200,000
British Airways/Iberia**		€1,250,000–1,500,000
Lufthansa	Yes	€350,000–400,000
Alitalia	No	N/A
Adria Airways	No	N/A
Aegean Airlines	No	N/A
Air Baltic	No	N/A
Air Berlin	Yes	< €50,000
Air Malta	No	N/A
Austrian Airlines	No	N/A
Brussels Airlines	No	N/A
Croatia Airlines	No	N/A
Cyprus Airways	No	N/A
Czech Airlines	No	N/A
Finnair	No	N/A
Iceland Air	No	N/A
Jat Airways	No	N/A
LOT Polish Airlines	No	N/A
Luxair	No	N/A
SAS Scandinavia Airlines	Yes	€15,000
Swiss International Air Lines	No	N/A
Tap Portugal	No	N/A
Tarom—Romanian Air Transport	No	N/A
Turkish Airlines	No	N/A
UIA—Ukraine International Airlines	No	N/A
Virgin Atlantic	No	N/A

Source: European Commission, Joint Transparency Register, available at <http://ec.europa.eu/transparencyregister/info/homePage.do> [accessed October 2013]; values correspond to lobbying expenses in Brussels during financial year 2012.

*AF and KLM have two separate registrations, whose total declared values are summed in this table. Both AF and KLM offices are located at the same address in Ave. Louise in Brussels.

**Based on values found in BA's registration; Iberia is not registered separately.

At times, however, CEOs may need to get involved and directly lobby the Commissioner. This is seen in the case of AF–KLM.[179] After official notification was made to the Commission on 30 December 2003, an investigation was launched. But by the third week of January 2004, the Commission stated that the investigation may be extended given potential competition concerns, namely on routes between Paris and Amsterdam. On 6 February, the Commission stated that on 11 February it would announce that it either approved the deal, or open up a more in-depth Phase 2 investigation where the chances of it getting quashed altogether would be higher. The day before the deadline, on 10 February, Competition Commissioner Mario Monti met with AF and KLM's CEOs. Within a day of this meeting, the Commission (along with the Department of Justice) announced it approved the deal. When later asked in a press conference if surprised by conditions placed by the Commission, AF's

Spinetta stated, '[N]othing in the Commission's decision was unexpected. Prior to the Commission's clearance, talks were held with the airlines. We knew exactly what we were willing to accept in terms of remedies to obtain their agreement.'[180]

The IAG acquisition of BMI, however, shows how chief executive lobbying may backfire. In mid-March 2012 Alex Barker of the *Financial Times* (13 March 2012, 1) reported that the deal was potentially going to enter a lengthy, deeper Phase 2 investigation. Yet, somewhat surprisingly, it was approved a month later. In order to understand this, Barker later described developments before his report in mid-March: Willie Walsh, who wanted speedy early approval, met with Competition Commissioner Joaquín Almunia who viewed the initial remedies offered as insufficient. This resulted in a disastrous 15-minute meeting where 'Almunia delivered a few home truths on competition law'.[181] Taking us full circle to the continuing importance of the state in life after privatization, Barker explains:

> The danger of the deal faltering over an irreconcilable Walsh–Almunia stand-off began to filter back to capitals. British ministers were warned that this could all result in a big political mess, with Lufthansa pulling the plug on its loss-making BMI unit, shedding thousands of jobs. Enter Justine Greening. The UK transport secretary apparently underlined the importance of the decision to the Commission in characteristically awkward British style (ministers never in theory lobby on merger cases, which are supposed to be impartial applications of the law). But the dangers in terms of BMI's future were made clear. Behind the scenes there was also a push to talk the two sides off a ledge and encourage IAG to sweeten the offer. There was a happy ending.[182]

Explaining the Beta—Alitalia

This section examines and explains the only Beta from the five countries, Alitalia. Given that it was a national flag carrier that was not taken over at the point of privatization and, in fact, was partially floated (X1), it theoretically had potential to become an Alpha. In order to understand why the Italian firm became a Beta, this section examines the intervening variables (X2). In an integrated discussion focusing on developments when AF–KLM attained 25 per cent control of Alitalia, it first examines the internal factors and then considers the more significant external ones at play, highlighting the role of liberalization, the state, and regulators.

Turning to internal factors, shortly after its (partial) privatization the airline continued to offer a poor quality service, low productivity, and aging fleets. As Beria et al. (2011, 215) discuss, it was only in 1996 that 'the Cempella plan, named after Alitalia's CEO, Domenica Cempella, was implemented in an attempt at solving some of the airline's problems [including] cutting costs and raising capital in the stock market to strengthen Alitalia's fleet'. Yet, the market share of formerly over 90 per cent when it was the national flag carrier had gone down to 80 per cent by the late 1990s, and fell to less than 50 per cent of the domestic market by 2003 (Beria et al., 215–16). Attempts at revival were led by management determined to restructure the company—including reducing the state's stake—but union opposition eventually resulted in the resignation of Chief Executive Francesco Mengozzi in February 2004 (Beria et al., 216; Doganis, 2006, 229). Such opposition continued with the next Chief Executive, Marco Zanichelli, who would later be replaced by Giancarlo Cimoli in May that same year. Alitalia's failure can thus in part be explained based on lack of continued leadership and managerial decisions not supported by labour. Increased competition, as well as shifting managerial strategies, resulted in losses of €256 million in 2000, which Amyot (2010, 257) highlights were characteristic of the airline's bottom-line over the next few years: losses of €900 million were incurred in 2001, €520 million in 2003, €850 million in 2004, €167 million in 2005, €625 million in 2006, and €495 million in 2007. Such poor performance hardly instilled confidence in potential foreign investors. As seen earlier, while firms such as BlackRock, Capital Group, Legal and General, and AXA have all invested in the Alphas, none invested in Alitalia after its privatization (with the exception of JP Morgan in 2007, as seen previously in Table 3.6).

While internal factors to the firm are important, other more political, external factors are of significance in explaining why Alitalia was eventually taken over. The first relates to the role of EU liberalization initiatives. The impact of the Commission's Third Package discussed previously resulted in the displacement of Alitalia's share on both domestic and European markets. Those such as Volare Airlines, Air Europe, and Air Dolomiti increasingly competed throughout the 1990s and 2000s. Air Dolomiti, in particular, was in a strong position to compete against Alitalia given that its global ultimate owner from the early 2000s was an Alpha, namely Lufthansa.

When turning to the role of the state, throughout the 1990s its main strategy to save the company included giving state aid. Between 1991 and 2002 Alitalia received a large amount of aid estimated at €2.5 billion worth of subsidies (Thatcher, 2009, 228). However, in contrast to Alphas such as Air France and Iberia, which were able to use the aid effectively as discussed before, shifting management teams were incapable of ensuring its 'long-term viability' throughout the 1990s and 2000s. As the 2000s continued, the airline continued to receive state aid, such as €400 million in 2004 which was approved by the Commission. As Thatcher (2009, 231) notes, 'Commission approval of recapitalization of Alitalia in 1997 and 2004 was linked to other reforms such as further liberalization, privatization (through recapitalizations that would reduce the state holding below 50%) and ending anti-competitive practices by Alitalia.' Nevertheless, given the Commission's overall strategy to reduce aid in the sector, particularly championed by Commissioner de Palacio, the state had to effectively abandon any type of long-term strategy reliant on aid.

Thus, after the mid-2000s the state's next overall strategy was to sell its remaining 49.9 per cent stake, finding a suitable partner to take over Alitalia. In December 2006 Prodi's government opened up a tendering process which eventually ended unsuccessfully without any offers by June 2007, reflective of the poor competitive position of an airline without clear plans (Beria et al., 2011, 216). This failure resulted in opening up a second process, but this time overseen by Alitalia itself, whose president, Maurizio Prato, had clear plans (henceforth referred to as the 'Prato Plan') to cut personnel, abandon loss-making routes, reduce fleets, and concentrate intercontinental routes from Rome's Fumicino, ditching them from Milan's second main airport Malpensa (Amyot, 2010, 258). Having received offers from the second principal Italian airline (Air One) and international carriers (Russia's Aeroflot and Lufthansa), in December 2007 AF–KLM was chosen as exclusive negotiating partner, happy to implement the Prato Plan (Amyot, 2010, 259).

However, when the Prodi government fell in the Senate in January 2008, the resulting election campaign saw Alitalia's sale to AF–KLM supported by Prodi becoming an issue. The Northern League (NL) led by Umberto Bossi, an important coalition partner for Berlusconi, openly rallied against any plan to relegate Malpensa and called for the AF–KLM deal to be scrapped (Amyot, 2010, 259–60). Aware that losing NL's support would damage its chances for victory, a month before the mid-April election Berlusconi:

> ...decided to come out decisively against the sale to Air France, stated that he would veto it if elected. He labeled the French bid 'colonial style,' called the proposed sale a 'sell-out', and promised to defend the *italianità* of Alitalia...
> (Amyot, 2010, 260)

After the beginning of April saw the breakdown of talks between Air-France's boss Jean-Cyril Spinetta and the trade unions, Berlusconi's newly elected centre–right government immediately orchestrated a three-dimensional plan for Alitalia's future (Amyot, 2010, 261–2). First, was a €300 million bridging loan from the state to keep the company alive, requested through the outgoing Prodi government.

The second dimension was to save Alitalia by changing regulations and splitting Alitalia into two: a 'bad company' assuming all the debts and liabilities 'that would ultimately fall on the government (taxpayers)' and a 'good company' consisting of Alitalia's profitable assets which were to be sold (Amyot, 2010, 263). Or, as the Bureau van Dijk reported on 28 August 2008:

the Italian government has changed bankruptcy and anti-competition rules to save Alitalia. Alitalia will be split into two parts. One of the parts will be moved to a new company, will contain all debt and non-profitable assets of Alitalia and will be put under bankruptcy regulations. The profitable assets of Alitalia will remain in the company and a group of Italian investors will then try to acquire Alitalia.[183]

This last point highlights the third dimension of the state's strategy: to spearhead the formation of an Italian-based consortium to acquire Alitalia and prevent a foreign takeover, eventually accomplished by August 2008. The consortium put together by Berlusconi was called Compagnia Aerea Italiana (CAI), was led by the Banca Intesa and included other Italian investors such as Carlo Toto, the owner of Air One, as well as those related to Piaggio and the Benetton Group. The plan was for CAI to take over Alitalia, merging it with Air One. Months of negotiation ensued, including getting the pilots finally on board in October after extensive talks moderated by the PMO's undersecretary Gianni Letta (Amyot, 2010, 264). But while CAI was finalizing the deal, behind the scenes negotiations were still taking place to find an industrial partner from the sector in order to add much-needed global expertise to the group. AF–KLM came back for 'round two' and was eventually offered a 25 per cent stake of CAI for three reasons, as highlighted by Amyot (2010, 265–6). First, CAI knew that if Alitalia left the Skyteam, a penalty of over €200 million would be given. Second, AF–KLM's Spinetta backtracked on earlier positions taken on Malpensa, offering more flights from the Milanese airport. Third, Berlusconi was of the view that AF–KLM represented the only 'viable alternative' even over the Northern League's first preference Lufthansa. To convince the NL of his plan, Berlusconi simply played his 'ace' and promised the League that he would accelerate the 'devolution of taxing and spending powers to the regions' (Amyot, 2010, 266).

Clearly, as Amyot's (2010, 260, 263, 265) work shows, Treasury funds were used to support the CAI offer, which was eventually more costly to the state than that originally made by AF–KLM. He argues that the original AF–KLM offer for 100 per cent of Alitalia amounted to a purchase price of €138.5 million, taking on Alitalia's debt of €1.78 billion, and injecting a further €850 million. The CAI offer included a higher purchase price of slightly more than €1 billion, but where the state assumed all of Alitalia's debts of the 'bad' company. That said, by later taking a controlling stake in CAI, AF–KLM was able to drive a good bargain in the end: in January 2009 it purchased 25 per cent of the merged airline, which would have a monopoly position on the Rome–Milan route, for €323 million.[184]

Ultimately, the main aspects of the deal were approved by the European Commission which could have potentially acted as veto-player. Previously, in 2004 the Commission had already shown predisposition towards the

AF–Alitalia alliance when it approved the cooperation agreement between the two, both of which agreed to surrender forty-two pairs of slots at Charles de Gaulle, Orly, Rome, Milan, and Venice.[185] However, as one interviewee stated,[186] it is doubtful that the remedy led to sufficient and timely entry of new competitors: the maximum number of new entrants expected that would have provided competition on routes such as Paris–Milan Malpensa, Paris–Rome, and Paris–Venice was eventually lower than expected. This is because one airline that covered these routes and mentioned by the Commission, Air Volare, declared bankruptcy shortly after the Commission's decision and was eventually taken over by Alitalia in 2006. Thus, the sufficient number of competitors envisaged by the Commission did not actually emerge.

When it came to the sale of Alitalia to CAI, this was ultimately approved by Mr Tajani, Vice-President of the Commission responsible for transport. Interestingly, he was appointed as Italian Commissioner on May 2008 shortly after Berlusconi was elected in April 2008. In November 2008 Tajani announced Brussels' approval of the sale to CAI, highlighting two decisions.[187] First, the €300 million bridging loan was deemed illegal and had to be reimbursed by Alitalia. Second, notwithstanding the first decision, because the sale of Alitalia's assets did not involve giving state aid that went directly to the purchasers, the deal could go through given that the price offered by CAI was deemed by the Commission to be fair.

To close, it is interesting to ask if there is evidence that the €300 million bridging loan was ever recovered by the state. In a 2013 ECJ judgment (in which the case was taken by Ryanair), the ECJ upheld the findings of the General Court's judgment and those of the Commission's decision when it affirmed that only Alitalia had to reimburse the loan.[188] In other words, because CAI was not regarded as the economic successor of Alitalia it was not obliged to repay the aid. The Italian government argued that there was an absolute impossibility to recover the aid because Alitalia had no funds. In the past, the ECJ has consistently maintained that the fact that a beneficiary would be insolvent or be subject to bankruptcy proceedings if it has to repay the illegal aid should have no effect on its obligation. The Court, however, also recognized, in this specific case, that 'the absence of recoverable assets is the only way for a Member State to show the absolute impossibility of recovering the aid'.[189] As such, despite constituting illegal aid, the evidence suggests that the €300 million was not recovered.

Conclusions

The first section considered the history of the five airlines, their sales, and the M&A (as well as Joint Ventures) they pursued before and after privatization.

Thereafter, Section 2 performed the Global Movers and Independence Tests, arguing that AF–KLM, Lufthansa, and IAG (the merger between BA and Iberia) can be defined as Alphas today, while Alitalia is a Beta.

In order to understand why firms became Alphas, Section 3 argued that the market positions of Alphas before and after privatization, as well as the goals of managers and shareholders, are all important. Attention was particularly paid to main asset management firms, such as BlackRock, showing that while they invested in Alphas, they generally did not do so in Betas (Alitalia), and even their investment in Alphas changes over time. Despite their importance, internal factors are not sufficient in explaining why firms could globally expand or not be taken over.

Rather, the more external, political, factors are necessary and sufficient, where one can conceptualize a type of sequential relationship binding the factors. The lack of liberalization in the sector shortly before or after Alphas were privatized, meant that the Alphas could become national champions and were generally protected. That is, Alphas consolidated their position and became dominant players in their home market. With liberalization, however, this set the foundation for *what could be done* with regard to expansion, allowing firm managers to negotiate deals that would allow Alphas to become world giants. In particular, with the Commission's 'Third Package' of the 1990s as well as the ECJ's 2002 decision, expansion could be (and had to be) pursued in order to maintain a leading position amongst peers. The Third Package thus set the foundation for alliances to form and, after the ECJ's 2002 ruling, mergers and acquisitions within the alliances to be pursued, starting with AF–KLM.

Once it was clear that major cross-border deals could take place in the wake of liberalization, the home states of Alphas, as well as other states keen to see the Alphas enter, acted accordingly and helped set the tone for *how expansion could be done*. Alpha home-states, historically important in building up their Alphas before and after privatization, were unable to continue to subsidize the firms as in the past given the European Commission's tight application of state aid rules. But they still helped shape the expansionary deals in the 2000s, as seen in AF/KLM, Iberia/Vueling, and IAG/BMI, as well as Lufthansa's joint ventures including that with DHL Worldwide. The ties between capital and the Alpha states are still maintained, as further reflected in the composition of the Alpha boards. Ex-ministers (in some cases involved in the previous privatization of the company), former civil servants, and former regulators (who still serve in public office, as seen in the case of IAG) serve on all Alpha boards even after privatization. Former public officials' ties to the firm were vital in some of the deals unfolding, as manifest in BA/Iberia. As seen in Air France/Air Ivoire, Lufthansa/BMI, Lufthansa/Air Dolomiti, and Lufthansa/Swiss, the evidence also highlighted that other states from abroad (i.e. states which the Alphas were not from) were equally keen to see Alphas enter and facilitated their expansion, sometimes even giving state aid in the transactions, as seen in Lufthansa/Austrian Airlines.

Finally, regulators at different levels of governance ensured *that expansion could be done*. By not vetoing major M&A, domestic- and supranational-level regulators ensured that Alpha deals were approved, mostly without tight conditions. Particular attention was paid to all of the Alphas' major cross-border deals in the 2000s investigated by the European Commission, none of which was blocked. Part of this approval can be explained given robust lobbying strategies pursued by Alphas. Given that merger decisions once made by the Commission cannot be undone, and comparing the Alphas' experience to Ryanair's failure to gain regulatory approval in its acquisition of Aer Lingus, the section underlined that Alphas' ties to their state—and their reputation to be 'trustworthy' partners—matter.

In order to understand why Alitalia is a Beta, it was argued that here, too, external factors are of significance, particularly the role of the state and the European Commission. Starting with factors internal to the firm, it first considered the role of Alitalia managers, which were faced with union opposition and unable to turnaround an airline which had suffered from poor service and obsolete fleets since the 1990s. As a result, its competitive market position continued to weaken. Turning to external factors, because competitors entered the market as a consequence of EU liberalization initiatives in the 1990s, the position of Alitalia was weakened on domestic and European routes. After the fall of Prodi's government in 2008, Berlusconi's state then played a crucial role in spearheading the sale of Alitalia to a group of investors, CAI, led by Banca Intesa, and the merging of the flag carrier with its main competitor, Air One. The deal was eventually approved by the European Commission, after which AF–KLM took a controlling 25 per cent stake in Alitalia, with the state's blessing. Further, the evidence suggests that aid given during the CAI takeover was not recovered.

In sum, taking the experience of the Alphas and Betas in the airline sector, a common explanatory thread lies in the importance of liberalization, the role of states, and the actions of regulatory authorities.

The next chapter examines and explains developments in the automobile sector.

Endnotes

1. History of Air France based on information found on AF–KLM website: <http://www.airfranceklm.com/en/group/background/> (last accessed 10 December 2013).
2. Air France, *Offering Memorandum*, dated 9 February 1999, page 11.

3. Data taken from Air France, *Offering Memorandum*, dated 9 February 1999, page 11.

4. Figures taken from <http://www.eurofound.europa.eu/eiro/1999/02/inbrief/fr9902 156n.htm> (last accessed 10 December 2013).

5. Privatization value based on that reported in <www.privatizationbarometer.net> (last accessed 10 December 2013).

6. Taken from the official company website: <http://www.airfranceklm.com/en/ group/background/> (years 2000–10; last accessed 10 December 2013).

7. Based on analysis of Bureau van Dijk's Zephyr database, BvD Deal ID Numbers 45717 and 56221.

8. For more on KLM, see its corporate webpage: <http://www.klm.com/corporate/en/ about-klm/index.html> (last accessed 10 December 2013).

9. Officials interviewed suggested that a 10 per cent cap (limit) of Iberia for any partner was the desired number. Interviews, September 2003.

10. Based on analysis of Bureau van Dijk's Zephyr database, BvD Deal ID Number 91510.

11. Based on analysis of Bureau van Dijk's Zephyr database, BvD Deal ID Number 130540.

12. Based on estimated deal values provided in BvD Zephyr database files with the following ID numbers: 130540, 301690, and 301717.

13. Based on analysis of Bureau van Dijk's Zephyr database, BvD Deal ID Number 130540.

14. Based on analysis of Bureau van Dijk's Zephyr database, BvD Deal ID Number 301690.

15. On French reductions, see Bureau van Dijk's Zephyr database, BvD Deal ID Number 301717. On the Netherlands' government's reductions in April 2005, see Zephyr file with ID number 333450.

16. Based on analysis of Bureau van Dijk's Zephyr database, BvD Deal ID Number 48032.

17. Based on analysis of Bureau van Dijk's Zephyr database, BvD Deal ID Number 1601172296.

18. Based on analysis of Bureau van Dijk's Zephyr database, BvD Deal ID Number 409908.

19. Based on analysis of Bureau van Dijk's Zephyr database, BvD Deal ID Number 1909017942.

20. 17 per cent was also acquired by Air Afrique (of which 68.4 per cent was controlled by eleven French-speaking African states). Based on analysis of Bureau van Dijk's Zephyr database, BvD Deal ID Number 74160.

21. The purchase was for an undisclosed amount, as seen in BvD Zephyr database files 352995 and 1601088607. For more on the US firm see: <http://www. aeromaintenancegroup.com/en/amg> (last accessed 10 December 2013).

22. Based on analysis of Bureau van Dijk's Zephyr database, BvD Deal ID Number 358355. On the date that the Cargo JV came into effect, as well as other JVs between AF–KLM and China Southern, see also the detailed report by the Center for Aviation <http://centreforaviation.com/analysis/skyteam-seeks-clarity-on-

proposed-china-southern-air-china-joint-a380-operation-97256> (last accessed 10 December 2013).

23. Please see AF–KLM's announcement on this at <http://corporate.airfrance.com/en/press/news/article/item/strengthened-cooperation-between-air-france-and-china-southern-with-the-signing-of-a-joint-venture-a-1/> (last accessed 10 December 2013).

24. For a history of the company in the 1920s, please see <http://www.lufthansagroup.com/en/company/history/1920s.html> (last accessed 10 December 2013).

25. For a history of the company in the 1940s, please see <http://www.lufthansagroup.com/en/company/history/1940s.html> (last accessed 10 December 2013).

26. For a history of the company in the 1960s, please see <http://www.lufthansagroup.com/en/company/history/1960s.html> (last accessed 10 December 2013).

27. On developments in the 1970s and 1980s see: <http://www.lufthansagroup.com/en/company/history/1970s.html> and <http://www.lufthansagroup.com/en/company/history/1980s.html> (last accessed 10 December 2013).

28. As explained by *The New York Times* (1994).

29. On the history of SunExpress, see <http://www.sunexpress.com/en/company-profile> (last accessed 10 December 2013).

30. As discussed by Coleman (1994).

31. Source: <www.privatizationbarometer.net> (last accessed 10 December 2013).

32. Based on analysis of Bureau van Dijk's Zephyr database, BvD Deal ID Number 74831.

33. Based on analysis of Bureau van Dijk's Zephyr database, BvD Deal ID Numbers 99075 and 1601011833.

34. On Eurowings/Germanwings, the BvD database offers no values for any of the deals as based on analysis of Bureau van Dijk's Zephyr database, BvD Deal ID Number 1601035653.

35. Based on analysis of Bureau van Dijk's Zephyr database, BvD Deal ID Numbers 390757 and 430199.

36. Based on analysis of Bureau van Dijk's Zephyr database, BvD Deal ID Number 50418.

37. Details on the 52 per cent purchase are found in BvD Zephyr database Deal ID Number 154270; the remaining 48 per cent is reported in BvD Deal Number 154278.

38. Based on analysis of Bureau van Dijk's Zephyr database, BvD Deal ID Number 52229.

39. Ownership data based on that found in the Amadeus database, where SAS has BvD Company ID number SE5566068499.

40. Based on analysis of Bureau van Dijk's Zephyr database, BvD Deal ID Number 517303.

41. Based on analysis of Bureau van Dijk's Zephyr database, BvD Deal ID Number 160051.

42. After Lufthansa's initial stake of 13 per cent, it had an option for another 10 per cent of Luxair which it did not exercise. The Luxembourg state still controls the

airline. On the shareholder structure of Luxair today, see <http://www.luxair.lu/cms/page?p=EN,13657,181,,1> (last accessed 2 December 2013).

43. Based on analysis of Bureau van Dijk's Zephyr database, BvD Deal ID Number 342030.

44. Based on analysis of Bureau van Dijk's Zephyr database, BvD Deal ID Numbers 165695 and 549886.

45. The Press release on this can be found on <https://www.swiss.com/corporate/EN/media/newsroom/press-releases/press-release-20080208> (last accessed 1 December 2013).

46. Quote as taken from Bureau van Dijk's Zephyr database Deal ID Number 14589.

47. Based on analysis of Bureau van Dijk's Zephyr database, BvD Deal ID Number 104515.

48. On the 2004 deal, see Done (2004).

49. This quote is taken from the corporate history of Brussels airlines, which is found on <http://company.brusselsairlines.com/en_be/corp/our-company/history.aspx> (last accessed 10 December 2013).

50. Based on analysis of Bureau van Dijk's Zephyr database, BvD Deal ID Number 1601012652. Note, BA and Hainan Airlines were also rumoured possible bidders for the controlling stake according to the file.

51. Based on analysis of Bureau van Dijk's Zephyr database, BvD Deal ID Number 640033.

52. For an overview of the main 'privatization steps' of Austrian Airlines see also the company's summary on <http://www.austrianairlines.ag/InvestorRelations/CompanyShare/PrivatizationSteps.aspx?sc_lang=en> (last accessed 10 November 2013).

53. In 2000 Austrian Airlines owned 36 per cent of Lauda Air, and the airline's founder, Niki Lauda, 30 per cent. Lauda left the company in November 2000 due to increasing tensions between the two main shareholders (CNN News, 2000). In the wake of Lauda's departure, Austrian Airlines became majority shareholder of Lauda Air within months, on 31 January 2001, ultimately gaining full control in 2002.

54. See the Zephyr Editorial which accompanies BvD Deal ID Number 625789.

55. Based on analysis of Bureau van Dijk's Zephyr database, BvD Deal ID Number 625789.

56. Based on analysis of Bureau van Dijk's Zephyr database, BvD Deal ID Number 625789.

57. Based on analysis of Bureau van Dijk's Zephyr database, BvD Deal ID Number 642649.

58. Based on analysis of Bureau van Dijk's Zephyr database, BvD Deal ID Number 1601109584.

59. Based on analysis of Bureau van Dijk's Zephyr database, BvD Deal ID Number 603696.

60. The rumour that it would sell its stake is seen in Zephyr Deal with ID Number 1601303207. On shareholdings in JetBlue, see JetBlue, 2012 Annual Report, page 14.

61. Based on analysis of Bureau van Dijk's Zephyr database, BvD Deal ID Number 550192.

62. Based on analysis of Bureau van Dijk's Zephyr database, BvD Deal ID Number 266493.

63. On the fate of Jade Cargo, see Cameron (2012).

64. Based on information provided at <http://www.lsgskychefs.com/en/about-us. html> (last accessed 4 November 2013).

65. See the following BvD Deal ID Numbers on the Zephyr Database: on Asiana Airlines catering business, 135170; on JV with HNA Air Catering, 1000011879; on the China Eastern Airline deal, 1000011877; and on the Cathay Pacific's (Hong Kong) catering service deal, 1601006494.

66. Figure on profits is based on data reported by the National Audit Office, *Report by the Comptroller and Auditor General, Department of Transport: Sale of Government Shareholding in British Airways plc*, 8 July 1987, page 2. For a discussion of developments in the airline in 1980, please see <http://www.britishairways.com/travel/history-1980-1989/public/en_gb> (last accessed 10 November 2013).

67. Please see <http://www.britishairways.com/travel/history-1980-1989/public/en_gb> (1980 and 1982; last accessed 15 November 2013).

68. The value in GBP is £849.7 million. On the sale's oversubscription, please see <http://www.britishairways.com/travel/history-1980-1989/public/en_gb> (1987; last accessed 16 November 2013). On net proceeds for BA as well as other previous sales in the UK see National Audit Office, *Report by the Comptroller and Auditor General, Department of Transport: Sale of Government Shareholding in British Airways plc*, 8 July 1987 (appendix 1 and 2).

69. Based on analysis of the Bureau van Dijk's Zephyr database, BvD Deal ID Number 655094.

70. Based on analysis of the Bureau van Dijk's Zephyr database, BvD Deal ID Number 54862.

71. The information presented on Dan-Air, TAT, and Air Liberté is a summary based on various European Commission merger rulings which will be referred to later in the chapter. None of these deals is found in the Zephyr database (whose data starts from 1997), so it is difficult to ascertain concrete deal values involved.

72. Based on analysis of the Bureau van Dijk's Zephyr database, BvD Deal ID Number 69789. The deal with an estimated value of €80.5 million.

73. Deal value of the management buyout in 2001 (£110 million) is based in EURO value reported in Zephyr database's deal with ID Number 85560. On the sale of Go, see <http://news.bbc.co.uk/2/hi/business/1388980.stm>; on easyJet's later purchase, see <http://news.bbc.co.uk/2/hi/business/1990691.stm> (last accessed 12 November 2013).

74. Based on analysis of the Bureau van Dijk's Zephyr database, BvD Deal ID Number, 488906.

75. Based on analysis of the Bureau van Dijk's Zephyr database, BvD Deal ID Number 276382.

76. Based on analysis of the Bureau van Dijk's Zephyr database, BvD Deal ID Number 276382.

77. Information is based on data in found in the Zephyr database's deal with ID Number 276382. The rationale behind the sale is found on the BvD file, as also seen in *The Guardian* report by Tran (2004).

78. Based on analysis of the Bureau van Dijk's Zephyr database, BvD Deal ID Number 451880.

79. Based on analysis of the Bureau van Dijk's Zephyr database, BvD Deal ID Number 1601034534.

80. See the company's webpage on initial history, which can be found (in Spanish) on <http://grupo.iberia.es/portal/site/grupoiberia/menuitem.449e959b2151b8e47c3f8 39ef34e51ca/;jsessionid=V1bYS6KQfHz1pV94HTr0p3002xcp32vHLQJb1P9VRpygc MXMhcNb!-980918419!719146073> (last accessed 10 December 2013).

81. Aerolíneas Argentinas was eventually sold off by the SEPI in October 2001, after the carrier filed bankruptcy in June 2001. Although its purchase had helped Iberia expand into, and increase the airline's own presence in, the Latin American market, Aerolíneas Argentinas was a financial burden with over a billion euros of accumulated debt by 2001. It was eventually taken over by Air Comet, which was jointly controlled by the Spanish tour operator Grupo Marsans and Air Plus Argentina, where Air Comet paid nothing for the airline but assumed half of Aerolíneas Argentinas's USD 1.2million debt (while SEPI took the other half). On the history of Aerolíneas Argentinas, including SEPI's eventual sale of it in 2001, see *El País* (2001), as well as deal with ID number 92208 found in the Zephyr database.

82. This discussion of the first stage of Iberia's privatization is taken from the author's previous work, Chari (2004).

83. As Chari (2004, 11–12) argues, there were three main reasons for seeking partnership with industrial and institutional investors: 'The *first* reason was related to the "equilibrium" that the investors represented. The idea here was to have a mix between Industrial and Financial partners, both with a proven track record in private enterprise. It was also crucial to not allow any one interest to gain control of Iberia as it was believed that the combination of both types of interests would offer a solid base. The *second* reason was related to future "management" of the airline. Given its track record and potential for the future, the company had to attain a strong management structure. However, if it were privatized outright through the sale of the company's entire stock to one investor, Iberia would not have had as solid a base or direction; both of these elements were necessary to ensure a solid foundation for its future performance. The *third* reason was "stability." The idea here was that reliable partners taking over 40% of the company would create a solid base in order to develop future commercial plans for Iberia, as industrial partners would offer, as well as financial stability in case of potential market shocks, as strong financial partners would assure.'

84. As Chari (2004, 12) argues, along with BA that offered complementary markets in northern Europe, 'AA offered Iberia a strategic link to the USA market given that Iberia had hubs only in Miami and New York while, at the same time, offering AA the opportunity to expand its own operations in South America'.

85. Quote taken from *The New York Times* (2001).

86. Based on value reported by <www.privatizationbarometer.net> (last accessed 10 December 2013).

87. See BvD Deal ID Number 177249.

88. These four other partners, all from Spain, included Grupo Cobra (an engineering services firm, which is a subsidiary of the Spanish construction firm ACS), Quercus Equity, Nefinsa (an investment trust), and Iberostar (hotel operator and travel agency). The deal had a total value of €50 million. Source BvD Deal ID Number 437925.

89. Based on analysis of the Bureau van Dijk's Zephyr database, BvD Deal ID Numbers 613607 and 1601119465.

90. Analysis of the merger between BA and Iberia is based on Zephyr Deal ID number 120266. The comments that the BvD compiles on the merger are some of the most extensive of all deals analysed in the book, discussing developments between June 2002 and January 2011 over several pages. Unless noted otherwise, the information in these two paragraphs of the book is based on main events in this BvD report.

91. Direct quote taken from BvD Deal ID Number 120266.

92. These included Vista Capital (equally owned by Banco Santander and Royal Bank of Scotland), Inversiones Ibersuizas (which is owned by the Spanish construction company, FCC), and Quercus Equity.

93. Other consortiums interested in Iberia that emerged in late 2007 include the Spanish operator Globalia Corporación, as well as a consortium led by Gala Capital (and included Spanish businesswoman, Alicia Koplowitz).

94. For more on IAG, see its webpage: <http://www.iairgroup.com/phoenix.zhtml?c=240949&p=aboutoverview>. On savings expected by the end of its fifth year, see <http://www.theguardian.com/business/2011/jan/20/british-airways-trades-last-time-merger> (last accessed 20 November 2013).

95. Based on analysis of the Bureau van Dijk's Zephyr database, BvD Deal ID Number 1601242539.

96. Based on analysis of the Bureau van Dijk's Zephyr database, BvD Deal ID Number 1601276109.

97. Based on analysis of the Bureau van Dijk's Zephyr database, BvD Deal ID Number 1601368703.

98. For a report on its final flight, see <http://www.bbc.co.uk/news/uk-england-nottinghamshire-19536090> (last accessed 22 November 2013).

99. In 1947 the British would also invest another 1.5 billion lira in 1947. Based on information found in the Amadeus company report, BvD ID Number ITRM0135156.

100. Based on information found on <http://corporate.alitalia.com/en/company/history/index.html>.

101. <http://corporate.alitalia.com/en/company/history/index.html> (1960; last accessed 27 November 2013).

102. Based on information provided in <www.privatizationbarometer.net> (last accessed 10 December 2013); see also Beria et al. (2011, 216).

103. Based on analysis of the Bureau van Dijk's Zephyr database, BvD Deal ID Number 382834.

104. Based on analysis of La Repubblica 20 ottobre 2006; La Repubblica 2 novembre 2006; and La Repubblica 3 novembre 2006.

105. Quote taken from European Commission (2004).
106. Based on analysis of the Bureau van Dijk's Zephyr database, BvD Deal ID Number 95082.
107. On the companies' announcement of the deal, please see: <http://www.etihad. com/en/about-us/news/archive/2014/alitalia-and-etihad-airways-finalise-1758- million-investment-deal/> (last accessed 2 October 2014).
108. Searches were performed in April 2013, verified in August 2013 with 2011 data, and then finalized in November 2013 using financial data from 2012. SAS AB, Ryanair, TAP, and IAG were specifically added to the search given that their NACE Rev 2 primary codes are not 51, but 6,420 (activities of holding companies).
109. The data for the Independence Test (and the BvD's independence ranking) are taken from the company reports with the following BvD ID numbers in the Amadeus database: AF–KLM, FR552043002; Lufthansa, DE5190000974; IAG, ESA85845545; Alitalia–CAI, ITRM1224709. The final tests were run between March 2013 and October 2103, and all reports were last accessed in October 2013.
110. This letter written by Mr Gurbindo (Director de Administración y Recursos, SEPI), with the title of *Comunicación de Hecho Relevante*, is found in the Zephyr database, in Deal 1601242539.
111. The exact wording from Mr Gurbindo's letter to the CNMV of 8 April 2011 is: 'Esta autorización no implica necesariamente la venta inmediata de las acciones citadas, que se realizará en todo caso cuando las condiciones de Mercado lo aconsejasen.'
112. See <http://www.sepi.es/default.aspx?cmd=0004&IdContent=430&idLanguage= &lang=%29&idContraste=> (last accessed 2 December 2013).
113. Interview was held on 3 December 2013 between the author and an official in the SEPI's Communications Department.
114. This does not mean, however, that in all cases this vision is maintained over time. Future CEOs can change the course of a company's strategy, and reverse deals previously envisaged or pursued. This is seen in the case of the no-frills airline Go. It was established when BA was led by Robert Ayling, but sold when Rod Eddington, who did not view the airline as part of the new 'full-service strategy', took over. See the BBC report from the BBC, which can be found at <http://news.bbc. co.uk/2/hi/business/1388980.stm>.
115. As reported in *The New York Times* article by Mitchener (1994).
116. Based on analysis of the Bureau van Dijk's Zephyr database, BvD Deal ID Number 625789.
117. On the BMI deal, Walsh stated, 'Buying BMI's mainline business gives IAG a unique opportunity to grow at Heathrow, one of our key hub airports. Using the slot portfolio more efficiently provides the option to launch new long-haul routes to key trading nations while supporting our broad domestic and short-haul network.' (Quote taken from Zephyr, deal ID number 1601276109.)
118. On Lufthansa's stake in Fraport, Chairman and CEO Mayrhuber stated: 'The stake in Fraport AG is a strategic investment in our core business.... It will allow Lufthansa to leverage influence in the airport's development, improve cooperation and enhance quality on the ground for the benefit of customers. That will

strengthen our competitive position. Moreover, Fraport AG generates strong returns. The investment in the airport operator will pay off,' as quoted in BvD Zephyr Deal ID Number 390757. On AF–KLM's acquisition of Miami-based Aero Maintenance Group, Air France Industries President Alain Bassil stated, '[T]his majority position enables AFI KLM E&M to consolidate its presence and market share in the Americas. It consolidates a long-term partnership with a highly skilled and performing Company, AMG which was initiated in 2004, and also allows us to bring more services to operators, offering enhanced proximity, reactivity and flexibility.' Source: BvD Zephyr Deal ID Number 1601088607.

119. Please see *The Guardian* (2011). It is also reported in the article that '(c)urrent BA chairman Sir Martin Broughton will remain in the post after the tie-up, but will also become deputy chairman of IAG and will earn €350,000 and an extra €175,000 next year to help with the demands of integrating the two firms.'

120. That is, the end of December for each year, except in the case of BA and Iberia where data for 2011 is based on shareholdings recorded by Amadeus as of 20 January 2011, before IAG was listed on the London and Madrid stock exchanges on Monday, 24 January 2011.

121. Based on information provided in the BvD database, Zephyr, with Deal ID Number 1601129354.

122. IAG's value of 258p in early July 2011 would drop the month later, and slowly recover to similar values by mid-March 2013. For a graph on the evolution of IAG's stock market prices in the same time period of Figure 3.5, please see <http://uk.finance.yahoo.com/echarts?s=IAG.L#symbol=iag.l;range=20110225,20131122;compare=;indicator=volume;charttype=area;crosshair=on;ohlcvalues=0;logscale=off;source=undefined>.

123. For a biography of Mayrhuber, see the UBS website: <http://www.ubs.com/global/en/about_ubs/corporate_covernance/board-of-directors/cv-wolfgang-mayrhuber.html> (last accessed 10 January 2013).

124. UBS's ownership in Lufthansa is recorded in Amadeus with the following dates: Aug-07, .68%; Oct-07, .63%; Dec-07, .78%; Jan-08, .5%; May-08, .99%; Jun-08, 1.33%; Jun-09, .22%; Sep-09, .16%; Dec-09 .14%; Jun-10, .13%; Sep-10, .26%; Oct-10, .27%; Mar-11, .29%; May-11, .27%; Jul-11, .26%; Aug-11, .21%; Oct-11, .17%; Dec-11, .17%; Aug-12, .2%; Apr-13, .1%.

125. On Mayrhuber's bid to become Lufthansa Chairman in May 2013 see Weiss (2013), and on his ability to have eventually gained the support to do so see Steen (2013).

126. Based on analysis of Zephyr file with ID Number 165695.

127. In the 2005 offer the BvD reported that 'the large Swiss shareholders will receive an earn-out in exchange for their shares; the maximum payout will amount to €250 million'. BvD Deal Number 165695.

128. Quote taken from Zephyr Deal with ID Number BvD 642648. One major shareholder in the transaction was Vienna Insurance Group (VIG), which sold its 1.4 per cent stake in Austrian Airlines.

129. Doganis, 2006, 45–6. Of course, not all EU initiatives were necessarily immediately implemented by all member states. For examples of French and Italian cases

where Community legislation was not implemented, see Van Houtte, 2000, 76–7. For Spain, see Chari and Kritzinger, 2006, 90–1.

130. European Commission 2002c.

131. The ECJ's November 2002 decision can be found on <http://eur-lex.europa.eu/LexUriServ/LexUriServ.do?uri=CELEX:61998C0466:EN:HTML:NOT>.

132. For a history of the Star Alliance, please see <http://www.staralliance.com/assets/doc/en/about/member-airlines/pdf/Star_Alliance_Chronological_May2012.pdf>. Information on Oneworld can be found on <http://www.oneworld.com/general/about-oneworld>. Finally, information on Skyteam is taken from <http://www.skyteam.com/en/About-us/Organization/History/> (all URLs last accessed 22 December 2013).

133. Quoted in *The New York Times* article by Landler (2002).

134. See the article by James (2002).

135. Quote taken from Tagliabue (2003).

136. As an example of US interests that ultimately bowed out of taking over a European airline, see the previous discussion on Iberia and the TPG consortium's failed bid.

137. An interesting case of why being part of the alliance matters is seen in the case of Lufthansa/Austrian. Austrian joined Star Alliance in 2000, but Air France had attained a minority stake (1.5 per cent) in Austrian in the early 2000s. When the Austrian state (ÖIAG) was selling its 41.46 per cent stake in 2008, Air France eventually left the process in late 2008 because the price was too high. But one may argue that Lufthansa could 'win' with a lower bid because of past association with Austrian: due to the idea that Austrian was in association with Lufthansa for years as a fellow alliance member, Lufthansa knew well which routes were profitable, which ones were not, and where Austrian airlines had problems. Lufthansa could hence provide an overall offer that was lower in price (than the French) but better in content. This argument is based on ideas raised in interviews, November 2013.

138. This aid, particularly those to Iberia, is discussed in Chari (2004, 1–14). For a complete list of other airlines that received aid see Doganis (2006, 246).

139. As discussed in Zephyr Deal with ID Number 625789.

140. As will be seen later when we discuss Commission approval of deal. See also Zephyr Deal with ID Number 642648.

141. Quote taken from Zephy Deal with ID Number 625789.

142. These ideas were raised in interviews in November 2013.The interviewee also stated that state-appointed board members of SAS rarely are involved in major decisions.

143. Quote taken from Bureau van Dijk's Zephyr database, BvD Deal ID Number 30717.

144. Based on analysis of completed acquisitions by Lufthansa as found on the Zephyr database between 1997 and 2012 (a total of twenty-eight deals).

145. In the case of Swiss, Lufthansa made its initial 11 per cent directly and then completed takeover via AirTrust AG. In the case of Austrian Airlines, while the initial 45 per cent of the privatized stake was bought directly by Lufthansa, the remainder was acquired through *ÖLH Österreichische Luftverkehrs Holding* GmbH.

146. The shareholder information of Deutsche Post is based on information provided in the Amadeus database, BvD company number ID DE 5030147191. Strong previous association between Lufthansa and Deutsche Post is also reflected in the idea that they had made a previous significant deal. In 2001 Deutsche Post had close to a majority stake in DHL, at 46.3 per cent. In 2002 Lufthansa Cargo sold its 25 per cent stake in DHL to Deutsche Post for an estimated €610 million, giving Deutsche Post a controlling 71.3 per cent stake in DHL. This is based on information found in the Zephyr Deal with BvD ID Number 103765.

147. The quote was made by Lufthansa CEO Wolfgang Mayrhuber, as found on the Zephyr database, taken from BvD Deal ID Number 550192.

148. See BvD Deal ID Number 177249.

149. As outlined in the AF–KLM Annual Report, 2011, 49.

150. Biographies on these members are as follows (as taken from the company report of AF–KLM, found in the Amadeus database):

- Jean-Cyril Spinetta, Chairman and CEO, has held positions within the National Education Ministry and has also served other positions throughout his career, including Auditor of the Conseil d'Etat (1976–8), Charge de Mission to the General Secretariat of the Government (1978–81), Head of the Information Department of Prime Minister Pierre Mauroy (1981–3), Minister of Transport and later Minister of Equipment (1984–6 and 1988–90), and Expert for France seconded to the European Commission (1997).

- Jaap de Hoop Scheffer, Director, formerly leader of the Christian Democratic Appeal (CDA) in the House of Representatives in the Netherlands from 1997–2001 as well as Dutch Foreign Minister from 2002–3. He also held the position of Secretary General of NATO and President of the North Atlantic Council from 2004–9.

- Jean-Dominique Comolli, Director, has served as Commissioner for State Holdings and Director General of French Government Shareholding Agency (APE) since 15 September 2010. Previous experience includes Assistant Director of the Budget Department (1986), and Chairman and CEO of SEITA (1993) that was privatized in 1995.

- Jean Marc Espalioux, Independent Director, served as financial controller in the Treasury Department from 1978–83.

- Claude Gressier, Director, Representative of the French State since June 2004.

- Marie-Christine Saragosse, Director, was Director for Cultural Cooperation and French Language Promotion at the French Ministry of Foreign Affairs from 2006–8 as well as a Member of the Board of Directors of the Agency for French Teaching Abroad from 2006–8.

151. This is based on information in the IAG Annual Report 2011, pages 36–8.

152. Biographies on the members are as follows (as taken from the company report of IAG found on the Amadeus database, and also cross-referenced and verified with the information found in the IAG Annual Report 2011, 36–8; unlike AF–KLM and Lufthansa, IAG provided brief biographies for all its Board members in 2011):

- Rodrigo Rato (as discussed in the text later), has served as Vice-President of Iberia since 2010, and was Former Minister of Economy and Finance under Aznar, 1996–2004.
- Baroness Denise Kingsmill, Non-Executive Director of BA since 2004, has served as Deputy Chairman of the UK's MMC (later renamed Competition Commission) from 1996–2003, and presently is a member of the House of Commons. On her resignation from the Commission, see <http://webarchive. nationalarchives.gov.uk/+/http://www.competition-commission.org.uk/press_ rel/archive/2003/jun/ html/19-03.htm>, and on her position in the House of Lords see <http://www.parliament.uk/biographies/lords/baroness-kingsmill/ 3788> (both URLs last accessed 5 April 2014).
- José Manuel Fernández Norniella, non-executive Director of Iberia since 2003, was elected as MP for Madrid in 1993 and served as the Partido Popular Secretary of State for Trade, Tourism, and SMEs. He joined Bankia in 2006.
- José Pedro Pérez-Llorca, has been Non-Executive Director of Iberia since 2000, and previously served as a career diplomat and a member of the Parliamentary Council. He was a former Cabinet Minister of the Presidency, Parliamentary Relations, Regional Government, and Foreign Affairs between 1980–1 (in Adolfo Suarez's UCD government during the Spanish transition to democracy).
- John Snow, Independent Director, served as US Secretary of the Treasury under George Bush from February 2003 to June 2006. He also held various other positions under the Ford and Clinton administrations.

  It should be noted that Kieran Poynter, Independent Director (who served on the President's Committee of the Confederation of British Industry and has also served as a member of an advisory committee to the Chancellor of the Exchequer on the UK's financial service sector competitiveness), is not considered to have past association in terms of having a long-term official role *per se*, although he has advised the government in the past.

153. This is based on information from the 2011 Annual Report, which can be found online at <http://reports.lufthansa.com/2011/ar/notes/boards/supervisoryboard. html>.
154. Biographies on the two are as follows (as taken from the company report of Lufthansa, Amadeus database):
    - Frank Bsirske, an employee representative on the Lufthansa Board, was involved in local politics earlier in his career: from 1978 to 1987 he was Secretary of Education in the district of Hanover of the Socialist Youth in Germany ('Die Falken'), and from 1987 to 1989 he was active as Assistant of 'Grüne Alternative Bürgerliste' in the city council of the state capital of Hanover.
    - Robert Kimmitt, a voting member, was a former US Ambassador to Germany (1991–3), previously serving as member of the National Security Council staff at the White House (1978–85) and then General Counsel of the Department of the Treasury (1985–7).

155. This is based on *El País* (2010). When Rato was named as being on the Board of Directors to Iberia the report stated in reference to the BA–Iberia deal that Rodrigo Rato 'continuará en la misma dirección para que la operación fructifique'.

156. On the organization of Brussels Airlines, see <http://company.brusselsairlines. com/en_be/corp/our-company/organisation.aspx> (last accessed 28 December 2013).

157. On BMI: Lufthansa's first 20 per cent stake in BMI was not referred to the UK Competition Commission. Further, when Lufthansa had purchased an extra 10 per cent of BMI from Mr Bishop in 2002, the deal had been given regulatory approval by the Bundeskartellamt (based on information provided in the Zephyr database, Deals with ID numbers 52229 and 125050). This approval is important in the context of SAS announcing its intention to sell its 20 per cent stake in 2007 (as a consequence of its S-11 strategy), which resulted in both BA and Virgin, which had previously been showing interest in BMI, expressing interest again in acquiring the SAS stake in 2007. However, Lufthansa having this 30 per cent stake gave it the first say in any sale and the option to buy out Mr Bishop, who owned 50 per cent, which it subsequently announced it intended to do in April 2008 (based on information provided in the Zephyr database, Deal with ID Number 517303). Eventually, the full takeover was approved by the European Commission in May 2009, as discussed later. On Eurowings: in September 2001 the Bundeskartellamt approved Lufthansa's intention to acquire 49 per cent in 2004 (based on information provided in the Zephyr database, Deal with ID number 99075). On Aerologic: this was approved by the Bundeskartellamt in 2007 (based on information provided in the Zephyr database, Deal with ID Number 550192).

158. Based on the information provided in the Zephyr database, file ID Numbers 92208 (Aerolíneas Argentinas) and 488906 (BA Connect).

159. Lufthansa's JV with Shenzen and the German government to form Jade Cargo received regulatory approval from China's General Administration for Civil Aviation (BvD 266493)—the formerly called General Administration of Civil Aviation of China is now referred to as the CAAC (the Civil Aviation Administration of China). See the regulator's webpage at <http://english.gov.cn/2005-10/22/con tent_81677.htm> (last accessed 1 December 2013).

160. In the words of the MMC, 'the merger would also have important beneficial results. It would strengthen the competitive position of BA, which is the only British company competing with major foreign airlines worldwide, and in future may have to face increasing competition from American mega-carriers'. From page 72 of the MMC report, which can be found at <http://webarchive. nationalarchives.gov.uk/+/http://www.competition-commission.org.uk/rep_pub/ reports/1987/219british_airways_caledonian_group_plc.htm>. On the MMC ruling see <http://news.bbc.co.uk/onthisday/hi/dates/stories/july/16/newsid_2503000/ 2503947.stm> (both URLs last accessed 7 December 2013).

161. The concern in this case was that the acquisition of VLM would '(l)essen competition between London City (LCY) and Amsterdam's Schipol (AMS)'. In OFT's words: 'On LCY–AMS (business), the transaction creates very high combined

shares of weekly capacity and frequency in excess of 70 per cent. Notwithstanding BA's recent entry, the merging parties are closest competitors on LCY–AMS: KLM and VLM remain by a large margin the top two choices for business passengers requiring morning and evening peak outbound and inbound flights between LCY and AMS.' The solution proposed by AF–KLM was 'divestment of up to three slots at LCY during the morning peak period and up to four slots at LCY during the peak evening period to be used by the purchaser for LCY–AMS'. See <http://www.concurrences.com/spip.php?action=acceder_document&arg=6775&cle=aa6a8817cf2e688244c99eab244f45e38017a4fa&file=pdf%2FAirFrance.pdf>.

162. BA/Dan-Air (Case No. IV/M.278) was originally deemed outside of the Merger Control Regulation (because the thresholds were not reached), but the Belgian government felt that the merger would restrict competition in Belgium, given that both fly between Belgium and the UK. So, the Commission looked at the case in 1993. The combined airline would have half the market between London and Brussels. Because British Midlands was serving the route, the Commission deemed there was effective competition, so it decided the takeover would 'neither create, nor strengthen a dominant position which would significantly impeded completion'. BA/TAT (1) 1992 (Case No. IV/M.259) was approved, but remedies prescribed for the Gatwick–Paris route (these were negotiated between BA and the Commission) were as follows: 'when a carrier(s) wishing to start or increase this service does not obtain the necessary slots for the airport coordinator, BA will make a maximum of 12 slots available in order to enable the operation of six additional daily frequencies (return flights) reasonably spread during the day.' When the rest of TAT was taken over in BA/TAT II (Case No. IV/M.806), the Commission approved it without opposition in August 1996. On BA/Air Liberté see the 1997 Case No. IV/M.857.

163. As demonstrated in comments from Zephyr file with deal ID number 130540.

164. Quote taken from a speech by Alexander Italianer (Director General, DG Competition) entitled 'Legal certainty, proportionality, effectiveness: the Commission's practice on remedies', given on 5 December 2012 at the Charles River Associates Annual Conference.

165. See European Commission 2011.

166. See European Commission 2013b.

167. When performing the Alpha/Beta tests previously outlined, we see that Ryanair appears in the latest Forbes 2000 List, ranks amongst the best compared to its peers in Europe (Table 3.3), and has an A$^+$ independence ranking as seen in its Amadeus database company report with ID Number IE249885. With regard to easyJet, it is on the Forbes list, and seen in Table 3.3. Its BvD Independence ranking, however, is B$^+$. This is because 38 per cent of the firm is owned by the Haji-Ioannou family, as recorded in the company's Amadeus file with ID Number GB03959649. Because this shareholder is a family, we can invoke exception 2 to this part of the test (as outlined in Chapters 1 and 2), thereby resulting in the firm being classified as an Alpha.

168. The comments made by Ryanair's Michael O'Leary were reported in *The Guardian* in an article by Webb and Wearden (2010). On BA/Iberia, easyJet's

Stelios Haji-Ioannou similarly reportedly stated in the same article that 'this is the classic story of two drunks that believe they can walk better together by supporting each other'.

169. Case No. COMP/*M*.4439—Ryanair/Aer Lingus.
170. On the case that was withdrawn, see Case No. COMP/*M*.5434—Ryanair/Aer Lingus II; on their third attempt, see Case No. COMP/*M*.6663—Ryanair/Aer Lingus III.
171. Quote taken from the European Commission (2013a.) Carswell (2013) reports the Commission highlighted that the 2013 decision was not political.
172. Interviews performed in Dublin, April 2012.
173. See the Press Release of the Minister, which can be found on the department's website: <http://www.dttas.ie/press-releases/2013/varadkar-welcomes-eu-commission-decision-prohibit-ryanair-takeover-aer-lingus>.
174. Interviews held in Brussels, March 2012.
175. Interviews held in Brussels, March 2012.
176. Based on analysis of Zephyr deal with BvD ID Number 642648.
177. Based on analysis of Zephyr deal with BvD ID Number 1601276109.
178. Based on analysis of Zephyr deal with BvD ID Numbers 1601134505 (BMI Deal) and 85560 (Go). Both the BA–Iberia and BA–BMI deals are also mentioned on Mr Whitman's webpage: <http://www.slaughterandmay.com/who-we-are/partners/david-wittmann.aspx>.
179. Based on analysis of Zephyr deal with BvD ID Number 130540. US regulators approved the deal at the same time as the European Commission.
180. On the conference call between journalists and AF and KLM bosses following the deal, see the Securities and Exchange Commission's webpage: <http://www.sec.gov/Archives/edgar/containers/fix011/56316/000119312504021087/d425.htm> (last accessed 5 January 2014).
181. Please see <http://blogs.ft.com/brusselsblog/2012/04/when-willie-let-fly-in-brussels/> (last accessed 6 January 2014).
182. Quote taken from Barker's FT blog which can be found on <http://blogs.ft.com/brusselsblog/2012/04/when-willie-let-fly-in-brussels/> (last accessed 6 January 2014).
183. Taken from the file in the Zephyr database with ID Number 637433.
184. Based on information provided in Zephyr's Deal with ID Number 1601039897.
185. See European Commission (2004).
186. Based on interviews with a competition lawyer based in Brussels, November 2013.
187. Decision 2009/155/EC of 12 November 2008. See also the European Commission (2008a).
188. On the ECJ's judgment in case C-287/12 P, 3.8.2013 (*Ryanair Ltd v Commission, Italy and Alitalia*), see the Court of the European Justice, Press Release No. 72/13, Luxembourg, 13 June 2013.
189. This reasoning was expressed in the European Commission (2007). The Commission justified its stance on this as follows: 'In the majority of cases involving an insolvent aid beneficiary, it will not be possible to recover the full amount of unlawful and incompatible aid (including interests), as the beneficiary's assets will

be insufficient to satisfy all creditors' claims. Consequently, it is not possible to fully re-establish the ex-ante situation in the traditional manner. Since the ultimate objective of recovery is to end the distortion of competition, the ECJ has stated that the liquidation of the beneficiary can be regarded as an acceptable option to recovery in such cases. The Commission is therefore of the view that a decision ordering the Member State to recover unlawful and incompatible aid from an insolvent beneficiary may be considered to be properly executed either when full recovery is completed or, in case of partial recovery, when the company is liquidated and its assets are sold under market conditions.' I am particularly indebted to Claire Micheau for clarifying the Commission's decision and ECJ's ruling on this case.

4

Automobiles: Get It In Gear

Introduction

In the first section, each company studied—Volkswagen (Germany), Renault (France), Jaguar (UK), SEAT (Spain), and Alfa Romeo (Italy)—is individually examined on three dimensions. First, a brief history of each firm is given. Second, the dynamics surrounding the firms' privatization are outlined. It shows that Volkswagen, Renault, and Jaguar were all successfully floated, while SEAT and Alfa Romeo were directly sold to sectoral leaders when privatized, namely VW and Fiat respectively. The third dimension considers life after privatization of each firm. With detail not heretofore presented in the literature, I specifically focus on the multiple mergers and acquisitions (M&A) by Volkswagen and Renault in Europe and globally. These deals will be first presented to the reader in this section and later referred to throughout the chapter.

The second section of the chapter comparatively classifies the firms today, performing the Global Movers Test and the Independence Test outlined in Chapter 2. It will be argued that while both the German and French automakers can be considered Alphas, Jaguar, SEAT, and Alfa Romeo are Betas.

In order to understand why the firms became Alphas or Betas, the third section first considers internal and external factors that explain why both Volkswagen and Renault have become global leaders. It then argues that Jaguar, although theoretically being in a position to become an Alpha, eventually became a Beta because of the firm's lack of competitiveness after its flotation, the goals of managers and shareholders, as well as the influence of the state in facilitating the firm being bought by Ford. The chapter closes by comparing and contrasting the cases of SEAT and Alfa Romeo, highlighting the importance of the state that desired that both loss-making firms be privatized to reliable, and 'safe', leaders in the sector.

4.1 Brief History of the Firms, Privatization, and Life Thereafter

This analysis starts with the first firm that was (partially) privatized, VW, and then turns to Renault, Jaguar, SEAT, and Alfa Romeo. There are three main dimensions to the discussion of each company: a brief history of the firm is presented, followed by discussion of its privatization and, in the case of Volkswagen and Renault, details on deals pursued as a privatized firm. This information will serve as the basis to better understand which firms are Alphas and Betas, and why, discussed in Sections 4.2 and 4.3 of the chapter. To keep the discussion on privatization consistent with that of Chapter 1, and unless otherwise noted, the values reported for the sales will be reported in US dollars as found in <www.privatizationbarometer.net>. For different M&A pursued by the firms (particularly VW and Renault), unless otherwise noted, deal values will be presented in euros, consistent with data found in BvD's Zephyr database.

Volkswagen—Brief History, Privatization, and Life Thereafter

The idea of mass production of an inexpensive, yet reliable, 'people's car' was something that had already started in Germany in the early 1900s (Volkswagen, 2013a, 1). Yet, production did not fully occur until the Nazi dictatorship: Volkswagen was founded in 1937 and officially named 'Volks-wagenwerk GmbH' on May 1938 (Volkswagen, 2013b, 1). At this time Hitler announced the beginning of production of the 'KdF-Wagen' ('Kraft durch Freude-Wagen', or the 'Strength Through Joy' car; Volkswagen, 2013b, 1, 2). He envisaged one to be owned by all German families. This car was based on prototypes (including the Type 12, Type 32, and Type 60, which had cheap air-cooled rear engines) previously designed in the early 1930s by the exceptionally gifted engineer Ferdinand Porsche, who had once worked with Daimler. Yet, dreams of everyone owning one were shelved during the Second World War due to serious economic problems, including a lack of materials. As a consequence the factory was used to produce military equipment. Many of those working in the factory during the Second World War were prisoners of war and concentration camp inmates, as recognized by present-day VW who state that '(a)pproximately 20,000 forced laborers who were allocated to the Volkswagen plant during World War II came from European countries occupied or dominated by Germany' (Volkswagen, 2013b, 1).

With three-quarters of the Wolfsburg factory destroyed by the end of the war, hopes for revival were renewed not by the Germans, but by the British: in June 1945, led by Major Ivan Hirst, the British Military Government took over the administration of VW in trusteeship (Volkswagen, 2013c, 1, 3). In so doing, production shortly began again and, as Nonnenkamp (2011, 65) explains, 'the cars built at the end of the war ... were virtually identical to the KdF-Wagen sedans built from 1938 until 1945'. The only difference was that the name of the car was changed to the Volkswagen 'Type 1' or, in common parlance, the 'Beetle' or 'Bug'. There were three decisive steps by the British to ensure the company's survival: a large order of cars in 1945 for the British Army of around twenty thousand; the establishment of a service department (including 'a parts warehouse, a technical department and service school') to service all VW cars; and the start of exporting to international markets, including the Netherlands, Switzerland, Belgium and Luxembourg, and Sweden (Volkswagen, 2013c, 1, 6, 9). In 1949 the British Military Government, which had unsuccessfully tried to sell Volkswagen to different firms such as Ford and Renault, who claimed that the Volkswagen was an 'inferior product' (Nonnenkamp, 2011, 65), turned VW over to West Germany, where the State (Land) of Lower Saxony assumed the company's administration (Volkswagen, 2013c, 7, 10.)

Throughout the 1950s VW became a leading European industrial firm under the direction of Heinrich Nordhoff, formerly of Opel, who was appointed Director General in 1948 when VW was still in British hands. In 1950 the firm introduced the larger Type 2 Volkswagen Bus (or, Transporter), which gained notoriety throughout the 1960s peace movement. The 1950s also witnessed internationalization into global markets outside of Europe, including that of North and South America where a plant was opened in Brazil in 1959 (Volkswagen 2013d, 1, 3, 24). Within the domestic market, the Beetle 'became a symbol of Germany's economic miracle ... (and was) the best selling automobile of the decade and had a market share of around 40 percent' (Volkswagen 2013d, 1). Over the next decades different models were developed and successfully sold throughout the globe—most notably the Beetle's successor, the Golf, introduced in the 1970s and marketed in North America at different times as 'the Rabbit'.[1]

With regard to its *privatization*, plans to sell the company were envisaged in the 1950s, relatively earlier than other state-owned car companies from other European states. However, the idea to privatize was not readily accepted by all. When discussions started in Parliament in 1956, there were predictably two opposing sides. On the one hand, the workforce was 'interested in protecting the financial and social benefits they had received and fought against the government's privatization plan', having the support of the opposition Social Democrats which were against the sale of national assets (Volkswagen 2013d, 2). On the other hand, VW management held the view that 'the privatization of Germany's most important automobile producer was unavoidable.... [It] was a company without an owner, administered by the state of Lower Saxony on behalf of and under the supervision of the federal government. In addition, public trusteeship did not conform to the liberal market economy principles of the coalition government led by the Christian Democrats' (Volkswagen, 2013d, 2). As such, by 1960 the Parliament had approved the ideologically driven (partial) privatization of the firm. Its initial listing on the market took place in April 1961, representing one of the first major sales of a state-owned enterprise in Western Europe. At the time, 60 per cent was sold as 'people's stocks' (*Volksaktien*), while 40 per cent was divided equally between the federal government and the state of Lower Saxony, both thus holding 20 per cent each (Volkswagen 2013d, 24).

In March 1988 all of the Federal Republic of Germany's 4.8 million shares of VW, equivalent to 20 per cent of the company, were floated on domestic and international stock markets.[2] This was done during the first small peak of German privatizations as seen in Figure 1.1 of Chapter 1, pursued in the context of both the government's wider privatization programme as well as the need for cash given the deficit at the time. The operation raised an estimated USD 675.8 million.[3]

In terms of its *life after privatization*, VW's first significant acquisition was made shortly after its initial 60 per cent sale. Based on analysis of VW's executive board meetings between 1960 and 1969, which was performed in Wolfsburg in March 2012,[4] it is clear that VW sought to acquire another European carmaker shortly after its privatization. In board meetings on 19 May 1964 interest was expressed in Peugeot in order to gain greater access to the French market. Similarly, in the same meeting, Lancia was considered because it potentially offered more access to the Italian market. In negotiations spearheaded by Nordhoff, it was finally decided to acquire another German competitor: on 28 September 1964 'Projekt XY', which was the term coined by Nordhoff regarding the acquisition of Auto Union in Ingolstadt from Daimler, was close to being finalized. As Nonnenkamp (2011, 103) explains, 'Auto Union (for whom Ferdinand Porsche had worked in the 1930s) was formed in 1932 from the merger of four car companies (Audi, Horsch, DKW and Wanderer)'. The board meetings of 22 October 1964 stated that a main reason for the acquisition was to enhance VW by increasing capacity to build 100,000 VW Beetles per year and take such a capacity 'away from a rival'. While the Ingolstadt factory was relatively new, the VW board also saw disadvantages: production costs, as well as car prices, were too high. The final price paid by VW to Daimler in two instalments in March 1965 and January 1966 was DM377,000, where DM80,000 was used towards a capital injection into the new acquisition. By 30 August 1966 concerns were raised regarding the low sales figures, especially in overseas markets. And while VW's initial plan was 'to use Ingolstadt's production capacity for building the VW Beetle', by 27 June 1967 the VW board concluded that developing new cars was to be beneficial to the Group and that 'it is wrong to think that selling Audi cars is harmful to VW cars/production'.[5] By 1968 the successful Audi 100 was produced and a year later Neckarsulm-based NSU Motorenwerke AG merged with Auto Union, where the new company was renamed 'Audi NSU Auto Union' AG. When NSU cars came off the production line in 1977, the company manufactured only Audi cars and was later renamed, to a more succinct, 'Audi AG' in 1985.[6]

After purchasing SEAT from the Spanish government between 1986 and 1990 (discussed in more detail later in the chapter), VW continued its expansion into other countries, acquiring more firms on the selling block: in 1991 VW bought a majority share in the Czech car manufacturer Škoda. It had started out as a bicycle manufacturer in 1895, later producing cars and planes. After the Second World War it was nationalized by the Czechoslovakian government, and 'became a national enterprise and took over all passenger car production' in the country.[7] With the end of the Cold War and in the context of seeking a leading international partner to ensure its longevity, the Czech Republic's government led by Václav Havel sought to sell Škoda. Volkswagen was chosen given that its 'chief executive Carl Hahn was committed to making high quality cars in the former Eastern Bloc', unlike the other bidder, Renault, which was perceived to want 'to produce low cost cars in the Czech Republic'.[8] The first 40 per cent of Škoda was sold in 1991 for an undisclosed amount; the second 30 per cent in May 2000, for €333 million[9], and the last 30 per cent that same month, for €222 million, even though the Czech government originally wanted 60 per cent more for this final tranche.[10]

Starting in 1998, with Ferdinand Piëch at the helm of the company, VW also purchased European luxury carmakers. One deal for an undisclosed amount in July 1998 was that of the luxury car manufacturer Bugatti International.[11] VW's takeover represented the revival of a company whose doors were closed since 1995. In September 1998 VW bought Automobili Lamborghini SpA, a sports car company founded in 1963, taken over by Chrysler in 1987, and then sold to a group of Indonesian investors in 1994 who later sold to VW for an undisclosed consideration.[12]

VW also took over production of Bentley cars in 2003, in a slightly complicated deal that was struck in August 1998 between Vickers (vendor of Rolls Royce), VW, and BMW. In terms of the company's history, Rolls Royce manufactured both Rolls Royce cars and Bentley cars after Rolls Royce acquired Bentley in 1931. Rolls Royce went into receivership, was nationalized in 1971, and floated in 1973 (as a separate entity from aero-engine manufacturing). Rolls Royce Motors was then bought by Vickers in 1980. On 25 March 1998, VW made an offer for Rolls Royce Motors, and a rival bid was placed two days later by BMW. On 6 June 1998 Vickers shareholders approved the sale to VW for £430 million.[13] However, Rolls Royce plc 'refused to allow any company other than BMW to use its name'.[14] By the end of July 1998 VW, BMW, and Rolls Royce reached an agreement with four dimensions: 'BMW would acquire the right to use the Rolls-Royce name for GBP 40 million'; 'until 2003, VW will produce Rolls Royce cars under license'; 'BMW will take over the production of Rolls-Royce cars from 2003'; and 'VW has the right to name and production of Bentley's in 2003'.[15] As such, starting in 2003, VW continued building Bentleys, while the BMW Group took over manufacturing Rolls Royce cars.

VW has also looked eastward by pursuing joint ventures and attaining minority stakes in Asian companies. Since the 1980s it has production facilities in China and in 2004 it signed an agreement to invest USD 171 million in an auto-parts joint venture with the state-owned Chinese First Automotive Works Group (FAW).[16] Within a year, both agreed to set up a jointly run car manufacturing plant in Chendu City.[17] Turning to Japan, in 2010 VW acquired a minority stake of close to 20 per cent in Suzuki Motors (which controlled over 30 per cent of the Japanese mini-vehicle market, and also served as a means to increase VW's share of the Indian small car market), for an estimated value of €1.681 billion.[18] The business alliance, however, was short lived given increasing differences between the two firms and allegations that the terms of the original contract had been breached.[19]

In an ongoing process starting in 2000 and lasting well over a decade, VW also completed the purchases of two heavy truck and bus manufacturers—Scania AB from Malmö, Sweden, and MAN AG from Munich, Germany. On 28 March 2000 VW completed the acquisition of 18.7 per cent of Scania (for an estimated value of €1.549 billion[20]). In so doing, VW became the largest shareholder in Scania, a company with whom VW had shared links since after the Second World War when Scania imported VWs into the Swedish market via Svenka Volkswagen AB. On 4 September 2006 MAN announced a hostile bid over Scania,[21] seeking the support of VW by offering it a stake in the new entity. However, on 18 September 2006 the board of Scania, of which VW was the main shareholder, rejected the takeover bid. Within two weeks, on 4 October 2006, for an estimated €1.571 million VW acquired a minority stake of around 15 per cent in MAN, where two-thirds of this was acquired from AXA.[22] Although denying such reports, a few days later VW intimated it wanted both Scania and MAN[23], and by 27 October 2006 VW increased its stake in MAN to 20 per cent for an estimated value of €490 million.[24] With around a fifth of a stake in both truck makers, sufficient momentum was effectively gained to help close the two deals over the next years in two conjunctures. First, by July 2008 VW had taken over a controlling stake in Scania by purchasing shares from Investor AB and other Swedish foundations owned by the Wallenberg family who supported the takeover.[25] Second, in February 2007 VW increased its stake in MAN from 20 to 29.9 per cent, in a deal worth an estimated €1.221 billion[26]. Four years on, in May 2011 VW made a hostile bid to increase its stake in MAN to 53.71 per cent for an estimated €2.083 billion.[27] VW presently owns 75 per cent of MAN.

Another acquisition in July 2012 (through VW's subsidiary, Audi) was of the Italian motorcycle manufacturer, Ducati, founded in 1926 as a producer of components for radio transmission. After the Second World War it produced the Cucciolo bike and its first motorcycle was constructed in 1949, starting its legendary status as a superbike manufacturer. In the midst of financial troubles, however, in early 2012 Ducati indicated its desire for a partner in order to sustain its future and increase its international growth. Two German firms—Audi and Daimler—had expressed interest. By May 2012 Audi was the first to put a firm offer on the table: it paid €875 million for Ducati, as well as an assumed €200 million of the Italian firm's debts.[28]

Finally, coming full circle is the saga between VW and Porsche, a company with which VW has had a long history from the days when Ferdinand Porsche designed the Beetle. In order to follow the different players in the saga, Figure 4.1 outlines the family tree of the Porsche–Piëch families based on information provided in a *Financial Times* Report by Schäfer (2009).

After the Second World War, Ferdinand Porsche along with his son 'Ferry' Porsche were arrested as war criminals by the French. Yet, within a few years, in 1949 the family returned to Stuttgart to restart the Porsche business. As Hawranek (2009a, 3) explains, at this time an agreement was made with Nordhoff's lead on three main dimensions: Porsche would receive a fee of 5 DM for every Beetle produced; VW would supply parts for Porsche's production plants; and Porsche would be the authorized dealer in Austria for all VWs. Hawranek (2009a, 2) explains that Ferdinand Porsche envisaged 'his son Ferry at the helm (of the sports car manufacturer) in Stuttgart and his daughter, Louise Piëch, in control of the dealership company in Salzburg'.

Some forty years after continued cooperation between VW and Porsche, and despite low profits in the early 1990s given falling US market sales, the

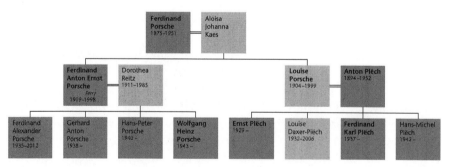

Figure 4.1. The Porsche–Piëch Family Tree
Source: Schäfer (2009)

sports car company later thrived throughout the decade under the leadership of CEO Wendelin Wiedeking. The Porsche CEO had the support of Wolfgang Porsche (the son of Ferry Porsche who played a key supervisory board role in the firm), although some personal tensions arose over time with the other 'half' of the Porsche family, namely that of the side of Ferdinand Piëch (as mentioned previously, the head of the VW group, who was also the grandson of Ferdinand Porsche, son of Louise Piëch, and first cousin to Wolfgang Porsche).

Fuelled by the family feud between the Porsche and Piëch families—where one could argue that 'Porsche' side of the family sought to gain more control within the Porsche empire and try to oust Piëch—Porsche's high cash reserves were used to purchase a minority stake of around 10.3 per cent of VW for €1.693 billion in September 2005.[29] In 2006 Wiedeking further increased this stake to over 27 per cent.[30] In March 2007 the carmaker had attained close to 31 per cent of VW, in a deal value of €1.128 billion, where credit facilities were provided by ABN AMRO Bank NV, Barclays Capital, Merrill Lynch, Commerzbank, and UBS.[31] By September 2008 their stake increased to over 35 per cent in a deal costing €2.949 billion.[32] After purchasing other minority stakes for unknown amounts, in January 2009 Porsche's acquisition increased from 42.6 per cent to 50.76 per cent, for an estimated value of €6.235 billion, with its eye set on taking up to a 75 per cent stake in VW.

The impossible almost seemed to become reality—the smaller company, Porsche AG, was at the point of taking over one of the world's automobile giants, VW. Then there were the rumours in May 2009 that it was VW that was going to be taking over Porsche (Davis, 2009). Only some months later did the rumours end and the deal close, as succinctly argued by *The Economist* (2009):

> ...tiny Porsche, which makes 100,000 cars a year, tried to take control of Europe's biggest car-maker, which makes 6 million a year. But the sport-car firm buckled under the debts it acquired along with 51% of VW's shares and options to buy yet more. Then VW tried to take over Porsche, but that deal also stalled until Porsche's boss (Wendelin Wiedeking) and finance chief (Holger Härter) resigned....

With Wiedeking and Härter out of the picture, a complicated deal was orchestrated by VW's boss Ferdinand Piëch with the help of the State of Lower Saxony, as discussed in more detail in Section 4.3: during the Summer of 2009 the creation of 'an integrated automotive group under the leadership of Volkswagen' was announced.[33] The integrated group was to be formed 'via the progressive participation of VW in Porsche AG, and the subsequent merger of Porsche Automobile Holding SE (hence Porsche SE) and Volkswagen AG'.[34] There were two main elements of the deal:

- The holding company, Porsche SE, would sell its automaker, Porsche AG, to VW in two stages.
    - First, an initial stake of 49.9 per cent at the end of 2009. At this stage, Porsche SE continued to hold a majority stake in VW, while VW owned 49.9 per cent of Porsche AG.[35]
    - Second, the remaining 50.1 per cent stake in August 2012. At this time, Porsche AG would be fully owned by Volkswagen, while Porsche SE maintained its over 50 per cent ownership of Volkswagen. The total consideration was approximately €8.4 billion.[36] To help finance the deals, in 2010 VW completed a capital increase of preference shares, with net proceeds amounting to €4.1 billion.[37]
- In March 2011 VW acquired the automobile trading business in Austria, Porsche Holding Salzburg, paying €3.3 billion.[38]

By 2012 Porsche AG and the large car dealer in Salzburg were thus absorbed into the VW Group. However, the question remains: who is the global ultimate owner of Volkswagen at the end of all this? We answer this when we consider the shareholder structure of the firm today and perform the 'Independence Test' in Section 4.2.

Renault—History, Privatization, and Life Thereafter

In terms of its *history*, the company was founded in 1898 by Louis Renault and his brothers, finding early success in motor racing.[39] During the First World War it produced vehicles for the military, including trucks, ambulances, and the FT-17 tank. With increasing competition from Citroën after the First World War, Renault pursued modernization initiatives, leading to the establishment in 1929 of a production line in Billancourt. Success was relatively short lived, however, starting with the Depression and then the onslaught of the Second World War. When the Germans arrived in France, Louis Renault made the fateful decision to cooperate with the Nazis. As such, when France was finally liberated Renault was arrested as a traitor, only to die a few months later.

As part of a larger policy of nationalization after the War, Renault's property and assets were taken by the state in 1945. Under the leadership of Pierre Lefaucheux, the 4CV (whose rear engine design was influenced by the Beetle) was developed after the Second World War and successfully sold to both the domestic and international markets (particularly ex-colonial ones). Over the next years development and sales of other cars—such as the Dauphine, the R4, and the R8—cemented the firm as one of the leaders in Europe. Even though the company continued to show signs of overall growth into the beginning of the 1980s, it lost heavily as the decade continued. Subsequently it was targeted to receive state aid from the French government.

In 1993 a merger between Renault and Volvo was being planned given both firms' desires for increased efficiency and cooperation. In this deal, the French state would own 65 per cent of the new entity and Volvo, 35 per cent. Yet, as Welch and Fremond (1998, 27–8) explain, there were 'fears in Sweden that... the French state would always put French interests first... (s)ome Swedes worried that if Renault-Volvo ever had to cut costs... it would be Swedish, rather than French jobs, that would go.' As a consequence, plans for the merger were squelched. In the wake of this, some months later the state decided that the initial public offering of the French care maker took place in 1994 during the second round of French privatizations as discussed in Chapter 1, starting the heavy cash generating sale of the company.

In the first stage of its *privatization*, slightly over 28 per cent of Renault's shares were floated in March 1994; 5 per cent of the company was also sold by way of private sale to a special Partner Shareholders Group. Occurring during the start of the second round of French privatizations discussed in Chapter 1, this first stage of Renault's sale is estimated to have fetched over USD 2.4 billion.[40] Within two years, and in context of attaining EU convergence criteria, another stake of around 13 per cent of the company was sold.[41] In 2002 and 2003, when Nissan took over 15 per cent of the company (discussed in more detail later), the government reduced its participation even further by selling two minority stakes equivalent to around 20 per cent of Renault. The estimated revenue for these two operations was over USD 2.6 billion.[42] As examined in Section 4.2, when the present-day ownership of the structure of the firm is presented, the French state (not unlike Lower Saxony in the case of VW) still owns 15.01 per cent of Renault.

Renault has been involved in a number of M&A in its life after privatization, where its first major deal involved Nissan. In the first stage of Nissan, Renault bought a minority stake equivalent to 36.8 per cent of the Japanese firm in 1999 (which also included a fifth of a stake of Nissan Diesel, the Japanese group's truck arm), for an estimated value of €5.189 billion.[43] Exercising its option to increase this stake to 44.4 per cent by 2004, in the second stage Renault bought an additional 7.6 per cent of Nissan in March 2002.[44] This alliance was cemented when Nissan purchased 15 per cent of Renault in two steps: first, a minority stake of 13.5 per cent in March 2002 and, second, a further 1.5 per cent within two months, where the consideration for both deals was €2.166 billion.[45] While to this day the Renault–Nissan alliance basically maintains the same ownership structure,[46] Renault did later sell its remaining shares of Nissan Diesel in the open market in March 2005 and, based on the closing price of the last day of trading, the value it fetched can be estimated at €2.262 billion.[47]

Another major acquisition in Asia, roughly during the same time as Nissan, was Renault's majority stake in the Korean company Samsung Motors. Under the terms of the deal, in September 2000 Renault paid approximately €618 million for around 70 per cent of the new company to be renamed the Renault–Samsung Motors, while the Samsung Group and creditors held 19.9 and 10 per cent respectively.[48] Throughout the decade, Renault continued its interest in Asia with two joint ventures. The first, in May 2004, was with Dongfeng Motor Corporation, China's third largest automaker.[49] The second, in July 2005, with Bombay-based Mahindra & Mahindra to establish a JV called 'Mahindra Renault'.[50]

While Renault consolidated its ties with Asian firms, it also flirted with Northern European ones in the early 2000s, particularly Sweden's Volvo, only to ultimately see its interest wane. One of its first transactions was to divest of Renault Vehicles Industriales (RVI), selling it to Volvo in January 2001 for a value of €1.860 billion.[51] As part of the sale, Renault attained a 15 per cent stake in Volvo, which was raised to 20 per cent in 2001.[52] Although Renault was rumoured to seek to take 100 per cent control of Volvo in 2003,[53] in 2010 it sold around 14 per cent of its Volvo stake,[54] and in 2012 the remaining 6 per cent, to institutional investors.[55] The deals raised a combined total of approximately €4.482 billion: the capital raised, particularly from the 2010 divesture which netted €3.012 billion, went towards reduction of its net automotive debt.[56]

Central and Eastern Europe also witnessed some major deals for the French automotive giant. Similar to VW's purchase of SEAT and Škoda, a major acquisition was Dacia: it was privatized by the Romanian government and acquired in two stages. The first included purchase of 51 per cent of the company in July 1999, where Renault paid approximately USD 50 million for the stake, plus USD 219.7 million over five years for future investments, restructuring, and modernization of the plants.[57] Renault's ownership in the Romanian firm increased to 92.77 per cent by May 2001 (when it acquired shares paying an estimated €181 million[58]), gradually attaining full owner-ship by 2004. The acquisition of Dacia complemented other activities in Central and Eastern Europe, such as in 2004 when Renault attained full ownership of the firm Revoz, the only car manufacturer in Slovenia and one with the highest number of workers of over two thousand.[59]

A major Russian deal in 2008 saw Renault pay over €659 million and attain a 25 per cent stake in the Samara region-based car manufacturer, Avtovaz, maker of the infamous Lada. In May 2012 it was announced that the Renault–Nissan alliance would gain a majority stake in a joint venture (with state-owned Russian Technologies) that would take 75 per cent control of Avtovaz by 2014.[60] Avtovaz was a continuation of having previously worked with the Russian government. For example, a joint venture between Renault and the Moscow City government, Avtoframos, was established in 2003. Although both parties equally owned Avtoframos on a 50:50 basis, in October 2005 Renault increased its stake to 76 per cent for a price of €33 million.[61]

If this series of acquisitions helped consolidate its presence in Eastern Europe and Asia, other deals have witnessed Renault strengthening its position in Africa and the Middle East. In 2000 Renault started its purchase of *the Société Marocaine Des Constructions Automobiles* (SOMACA), a Casablanca-based car-assembly plant of which the Moroccan state was the principal owner. Different stages of Renault's purchase included: in 2000 a minority stake of 8 per cent held by the state for an undisclosed value; in 2003 a further 26 per cent held by the state for €8.6 million; in 2005 a further 20 per cent for €4.5 million that was held by Fiat; in 2005 the remaining 12 per cent held by the Moroccan government, where the consideration was not disclosed; and, in 2006, 14 per cent of shares held by individual minority shareholders.[62] Beyond producing cars for the African market, the SOMACA plant today serves as a key producer of the Dacia Logan for the French and Spanish markets, in a similar vein that 'Mahindra Renault' manufactures and sells the same car for the Indian market.[63] In the Middle East, Renault agreed to a joint venture with the Industrial Development and Renovation Organization of Iran (IDRO), the Iranian state-owned venture capital firm, to create a company to manufacture and retail Renault cars.[64]

The most recent deal is a 2010 cross-shareholding agreement between the Renault–Nissan alliance and Daimler, known for its successful division of Mercedes-Benz cars. The rationale was to increase cooperation between the firms and embark on wide-ranging strategic cooperation. The Renault–Nissan alliance acquired a 3.1 per cent of Daimler's shares, where both Renault and Nissan each hold a 1.55 percentage stake. Based on Daimler's closing price on the last day of trading before the announcement, this total stake can be valued at €1.168 billion.[65] Under the equity exchange, Daimler acquired a stake of 3.1 per cent in Renault and in Nissan, where Renault sold newly issued shares (with an estimated value of €338 million) and Nissan sold existing ones (with an estimated value of €923 million).[66]

Jaguar—History, Privatization, and Life Thereafter

In 1922 Sir William Lyons established the 'Swallow Sidecar Company' in Blackpool. The company moved from producing sidecars to then automobiles by the late 1920s, with the first 'SS Jaguar' to appear in 1935 (Jaguar, 1984, 1). At the end of the Second World War, the company's name changed to 'Jaguar Cars Limited' in 1945, taking over its historical 1 million square foot factory in Brown's Lane, Coventry in 1951/2 (Jaguar, 1990). By the end of the decade, a record of over twenty thousand luxury motor cars had been produced for the market and, on the race track, the XK120 had won LeMans five times during the 1950s (Jaguar, 1984, 1). Seeking to increase strength, Jaguar and the British Motor Corporation Limited merged in 1966, and this new entity

(British Motor Holdings Limited) merged in 1968 with the Leyland Motor Corporation Limited, to form British Leyland Motor Corporation Limited (Jaguar, 1984, 1). This same year, the XJ6 was launched and over the next five years the larger engine model XJ12 and XJ-S sports car appeared. Amidst the economic crisis of the 1970s, BMLC was crippled by the wide array of cars it produced, many of which were in direct competition with each other, including Jaguar, Rover, Triumph, Austin, Morris, and MG. With the government-commissioned 'Ryder Report', the Wilson government subsequently bailed British Leyland out with £2.4 billion of state aid, and took control of BL as the major shareholder in 1975. As Vickers and Yarrow (1988, 163) explain, the immediate years after state injections in BL were followed by 'heavy losses, labour union problems, and declining market shares, despite successive attempts to rationalize the company's operations'. Therefore, by the late 1970s manufacturing problems plagued Jaguar, resulting in low production levels.

But starting in 1980 Jaguar's was the story of a come-back kid: under the leadership of Sir John Egan, and with the development of the Jaguar XJS which proved to be very successful in the European and US markets, by the early 1980s the company had started to turn itself around and demanded its independence from BL (Robson, 2009, 22). This was a consequence of drastic cost-reductions pursued by Egan and his team, which resulted, on the one hand, in job losses (from 10,500 workers in 1980, to 7,400 in 1982), but, on the other, in productivity increases (14,105 cars were produced in 1980, compared to 22,046 in 1982; Jaguar, 1990, 2). A company losing over £40 million by 1980 was thus achieving profits of £55 million by 1983 (Jaguar, 1990, 3; Maloney and McLaughlin, 1999, 49). Seeking to sell off the more profitable part of the business, the Tories were determined to privatize Jaguar.

Interviews conducted during this study suggest that the subsequent 1984 privatization of Jaguar was ideologically based, seeking to create shareholders (and future voters) by selling shares at an under-priced value of 165p.[67] A trade sale of Jaguar to another firm in the sector, moreover, was not considered at the time because the Thatcher government did not want to give the perception that a foreign corporate power was taking over one of the perceived 'crown-jewels'. This is reflected in Jaguar's Offer for Sale, which clearly outlined 'limitations on shareholdings' which effectively amounted to a 'Golden Share' for the state: until the end of December 1990, no one shareholder could hold more than 15 per cent of the company's shares unless the government agreed (Jaguar, 1984, 33). Jaguar was subsequently floated on the London Stock Exchange in July 1984, where the Offer for Sale was eight times oversubscribed (Jaguar, 1984, Annual Report, page 7). The proceeds from the sale amounted to USD 397.7 million.[68]

After its privatization, Jaguar immediately witnessed increasing profits and sales for the next few years. However, as discussed in the final section of the chapter, which examines why firms become Alphas or Betas, with financial difficulties arising in the late 1980s and lack of competitiveness in the sector to 'go it alone', the company was fully taken over by Ford of Europe in December 1989 despite the 'in principle' Golden Share constraint. After the takeover, Ford invested heavily and helped create the successful Jaguar XK8 car in the 1990s and 2000s. In 2000 Ford acquired Land Rover from BMW[69] and in 2002 united it with Jaguar, forming Jaguar Land Rover (JLR). JLR was later sold to India's Tata Motors in 2008, which has become a strong player in the European market, as seen in Section 4.2.

SEAT—History, Privatization, and Life Thereafter

SEAT (*Sociedad Española Autómoviles de Turismo*) was founded in 1950 with a capital of 600 milllion Pesetas (approximately 3.6 million EUR) by the fascist dictator Francisco Franco, who started and later won the Spanish Civil War (1936–9), toppling the democratic regime of the Second Republic of 1931. Compared to other states in Western Europe, at the time Spain suffered from an agrarian-based economy, with one of the lowest number of users of motor vehicles. The majority partner in SEAT was the Ministry of Industry's holding group *Instituto Nacional de Industria* (INI, or National Industry Institute), and included several Spanish banks, such as Banco Urquijo, which had close links to Franco's dictatorship, as well as Banco Bilbao, Vizcaya, Central, and Hispano Americano. The Italian carmaker Fiat also held 7 per cent of SEAT's capital (Chari, 1998). The factory was based in Martorell (Barcelona). While the first SEAT 1400 proved too expensive for the Spanish market, the SEAT 600 introduced in the mid-1950s was a huge success: it was a small, reliable car, effectively a replica of the Fiat 500, which was within economic means of the population. Over the next decade the Opus Dei-led Stabilization Pacts of 1959 that resulted in the economic boom of the 1960s (Heywood, 1995) ensured that the SEAT 600 was in the reach of many more households. Starting in the late 1960s, the SEAT 600 was also exported to both European and international markets. With other popular models such as the SEAT 124, by the early 1970s the company thus had a dominant share of the Spanish market, competing successfully against FASA-Renault and Citroën-Hispania. With approximately twenty-four thousand workers, by the beginning of 1975 it was one of the state's principle undertakings, ranked twenty-third amongst all public firms in terms of total assets (Carreras et al., 2000, 211.)

The end of dictatorship with Franco's death in 1975, coupled with the pressures of the entrance of other foreign carmakers during the transition to democracy (1976–81), meant that SEAT's fortunes reversed. By 1976 SEAT had experienced its first losses and Fiat, not wanting to invest further in the firm amidst financial difficulties that required fresh capital investment, eventually pulled out in 1980. However, keen to establish cooperation agreements with other carmakers, in 1982 SEAT agreed to produce the VW's Polo, Passat, and Santana models with the German automaker for both the domestic and European markets. By 1984 VW had expressed interests to members of the INI to purchase SEAT for two main reasons. First, labour costs were relatively lower in Spain than much of the EU, with the added advantage that it was close to the continental market. Second, SEAT showed some signs of promise. In terms of the domestic market, by the end of 1983 SEAT's production had increased by 1.6 per cent from the previous year, representing around 20 per cent of the 1.2 million vehicles made in Spain.[70] Yet, despite the introduction in 1984 of the legendary SEAT Ibiza, whose gearbox is designed by Porsche, difficult financial times continued. By 1985 Felipe González's Socialists—cognizant of SEAT's financial difficulties and VW's desires to acquire SEAT—sought to get rid of it, along with several INI companies.

There were subsequently two stages to the privatization that will be discussed in more detail in the last part of the chapter, which explains why firms become Alphas or Betas. In the first, prior to the sale, the state reimbursed loans granted over the previous years by Spanish banks to SEAT. The second stage was the negotiation of the direct sale of SEAT to VW: the Germans gained majority (51 per cent) control of SEAT in June 1986, which rose to 76.1 per cent by December 1986. VW gained full control within four years and, as explained in Section 4.3, the German automaker eventually received several million pesetas from the Spanish state when taking over SEAT.

After Audi, SEAT represented the second major acquisition of VW. To this day it represents an integral part of the VW group, continuing to produce the best-selling Ibiza as well as the Leon and Toledo. In 2012 the SEAT brand 'sold 429 thousand vehicles, 18.8 per cent more than the previous year' (VW, Annual Report, 2012, 133), not only in European markets, but also those in Latin America, Asia (including China), Africa, and the Middle East.[71]

Alfa Romeo—History, Privatization, and Life Thereafter

Alfa Romeo was originally founded in 1910 as *Anonima Lombarda Fabbrica Automobili* (A.L.F.A, or Lombard Automobile Factory), whose production consisted of racing sports cars during its first years. After being acquired by Nicola Romeo, it turned to producing war supplies during the First World War, before turning back to racing during the 1920s with the collaboration of Enzo Ferrari and the successful Alfa P2. While there was some success in the racing circuit, it had lesser fortunes in terms of commercial success, which resulted in Mussolini's state needing to step in to keep the company alive. Therefore, in

1933 the company became part of the state holding corporation IRI (*Istituto per la Ricostruzione Industriale*—Institute for Industrial Reconstruction) and, in 1948, formed part of the sub-holding within IRI, Finmeccanica (Felice, 2010, 612). The 1950s witnessed attempts to mass-produce, first with the 1900 and then the beautiful Giulietta. The heir to the latter, the Giulia, saw its large-scale production begin in the 1960s, ultimately selling over 1 million during its time.[72] By the late 1960s, and seeking an opportunity to increase employment in the South of Italy, it was decided that a new car should be produced to cater to an end of the market heretofore untapped. Consequently, AlfaSud was set up in 1968, with factories in Naples rather than Milan (where all previous Alfas were made).

But three problems ensued over the next two decades. First, 'AlfaSud had its own troubles, mostly because of Southern Italy's problematic sociopolitical environment' (Felice, 2010, 64), and its full success did not materialize. Second, was the oil crisis of the 1970s: in 1973 alone, the firm lost 555 billion lira (Santagostino, 1993, 17). As explained in more detail in the last section of the chapter, Alfa never fully recovered from the crisis—it continued to receive billions of lire of state aid on a yearly basis from 1979–86. Third, the early

Table 4.1. VW, Renault, Jaguar, SEAT, and Alfa Romeo Deals

Privatized Company	Date(s) of Sale	Main Mergers & Acquisitions
VW	1961 (60%); 1988 (20%); 20% still owned by Lower Saxony	VW Group acquired Audi (1965, 1966); SEAT (which was privatized by Spanish government (1986, 1990)); Škoda (which was privatized by Czech government (1991, 2000)); Bugatti (1998); Lamborghini (1998); Bentley Motors (1998–2003); Scania (2000–8); 20% of Suzuki (December 2009), but later sold in 2011; MAN SE (2006–11); and Porsche AG (2009–12); Ducati (through Audi, 2012).
Renault	1994, 1996, 2002, 2003. 15% still owned by French state	Alliance is formed where Renault acquires 44% of Nissan and Nissan 15% of Renault (1999, 2001); Dacia (on its privatization by the Romanian government, 1999); 70% stake in Samsung Motors (2000); SOMACA (Morocco, 2000–6); Revoz (Slovenia, 2004); 25% stake in Avtovaz (Russia, 2008; with controlling stake in sight). Share-swap between Renault–Nissan and Daimler, 3.1% each (April 2010).
Jaguar	1984	Jaguar floated in 1984 and then acquired by Ford (1989); Ford later sold it to Tata Motors (India, 2008).
SEAT	1986, 1990	Bought by VW when privatized by the Spanish government (51%, 1986; 49%, 1990). See VW Group for other activity.
Alfa Romeo	1987	Alfa Romeo sold to Fiat (1987). Fiat Group today includes: Ferrari (since 1969), Lancia (1969), New Holland (1991), Maserati (1993), Iveco (1993), and Chrysler (full acquisition in 2014).

1980s joint venture with Nissan (intended to create new products, gain new customers, and learn from each other) proved a failure, with the development of an unsuccessful light car (Arna) produced in Naples which sold poorly (Santagostino, 1993, 24).

In 1985 and early 1986 Alfa's privatization was imminent: both the IRI (led by Romano Prodi, Head of IRI and member of the DC) and Finmeccanica (led by Fabiano Fabiani) concluded that Alfa Romeo could not last for long as an independent company. As examined in more detail later when I explain why firms become Alphas and Betas, Alfa Romeo was eventually sold to Fiat. The activities of Alfa would be merged with Lancia, which Fiat had acquired in 1969, resulting in the Alfa–Lancia group which came into operation in January 1987. After Ferrari and Lancia, Alfa represented the third major acquisition by Fiat, which later purchased companies including New Holland (1991), Maserati (1993), Iveco (1993), and a stake in Chrysler (2009).

To conclude the section, taking all five firms together Table 4.1 summarizes the main findings, highlighting the details on their privatization and, in the cases of VW and Renault, main M&A.

4.2 Determining Alphas and Betas

The main goal of this section is to determine which of the privatized firms can be considered Alphas and Betas today. In a comparative discussion I first turn to the 'Global Movers Test', demonstrating the results of its two dimensions. In the first, which seeks to understand the position of the firms amongst leading ones from around globe, I consider whether or not the firm appears in the latest Forbes 2000 index, which measures the performance of companies based on four metrics—sales, profits, assets, and market value. In the second, I examine how the firms compare, more specifically, to their European peers in terms of different metrics found on the Bureau van Dijk's Amadeus database, including operating revenues, assets, shareholders funds and number of employees. Thereafter, I examine the shareholder structure of the firms and seek to better understand their shareholder structure by performing the Independence Test. The end objective of this is to ascertain whether or not the firms are independent, or are ultimately owned by another firm.

The Global Movers Test

Examining the world's leading auto and truck manufacturers on the Forbes 2000 list from 2014 shows that Volkswagen and Renault are on the list.

As seen in column 3 of Table 4.2, when compared to all the other leading 2,000 firms in the world, Volkswagen ranks close to the highest and within the

Table 4.2. Privatized Automobile Firms Studied on Forbes 2000 List, 2014

Company	Country	Ranking of the Company in the Forbes 2000 list	Sectoral Ranking (out of 26 companies in Forbes 2000 from the Automobile Sector)
Volkswagen	Germany	19/2000	2/26
Renault	France	262/2000	12/26
Jaguar	UK	Not Ranked	Not Ranked
Alfa Romeo	Italy	Not Ranked	Not Ranked
SEAT	Spain	Not Ranked	Not Ranked

Sources for classification: Forbes 2000 Index, May 2014 <http://www.forbes.com/global2000/list/> [accessed 6 June 2014]

top 1 per cent of all on the list in 2014. It even surpasses leading global companies such as Gazprom, Samsung Electronics, AT&T, Microsoft, and Pfizer. Renault, while not as strongly positioned when compared to Volkswagen, nevertheless is found within the top 15 per cent of the world's leading 2,000 firms. When examining how both are placed within their sector in 2014, Volkswagen is second in the world only behind the Japanese giant Toyota, which VW was actually ranked above in 2013. In 2014 Volkswagen was ahead of European leaders such as Daimler and BMW, the US's Ford and GM, Japan's Honda and Nissan, and South Korea's Hyundai and KIA Motors. Renault places a respectable twelve out of all twenty-six firms from the sector, ranked higher than those such as Japan's Suzuki and France's Peugeot–Citroën. Given that Jaguar, SEAT, and Alfa Romeo are not on the Forbes list, they can be considered Betas at this stage.

The second dimension of the Global Movers Test seeks to better understand how the privatized firms compare to their European peers. As discussed in the previous chapter, to be deemed an Alpha a firm must appear today within the top 1 per cent of all firms in their sector in the EU-27 in terms of a variety of metrics, including operating revenue, assets, shareholder funds, and number of employees. In order to calculate what constitutes the top 1 per cent, a search was done on the Amadeus database of all active companies in the EU-27, with a primary NACE Rev. 2 code of 291 (manufacture of motor vehicles) and which all had accounts available in the latest year, which in this case was 2012. The number of companies that were yielded in the Amadeus search was 1,311.[73] This means that, in order for the company to be within the top 1 per cent of all firms according to the various metrics, they had to fall within the top thirteen. In order to see how each of the companies ranked comparatively to their peers—and whether or not they fell within the cut-off point of 'top thirteen'—Amadeus allows the user to comparatively analyse, and then rank, these five metrics of the top 100 (of the 1311) companies in the sector.

Table 4.3. The Automobile Sector: The European Giants, 2012

Company name	Operating revenue (turnover) mil EUR		Total assets mil EUR		Shareholders funds mil EUR		Number of employees	
2012		Rank (amongst top 100)		Rank		Rank		Rank
VOLKSWAGEN GROUP	203,172	1	309,644	1	81,825	1	469,497	1
DAIMLER	115,804	2	162,978	2	45,510	2	274,605	2
BMW	77,677	3	131,850	3	30,402	3	102,232	5
PEUGEOT	55,463	4	64,849	5	9,822	6	204,287	3
RENAULT	42,194	5	75,414	4	24,292	5	127,086	4
JAGUAR LAND ROVER	18,640	6	15,160	7	4,179	7	17,832	9
FIAT GROUP	16,470	7	11,772	10	922	21	22,792	7
ADAM OPEL	15,768	8	10,147	11	−3,404	96	18,850	8
VOLVO	12,496	9	6,268	12	1,487	12	15,085	10
FORD MOTOR EUROPE	10,519	10	3,354	15	−1,310	95	10,719	13

Source: Amadeus

The findings are summarized in Table 4.3. Column 2 of Table 4.3 shows the top ten firms with the highest operating revenues, plus how this figure ranks compared to the top 100 firms in the database with the highest revenues. Moving down the column, one sees that Volkswagen had the highest value of all firms in the sector, Daimler the second, BMW the third, and so on. Analysing the various rankings obtained by the two firms across all metrics, the table demonstrates that both VW and Renault have passed the second part of the Global Movers Test: they attain values within the top 1 per cent of European firms in the sector. Given its strength in the Forbes test, it seems little surprise that Volkswagen attained the highest rankings of all firms across all metrics. Renault also consistently performed well on all metrics, even better than its French counterpart Peugeot. Interestingly, some of the firms in the Table which attained high operating revenues did not necessarily perform well in other areas, as seen in the case of the firms at the bottom of Table 4.3. Although neither SEAT nor Alfa Romeo is found in the Table, the Jaguar Land Rover Group fares respectively within the top ten, even though it does not make it onto the Forbes 2000 list.

The Independence Test

I now turn to the shareholder structure of the five companies and perform the Independence Test as outlined earlier.[74] As a brief reminder, for a firm to be considered an Alpha it must have demonstrated that, either during or after its privatization, it has not been acquired by another firm and maintains its independence. To this end, I rely on two sources. The first includes the latest available annual company reports which outline the shareholder structure of the firm in question. The second, which also compiles and analyses such reports, is the information available in the Amadeus and Zephyr databases, which show the Bureau van Dijk 'Independence Indicator' assigned to each of the firms (as discussed in the methods section in Chapter 2). For a firm to be considered an Alpha it must have obtained a BvD independence indicator of 'A⁺', which is given to any company with known recorded shareholders, none of whom has more than 25 per cent of direct or total ownership. An 'A' indicator contrasts to 'B', 'C', and 'D' indicators, which characterize different scenarios in companies where one shareholder owns more than 25 per cent of the firm, as discussed in Chapter 2. Firms which attain BvD indicators of A⁺ are considered Alphas, whereas those with 'B', 'C', or 'D' will generally be considered Betas *unless* they fall into one of the two reasonable exceptions outlined in Chapter 2. The first is applicable to cases where the state has not fully privatized the company and may hold 25 per cent or more of the shares. The second is applicable to cases where a family with historical ties to the firm maintains more than 25 per cent ownership today. As discussed in Chapter 2, a scenario of owning large stakes in automobile firms is somewhat common-place within the sector, as seen with the Peugeot, Agnelli (Fiat), and Quandt (BMW) families.

When turning to Renault, Figure 4.2 outlines the company's latest share-holder structure, consistent with information related to Nissan and Daimler discussed earlier.

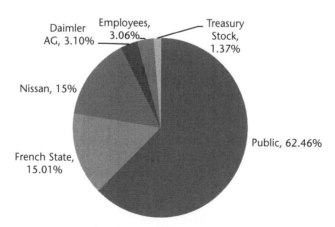

Figure 4.2. Renault Shareholder Structure, 31 December 2011

Source: <http://www.renault.com/en/finance/action/pages/repartition-du-capital.aspx [last accessed 27 August 2013]. Note, as outlined by Renault, Nissan Finance Company (15%) cannot exercise the voting rights attached to these shares; nor do the Treasury stock shares carry voting rights.

Given its structure, Renault attains an 'A$^+$' BvD Independence ranking. Yet even though no one shareholder owns more than 25 per cent of the company, the French state still continues to own around 15 per cent of the firm.

In terms of its shareholder structure, even though VW reports the structure as a percentage of subscribed capital,[75] it also reports it in terms of the distribution of voting rights. This latter data is thus presented in Table 4.4, consistent with the information also reported by BvD's Amadeus.

Table 4.4 demonstrates that Porsche SE, with a stake of ordinary shares of over 50.7 per cent, is effectively the largest shareholder of the Volkswagen Group.[76] As of June 2013, Porsche SE is owned 100 per cent by the Porsche–Piëch families.[77] Because Amadeus calculates a firm's independence based on data found regarding shareholder voting rights, as seen in Table 4.5 it assigns an independence indicator of 'D' to the VW Group given that the global

Table 4.4. Current Voting Rights Distribution in the VW Group, 31 December 2012

Shareholder	Voting Rights
Porsche Automobile Holding SE, Stuttgart	50.73%
State of Lower Saxony, Hanover	20.00%
Qatar Holding	17.00%
Porsche GmbH, Salzburg	2.37%
Others shareholders which own ordinary shares	9.90%

Source: <http://www.volkswagenag.com/content/vwcorp/content/en/investor_relations/share/Shareholder_Structure. html> [last accessed 27 August 2013]; data also reported in VW Group Annual Report, 2012, page 169

Table 4.5. Summary of the Independence Test Findings for Automobile Firms

Privatized Company	BvD Independence Ranking	Exception 1: Does the state still own more than 25% of the firm?	Exception 2: Does a family with historical relations own more than 25%?	Has the firm been taken over by another firm during/after privatization? If so, which firm is the Global Ultimate Owner?	Given exceptions (if applicable), did the firm pass the Independence Test?
VW	D	No, but Lower Saxony owns 20%	Yes, the Porsche–Piëch families	No	Yes
Renault	A$^+$	No, but French state still owns 15%	No	No	Yes
Jaguar	D	No	No	Yes, after its flotation was first taken over by Ford, then TATA	No
SEAT	D	No	No	Yes, sold to Volkswagen when privatized	No
Alfa Romeo	D	No	No	Yes, sold to FIAT when privatized	No

ultimate owners of Porsche SE are the Porsche and Piëch families.[78] Interestingly, despite having little love lost between them, as principal players in the largest automotive group in the world the Porsche–Piëch dynasty seems to eclipse even that of the Quandts, Agnellis, and Peugeots.

It was earlier argued that 'Exception 2' can be considered when performing the Independence Test—having a family with historical links to the firm with more than 25 per cent control, as seen in many automobile firms in Europe—so the BvD Independence Indicator will not be relied on in the VW case. Moreover, adding more dimensions of complexity to VW, Lower Saxony controls 20 per cent of the company in terms of voting rights. And, as will be discussed later, a consequence of the so-called Volkswagen-Law, this 20 per cent stake allows the state to effectively have the right to veto decisions taken in the firm. This represents a special case where the state, not even owning a majority of the firm, is still in a position to exercise a blocking minority on decisions, as discussed later in the chapter when I consider the importance of the role of the state in explaining life after privatization.

When turning to the three remaining privatized automobile companies studied, each was taken over either during or slightly after privatization. As mentioned earlier, at the point of privatization SEAT was acquired by VW, Alfa Romeo by Fiat. Five years after its flotation, Jaguar was taken over by Ford, later to be sold along with Jaguar Land Rover to TATA. Consistent with this, analysis of the BvD indicators assigned to the firms indicates that they have a 'D' Independence Indicator: since the 1980s they have been ultimately owned by another firm. Table 4.5 summarizes this test's findings.

Given the results of both parts of the Global Movers Test, Table 4.6 summarizes the main findings of this section concerned with determining which firms are Alphas and Betas. It highlights that while VW and Renault can be considered Alphas, Jaguar, SEAT, and Alfa Romeo are all Betas.

Table 4.6. Summary of Empirical Tests to Determine Automobile Alphas and Betas

Firm	Global Movers Test, 1st Dimension: Is the firm on Forbes List?	Global Movers Test, 2nd Dimension: Is the firm ranked as a leading European firm amongst its peers?	Given exceptions, did the firm pass the Independence Test?	Alpha or Beta?
VW	Yes	Yes	Yes	Alpha
Renault	Yes	Yes	Yes	Alpha
Jaguar	No	Not individually, but JLR appears	No	Beta
SEAT	No	No	No	Beta
Alfa Romeo	No	No	No	Beta

4.3 Explaining Why Firms Become Alphas and Betas

This section offers a comparative analysis of all firms studied, discussing which factors are of importance in explaining why the firm is an Alpha or Beta. This is the only chapter where we will rely on both of the main theoretical conceptualizations (outlined in Chapter 2) to explain why firms become Alphas and Betas.

We turn first to the discussion of VW, Renault, and Jaguar. The theoretical conceptualization is presented in Figure 4.3, a slightly modified version of Figure 2.2 in Chapter 2. This serves as a framework for discussion of all three firms. It outlines initial conditions (X1), intervening variables (X2), and the outcome Variable (Y), where VW and Renault are Alphas and Jaguar is a Beta (as discussed in Section 4.2). The analysis starts with comparative examination of the two Alphas, VW and Renault. Relying on the same model, attention is then paid to Jaguar, which had theoretical potential to become an Alpha, but eventually became a Beta five years after privatization when it was taken over by Ford. The reason that the same model is used is because VW, Renault, and Jaguar were not taken over at the point of privatization, as seen in the case of SEAT and Alfa Romeo, which will be turned to later in the chapter when we present the other theoretical conceptualization.

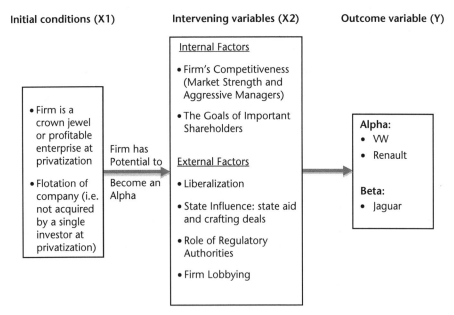

Figure 4.3. The Second Model: How an Automobile Firm May Become an Alpha or a Beta (Y) Based on Initial Conditions at Privatization (X1) and Intervening Variables Post-Privatization (X2)

The Firms that are Alphas after Privatization: VW and Renault

Why are Volkswagen and Renault Alphas? In terms of initial conditions (X1), both were profitable crown jewels that were successfully floated. As such, it is necessary to examine the intervening variables in order to explain why the firms became Alphas in their life after privatization. I first consider developments internal to the firm, including market strength, the goals of managers, and (non-state) shareholders. Thereafter, attention is paid to those more political, external factors.

VW AND RENAULT: INTERNAL FACTORS

Turning first to the internal factors that help explain why both VW and Renault are Alphas, both have represented leaders in the sector, competitive compared to their peers before and after their privatization. This was indicated when the Global Movers Tests were performed earlier. Further, analysis of the BvD Amadeus data throughout the 2000s demonstrates that in 2012 Volkswagen had the highest net income amongst all of its peers in Table 4.4, having attained EUR21.885 billion, while Renault was ranked fifth with EUR1.772 billion.[79]

In terms of market shares, both have continued to be dominant at home and in European markets since their privatization. Considering data in the late 1990s, Maloney and McLaughlin (1999, 191) highlight that the main European automakers were:

> Fiat, Ford, General Motors, Peugeot, Renault and Volkswagen, (which) produce 10 million cars per year (78% of West European production). The market share is (almost) evenly distributed between these six manufacturers, ranging from 10.3% to 12.0%, with the exception of VW who have a 'clear' market lead with 16.7% mainly as a result of the purchase of SEAT and Škoda.

Data for these same six firms in 2013 shows that two Alphas have increased their market shares in the EU-27 (as well as Iceland, Norway, and Switzerland), where Volkswagen now enjoys 23 per cent and Renault 12.9 per cent.[80] Other firms have seen a decline, such as Fiat (6.3 per cent), Ford (7.7 per cent), and GM (7.4 per cent).

When turning to the role of management, having leaders such as Ferdinand Piëch, a trained engineer, has resulted in Volkswagen particularly championing technological advancements, which has allowed it to consolidate its position as a leader in the sector. Seeking to maintain a technological leading edge in the firm, Renault–Nissan's CEO, Carlos Ghosn, is currently earmarking €4 billion for the further development and production of electric cars.[81]

Without doubt, as seen in the M&A pursued, directors and managers have aggressively championed acquisitions of firms both at home and abroad in order to extend their global production. Production costs in such countries where acquisitions were made and JVs pursued—such as Spain, the Czech Republic, Romania, Morocco, China, and India—could also be reduced given relatively low wages compared to home. As an illustration of VW's expansion into cheaper labour markets, one may consider labour costs per hour in Spain compared to the rest of the EU shortly after Carl Hahn spearheaded VW's purchase of SEAT. Abraham's (2001, 20) work, for example, shows that Spain's labour costs per hour in 1996 were some of the lowest in the EU-15: they were less than half that of Germany and above only Portugal and Greece.

Beyond those at the helm, the goals of shareholders (not including the state, discussed in more detail later) are also important in explaining both firms' desires to see their companies grow through acquisitions. On VW's takeover of MAN, for example, VW's chief executive Martin Winterkorn underlined in 2011 that having both Scania and MAN as part of VW laid 'the foundations for generating synergies for the benefit of all shareholders'.[82] After that announcement, the stock price of Volkswagen went up.[83]

Chapter 2 also specifically considered the importance of certain asset managers that may hold interests in the firm, seeking investment in safe places in order to gain the best returns. If we consider the top ten asset managers (Chapter 2), Figure 4.4 illustrates their ownership in Renault between 2007 and 2011.[84]

Figure 4.4 demonstrates that asset managers such as AXA as well as Capital Group have owned a significant amount of shares in Renault, with notable fluctuations from highs of well over 8 per cent to lows of over 1 per cent. Others, such as BlackRock and the Vanguard Group, held more than .5 per cent of Renault in 2011. One sees that although fewer of the top asset management firms invested in Volkswagen when compared to Renault, 2007–10 figures indicate that BlackRock, State Street, and AXA have all been shareholders, from a high of over .7 per cent in BlackRock (over three years between 2007 and 2009) to a low of .1 per cent held by the Vanguard Group (in 2010). There may be many factors which explain why the percentage of ownership of asset managers ebbs and flows over time, but, as argued in Chapter 3, a main objective of these firms is to invest in stable companies and potentially sell over time as the stock price increases.

While the goals of managers and shareholders in leading the firms are important, it is necessary to turn to the next set of intervening variables that focus on developments outside the firm.

VW AND RENAULT: EXTERNAL FACTORS

In order to better understand the more political factors of salience, attention is now paid to the role of liberalization, the influence of the state (in terms of providing state aid even after privatization, acting as a strategic shareholder

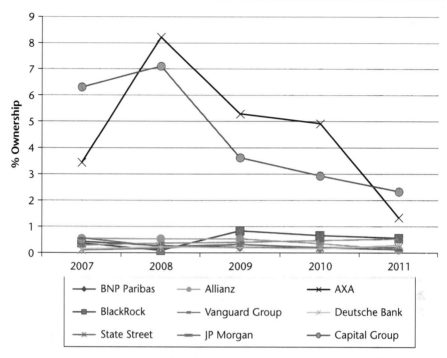

Figure 4.4. Global Asset Managers Holding Shares in Renault, 2007–11
Source: Analysis of data on the Amadeus database, performed September 2012

in both firms, and helping in some foreign acquisitions), regulators (in approving major deals discussed earlier in the chapter), and lobbying resources of the firms (employed especially when regulatory decisions are taken).

Liberalization

At first glance one may downplay the importance of liberalization in the sector given its 'globalized' image today, especially when compared to specific liberalization initiatives in the airline or electricity sectors. But, the different conjunctures of European single market evolution help explain, first, consolidation at home, followed by expansion into Europe and Asia after the Single European Act (SEA, signed in 1986). I consider both the pre- and post-SEA dynamics in turn, paying reference to some of the deals discussed in Section 4.1.

Before the SEA, one can see a broad consolidation of automobile makers at the domestic level in various EU states in the late 1960s and 1970s, no different to the airlines as seen in the previous chapter and electricity companies examined in the next. This includes VW acquiring Audi in Germany; Fiat acquiring Lancia and Ferrari in Italy; the formation of British Leyland; and

Peugeot's acquisition of Citroën, forming PSA in France. Particularly in the context of the economic crisis in the 1970s, member states were protective of their industries and gave state aid if necessary to help guarantee employment that translated into votes, all with the view to strengthen their national champions (Hanson, 1998, 74). In light of this, one can better understand VW's purchase of Audi: as much as the internal files on *Projekt XY* (as discussed in Section 4.1) discuss how the Germans also considered the acquisition of Peugeot and Lancia at the same time they were eyeing Audi, this may have really been no more than wishful thinking. Because both the French and Italian states were the sectors' two most protective member states, they would have almost certainly enacted barriers to any such deals.

Yet, the environment changed with the SEA. The Act meant that state intervention in terms of preventing the free movement of goods and capital within the EU could no longer take place, unless the states sought legal battles in Luxembourg. In terms of trade, previous national measures that 'allowed for protectionist member states to block the importation of cars from both member and non-member states' could no longer hold (Hanson, 1998, 78). Further, unlike the airline sector, there were no ownership rules in the sector for which further legislation was required, allowing capital to freely move and fully acquire other firms within other parts of the Union post-SEA. As Hanson (1998, 78) additionally explains, the internal market meant that 'explicit border measures were outlawed and technical requirements were harmonized, so that auto producers only needed to meet one set of standards to sell their vehicles in the EU'.

Accordingly, in the same year that the SEA was signed VW immediately made the first of the Alphas' main acquisitions, SEAT, in one of the newest EU states keen to prove its credentials, Spain (discussed in more detail later). Establishing the counterfactual, we can establish the significance of the creation of the single market by demonstrating that, before it, neither of the Alphas made acquisitions of (or share-swaps with) other firms in the Union that were outside their own country (see Table 4.1). But, after it, a whole host of deals took place, especially seen in the case of VW which later acquired Bugatti, Lamborghini, Bentley, Scania/MAN, Porsche, and Ducati.

The case of Renault highlights that its first big move, the alliance with Nissan, can also be understood in the wake of EU trade liberalization initiatives in the sector, a direct consequence of the SEA. With increasing imports from Japan in the 1970s and 1980s, protectionist member states (such as France and Italy) sought to limit the number of imports through bilateral trade agreements (Mason, 1994, 436), ostensibly to protect their own industries. But, in anticipation of the SEA, in the 1980s Japanese firms set up shop in the EU—particularly the UK, where Nissan assembled its Bluebirds—with the view that it would be impossible to stop the movement of Japanese production once inside fortress Europe (Hanson, 1998, 78–9). That is, once a good was produced in the single market, Japanese firms, as any another operating in the free trade zone, could sell their products within it. Many member states were:

> alarmed by the possibility of Japanese transplant production being imported into their markets without restraint.... (Therefore) reestablishing protection from Japanese auto imports could not be accomplished through national policy, but required the EU-wide negotiation with Japan (Hanson, 1998, 79).

As a consequence of the SEA, previous bilateral agreements spearheaded by member states and Japan were thus replaced with a 1991 EU-wide agreement with Japan that started to liberalize Japan's car imports into the EU (Hanson, 1998, 76).

In light of these developments, the Renault–Nissan alliance in 1999 can be better understood: in the early 1980s, in their drive to 'transplant production', Japanese firms' market share was significant in many member states (with 24.7 per cent in Belgium; 26.4 per cent in the Netherlands; 30.9 per cent in Denmark; 30.8 per cent in Ireland; 42.9 per cent in Greece; 11.9 per cent in the UK; and 10.4 per cent in Germany), while French protectionist measures at the time meant that their shares were concomitantly low in France, with 1.2 per cent of the market (Mason, 1994, 436). Even though bilateral agreements in the 1980s would 'brake or restrain' Japanese growth in the EU during the rest of the 1980s (Mason, 1994, 437), the EU trade liberalization agreement in 1991 meant that Japanese firms' overall shares in the EU would increase over the decade. As Hanson (1998, 75) argues, 'after this (EU) agreement took effect market shares of Japanese cars shot up in previously restricted member states', such as Italy and Spain. The net effect was that this would augment Nissan's shares in the rest of the EU, and give Renault a Japanese partner with a solid European base whose trade and profits the French could tap into. Further, forming an alliance with an Asian partner meant that the French firm would have greater access to a market not heretofore tapped, namely the Asian one. A similar logic helps explain VW's partial acquisition of Suzuki in the 2000s.

But, as much as liberalization's impact set the tone for what Alphas could do, and the timing of when they could do it, it does not explain why firms made acquisitions in states such as Morocco and Romania. Nor, does it fully explain the nature of the deals and how the state—which has had historical vested interest in the Alpha—may have shaped them. To this end, we consider the role of the state.

The role of the state
There are three dimensions to the state's role in fostering Alphas' development and expansion: state subsidies, the state acting as a strategic shareholder, and its role in crafting deals. The three are considered in turn.

First, public subsidies have been earmarked towards both firms, before and after their privatization. Along with others such as Alfa Romeo (discussed later), both Renault and VW received large amounts of aid similar to many European manufacturers which faced difficult times in the 1970s and 1980s. Stephen's data (2000, 66) demonstrates that between 1977 and 1987 Renault (receiving well over ECU 4,400 million) received even more aid than Alfa Romeo (at around ECU 3500 million), and VW (at over ECU 1,500 million) more than Peugeot (slightly more than ECU 1,100 million).

Is there any evidence that after their privatization the Alphas continue to receive state aid? Setting up this part of the investigation, it is important to consider ideas raised in Schütte's work (2013), which highlights that throughout the 2000s firms in the automotive sector have been beneficiaries of regional and training aid. Regional aid is earmarked towards large, long-term investment projects related to the development of factories. As Schütte (2013, 8) argues, 'each factory will be used for several product cycles, each cycle being around seven years or more (for each car model) and more for key components'. Training aid is given by states, particularly in less developed areas of the Union, in order to foster training in computer skills and languages which are required for the development of new technologies applied in production.

Examining evidence provided by the Commission, one can see that throughout the 1990s and 2000s both Volkswagen and Renault received significant amounts of regional and training aid. Such aid is given by their own governments as well as those where firms have expanded. For example, in 2002 the Commission authorized an aid of €22 million that was given by Spain towards the production of diesel and gasoline engines to invest in Renault's Valladolid plant.[85] More extraordinary, Table 4.7 outlines the multiple amounts of aid given by Germany and other member states to Volkswagen after its privatization, including even further aid to SEAT.

Table 4.7 highlights that, except for a small number of cases, all aid was approved by the Commission without reductions in the original amount of aid requested.

One reason for this is that competitors rarely object to automakers receiving aid, as they themselves make similar requests (Schütte, 2013, 7). Evidence of this is seen in firms such as Fiat, which received millions from the Italian government related to large investments throughout the 1990s and 2000s.[86] If Fiat, for example, were to object to an aid given by the German government (or any other government, for that matter) to VW, it runs the risk that VW could in the future object to aid that Fiat might receive. It thus makes rational sense for firms in the same sector not to object to their competitors receiving aid.

The underlying justification why states are keen to incentivize automotive investments is to help create jobs in one of Europe's largest industries

Table 4.7. Major State Aid Received by Volkswagen, 1993–2009

Year	Amount	Concept
1993	5.539 billion pesetas (35.9 MECU)	Regional and training aid to SEAT, supporting investment plan in Arazuri (Pamplona) given by government of Navarra
1995	46 billion pesetas (283 MECU)	Aid towards restructuring of SEAT plant, given by Spanish central and regional authorities (condition stated that no further aid to SEAT can be given)
1996	DM 539.1 million	Regional aid given by German government for investment project in Mosel and Chemnitz, Germany; (aid originally offered by German government DM779.8; remainder deemed incompatible and not approved by Commission)
2001	DM 145 million	Regional aid from German government for new factory in Dresden (aid of extra DM 25.7 million deemed incompatible)
2003	€15 million	Regional aid from Spanish government for Volkswagen Navarra for its Arazuri plant (Pamplona)
2003	€84 million	Regional aid by Germany towards construction of a new company (VW Mechatronic, a JV of Siemens Automotive and VW) in Stollberg (Germany)
2009	€14.3 million	Regional aid given by Slovak authorities for transformation of existing plant, in Bratislava

Source: European Commission (1993, 1995, 1996, 2001b, 2003a, 2003b, and 2009b)

(Hanson, 1998, 74). From this perspective, deals done between business and the state in the automotive sector is something that the Commission simply passively reacts to rather than leads, offering evidence to support Stephen's (2000) and Maloney and McLaughlin's (1999) argument that tight industry and government relations ensure that large amounts of aid allow European manufacturers to consolidate their position in home markets, while expanding in the EU, thereby making European firms competitive in world markets.

Beyond giving aid, a second dimension of state influence is based in the ownership structure, and the states' sizeable ownership previously seen in Section 4.2: even after privatization, Lower Saxony owns 20 per cent of VW, while the French state's stake in Renault is around 16 per cent. The rationale is simple: maintain a privileged position, continue to reap financial benefits, and prevent takeover. This is amply demonstrated through the legacy of the 'Volkswagen Law', whose evolution is worth examining in detail in order to better understand how the interests of the state and the firm go hand in hand.

In terms of its history, the Volkswagen Law was enacted during the firm's partial privatization in the 1960s, capping 'the voting power of any shareholder at 20 percent' (Enriques and Volpin, 2007, 120). Even after 20 per cent of the Federal government's share in VW was sold in the 1980s, this still meant that with its over 20 per cent ownership the 'State of Lower Saxony...retain(ed) its blocking minority in order to maintain its veto power in cases of radical changes, such as shutting down or relocating assembly plants' as well as takeover (Goutas and Lane, 2009, 335). In 2005 the European Commission 'brought an action against Germany on the ground that the Volkswagen Law adversely affects the free movement of capital', something the ECJ upheld in 2007 at the time Porsche was increasing its ownership of VW.[87] As a consequence, in May 2008 the German government amended the law by taking away restrictions on ownership, but it 'left untouched the rules that give Lower Saxony a blocking minority on major VW decisions with its 20 per cent stake in the company'.[88] Even though Internal Market Commissioner Michel Barnier sought to impose a retroactive fine in 2011 for non-compliance with the ECJ decision, the golden share was defended by both Angela Merkel and Economy Minister Philipp Roesler.[89] As of the time of writing the ECJ has yet to make a final ruling on whether or not VW should be fined. But, in May 2013 an Advocate General of the ECJ, Nils Wahl, offered a preliminary opinion that 'Germany has "fully complied" with the 2007 decision of the EU Court on the free movement of capital within the EU... despite the fact that Germany has not revoked the government's veto power over board decisions'.[90]

The maintenance of Lower Saxony's veto with the amended VW-Law can, on the face of it, be explained by the state's desire to maintain a decisive position in the firm and continue to reap large treasury benefits as a shareholder in VW: by holding a 20 per cent stake in VW, 20 per cent of VW's profits go the state.[91] On deeper investigation, however, the maintenance of Lower Saxony's veto can also be explained because it was agreed to by Ferdinand Piëch when VW's takeover of Porsche was being negotiated, highlighting the continued ties between the state and firms in life after privatization.

This becomes apparent when examining developments in the spring of 2008. With Porsche's takeover of VW becoming imminent, Wolfgang Porsche was seen as holding the principal place within the Porsche–Piëch dynasty, much to the chagrin of Ferdinand Piëch. As Hawranek (2009b, 3) explains:

> [a]t that point, in the Spring of 2008, Ferdinand Piëch seemed to have lost his power. He was still the chairman of VW's supervisory board, but the more shares in VW that Porsche acquired, the stronger was the Stuttgart executives' influence on the Wolfsburg-based automaker.... The VW board would have been forced into a subordinate position if (Wolfgang) Porsche had managed to conclude a so-called control agreement with Volkswagen.... Only two conditions had to be met to conclude such an agreement. First Porsche needed 75 percent of the VW shares. Second, the so-called VW Law had to go.

In this context, Piëch sought to increase alliances with the state of Lower Saxony Prime Minister, Christian Wulff: by retaining the VW-Law, Piëch ensured that the state was on his side in his attempt to become the main leader of the Porsche–Piëch clan. Once assurances had been granted by Wulff to maintain the spirit of the VW-Law, all it needed was the support of Chancellor Merkel who readily consented, as discussed by Hawranek (2009b, 4):

On April 15, 2008, Wulff met with Chancellor Angela Merkel at Sale e Pepe, a small Italian restaurant in Berlin's Charlottenburg district. Their conversation would prove to be critical to subsequent developments in the power struggle between Porsche and VW. If the European Commission had overturned the VW Law, as it intended to do, (Wolfgang) Porsche would have free reign in Wolfsburg. But, on that evening, Wulff managed to win over the Chancellor. After that, she made sure that Lower Saxony would keep its blocking minority, even with an amended VW Law (which was subsequently passed by the Cabinet on May 27, 2008 as discussed above).

Maintenance of the VW-Law thus represented a positive sum game for both the state and the firm. On the one hand, it allowed Piëch to be at the 'helm' within Porsche's empire, and, on the other, the state continued to gain substantial revenue as well as exercise considerable influence in VW, a firm then also expanding into new markets such as heavy trucks, all in the name of national interests. The latter is reflected in comments made by Wulff shortly after the 2009 Porsche deal was announced when he stated that 'the solution accommodates the interests of all concerned and safeguards the strength and performance of Germany's automotive industry'.[92]

When turning to Renault, there is no doubt of the state's significance as the largest shareholder with 15 per cent ownership, highlighting the close links between the firm and the state. Such links are seen with the former Chairman before Ghosn, Louis Schweitzer. He had ample government experience (including as Prime Minister Laurent Fabius' Chief of Staff in the 1980s), was in charge of Renault when it was privatized, and had the support of the government when he spearheaded the Nissan deal.[93] With his experience in mind, analysis of Renault's board of directors (BoDs) was made to see which members have held previous government posts or any links to the state in general, such as being ex-ministers or civil servants. A search was thus performed on Amadeus, which offers names and biographies of BoDs for most registered companies, and this information was crosschecked with company reports.[94] Findings in the case of Renault in 2011 are reported in Table 4.8.

The Table indicates that seven of the nineteen members of Renault's BoD have experience with the French state. This represents over 35 per cent of the Board (well over the 15 per cent of the state ownership in the firm), many of whom held high-ranking positions in key Ministries.[95]

Beyond having important stakes, a third dimension of state influence relates to firms expansion both within Europe and globally. As discussed previously in Mark Thatcher's work, such areas where firms expand may include those where the state has historical association. The rationale behind this is that car-making is massively employment generating, directly and indirectly (Haugh et al., 2010), perhaps even more so than other sectors studied in this book. Accordingly, there are potential votes associated with the national firm's consolidation in home markets or expansion abroad. As an example, the

Table 4.8. Renault's 2011 Board of Directors with State Experience

Name	Former State Position
Charles De Croisset	Served in several positions, including: Chief of Staff and assistant to the Minister of Industry and Energy (1978), Deputy Head of the Minister of the Economy and Finance's private office (1987–8), later becoming Chief of Staff of the State Minister of Economy, Finance, and Privatization.
Bernard Delpit	Throughout the 1990s has held several positions in the Ministry of Economy and Finance.
Thierry Desmarest	Served as Director of Mines and Geology in New Caledonia. Other positions include being a technical advisor in the Ministry of Industry and the Ministry of Economy.
Alexis Kohler	Served as Division Director at Transports and Media-French Government Shareholding Agency, Ministry for the Economy, Industry, and Employment. He also serves as a director as representative of the state for TSA, GIAT Industry, STX France Cruise, Société de Valorisation Foncière et Immobilière, and La Monnaie de Paris.
Philippe Lagayette	Throughout the 1970s and 1980s has held various high-level positions in the Ministry of Economy and Finance, and the Bank of France.
Luc Rousseau	Served as Chief Executive Officer of Enterprises at the French Ministry of Economy, Finance, and Industry, as well as member of the Atomic Energy Committee and government commissioner at the Board of Directors of the French Postal Service.
Pascale Sourisse	Throughout the early 1990s has held high-level state positions, including in the Ministry of Industry.

Source: BoD composition verified in Renault Annual Report, 2011, page 6 (available on <www.renault.com>, last accessed 2 October 2013). Biographies based on data found in Amadeus, obtained July–September 2012.

above highlighted the significant role of the state of Lower Saxony in the VW-Porsche deal, as well as VW's acquisition of MAN, ensuring consolidation of the German automotive industry. Before considering examples of the state's impact in helping foster deals globally, it is first worth over-viewing where Alphas have globally expanded.

To this end, a search was done to isolate all deals involving Renault on Zephyr (including M&A, JVs, and Share-Buybacks) between 1997 and 2012, which resulted in fifty-eight completed cases. A further breakdown was done on these fifty-eight cases to see which countries they took place in, and what percentage this represented of the total number of deals. Although a break-down could have been made regarding the deal values for each case and what percentage this represented based on aggregate deal value, there were several cases with unknown values, resulting in incomplete data. As such, Figure 4.5 subsequently highlights the geographic distribution of deals pursued by Renault based on the number of deals in various target countries.

Figure 4.5 highlights that while a majority of deals have been pursued at home, expansion has taken place throughout Europe, Asia, and (to a lesser degree) the Americas. This general observation is also seen in the case of Volkswagen, although it sees relatively more deals in China.[96] Renault has also pursued M&A in countries with which France has historical colonial association, including Mauritius and Morocco.

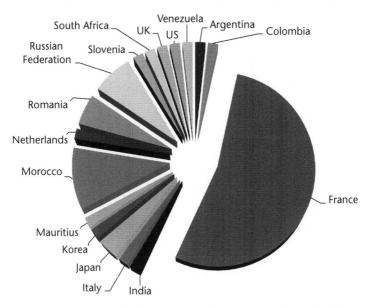

Figure 4.5. Geographic Breakdown of Renault's Deals, 1997–2012
Source: BvD, Zephyr database; analysis performed September 2012

Past state historical association was essential in providing the backdrop of some of the deals, as seen in the case of Renault's purchase of Dacia. By 1968, some two years after the Mioveni plants began construction, the French and Romania governments signed an agreement where the Dacia 1100 was built under the R8 licence, given France's desire to expand into Central and Eastern Europe.[97] By 1969 this was extended to build the Dacia 1300 under the R12 licence. In fact, the first 100 per cent Romania-designed vehicle was not produced by Dacia until 1995, four years before its privatization. Dacia having a close previous relationship thus allowed Renault a privileged position when Dacia was privatized in the late 1990s, not dissimilar to that VW had when SEAT was sold in the 1980s, as seen in more detail later.

Similarly, the state-owned Renault was present in Morocco since the 1930s where it has since been a key player[98] and the French state's ties with the firm were essential in its ex-colonial expansion on at least two related fronts. First, given its historical relations with France, the Moroccan government chose Renault's bid for SOMACA over the Malaysian company Proton which had 'no connections in Morocco's car-market', even though Proton enjoyed the 'support of Malaysian Prime Minister Mahathir Mohamad'.[99] Second, the 2003 deal to acquire 38 per cent of SOMACA was negotiated and eventually signed off by the Moroccan Minister of Industry, Trade, and Telecommunications (Rachid Talbi El Alami), the Moroccan Minister of Finance and Privatization (Fathallah Oualalou), and Renault's Senior Vice President of International

Operations, Luc-Alexandre Ménard.[100] Like many members of Renault's BoD seen previously, Ménard had previous ties with the state: he started his career in the French civil service 'working in the government accounting office, the DATAR (national and regional development department), and subsequently as Sub-prefect and Secretary General of the Aube region of France',[101] before joining Renault in the 1980s when it was fully state-owned. Interestingly the same advisers to Ménard and Renault on the SOMACA deal later advised Renault when it negotiated with the Moroccan government a €1 billion investment in Tangier.[102]

Yet, as much as the state may have played a key role in subsidizing Alphas and crafting deals, its sole explanatory power is limited because it does not necessarily account for how all deals attain regulatory approval. As such, it is necessary to consider the actions of regulators at different levels of governance in order to understand Alphas' global expansion.

Regulators

Regulatory authorities could have theoretically vetoed mergers and acquisitions. As discussed, the European Commission has rarely deemed state aid given to Alphas after their privatization as being incompatible with the Common Market, therefore allowing them to go through. Yet, dynamics surrounding M&A are somewhat more complex, potentially involving approval at different levels of governance, both inside and outside the EU.

When turning to M&A pursued by Alphas one sees two main scenarios which highlight that regulators, at different levels of governance, did not veto the deals by Volkswagen and Renault seen in Section 4.1: outright approval without conditions, or no investigation at all. I consider each in turn, demonstrating that few barriers have been constructed when acquisitions are made in order to foster consolidation of European-based global champions.

In the first scenario, the acquisitions proposed by Alphas were readily approved by regulators without any conditions being placed on them. At the supranational level, VW's takeover of Bentley, Scania, Porsche, Ducati, and MAN all were readily approved by the European Commission with no conditions.[103] When turning to Renault, both the Nissan deal, as well as Avtovaz, received the green light from DG Competition.[104]

Without doubt, gaining Brussels' regulatory approval does help consolidate Alphas' position as market leaders in Europe and globally. But, the seeming ease of Brussels' regulatory approval begs the question: are Alphas treated as 'special' by the Commission? This question stems from interview comments from competitors in the automobile sector.[105] The argument here is that VW's deals, in particular, are not vetoed because Brussels seeks to create European and global champions from Germany. As such, the criteria the Commission uses when evaluating these M&A is not the same as that used when it evaluates other deals involving firms from other parts of the EU. As an example, two firms from Sweden seeking to merge will have a tougher time gaining Commission approval than two firms from Germany seeking to do the same thing, precisely because 'German interests' are deemed more significant.

This argument is almost impossible to verify. For one, even if true, no one from the Commission would admit to it. Yet, because merger control rules are, theoretically, based on 'competition only criteria' we can compare some elements of two similar cases: Volvo/Scania (both of Sweden, whose 2000 deal was blocked by the Commission after deeper Phase 2 investigation) and VW's acquisitions of Scania in 2008 and then Germany's MAN in 2011 (both cleared after Phase 1 investigation). By so doing, we can see if different criteria were used during the Commission's investigations. Analysing these cases is significant for two reasons of relevance to both Alphas discussed in this chapter. First, one may argue that the Commission's blocking Volvo/Scania in 2000 effectively set the stage for VW's expansion into the heavy truck and bus market. After the Commission blocked Volvo/Scania on 15 March 2000, within two weeks VW bought its first stake in Scania of close to 20 per cent on 28 March 2000.[106] As discussed in the chapter's first section, this allowed VW to become a main shareholder in Scania, prevented MAN's takeover of Scania some years later, and paved the way for VW to eventually take over first Scania and then MAN. Second, the Commission's decision is significant because it also set the stage for Volvo's acquisition of Renault Trucks (RVI) from Renault (completed January 2001), even though RVI represented a company with a much smaller market share than Scania as a producer of heavy trucks. This ultimately resulted in Renault selling its stake in Volvo some years later for a significant amount, as discussed in the first section.

Volvo/Scania, if approved by the Commission in 2000, would have resulted in the European Economic Area's (EEA) largest producer of heavy trucks (i.e. trucks over 16 tonnes) and the second largest of buses.[107] According to the Commission's data, the combined overall market share between Volvo and Scania in heavy trucks would have amounted to 30.8 per cent.[108] After VW's purchase of Scania, which the Commission approved by stating that there was no overlap in terms of their core businesses,[109] the Commission similarly argued in 2011 that VW's acquisition of MAN also resulted in the largest producer of heavy trucks in the EEA and the second largest of buses. According to Commission data, again, the combined market share of VW/Scania/MAN in heavy trucks was estimated at 29.4 per cent, almost the same as Volvo/Scania which was blocked some years earlier.[110]

Even though the end market share in heavy trucks was virtually the same in the two transactions, one sees that the Commission decided to block Volvo/Scania based on selective investigation which focused primarily not on market shares throughout all of the EEA, but, rather, on Northern Europe (Denmark, Finland, Norway, and Sweden) and Ireland, where heavy truck combined market shares ranged between 59 per cent and 90 per cent.[111] Such a selective investigation did not take place during the VW/MAN deal: one may argue that when VW acquired MAN, Commission officials focused almost exclusively on the impact of the deal on competition in the EEA and did not perform a complete analysis of particular geographic markets.

To be fair, the Commission may have seen no need to pursue deeper investigation in Phase 2 investigation because VW's newly merged entity would never attain more than 50 per cent of the market share in any one EEA country, something which the Commission used to justify blocking Volvo/Scania. However, one may argue that competition in the future may be effectively impeded, given the new dominant position of VW over competitors such as Daimler, Volvo, DAF, and Iveco. This is seen in Table 4.9, which is based on the European Commission's own data on main companies that manufacture heavy trucks. As a consequence of the Commission's

Table 4.9. Market Structure in Heavy Trucks, 2010

Country	VW/Scania	MAN	VW/Scania/MAN (Combined)	Daimler	Volvo	DAF	IVECO
EEA	13.38	16.06	**29.43**	21.21	24.44	15.5	8.52
Austria	11.86	35.14	**47.00**	17.17	15.44	13.87	6.37
Belgium	13.82	18.44	**32.26**	12.19	26.73	22.46	6.20
Bulgaria	14.46	9.07	23.53	**36.19**	20.34	9.17	9.97
Czech Republic	17.40	17.91	**35.32**	17.81	16.92	20.87	5.79
Denmark	22.97	20.92	**43.89**	12.44	24.98	15.25	3.26
Estonia	24.46	17.65	**42.11**	20.43	29.72	6.19	.93
Finland	39.83	4.61	**44.44**	15.36	33.42	3.42	1.95
France	8.79	8.35	17.14	15.00	**44.52**	14.49	8.46
Germany	8.8	27.25	36.05	**37.32**	10.33	11.56	4.55
Greece	10.07	13.62	23.69	**37.02**	16.88	6.95	12.48
Hungary	17.44	11.63	**29.07**	13.39	24.67	27.70	2.25
Iceland	29.62	15.38	**42.31**	30.77	3.85	19.23	3.85
Ireland	20.73	11.74	**32.48**	16.15	25.87	19.27	2.57
Italy	11.42	7.72	19.15	10.37	20.84	12.00	**37.37**
Latvia	29.15	3.40	**32.55**	15.74	27.23	20.21	3.40
Luxembourg	11.13	11.55	22.68	28.73	**29.58**	13.10	5.92
Netherlands	16.77	10.12	26.89	12.48	21.49	**34.98**	2.41
Norway	38.92	7.48	**46.40**	12.96	36.41	3.01	1.06
Poland	16.11	16.28	**32.38**	14.05	27.54	19.90	6.13
Portugal	10.19	9.42	19.61	10.97	**42.38**	23.89	3.15
Romania	8.62	18.54	**27.17**	12.38	15.39	19.10	23.27
Slovakia	20.06	13.3	**33.37**	19.25	28.66	10.44	7.95
Slovenia	20.60	13.45	**34.05**	24.75	25.89	4.15	11.16
Spain	10.84	14.39	25.24	13.22	**30.77**	14.33	16.06
Sweden	41.78	3.43	**45.20**	8.37	43.75	1.94	.2
UK	17.41	10.73	**28.14**	19.61	22.93	20.43	5.09

Source: European Commission, Case No. COMP/M.6267—Volkswagen/MAN, pages 6, 13, and 14; **bold** indicates market leader.

approval there are several countries where VW/Scania/MAN has attained a dominant position, ranging between 35 per cent and 47 per cent of national markets. This includes Austria, the Czech Republic, Denmark, Estonia, Finland, Germany, Iceland, Norway, and Sweden. Moreover, given that no conditions were imposed by Brussels in its 2011 decision, the merged entity is now *the* national market leader in seventeen out of the twenty-six observations the Commission refers to in its decision, representing close to 65 per cent. In nine of these countries—Belgium, Denmark, Estonia, Ireland, Poland, Slovakia, Slovenia, Sweden, and the UK—VW now displaces Volvo from its leadership position.

Beyond regulatory approval at the EU level of governance, Alphas have also gained it in other countries throughout the world. For example, the jointly run car manufacturing plant between VW and FAW was a venture welcomed by China's State-Owned Assets Supervision and Administration Committee.[112] Similarly, VW's bid for MAN received approval by Chinese competition authorities.[113] The Competition Commission of India did not veto Renault's joint venture with Mahindra & Mahindra. And Renault's 25 per cent acquisition of Avtovaz was approved by Russia's Federal Antimonopoly Service.[114] The latter helps demonstrate the seriousness of investigation of some of these regulatory decisions: regulators from Russia took only five days to make a decision to approve the Avtovaz transaction.[115]

In the second scenario, some deals were not investigated at all, falling outside of any 'regulatory radar'. Because states themselves were driving the sales of SEAT (VW), Škoda (VW), and Dacia (Renault), national concerns regarding the competition aspects of the deals in Spain, the Czech Republic, and Romania were of little relevance in the privatization process. Because both Škoda and Dacia represented firms from non-EU states that had no market strength within the Union at the time of their sales, they fell outside the scope of the Union's merger control rules.[116] The sale of the Moroccan state-owned SOMACA similarly saw no formal regulatory process. These cases highlight that without making decisions, national and supranational regulatory authorities implicitly approved (or did not stop) M&A pursued by both VW and Renault, in a similar vein to the MMC in the Jaguar case discussed later.

Lobbying resources

In order to understand the success of the Alphas in attaining regulatory approval, the direct lobbying of firms is essential. For example, at the supranational level, both Renault and Volkswagen have representation offices in Brussels. These in-house corporate lobbyists seek to influence the main institutions of the EU, particularly the Commission and the European Parliament. Both firms also belong to the umbrella organization Association des Constructeurs Européens d'Automobiles (ACEA), which represents the interest of the major automakers based out of Europe. Because ACEA plays no role when firms seek to influence the Commission during the M&A process (in a similar vein to the AEA as discussed in Chapter 3), in-house corporate lobbyists will work alongside deal professionals and lawyers.

Building on previous work that has reported on lobbying registration and costs in 2008 (Chari and O'Donovan, 2011), Table 4.10 considers all the companies represented by ACEA, their status as possessing a registered in-house representative in 2008 (on the Commission Register) and 2013 (on the Joint Transparency Register), and estimated costs directly related to representing interests to EU institutions.

It highlights that while all automobile firms registered with the Commission declared roughly the same amount in 2008, values increased by 2013. The highest increase is seen in Daimler, while in the case of Renault the amount almost doubled and VW's spending increased fourfold. Taking all of ACEA's members which registered in the Commission Register and the Transparency Register, VW's increase between 2009 and 2013 is second only to Daimler. Part of this increase may be explained based on acquisitions being made (and needing approval) during this time period, including that of MAN, Porsche, and Ducati.

Table 4.10. Automobile Lobbying Costs in Brussels

Company Name	Registered with European Commission (2008)?	Lobbying Costs Declared on Commission Register (2009)	Registered in Joint Trans. Register (2013)	Lobbying Costs Declared in Transparency Register (2013)
ACEA	Yes	€550–600,000	Yes	€2,000,000–2,250,000
BMW Group	Yes	€200–250,000	Yes	€700–800,000
DAF Trucks	No	N/A	No	N/A
Daimler AG	Yes	€300–350k	Yes	€2,834,700
Porsche	No	N/A	No	N/A
Fiat Group	Yes	€200–250k	Yes	€400–450k
Ford Motor	Yes	€100–150k	Yes	€500–600k
Opel	Yes	€350–400k	Yes	€800–900k
Hyundai	Yes	€100–150k	Yes	€350–400k
Jaguar Land Rover	No	N/A	Yes	€150–200k
MAN	Yes	€80k	Yes	€80k
Peugeot Group	Yes	€150–200k	Yes	€300–350k
Renault	Yes	€250–300k	Yes	€400–450k
Scania	Yes	Less than €50k	Yes	€450–500k
Toyota Motor	Yes	€200–250k	Yes	€300–350k
Volkswagen	Yes	€200–250k	Yes	€800–900k
Volvo Group	Yes	€250–300k	Yes	€350–400k

Source: Conceptualization developed by Stacey (2010); Columns 2–3, Chari and O'Donovan (2011); Columns 4–5, Transparency Register Data (May 2013). In 2008 Hyundai was not a member of ACEA. MAN, Scania, and Porsche left the main ACEA board in 2012 (because they joined the VW Group), although MAN and Scania remain 'in' ACEA as members of its Commercial Vehicles Technical Committee.

Relying on the same model to explain why these two firms became Alphas (Figure 4.1), we now consider the case of Jaguar: a firm that had theoretical potential to become an Alpha, but ended up a Beta.

Potentially an Alpha, the Firm that Became a Beta after Its Sale: Jaguar

While SEAT and Alfa Romeo became Betas when they were privatized, Jaguar represents a case of a profitable firm that was floated successfully in 1984 which, theoretically, could have become an Alpha given initial conditions. As such, the theoretical conceptualization outlined in Figure 4.1 is applicable to it: it was a crown jewel that was successfully floated (initial conditions, X1). However, it became a Beta (outcome variable, Y). In order to understand this development, I consider the intervening variables (X2) of salience, including factors internal to the firm, as well as those external to it.

When turning to Jaguar's internal factors, one can see that while the firm's profits increased after its flotation, by the turn of the decade there was a slide. Table 4.11 shows that profits after taxes in 1985 were at GBP 87.6 million, only to continuously fall to negative values by mid-1989.

Low profits can be understood as being a consequence of at least three factors. First, with liberalization, there was increasing competition throughout the 1980s from French, German, and Italian firms that were establishing themselves in the UK market. Second, there were increasing costs associated with production of the XJ40 which suffered from technical problems.[117] Finally, adverse exchange rates also explain profit reductions, as highlighted by Jaguar's Chairman, John Egan (Annual Report, 1988, 8):

> A major reason for the profit reduction was a further sharp deterioration in the revenue we received from our export business as a result of the strength of sterling, particularly against the US dollar, and our inability to increase volume or pricing in North America to compensate this.

This is reflected in Table 4.12: even though sales increased in the UK and EU markets, the larger US market saw decreasing sales by the end of the decade.

Recognizing their problems, and not unlike SEAT and Alfa Romeo before their privatizations, by mid-1988 the Jaguar Board sought to collaborate with

Table 4.11. Jaguar: Profits After Taxes, 1984–9

	1984	1985	1986	1987	1988	1989*
Profits After Taxes (Million GBP)	42.6	87.6	83.4	61.3	28.4	−1.1

*1989 profit after taxes for the half-year to 30 June 1989.
Source: Jaguar Annual Reports 1984 to 1988; Jaguar Interim Report, 1989.

Table 4.12. Jaguar Sales by Market, 1985–9

	1985	1986	1987	1988	1989
US	20,528	24,464	22,919	20,727	18,967
UK	8049	7579	11,102	14,504	14,243
Canada	1315	2032	2660	2154	1606
Europe	4838	4332	6550	7876	8199
Overseas	3015	2586	3412	4233	4385

Source: The Jaguar Story—A legend in its lifetime (1990, page 4)

leading international car manufacturers 'to explore ways of broadening Jaguar's product range and achieving access to world class technology' (Jaguar, 1990, 5). At first, discussions to enter into a manufacturing and marketing agreement were held with General Motors, which also expressed an interest in attaining a minority interest in Jaguar. Later, similar negotiations were held with Ford.

The result was a bidding war between the two firms, defined by an interviewee as one where 'common sense was thrown out the window'.[118] Ford, like GM, was interested in having a global presence in the luxury car market and both realized that one of the most important markets for Jaguar was the US. Further, more concerned with long-term (as opposed to short-term) profits, Ford was happy to pay a hefty price in order to attain a potentially strong place within the European internal market before its completion in 1992. This can be seen in a similar vein to Japanese firms that sought to move their operations to Europe in response to the completion of the single market, as discussed earlier. Additionally, one may argue that pressure was on Ford to complete the deal given that it had previously failed in buying into Rover, Saab, and Alfa (as discussed later).

After Jaguar's 1989 half-year figures were published in September 1989, Ford thus announced its intentions to acquire 15 per cent of Jaguar. As Clausager (1990, 188) notes, this was 'the maximum allowed permitted until the expiry of the government's golden share at the end of 1990'. Despite the golden share, Ford sought to negotiate in October 1989 a full buy-out of Jaguar. After the state rescinded its golden share (discussed shortly), the deal was signed in December 1989.

From this perspective, Jaguar shareholders were happy given Ford's willingness to amply pay: the agreed price was for 850p per share, for a total value of approximately GBP 1.6 billion. This represented a five-fold increase on the price paid by shareholders who bought at 165p during the original flotation in 1984. And it represented almost double the value of shares that had a market value of 404p on 18 September 1989, the day before Ford announced its intentions to take 15 per cent.

One may also argue that Jaguar Directors, who had been talking to both Ford and GM since mid-1988 but did not finalize the sale until December 1989, also had vested interests in selling to Ford. Table 4.13 shows the number of ordinary shares and options (including Senior Executive Share Option, Employee Share, and Savings Related Share Option Schemes) held by the Directors of Jaguar in December 1988 and compares that to figures of November 1989, shortly before all Jaguar shares were sold to Ford. It suggests that the Directors' interests in the share capital of Jaguar were not only significant, but also increased between the two time periods.

While this helps explain why shareholders and managers sold Jaguar to the eager US firm, attention must be paid to the more political factors at play: the sale could not have taken place without the influence of the state and the position it took. The reason why the state was essential is because it could have acted as a veto player, holding a golden share which prevented any single investor from having more than 15 per cent of Jaguar. As the Secretary of State for Trade and Industry Nicholas Ridley explained, the rationale behind the original golden share established when the firm was privatized in 1984 was to prevent it from being taken over by another firm until the end of 1990:

> These provisions of the company's articles were put into place to preserve Jaguar's independence in its formative years as a free-standing company and so allow its management to concentrate on developing the business without the constant distraction of unwelcome takeover bids.[119]

Yet, throughout the negotiations in October 1989 when Ford sought Jaguar's complete takeover, it was clear that the golden share was an impediment. One interviewee stated that throughout the negotiation process Jaguar's Finance Director John Edwards was in discussions with the state, effectively lobbying for the golden share removal. Highlighting the confluence of interests between the firm and the state, on 31 October 1989 Ridley subsequently announced that:

> [i]n recent months, however, I understand that the chairman of Jaguar has been talking to a number of companies that are interested in forming links with Jaguar. There is a widespread perception that the company's financial and technological base needs strengthening in this way. The restrictions on shareholdings entrenched by the Government's special share are now clearly causing uncertainties about the company's future by prompting speculation over how my powers may be exercised, so distorting the basis on which all parties involved have to reach their decisions. I have accordingly told the Jaguar management that, if shareholders pass a special resolution by the requisite 75 percent majority amending the ownership provisions of the articles, I shall be ready also to give my consent. I am clear that it is in the best interests of Jaguar's management, shareholders and work force for the company's future to be assured and the present climate of uncertainty resolved as quickly as possible.[120]

Table 4.13. Directors' Interests in Jaguar, 1988–9

Directors	Position	1988 Ordinary Shares	1988 Options	1988 Total	1989 Ordinary Shares	1989 Options	1989 Total	Difference (1989–1988) Total
Sir John Egan	Jaguar Chairman and Chief Executive	32,150	237,047	269,197	32,970	260,518	293,488	**24,291**
Michael Beasley	Assistant Managing Director	3000	109,415	112,415	3820	129,296	133,116	**20,701**
Edward Bond	Non-Executive Director	1000	0	1000	1000		1000	**0**
John Edwards	Finance Director	10,000	94,806	104,806	10,820	108,832	119,652	**14,846**
Kenneth Edwards	Personnel Director and Company Secretary	10,000	69,585	79,585	10,820	68,824	79,644	**59**
Sir Austin Pearce	Non-Executive Director	2000		2000	2000		2000	**0**
Graham Whitehead	President of Jaguar Cars Inc. and Chairman of Jaguar Canada Inc.	33,751	152,859	186,610	34,571	171,939	206,510	**19,900**

Source: 1988 figures based on those as outlined in Jaguar's Annual Report 1988, page 41. 1989 figures outlined in the Offer of Sale to Ford, page 52, refers to that held as of 6 November 1989, weeks before the sale was approved in December 1989. Positions of the Board of Directors taken from page 6–7, Jaguar Annual Report 1988.

Interviewees stated that, as far as the state was concerned, they were happy with Jaguar to be taken over by Ford for at least three reasons.[121] First, Jaguar needed a partner in order to increase technological development: the US firm was perceived to have 'deep pockets' in order to fund ambitious capital investment and new model programmes. Related, saving the jobs of 12,500 workers who may have otherwise been let go if the company folded would have proven unpopular amongst the electorate.

A second related reason is that although a direct sale of Jaguar to a US multinational may have been unpopular amongst the electorate when the firm was privatized in 1984, by the late 1980s the state did not fear a political backlash. This is because the firm had already been privatized and, in order to survive, was in need of a strategic partner.

Third, the state could 'walk away' without having to give future state aid. Thus, this represents a case of a firm that may have had potential to become an Alpha, but which did not receive potential aid from the state for its continued independent survival. The firm was ultimately situated in a position to be taken over by another firm, with the state's blessing. The UK government felt that state intervention in any form (such as aid) was not only against its ideological principles, but also could have been frowned upon by the European Commission as reflected in its investigation into Alfa Romeo's aid discussed at the end of the chapter. Ford thus represented a 'new saviour' from the US, a trusted historical ally that could take over Jaguar and not result in the state having to potentially bail out the company.

This is consistent with the idea that the British state encouraged other (less successful) companies within BL to be taken over by other sectoral giants, including Mini (BMW) and Land Rover (BMW, Ford, and later Tata) in order to prevent any potential future budgetary drain. Interestingly, when performing the tests to determine whether or not a firm can be considered an Alpha or a Beta (Section 4.2), one sees that BMW, too, can be considered an Alpha.[122] Considering that other manufacturers—such as Bentley which is now owned by VW, and Rolls Royce cars which is owned by BMW—were also sold off, one may argue that Jaguar represents another case of once UK-owned car manufacturers now being in the hands of non-native capital, including Alphas.

Turning to the role of regulatory authorities, the deal witnessed no intervention by either the UK or European regulators, effectively resulting in the deal going under the regulatory radar. Shortly before the sale was finalized in December, Minister Ridley announced that the takeover 'would not be referred to the Monopolies and Mergers Commission',[123] highlighting that a 'no-decision' by regulators effectively determined developments in the market. Nor did the European Commission investigate the merger (in fact, its first rulings under the 1989 Merger Control Regulation had not taken place until 1990[124]).

In sum, in order to understand why Jaguar became a Beta it is necessary to examine factors both internal and external to the firm. It has been argued that while firm-specific factors are important in setting the stage for Ford's purchase, they are not sufficient. Rather, political variables—particularly the impact of liberalization to the role of the state that rescinded its golden share, and the (lack of) role of regulators that never investigated the sale and potentially stopped it—were necessary in order for the deal to go through.

Attention is now turned to the remaining Betas, SEAT and Alfa Romeo.

Firms that Became Betas at the Point of Privatization: SEAT and Alfa Romeo

Chapter 2 theoretically argued that a privatized firm may become a Beta based on its initial conditions (X1): in a first dimension, it is a loss-making firm prior to its sale and, in a second, the state promotes the SOE's takeover by another leading sectoral firm. This was originally outlined as Figure 2.1 in Chapter 2. A slightly modified version is reproduced in Figure 4.6, highlighting that both SEAT and Alfa Romeo are Betas (Y, the outcome variable) based on Section 4.2's results.

On the first dimension, both SEAT and Alfa Romeo were, quite simply, firms in the red. Regarding SEAT, by 1976 it had experienced its first losses which, except for the following year, plagued it for the next decade. By 1982 it had losses of over 23.6 billion pesetas, which culminated to almost twice that in 1983.[125] After Fiat abandoned its minority shares and collaborative

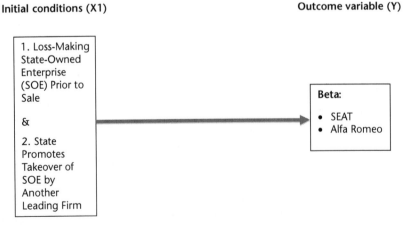

Figure 4.6. The First Model: How an Automobile Firm May Become a Beta (Y) Based on Initial Conditions (X1)

interests because of SEAT's continued inability to attain profits, in 1982 the Socialist government sought alternative financing for SEAT through private banks rather than proceeding with the closure of the company. Based on examination of the internal files of the INI performed by the author, these banks included, amongst others, Banco Hispano, Caja Madrid, Banco Bilbao, and Banco Vizcaya.[126] Yet, by the end of 1985 the banks sought repayment of the close to 100 billion pesetas they had loaned to SEAT, something approved by the core-executive (although not discussed in the House or Senate) just days before Spanish entry into the European Community on 28 December 1985.[127]

In the case of Alfa Romeo, its losses between 1979 and 1986 were acute. The subsequent state contributions to the firm were significant throughout most of those years, as seen in Table 4.14.

The Table demonstrates that over eight years, the firm suffered losses of close to 1,500 billion lira between 1979 and 1986. To keep it alive, close to 1,400 billion lira had been given as state aid, something unsustainable over the short and long term. Consistent with overall goals to reconstruct the IRI, Finmeccanica and IRI decided that because Alfa could not become profitable as an independent company it should not be shut down but, rather, merge with a sectoral leader to guarantee Alfa's survival.

Turning to the second related dimension, in the context of keeping the companies alive both the Spanish and Italian states promoted their takeover by leading European automakers. In the case of SEAT, one may argue that the Spanish Socialists allowed VW to, literally, drive a good bargain: the Spanish state was a willing partner to pump state funds into SEAT during the privatization process. Without doubt, VW officials at the time expected that adding the SEAT brand would help consolidate the VW Group as the European market leader ahead of Fiat.[128] Yet, VW's top concern was SEAT's potential future losses. The Spanish government was aware that selling SEAT would

Table 4.14. Alfa Romeo Losses and Aid Received, 1979–86

Year	Losses (billion lira)	State Contributions (billion lira)
1979	91,8	131,6
1980	75,5	201,4
1981	114,4	134,0
1982	91,4	133,7
1983	121,7	1,5
1984	210,9	0,0
1985	465,5	376,4
1986	313,3	408,9
Total	1484,5	1387,5

Source: European Commission, Case No. 89/661/EEC, 31 May 1989, Section VII (page 5 of Decision)

prevent long-term future losses and therefore seemed willing to take some short-term pain to allay VW's concerns. Analysis of INI internal documents (Chari, 1998) shows that prior to the sale, the state secured a series of loans, guaranteed to purchase SEAT's unprofitable subsidiaries, earmarked funds for workforce reduction, and recapitalized SEAT. Additionally, after the majority sale in 1986, over the next four years the state paid various retroactive contributions demanded by VW. In terms of the sale price, it can be estimated that VW paid 39.2 billion pesetas for INI shares sold between December 1986 and 1990; however, state payments towards SEAT before and after its majority sale to VW were close to 73.6 billion pesetas, leaving an approximate difference of 34 billion pesetas in VW's favour (over USD 250 million).

Not dissimilar to the Spanish state, in the case of Alfa Romeo both IRI and Finmeccanica were keen to offload and integrate Alfa within a larger automobile group for a sustainable future.[129] Although early in the privatization process the state had approached leading international carmakers, only two answered the call: Ford and Fiat. State officials started negotiations first with Ford in the spring of 1986 and then with Fiat later in the autumn. On the one hand, Ford sought to strengthen its position in the European market (as with Jaguar, discussed earlier); on the other, Fiat sought to consolidate its position in the Italian one, where in 1986 it had already close to 62 per cent of it. After agreeing to assume 700 million lira of Alfa Romeo's debt, as well as to pay a price of 1,050 billion lira, in November 1986 Finmeccanica's board agreed to sell to Fiat over Ford. Linked to its investigation of unnotified aid from the Italian state to Alfa during 1985 and 1986, the European Commission investigated whether or not the Fiat offer was really better than that of Ford. It concluded that 'while Ford's offer was on average slightly higher in financial terms, it included future commercial risks for Finmeccanica linked to the development of Alfa Romeo's net results during the period 1987 to 1993. In contrast, Fiat's offer excluded these kinds of risks'.[130]

Comparing privatization developments in both SEAT and Alfa Romeo sees both states playing key roles, motivated similarly on at least three grounds. First, just as Alfa Romeo had been receiving large amounts of state subsidies over the years, SEAT was a large drain. Selling SEAT was consistent with decreasing state transfers to the INI which was home to several loss-making companies, in a similar vein to the Italian state seeking to reconstruct the IRI. In the case of SEAT, for example, the data demonstrates a decrease of state budget transfers to the INI from approximately 400 billion pesetas in 1985 (before SEAT was sold in 1986) to less than 100 billion pesetas by 1991.[131]

Second, not closing down the companies meant saving jobs, which also helped gain, save, or not drastically lose votes in the short term. For example, in 1986 SEAT employed 22,197 workers, which was virtually the same in 1991 with 21,592, although this number declined to almost half by the end of 2012, to 11,465.[132] Particularly important in the case of Spain, by selling to a European champion such as VW, and not forcing massive job losses with the closure of the firms, leaders such as González were able to maintain a key industry located in a key autonomous community, Catalonia, which is sometimes at odds with Madrid. In the case of Alfa Romeo, the press at the time highlighted that one of the advantages of the Fiat offer over Ford was that Fiat guaranteed 23,000 of the 34,000 jobs in Alfa (*La Stampa*, 7 November 1986).

Third, was the credibility both states attained by choosing the 'right' buyer. Having SEAT taken over from an established Community member gave Spain the credibility it needed: it had recently joined the EU and sought to establish itself as a 'trustworthy' member state. As stated in an interview with a former PSOE official, attracting German investment was consistent with the broader goals of the single European market and choosing VW was the right 'political thing' to do for the young democracy seeking to establish a place for itself in Europe.[133] This highlights the importance of states from abroad (i.e. those states that are not Alpha home states) in fostering Alpha expansion. One may argue that this 'SEAT-dynamic' also occurred when the Czech government sold Škoda to VW and the Romanian government sold Dacia to Renault. It was also manifest in other states outside the EU which were keen to demonstrate to the rest of the world that they were modernizing and pursuing liberal market reforms, such as when the Russian government facilitated Renault's entry (and scheduled majority control) of Avtovaz. In the case of Alfa Romeo, one may reasonably argue that, regardless of whether or not whoever's offer was better or worse, the state's choice of Fiat was a prudent one: selling to a US-based firm (Ford) over the leading firm in Italy (Fiat) may have proved unpopular amongst both politicians and citizens alike.

The one point of contrast in both sales was the role of the EU in investigating aid that was linked to the sales, ultimately sealing the deals for firms to expand without having to pay anything back. There is no evidence that any of the contributions by the Spanish state during the SEAT privatization—which were never notified to the European Commission—were ever investigated by the Commission, as verified by correspondence between the author and DG Competition.[134] A former state official in Spain somewhat complacently argued that, 'Yes, we probably should have informed and sought approval from Brussels...but I am sure, that if we did inform the Commission, they would have accepted the proposals in any case.'[135] Ultimately, if the aid was deemed incompatible with the Common Market, it should have been recovered from Volkswagen (Chari, 1998). This lies in some contrast to developments surrounding the privatization of Alfa Romeo: the unnotified aid given by the Italian state in 1985 and 1986 was eventually scrutinized by the Commission in 1989, which sought to determine if it was linked to Alfa's privatization. The Commission finally concluded that around 650 billion lira were, indeed, incompatible with the Common Market. But, the Commission concluded that the aid did not have to be recovered from Fiat, which one may have otherwise expected considering that it directly benefited by buying Alfa after the injections into the struggling firm. Rather, in a surprising case of having an aid recovered from one arm of the state to the other, the Commission decided the aid had to be recovered by the Italian government from Finmeccanica, which the Commission argued was the 'sole beneficiary of all the revenue generated by the sale of the assets of the former Alfa Romeo Group'.[136] Although the Italian state appealed the decision, the Commission's ruling was upheld by the European Court of Justice in 1991.[137]

Conclusions

This chapter started by examining the history of the firms, their privatization, and, in the case of Volkswagen and Renault, their M&A. Thereafter, based on the results of the Global Movers and Independence Tests, the second section argued that both VW and Renault can be considered Alphas, while Jaguar, SEAT, and Alfa Romeo are Betas. The third section then considered which factors help explain why some are Alphas, while others Betas.

The cases of Volkswagen and Renault saw a contrasting situation to the other three firms because the state never fully privatized them, maintaining 20 and 15 per cent ownership, respectively. Both Alphas are also at the cutting edge in terms of technological developments and have been world leaders in the sector for years. Yet, one may argue that a similar dynamic to the Betas was witnessed in terms of which factors help explain why the firms have become Alphas: managers and shareholders are important, but the impact of liberalization, the roles of states, and the actions (or inactions) of regulators were necessary and sufficient.

As in the previous chapter, three principal external factors are sequentially bound. First, the SEA firms consolidated their position at home. The impact of the SEA and the creation of the single European market meant that firms could acquire in the EU and also form alliances with Japanese players. From this, liberalization initiatives helped define *what could be done*, or, where the firms could expand and when. Second, the state maintained strong, cooperative links with Alphas: it continues to exercise influence as a shareholder with board representation given its ownership in the firms; it gives state aid for investment projects (along with other states in the EU); and it positions itself to help craft deals in Europe and overseas, as seen in VW/Porsche and Renault/SOMACA. Taken together, the state helped define *how expansion could be done*, while also playing a key protectorate role, as seen in

VW. Finally, domestic and supranational regulatory authorities ultimately approved aid given to Alphas after privatization. Most importantly, they approved M&A planned by Alphas. Such regulators could have potentially vetoed deals. But the evidence showed that no major deals pursued were vetoed by regulatory authorities at any level of governance; almost all those reviewed were approved without any conditions; and some even escaped any regulatory review. Thus, regulatory decisions (and, sometimes, non-decisions) ensured *that expansion could be done*. Money spent on lobbying political institutions explains why firms are able to gain regulatory approval, especially at the EU level. But the evidence also suggests that the Commission's relatively easy approval may be explained because Brussels may use different criteria when investigating deals proposed by Alphas, when compared to other deals it blocks as seen when comparing Volvo/Scania with Volkswagen/Scania/MAN.

Even though Jaguar can be considered a Beta, it contrasts to the Southern European ones: with its successful flotation it was in a theoretical position to become an Alpha after privatization. But, it was eventually taken over by Ford in the late 1980s, a firm keen to set up shop in the internal market. In order to understand why the firm became a Beta, factors internal to the firm— including the goals of managers and shareholders—while important, are not sufficient. Declining profits in the wake of foreign competition with increased liberalization, technical problems with the cars, and adverse exchange rates in the 1980s, meant that the firm was in decline after privatization. The state was thus motivated to see the firm (and workers' jobs) survive, while not having to consider a future bailout given Jaguar's financial difficulties. With a keen buyer from the US keen to set up shop in the European single market after already having suffered blows in making European acquisitions, the state intervened and allowed the sale to Ford to occur by rescinding the 'golden share' which prevented takeover. Nor did the UK's regulator at the time, the MMC, veto the deal.

Finally, focusing on SEAT and Alfa Romeo, it was argued that both firms were suffering losses and represented a drain on the state, which sought to sell them to sectoral leaders. To this end, both the Spanish and Italian states were willing to give generous amounts of aid, which ultimately benefited Volkswagen and Fiat who purchased SEAT and Alfa, respectively. Although the Italian case saw investigation into state aid by the European Commission, such aid given during both sales was never recovered from those that purchased the companies at privatization. Beyond desires to reduce state expenditure towards these firms, the states were motivated to keep jobs as well as to sell to the 'right' buyer. Spain, as a new democracy entering the EU in 1986, was particularly willing to sell to a firm from an established EU state in order to gain a reputation of being 'trustworthy'. It thus facilitated Volkswagen's first main expansionary deal in the continent. Nor was there evidence that domestic regulators approved the sales; hardly surprising considering the firms were on the selling block.

In sum, taking all of the five cases together, a common thread that explains why firms become Alphas or Betas is the impact of liberalization, the influence of states, and the actions, and sometimes inactions, of regulatory authorities.

The next chapter examines and explains life after privatization in the electricity sector.

Endnotes

1. On marketing and name changes of the Rabbit, see Garrett (2009).
2. On the sale, see *The New York Times* (1988).
3. The US dollar value of the privatization is based on data from <www.privatizationbarometer.net> (accessed 14 July 2013). The estimated Deutsche Mark value is over DM1.1 billion.
4. Analysis of the VW company archives was performed on-site in the company in March 2012 by a native German speaker who worked as a research assistant for the project, Laura Schwirz, to whom the author is grateful. As there is a thirty-year freeze on documents to be released for archival research, access was offered only on internal documents which were dated before 1982. As a result, analysis was focused on the Audi acquisition.
5. See Audi's webpage, on its history, <http://www.audi.com/com/brand/en/company/audi_history/model_evolution.html#source=http://www.audi.com/com/brand/en/company/audi_history/companies_and_brands/rebirth_of_the_brand.html&container=page> (accessed 20 July 2013).
6. See: <http://www.audi.com/com/brand/en/company/audi_history/model_evolution.html#source=http://www.audi.com/com/brand/en/company/audi_history/companies_and_brands/merger_with_nsu.html&container=page> (accessed 20 July 2013).
7. See: <http://www.skoda.co.uk/skoda-history> (accessed 20 July 2013).
8. See: <http://www.telegraph.co.uk/motoring/car-manufacturers/skoda/8458395/Skoda-celebrates-20-years-of-success-under-VW.html> (accessed 20 July 2013).
9. Based on analysis of Bureau van Dijk's Zephyr's database, BvD Deal ID Number 61508.
10. Based on analysis of Bureau van Dijk's Zephyr's database, BvD Deal ID Number 62473.
11. Based on analysis of Bureau van Dijk's Zephyr's database, BvD Deal ID Number 37022.
12. Based on analysis of Bureau van Dijk's Zephyr's database, BvD Deal ID Number 38124. Also, for a history of the company, please see: <http://www.lamborghini.com/en/heritage/history/1963-1964/> (last accessed 17 July 2013).
13. Based on analysis of Bureau van Dijk's Zephyr's database, BvD Deal ID Number 35758.

14. Based on analysis of Bureau van Dijk's Zephyr's database, BvD Deal ID Number BvD 35758, from where quotes are taken.

15. Based on analysis of Bureau van Dijk's Zephyr's database, BvD Deal ID Number 35758, from where quotes are taken.

16. On VW in China since the 1980s see *The New York Times* (2013). The analysis of the 2004 deal is Zephyr's database deal with ID Number 266355.

17. Based on analysis of Bureau van Dijk's Zephyr's database, BvD Deal ID Number 330728.

18. Based on analysis of Bureau van Dijk's Zephyr's database, BvD Deal ID Number, 1603029502.

19. In more detail, in November 2011 VW 'served notice to Suzuki of an alleged infringement of the cooperation agreement...the notice concerned that Suzuki breached Volkswagen's contract by deciding to purchase diesel engines from Fiat of Italy, in June 2011.' Taken from MarketLine, *Company Profile Volkswagen AG*, 28 September 2012, published on <www.marketline.com>.

20. Based on analysis of Bureau van Dijk's Zephyr's database, BvD Deal ID Number 44098

21. Based on analysis of Bureau van Dijk's Zephyr's database, BvD Deal ID Number 421295.

22. Based on analysis of Bureau van Dijk's Zephyr's database, BvD Deal ID Number 481493.

23. Based on analysis of Bureau van Dijk's Zephyr's database, BvD Deal ID Number 421295.

24. Based on analysis of Bureau van Dijk's Zephyr's database, BvD Deal ID Number 484137.

25. Based on analysis of Bureau van Dijk's Zephyr's database, BvD Deal ID Numbers 520765 and 579851.

26. Based on analysis of Bureau van Dijk's Zephyr's database, BvD Deal ID Number 487707.

27. Based on analysis of Bureau van Dijk's Zephyr's database, BvD Deal ID Number 623570.

28. Based on analysis of Bureau van Dijk's Zephyr's database, BvD Deal ID Number 1601297714.

29. Based on analysis of Bureau van Dijk's Zephyr's database, BvD Deal ID Number 38012.

30. Based on analysis of Bureau van Dijk's Zephyr's database, BvD Deal ID Numbers 495834 and 38466.

31. Based on analysis of Bureau van Dijk's Zephyr's database, BvD Deal ID Number 495819.

32. Based on analysis of Bureau van Dijk's Zephyr's database, BvD Deal ID Number 653786.

33. VW Press Release, 23/07/09, which can be found on <http://www.volkswagenag.com/content/vwcorp/info_center/en/news/2009/07/VW_AR_July_09.html> (last accessed 20 October 2013).

34. Based on analysis of Bureau van Dijk's Zephyr's database, BvD Deal ID Number 1601075545.
35. Based on analysis of Bureau van Dijk's Zephyr's database, BvD Deal ID Number 1601317352.
36. Based on analysis of Bureau van Dijk's Zephyr's database, BvD Deal ID Numbers 1601071668 and 1601317352.
37. Based on information found on: <http://www.volkswagenag.com/content/vwcorp/info_center/en/news/2010/04/Bezugspreis.html> (last accessed 10 July 2013).
38. Based on analysis of Bureau van Dijk's Zephyr's database, BvD Deal ID Number 1601104221.
39. On the history of Renault see: <http://www.renault.com/en/groupe/chiffres-cles/pages/dates-cles.aspx>
40. Source: <www.privatizationbarometer.net> (accessed 11 July 2014).
41. Based on analysis of the data for 1996, found on the Renault's webpage, <http://www.renault.com/en/finance/action/pages/repartition-du-capital.aspx> (last accessed 31 July 2014).
42. Based on values reported by <www.privatizationbarometer.net> (this case last accessed December 2013). Both the 2002 and 2003 sales, with values of €2.9 billion, are also found on the BvD Zephyr database. The cases are identified with the following Deal ID Numbers: 101279 (minority stake sale of 10.7% of Renault, completed 02/04/02) and 180923 (minority stake sale of 9.35%, completed 08/08/03).
43. Based on analysis of Bureau van Dijk's Zephyr's database, BvD Deal ID Number 45458.
44. Based on analysis of Bureau van Dijk's Zephyr's database, BvD Deal ID Number 83387.
45. Based on analysis of Bureau van Dijk's Zephyr's database, BvD Deal ID Numbers 100430 and 115694.
46. That is, today Nissan Motors owns 15% of Renault, although Renault would see a slightly reduced stake in Nissan from its initial 44.4% discussed in the text, to 43.4% it has today which one sees after the Daimler deal discussed here. Source, Zephyr Company Report on Nissan Motor Corporation, BvD ID Number JP000000941JPN (last accessed 7 July 2013).
47. Based on analysis of Bureau van Dijk's Zephyr's database, BvD Deal ID Number 324531.
48. Based on analysis of Bureau van Dijk's Zephyr's database, BvD Deal ID Number 69601.
49. Based on analysis of Bureau van Dijk's Zephyr's database, BvD Deal ID Number 246247.
50. Based on analysis of Bureau van Dijk's Zephyr's database, BvD Deal ID Number 296048.
51. Based on analysis of Bureau van Dijk's Zephyr's database, BvD Deal ID Number 61243.
52. Based on analysis of Bureau van Dijk's Zephyr's database, BvD Deal ID Number 61243.

53. Based on analysis of Bureau van Dijk's Zephyr's database, BvD Deal ID Number 175573.

54. Based on analysis of Bureau van Dijk's Zephyr's database, BvD Deal ID Number 469312.

55. Based on analysis of Bureau van Dijk's Zephyr's database, BvD Deal ID Number 1601429365.

56. Based on analysis of Bureau van Dijk's Zephyr's database, BvD Deal ID Number 469312.

57. Based on analysis of Bureau van Dijk's Zephyr's database, BvD Deal ID Number 69497.

58. Based on analysis of Bureau van Dijk's Zephyr's database, BvD Deal ID Number 90744.

59. Based on analysis of Bureau van Dijk's Zephyr's database, BvD Deal ID Number 219128.

60. On the initial 25% stake taken in 2008, see Zephyr deal with ID Number 446877. On the deal regarding the controlling stake, see Zephyr file with ID Number 1601465455. See also the report on the deal by *The New York Times* (2012).

61. Based on analysis of Bureau van Dijk's Zephyr's database, BvD Deal ID Number 207147.

62. Based on analysis of several deals in Bureau van Dijk's Zephyr's database with the following ID Numbers: 76257; 147354; 315583; and 416053.

63. See: <http://www.renault.com/en/Groupe/renault-dans-le-monde/Pages/renault-au-maroc.aspx> (last accessed 15 September 2013).

64. Based on analysis of Bureau van Dijk's Zephyr's database, BvD Deal ID Number 156250.

65. Based on analysis of Bureau van Dijk's Zephyr's database, BvD Deal ID Number 1601168453.

66. Based on analysis of Bureau van Dijk's Zephyr's database, BvD Deal ID Numbers 1601168456 and 1603056821.

67. The term 'underpriced' was used by economic actors once associated with the company that were interviewed in this study, February 2012.

68. Based on value of the transaction reported by <www.privatizationbarometer.net> (where this data was last accessed 4 December 2013). The value in GBP, as reported by Vickers and Yarrow (1988, 163), is £294 million.

69. See: <http://news.bbc.co.uk/2/hi/business/761794.stm> (last accessed October 2013).

70. SEAT, *Memoria y Balance*, Ejercicio 1983, 23.

71. See: <http://www.seat.com/content/com/com/en.html>.

72. Information taken from <http://www.alfaromeo.com/com/#/history/timeline> (1960) (last accessed 21 October 2013).

73. Searches were performed on the Amadeus database in August 2013 and verified in November 2013. Peugeot SA and Renault were specifically added to the search given that their NACE Rev 2 primary codes are not 291, but 7010 (Activities of Head Office) and 6420 (Activities of holding companies), respectively.

74. The data for the independence test (and the BvD's independence ranking) are taken from the company reports with the following BvD ID Numbers in the

Amadeus database: VW, DE2070000543; Renault, FR441639465; Jaguar Land Rover, GB06477691; SEAT, ESA28049161; Alfa Romeo, ITTO0577851. The final tests were run between March 2013 and October 2013, and all reports were last accessed in October 2013.

75. For a graph on the structure of the Group as a percentage of subscribed capital, see: <http://www.volkswagenag.com/content/vwcorp/content/en/investor_relations/share/Shareholder_Structure.html> (last accessed 27 August 2013); data also reported in VW Group Annual Report, 2012, page 168.

76. See also: <http://www.porsche-se.com/pho/en/porschese/holdingstructure/> (last accessed 27 August 2013).

77. This 100% control occurred after a remaining 10% that was held by the Qatar Holding Company GmbH was sold back to the families. See: <http://www.porsche-se.com/pho/en/press/newsarchive2013/?pool=pho&id=2013-06-17> (last accessed 27 August 2013).

78. See BvD Company Report on the VW group, BvD ID number DE2070000543.

79. VW's profits in 2011 were 15,800 million EUR (ranked first amongst its peers in the sector), while those of Renault were €2,092 million (ranked fourth). Source: Bureau van Dijk, Amadeus Database.

80. This data on new registrations in 2013 in the EU is that reported by the trade association that represents the main European car manufacturers, ACEA. The data for Renault is based on the market share of Renault (9.6%) and Nissan (3.3%). The data can be accessed on <http://www.acea.be/statistics/tag/category/by-manufacturer-registrations> (last accessed 11 March 2014).

81. On this, see the report by Kurylko and Specht (2013).

82. Comments made on 10 May 2011 and reported in the Zephyr database, BvD Deal Number 623570.

83. See: <https://www.google.com/finance?cid=661748>.

84. Of the top ten asset management firms outlined in Chapter 2, Fidelity owned no shares in Renault and is therefore not graphed.

85. See European Commission, 2002a.

86. As examples, Fiat received €27.9 million for its engine plant in Termoli, Italy in 1999 and €46 million for the new car development in Sicily in 2009. See European Commission 1999 and 2009a.

87. Case C-112/05, 23 October 2007.

88. Quote taken from the *Financial Times* report by Alex Barker (2011).

89. As discussed in the *Financial Times* report by Alex Barker (2011).

90. Quote taken from *The Wall Street Journal* report by Laurence Norman (2013).

91. See: <http://www.mf.niedersachsen.de/themen/beteiligungen/volkswagen-ag-wolfsburg-1590.html> (last accessed 1 October 2013).

92. Volkswagen, Press release, 23/07/09.

93. See *The New York Times* report by Tagliabue (2000).

94. The Amadeus searches were performed in July 2012 and September 2012. The Companies' annual reports with which data was cross-referenced were those of 2011. Company reports were used as the ultimate source in case of inconsistent or out-of-date information in Amadeus.

95. While still having ties to the state, the case of Volkswagen's BoD somewhat differs as only two of the twenty-two members (around 10%) of the supervisory board have state association, corresponding to the two board members of Lower Saxony, which maintains a veto power as discussed previously. This is based on analysis of Amadeus and VW's Annual Report, 2011, page 142. The two members from Lower Saxony in 2011 include: Jörg Bode (Minister of Economic Affairs, Labour, and Transport for Lower Saxony) and David McAllister (Prime Minister of Lower Saxony).

96. When a similar search was done on the BvD Zephyr database on completed deals between 1997 and 2012 where VW was the acquirer, thirty-seven cases were isolated. In terms of target distribution, the main countries were: Germany (49%), Sweden (16%), China (5%), UK (5%), Japan (5%), and the Czech Republic (5%). Search performed in September 2012.

97. See: <http://www.daciagroup.com/en/about-us/dacia-industrial-site/background> (accessed June 2013).

98. See: <http://www.renault.com/en/groupe/renault-dans-le-monde/pages/renault-au-maroc.aspx> (accessed 20 September 2013).

99. Quote taken from the Bureau van Dijk's Zephyr's database, BvD Deal ID Number 14735.

100. For more details, please see Zephyr Deal Number 315583 as well as: <http://www.leconomiste.com/article/somaca-renault-remet-le-cheque-le-26-septembre> (accessed 1 October 2013).

101. As taken from a Press Communication by Renault itself, found at: <http://www-nocache.renault.axime.com/SiteCollectionDocuments/Communiqué%20de%20presse/en-EN/Pieces%20jointes/355_Appointments_37303.pdf> (accessed 2 October 2013).

102. The BvD database states that advisors to Renault in the September 2003 SOMACA deal in Morocco were CMS Bureau Francis Lefebvre, where the deal professionals involved included Mr Jean-Pierre Andrieux and Mr Frédéric Elbar (BvD, Deal Number 147354). The latter has since set up his own consultancy—Maghreb Consulting and Training—which was involved in the Tangier investment, where production started in 2012. See, on Mr Elbar, <http://www.maghreb-consulting.com/maghreb-consulting/pagesEn/track-record.asp>, and, on Renault in Tangier, <http://www.renault.com/en/groupe/renault-dans-le-monde/pages/renault-au-maroc.aspx> (last accessed 2 October 2013).

103. The Commission case numbers of the deals are as follows: VW/Bentley/Rolls Royce, Case No. IV/M.1283; Volkswagen/Scania, Case No. M/5157; VW/Man, Case No. COMP/M6267; VW/Porsche, Case No. COMP/M.5250; Audi/Ducati (2012) No. Comp/M.6593. As with all Competition decisions, these can easily be searched for on: <http://ec.europa.eu/competition/elojade/isef> (last accessed 4 July 2014).

104. Based on analysis of Bureau van Dijk's Zephyr's database, BvD Deal ID No. 446877. For the Commission's decisions see: Case No. IV/M.1519—Renault/Nissan, 12/05/1999; and Case No. COMP/M.5061—Renault/Russian Technologies/ Avtovaz, 08/04/08.

105. Two interviews with officials working in the automobile sector, April 2011 and August 2013.
106. Information of VW's 18.7% purchase of Scania in March 2000 based on evidence in BvD Deal Number 44098.
107. Case No. COMP/M. 1672—Volvo/Scania, 15/03/00 see pages 5 and 52.
108. Case No. COMP/M. 1672—Volvo/Scania, 15/03/00, page 19. The Commission provides no comparable concrete figures for market shares for bus markets (city buses, intercity buses, and coaches). See page 58.
109. Case No. COMP/M.5157—Volkswagen/Scania, 20/12/06.
110. Case No. COMP/M.6267—Volkswagen/MAN, 26/09/11, page 6. Again, the Commission provides no comparable concrete figures for the bus market in this case. See pages 20–53 of its decision.
111. Case No. COMP/M.1672—Volvo/Scania, pages 19–52.
112. Based on analysis of Bureau van Dijk's Zephyr's database, BvD Deal ID Number 330728.
113. Case No. COMP/M.6267—Volkswagen/MAN.
114. Based on analysis of Bureau van Dijk's Zephyr's database, BvD Deal ID Number, 446877.
115. Based on analysis of Bureau van Dijk's Zephyr database, BvD Deal ID Number 446877.
116. This is based on discussions with Commission officials in September 2013. The purchases of both Lamborghini and Bugatti saw no case decisions by the Commission. This is not much of a surprise, though, considering that Bugatti was revived with VW's purchase, and Lamborghini was a small company: the 1998 deal did not surpass the thresholds to be investigated by the Merger Task Force.
117. Based on interviews with an Ex-Jaguar official, February 2012.
118. Based on interviews with an Ex-Jaguar official, February 2012.
119. House of Commons Debate, *31 October 1989 vol. 159 cc177–87*, found at: <http://hansard.millbanksystems.com/commons/1989/oct/31/jaguar-plc#S6CV0159P0_19891031_HOC_221> (last accessed 22 September 2013).
120. House of Commons Debate, *31 October 1989 vol. 159 cc177–87*, found at: <http://hansard.millbanksystems.com/commons/1989/oct/31/jaguar-plc#S6CV0159P0_19891031_HOC_221> (last accessed 22 September 2013).
121. This is based on interviews with three former Jaguar and Ford officials in February 2012 and April 2012.
122. BMW can be classified as an Alpha because it appears on the Forbes 2000 list, ranks as one of the top European companies (Table 4.3), and would pass the Independence Test (when invoking the Exception 2 to the test because the Quandt family owns more than 45% of the firm).
123. Quote taken from the Associated Press (1989). See also the report from the *Chicago Tribune* (1989).
124. For full yearly statistics of Commission Merger cases, see: <http://ec.europa.eu/competition/mergers/statistics.pdf> (last accessed 3 November 2013). Further analysis of DG Competition's website devoted to merger cases <http://ec.europa.eu/competition/mergers/cases/>) found no investigation of the takeover of Jaguar by Ford.

125. SEAT, *Memoria y Balance*, Ejercicio 1983, 47, 53. Accordingly, the state (thorough the INI) would continue to give SEAT extra financial contributions (aportaciones) which, for example, in 1982 amounted to over 18.7 billion pesetas.
126. Analysis of the INI files was performed by the author in 1996 in the offices of the SEPI in Plaza de Marques de Salamanca, Madrid. The main findings from this research are also highlighted in Chari (1998).
127. The quick approval by the core-executive is inexorably linked to the ties held between Socialist leaders of the Ministry of Economy, Finance and Industry (such as Solchaga, Croissier, and Aranzadi; all having roots in financial capital) and the Spanish banks which held the loans. See Chari (1998).
128. Ray Moseley, 1986, 'Spain's Automaker Driven to Join Volkswagen', *Chicago Tribune*, 9 May.
129. As seen in *La Stampa*, 29 May 1986, 1. See also European Commission, Case L 394/9, Section 5, page 4.
130. European Commission, Case L 394/9, Section 7, page 7.
131. Based on analysis of Section 20 (Transfers to the INI) of the Spanish State Budget between 1985 and 1991, performed in June 1997 by the author.
132. Sources for data: 1986, SEAT SA *Informe Anual* 1986, page 33; 1990, SEAT—*Informe del Ejercicio* 1990, page 21; SEAT, *Informe Anual* 2012, page 123.
133. Interview with the author, September 1996.
134. See Chari (1998), which outlines correspondence between the author and DG IV (later renamed DG Competition). To verify these previous findings, a recent search was done in October 2013 of the EU's database <www.euro-lex.eu>, where all Community decisions are published, and no decisions of the state aid towards SEAT during the privatization have yet to be reported.
135. Interview with the author, 7 May 1997 (in the PSOE central offices).
136. European Commission, Case L 394/9, Section XI (page 10 of decision).
137. Judgment of the Court, Case C-305/89, 21/03/91.

5

Electricity: Powering Up

Structured in a similar fashion to the other empirical chapters, the first section offers a brief history of the firms—EDF (France), E.ON (Germany), SSE (UK), ENEL (Italy), and Endesa (Spain). It then considers aspects of its privatization as well as M&A developments. Given that the volume of deals in the sector out-flanks that found in the automobile and airline chapters, only the key deals will be presented. EDF's and E.ON's discussion highlights their plethora of acquisitions in the UK, continental Europe, as well as overseas. Endesa shows the firm's eventual takeover by ENEL, which occurred after E.ON was unsuccessful in its previous bid. The discussion of these main deals for all firms is particularly important because it offers the reader the foundation and reference point to better understand which firms are Alphas and Betas, and why, as discussed in Sections 5.2 and 5.3.

The second section thus performs the Global Movers and Independence Tests. It argues that EDF, E.ON, SSE, and ENEL can be considered Alphas today. Endesa, although clearly showing signs of being a world leader after its privatization, with potential to be an Alpha today, nevertheless became a Beta.

In order to understand why Alphas have become so, Section 5.3 argues that it is necessary to consider several of the variables outlined in Chapter 2. It first argues that the firms' strong domestic market position before and after privatization is important, as are managers' roles in acquiring European and global assets (including taking over other former state-owned electricity companies). It also highlights the importance of shareholders, such as global asset management firms including BlackRock. Similar to previous findings, it shows that they are more likely to have invested in the Alphas than in the Betas (Endesa) in life after privatization. Nevertheless, in order to understand why Alphas could globally expand and become world giants, factors external to the firm are necessary and sufficient. The first factor relates to liberalization (or lack thereof) in the sector, which sets the stage for what will be referred to as 'Alpha invasions' into the UK and Central and Eastern Europe before their accession to the Union, followed by expansion into other parts of the EU. A second factor of salience is Alphas' home states', as well as other states' role in terms of helping craft deals. Finally, multi-level regulatory decisions that did not block any deals, as well as lobbying pursued by firms when such decisions were made, are essential in order to understand why Alphas became global giants.

Section 5.3 closes by explaining why Endesa became a Beta, underlining the importance of external, more political, factors. It argues that while Endesa showed characteristics of becoming an Alpha—in fact, in the early part of the 2000s it was ostensibly one of the world's leading utility companies—the role of the state and the decisions of regulatory authorities are crucial in explaining why it did not. The discussion also demonstrates a clear manifestation of what I refer to as 'Alpha Wars', where Alphas competed against each other and targeted the same firm. However, such wars may actually see both combatants winning: even though E.ON and ENEL targeted Endesa, both Alphas could ultimately claim some victory in the end because the Spanish firm's assets were divided out, highlighting the positive sum nature of Alpha Wars.

5.1 Brief History of the Firm, Privatization, and Life Thereafter

This section first offers a glimpse of the history of the firms and their privat-ization, before considering the M&A as well as Joint Ventures (JVs) pursued. It starts with France's giant EDF, a firm that has ostensibly pursued the highest number of M&A on a global scale, and then turns to E.ON, SSE, and ENEL. It closes by examining Endesa, a firm eventually taken over by ENEL and whose assets were also partially sold to E.ON. Privatization transaction values are reported in USD, based on data provided by <www.privatizationbarometer. net>, keeping the discussion consistent with previous chapters. Because the M&A referred to are primarily based on data found in Bureau van Dijk's Zephyr database, and in order to ensure comparative consistency, deal values are reported in euros unless otherwise noted.

In terms of background information, and in order to contextualize the deals pursued, it is important to note that the electricity supply sector can be subdivided into three activities: generation, transmission, and distribution. Power plants generate electricity, where generators (that transform mechan-ical energy into electric power) are spun, in most cases by a steam turbine. Resources which are important in electricity generation, as discussed by Bryce (2011, 48), include coal, petroleum, natural gas, fission by nuclear fuel, as well as renewable energy such as wind and the sun. After leaving the plant, electricity's voltage is 'stepped up' at a substation and transmis-sion occurs on a grid. Once the power is 'stepped down' after coming off the grid, electricity is then distributed to homes and businesses. In a purely deregulated market, consumers can buy electricity from whichever distributor they choose.

EDF

In the wake of the Second World War, in 1946 the French government nationalized over 1,450 electricity and gas generation, transmission, and distribution companies under the single banner of *Électricité de France* (EDF).[1] By the early 1970s 'oil was the primary source of electrical power',[2] and the aftermath of the OPEC crisis of 1973 saw a change in the French strategy in order to guarantee its energy independence, where EDF focused on nuclear-powered electricity generation.[3] The early 1980s subsequently saw 'the commissioning of new nuclear power plants and the modernization of the transmission grid'.[4] In the early 1990s EDF had a dominant, virtual monopoly, position in the French market almost fully controlling generation capacity, the transmission grid, and the distribution network (Chick, 2007, 128).

In terms of its privatization, the company was (partially) sold relatively later than its counterparts in Europe, although its revenues represented some of the highest.[5] First, in November 2005 a 12.7 per cent stake of the company was sold for a value of over USD 8.4 billion. This was followed by 2.5 per cent in December 2007 for an estimated USD 5.45 billion. The state's stake in EDF remains, to this day, close to 85 per cent, as examined in more detail in Section 5.2.

The M&A pursued by the firm (when it was 100 per cent controlled by the state and after its partial privatization) can only be described as remarkable. This is because there is no region of Europe where it has not pursued deals and it has targeted many parts of the globe.

Turning to the UK, where the firm has been branded EDF Energy since 2003, the French giant has made the following notable acquisitions since the late 1990s:

- London Electricity was acquired in November 1998 from US-based Entergy Corporation for a consideration of €2.69 billion.[6]
- South Western Electricity Board (SWEB) supply business, jointly owned by US-based Southern Company and PP&L Resources, was acquired by EDF in July 1999 (through London Electricity) for €160 million.[7]
- Sutton Bridge Power Station was sold by US-based Enron Corporation in April 2000 for approximately €256 million.[8]
- Cottam Power Station was sold by the UK's Powergen in December 2000 for an estimated €631 million.[9]

- West Burton Power Station was bought from the TXU Europe Group for around €695 million in December 2001.[10]

- Eastern (the subsidiary of TXU Europe which owned the electricity distribution company in the eastern region of England) and 24Seven (the firm that managed and operated London Electricity's and Eastern's distribution network) were bought in 2001.[11]

- Seeboard Group was sold to EDF by US-based AEP in 2002.

Beyond these, EDF's major UK acquisition was British Energy (henceforth BE), the country's leading producer of nuclear power generators. Although privatized in the 1990s,[12] in 2008 the British state still held a 35.2 per cent stake. In its life after (partial) privatization at home, BE purchased the South Wales Electricity Board (SWALEC) in 1999 only to later sell to Scottish and Southern Energy. Abroad, British Energy, the Cameco Corporation (of Saskatoon, Saskatchewan, Canada), and others founded Bruce Power as a Limited Liability Partnership in 2001. But given BE's financial difficulties the LLP became a fully Canadian-owned operation in 2003. Throughout 2008 BE entered into takeover talks with some of Europe's main energy companies, including EDF, E.ON, Germany's RWE, Spain's Iberdrola, and the UK's Centrica. The firm was eventually 100 per cent acquired in January 2009 by EDF for an estimated €13.853 billion, although 20 per cent was later sold to Centrica in a deal linked to EDF's acquisition of SPE in Belgium, as discussed shortly.[13]

In 2010 one divestment in the UK was of 'EDF Energy Networks, the part of the business that owned and operated the cables and power lines that distribute electricity around London, the South East and the East of England', selling it to the Cheung Kong Group of Hong Kong.[14] As a consequence of deals, EDF Energy today forms one of the UK's 'Big Six Energy Companies', where it is the largest electricity producer with 5.7 million customers.[15]

EDF's UK expansion is reflected in other firms studied in this chapter, whose general phenomenon is more fully explained in Section 5.3 in the context of liberalization policy in the UK. This was seen when E.ON purchased Powergen and, though not directly related to the main firms examined, Scottish Power. Privatized in 1991, in its life thereafter Scottish Power acquired the Regional Electricity Company *Manweb*, supplier to Merseyside and North Wales, in 1995. It later purchased Southern Water in 1996 (later sold in 2002), only to turn west by later acquiring Pacificorp, operating as Pacific Power in Washington state, Oregon, California, and Wyoming in 2000 (later sold in 2005). That same year Scottish Power also bought Utah Power (in Utah and Idaho). But within years the firm was a takeover target of E.ON, eventually rejected by the Scottish Power board in 2005. The firm was eventually acquired by Spain's Iberdrola in 2007 for €17.2 billion,[16] creating one of the EU's largest utility companies that continued its expansion with its purchase of US-based Energy East in 2008.

Considering other parts of the EU where the French giant has made acquisitions, one sees the case of Belgium where EDF has come, gone, and then comeback once again following the British Energy acquisition. In exchange for 20 per cent of British Energy to Centrica, EDF acquired Centrica's 51 per cent stake in the Belgian electricity producer and distributor SPE (later renamed EDF Luminus) in August 2009, thereby gaining a stronghold in the Belgian market. This was years after EDF sold in 2003 its original 10 per cent stake in SPE, previously bought in 2001, claiming that Belgium was no longer considered by the French firm as a core-market.[17] Centrica, a leading British energy company that was formed following a demerger from British Gas in 1997,[18] took a controlling stake in SPE in 2005. The Belgian company almost immediately grew thereafter and shortly became Belgium's second largest power provider, just behind Electrabel which had 2.1 million customers.[19] In 2010 Dexia Banque Belgique and other shareholders sold EDF a minority stake they held in SPE (whose total value was an estimated €1.72 billion), increasing the French firm's ownership to 63.5 per cent which it holds today.[20]

Turning to Italy, in 2012 EDF took full control of Edison, a company dedicated to the generation and distribution of electricity (and also involved in gas supply services), considered the country's second largest player. In terms of EDF's previous association with Edison, in the early part of the 2000s EDF, Fiat, and Banca Intesa amongst others formed an electricity investment holding company called Italenergia. The year 2002 saw the merger between Edison, Montedison, Sondel, and Fiat Energia, all under the banner of the Edison name brand, which was taken over by Italenergia.[21] In 2005 EDF's stake would increase when 90 per cent of Edison was acquired by the electricity producer holding company called Transalpina di energia, whose two co-owners were EDF and Delmi (where Delmi was majority owned by A2A, and other shareholders included Dolomiti Energia, Mediobanca, Iren Spa, and SEL).[22] By May 2012, after buying out its partner, EDF eventually acquired 99.5 per cent of the share capital of Edison, valued at €4.611 billion.[23]

Opposite to Belgium's SPE, the case of Germany's EnBW (*Energie Baden-Württemberg*) represents EDF coming in and then, literally, taking the money and running. The Karlsruhe-based electricity manufacturer and distributor, whose generating assets included four nuclear reactors, was partly owned by the state of Baden-Württemberg. Privatization took place in the early 2000s: not dissimilar to several firms in Central and Eastern Europe (discussed later), the German state privatized to the then 100 per cent French state-owned firm. This included an initial 9 per cent stake in 2000, a further 25 per cent in 2001, and a third tranche of 4.5 per cent in 2004.[24] After both Deutsche Bank and HSBC sold EDF a minority stake in 2005, EDF attained an overall ownership of 45.01 per cent.[25] Summing the amount paid during the various transactions, EDF paid approximately more than €3.6 billion for this controlling stake in EnBW. As the decade continued, cooperation between EDF and EnBW increased. This is seen in the 2009 deals in which both firms gained joint control of Poland's Kogeneracja and Elektrownia Rybnik (ERSA), whose business activities included the generation of electricity and heat. EDF eventually gained full control of both Polish firms in 2012. Nevertheless, as discussed in more detail when we examine the role of the state in Section 5.3, EDF and EnBW eventually parted ways: in 2011 the state of Baden-Württemberg somewhat surprisingly re-acquired the 45 per cent stake of EnBW, paying EDF €4.7 billion.

When turning to Northern Europe, in 1998 EDF acquired a controlling stake in the Swedish electric power company Graninge.[26] The firm was later sold to Sweden's Sydkraft in the early 2000s, however, and became an integral asset in a significant deal between E.ON and Norway's state-owned Statkraft. The year 2007 also saw that, along with Delta NV, EDF would jointly build and operate Sloecentrale, a gas-fired combined-cycle power plant in Vlissingen-Oost, the Netherlands. The plant, in which EDF invested an estimated €550 million, was finalized in 2010 and had the 'capacity of approximately 870 megawatts which is enough to supply the needs of more than 2 million households'.[27]

Similar to E.ON and ENEL, EDF would also purchase several firms in Central and Eastern Europe that were being privatized, as seen in the following examples:

- In 1998 EDF acquired a 25 per cent stake in the privatized Austrian energy company ESTAG (*Energie Steiermark AG*). The deal was estimated at €407 million.[28]

- The Hungarian electricity supplier and distributor DÉMÁSZ (*Delmagyarorszagi Aramszolgaltato*) was privatized in 1996. A target with a total value of €288 million, EDF attained a 60.91 per cent stake in 2001 and finalized full takeover in 2006.[29]

- In the late 1990s EDF gained a 58 per cent stake of the electricity company Elektrocieplownia Krakow.[30] This increased to 94 per cent by 2009 (where the remainder was held by employees), when Poland's Treasury Ministry completed the Krakow-based firms' privatization.[31]

- In 2002, 49 per cent of Stredoslovenská Energetika, the second largest Slovakian electricity distributor, was privatized and sold to EDF for €158 million.[32] In May 2013, however, EDF announced the sale of this stake for €400 million, representing a value about two and half times the original purchase price.[33]

Turning to Latin America, in 1999 EDF acquired 23.11 per cent in the Rio de Janeiro-based electricity company, Light Serviços de Electricidade (henceforth, Light) that was privatized by the Brazilian government.[34] A year previously, Light had taken a 30 per cent stake in the electric utility Eletropaulo Metropolitana Electricidade de Sao Paulo (henceforth, Eletropaulo). Within two years of gaining a minority stake in Light, EDF attained 88.2 per cent of Light which was valued at over €1.4 billion in a share exchange with US-based firm AES Corporation. The nature of the deal was as follows: AES had increasingly taken control of Eletropaulo and both the French and US firms sought to separate the activities of Light and Electropaulo; so, in exchange for EDF's stake in Eletropaulo, AES offered EDF its shares in Light.[35] Yet, given Light's debts over the next years, coupled with EDF's strategic plan to refocus on European operations as well as its position in the US market, EDF eventually sold Light in 2006 to the Brazilian holding company Rio Minas Energia Participações.[36]

A year after selling Light, a 50/50 Joint Venture was thus signed with the Constellation Energy Group to create UniStar Nuclear Energy, set up to further develop nuclear energy in the US. Within three years, in 2010 EDF bought out Constellation's stake and became the sole owner of the Maryland-based development company. EDF's payment for this stake in UniStar consisted of €180 million in cash plus the 3.5 million shares the French giant previously held in Constellation, a firm that eventually merged with Exelon Corporation in March 2012.[37] Further north, EDF's has a strong presence in Canada through EDF EN Canada Inc., which is a subsidiary of EDF Energies Nouvelles.[38] Examples of the several renewable energy projects that have been spearheaded include those in Quebec, such the recently authorized La Mitis Wind Project. It is estimated that by the end of 2015 EDF will have invested close to CDN 2 billion in the French-speaking province.[39]

In Asia, EDF has taken over various firms and been involved in significant Joint Ventures in the area since the 2000s. For example, with regard to ownership in clean coal electricity generation, through its 100 per cent controlled subsidiary FIGLEC the French firm owns the Guangxi Laibin B Thermal power plant as well as 85 per cent of the plant's operator.[40] Since 2006 EDF has also had close to a one-fifth stake in the Shandong Zhonghua Power Company, supplying electricity to over 4.5 million customers.[41] Turning to nuclear energy, in 2008 the firm offered its worldwide expertise in the area and entered into a JV with the state-owned nuclear power station operator China Guangdong Nuclear Power Holding, forming Tiashan Nuclear Power Company which is scheduled to launch into service by 2014.[42] EDF is also present in Vietnam, owning a majority in the firm Mekong Energy Company, MECO, since 2005. MECO operates the Phu My 2.2 power plant 'which is able to produce roughly 40% of the maximum electricity demand in Vietnam'.[43]

Table 5.1. Main EDF deals (in chronological order)

Privatized Company	Date(s) of Sale	Main Mergers & Acquisitions
Électricité de France (EDF)	2005, 2007 (remains 84.00% remains state owned)	Takeover of DÉMÁSZ (privatized by Hungarian government, 1996–2009); 94% ownership of EC Krakow (privatization, Poland, 1997–2009); 38% stake in Azito Energie (Ivory Coast, 1997, but stake is later sold in 2010); 25% of ESTAG (privatization, Austria, 1998); takeover of London Electricity (1998); acquires SWEB (UK, 1999); purchase of Light (privatization, Brazil, 1999, later sold in 2006); purchase of Sutton Bridge Power Station, Cottam Power Station, and West Burton Power Station (UK, 2000–1); 45.01% of EnBW (privatization, Germany, 2001–5, but later sold to the state of Baden Württemberg in 2011); full acquisition of Edison (Italy, between 2002 and 2012); 49% stake in Stredoslovenská Energetika (privatization, Slovakia, 2002, but later sold in 2013); majority shareholder in Mekong Energy Company, MECO (2005, Vietnam); 19.6% stake in Shandong Zhonghua Power Company, SZPC (China, 2006); JV with China Guangdong Nuclear Power Holding, forming Tiashan Nuclear Power Company (2008); acquisition of British Energy (including 35% stake owned by British state, 2009); sale of 20% of British Energy, sold to Centrica (UK, 2009); acquires 63.5% stake of SPE (Belgium, 2009–10, of which 51% stake was bought from Centrica in British Energy deal); along with EnBW, joint control of Kogeneracja and ERSA (Poland, 2009; full control attained 2012); UniStar Nuclear Energy (US, 2007–10).

Elsewhere in Asia, EDF is also present in Laos where it owns 40 per cent of the Nam Theun 2 Power Company (NTPC) established in 2002.[44]

The final continent EDF has been present is Africa. For example, in the late 1990s it formed part of the consortium chosen by the Ivory Coast government to construct the combined cycle gas turbine power station Azito Energie.[45] This 35.85 per cent stake in Azito, however, was sold to the UK-based Globeleq Generation in 2010 for an undisclosed amount.[46]

Table 5.1 summarizes the main M&A and Joint Ventures that EDF has pursued as a fully state-owned enterprise as well as a partially privatized one.

E.ON

E.ON, whose name symbolizes energy (E) and illumination (ON),[47] has its roots in two German ex-state-owned enterprises, VEBA AG and VIAG AG. VIAG was founded in 1923 and VEBA in 1929, and they originally had a wide portfolio of industrial interests such as energy, chemicals, telecoms, and real estate.[48] A majority of VEBA was privatized by the Federal Republic in 1965. This was followed by two sales in 1983 and 1987, where the latter represented 25.55 per cent valued at USD 275.5 million. VIAG followed a similar process where a major stake of 60 per cent was sold in 1988 with a transaction value of USD 129.7 million.

The wake of privatization witnessed restructuring in the firms and the foundation for the two to join, forming E.ON in June 2000. Although the formation of E.ON is generally considered a merger, technically the BvD Zephyr database characterizes the deal as one where VIAG was the target that was acquired by VEBA.[49] In a deal whose value was €13.9 billion, VIAG shareholders received one VEBA share for every 2.8 VIAG shares owned. Further, VEBA acquired 10 per cent of the 25.1 per cent stake of VIAG still held by the Bavarian state. This resulted in the Bavarian State's Ministry of Finance (*Freistaat Bayern Bayerisches Staatsministerium der Finanzen*) holding around 5 per cent of E.ON throughout the 2000s. This was subsequently reduced to 1.9 per cent in mid-2010, and represents the same percentage still owned by the state as of January 2014.[50]

In their drive to concentrate on the energy sector, both VEBA and VIAG had already sold several established operations considered of tangential interest even before E.ON was formed. Four main transactions help illustrate the nature of divestments and the funds raised. First, in late 1999 VEBA entered into negotiations with the US-based cable communications operator NTL, to sell VEBA's UPC Cabelcom for €3.66 billion.[51] A month later, France's Saint Gobain acquired VEBA's building materials wholesaler Raab Karcher Baustoffe for €477 million.[52] A third example is seen in February 2000 when Bellsouth Corporation and Netherlands-based KPN paid over €9.3 billion for the mobile telecommunications operator E-Plus Mobilfunk that was owned by VEBA, RWE (a major German utility company), and Vodafone Airtouch.[53] And, finally, a month before E.ON was formed, VIAG sold its tubular and specialty glass packaging systems manufacturer Gerresheimer Glas for an estimated €216 million.[54]

Following the formation of E.ON, this overall policy of selling its non-core assets continued to be respected in the early 2000s, resulting in sizeable sums that proved essential in its global M&A drive throughout the decade. For example, in February 2001 E.ON completed the sale of its 42.5 per cent stake in Orange Communications (Switzerland) to France Télécom for close to €1.6 billion, increasing the French ex-SOE's ownership in the mobile phone operator to 85 per cent.[55] That same month a 45 per cent stake in Viag Interkom, at the time Germany's fourth ranked mobile phone operator with 2 million customers, was sold to British Telecommunications (BT) for approximately €11.4 billion.[56] In 2002 British Petroleum acquired E.ON's Veba Oel, whose activities included petrol refining services as well as operating the largest chain of service stations in Germany through the firm Aral: 51 per cent was first acquired for €2.83 billion, followed by the remainder for €3.3 billion.[57]

With plenty of cash in hand, the Germans marched to the UK. One of its first major acquisitions was of the electricity generator and distributor Powergen, not dissimilar to EDF which spearheaded some of its first European acquisitions in the UK. In terms of its history, Powergen—which is today rebranded as E.ON UK—was privatized in 1991 (60 per cent) and 1995 (40 per cent). In its own life after privatization, it formed a consortium with NRG Energy and Morrison Knudsen, and in 1995 purchased MIBRAG, a brown coal producer in former East Germany. Powergen then acquired East Midlands Electricity in 1998. Despite these initial acquisitions, Powergen (as well as its US subsidiary LG&E Energy which it acquired in 2000) was ultimately purchased by E.ON in July 2002 for a total consideration of €14.84 billion.[58] As discussed in Section 5.3, the deal saw shareholders making significant profits.

As the decade continued, more UK deals were signed. After acquiring TXU Europe Group's remaining electricity generation assets in the UK, in 2003 Midlands Electricity was targeted. The latter deal, valued at GBP 1.2 billion, led to the merger of both East Midlands and Midlands Electricity in 2004, rebranded as Central Networks which by the end of the decade would become 'UK's second largest electricity distributor and operat(or) of the regional grid that covers the UK Midlands'.[59] Finally, in 2008 E.ON acquired a 50 per cent stake (along with Denmark's Dong Energy) in the wind farm operator London Array, which was sold by Shell for an undisclosed amount.[60] Given its purchases, E.ON joins EDF as one of the 'big-six' energy companies in the UK, where it 'supplies energy to 5.3 million homes and business across the nation'.[61]

After Powergen, E.ON took a sojourn back home between 2002 and 2003. It acquired the leading natural gas distributor Ruhrgas, a sizeable deal which had an estimated total value of €10 billion.[62] A 96.6 per cent control of the Munich-based energy supplier Thüga was also completed in 2004, a firm whose value was an estimated €4.45 billion.[63]

Turning to Scandinavia, one of its most important (if not complicated) acquisitions in the 2000s was of Swedish Sydkraft, the country's second largest electricity producer and distributor. After gaining less than 30 per cent control in 2000, E.ON gained almost full control of the Swedish firm in 2001, except for the 35.7 per cent owned by the Norwegian state utility Statkraft, which refused to sell its part at the time.[64] E.ON would sell Statkraft an additional 8.9 per cent of Sydkraft in 2002, bringing the Norwegian's stake to 44.6 per cent.[65] Sydkraft's assets increased in 2003 when EDF sold its stake in Swedish electricity producer Graninge, to Sydkraft.[66] After Graninge was purchased, Sydkraft was rebranded 'E.ON Sverige', and continued to be roughly owned 55 per cent by E.ON, and 45 per cent by Statkraft. In a deal rumoured since October 2007, by December 2008 E.ON consolidated its position in Sweden through a €4.495

billion asset-swap agreement with Statkraft: E.ON gained control of Statkraft's 44.6 per cent stake in E.ON Sverige (thereby becoming the sole owner of a firm valued at approximately €10.1 billion) and, in exchange, Statkraft attained shares in E.ON that represented a stake of 2.74 per cent of the German firm (with a value of €2.18 billion) and took over more than sixty power and district heating plants in Sweden, Germany, and the UK.[67]

In other west European deals, in May 2005 and June 2005 E.ON purchased the fifth largest power company in the Netherlands, NRE Energie, in a deal valued at €76.5 million.[68] This was acquired from the city of Eindhoven and other Dutch local authorities, securing 275,000 electricity and gas customers (as will be seen, an original agreement whereby Endesa would take over NRE was squashed). Finally, after an unsuccessful takeover bid of Endesa in 2006 (discussed in Section 5.3), E.ON nevertheless reached an agreement with ENEL to take over some of its assets (as well as others belonging to Endesa). This included Electrica de Viesgo (which ENEL had previously acquired from Endesa). The German firm later strengthened its Italian market position when in 2009 it gained 100 per cent control of MPE Energia, a Milan-based electricity company.[69]

Similar to EDF, several acquisitions were also pursued in Central and Eastern Europe, including:

- In 2003 it gained close to an over 84 per cent controlling stake in the Czech generator and distributor Jihoceska Energetika from Austria's state-owned Energie AG Oberösterreich, as well as the Czech government-controlled operator involved in generation, transmission, and distribution, CEZ.[70]

- Between 2002 and 2004 E.ON attained 98 per cent control of the Hungarian electricity distributor *Eszak-Dunantuli Aramszolgaltato* (Edasz), where the target's total value was estimated at €238 million.[71] Within two years, E.ON also acquired the gas business of the Hungarian firm MOL.

- In 2005 a 67 per cent stake was attained in two regional utilities in Bulgaria—EDC Gorna Oryahovitza and Varna—privatized by the Bulgarian government, accounting for around 25 per cent of the Bulgaria's market.[72]

- In 2005 it bought a controlling 51 per cent stake (for an estimated €99.73 million) in the electricity generator and distributor Electrica Moldova, which was privatized by the Romanian government.[73]

- In 2006 a 49 per cent stake in the Czech natural gas distribution company Pražská plynárenská (PP) was purchased from RWE for an unknown value.[74] The company was subsequently jointly controlled by E.ON and the City of Prague, until it was finally fully taken over by E.ON in 2010.

During the latter part of the decade, however, there was a change of strategy where some of E.ON's domestic assets were either swapped with other firms, or simply sold off. Notable deals in this regard were, for example, a 2009 swap with Electrabel, where E.ON would acquire some of Electrabel's assets (such as in biomass power stations in Belgium) and, in exchange, E.ON would reduce generation capacity in Germany by granting Electrabel 'drawing rights from a number of its nuclear power plants in Germany'.[75] This was followed by the 100 per cent sale of Thüga for €2.9 billion in 2009.[76] Thereafter, the sale of its high voltage network, Transpower, took place. Announced in 2009, Transpower attracted the interest of several bidders, including ACS (the Spanish construction company that owned around 15 per cent of the Spanish giant Iberdrola), Allianz, and the UK-based National Grid. The acquirer eventually chosen, TenneT Holding BV which managed the national transmission grid of the Netherlands, purchased Transpower for €885 million.[77]

The sell-off of domestic assets served as a prelude for a new plan post-2010 that consisted of selling off some of its assets abroad, increasing investment in markets where it sought a stronger position, and entering into other markets in which it was previously absent. Examples of sell-offs abroad which generated large sums included the 2011 sale of UK-based Central Networks (a product of the merger of East Midlands and Midlands Electricity) to US-based PPL Corporation of Allentown for an estimated €4.6 billion.[78] PPL had previously bought E.ON US's power gas business in 2010, for an estimated

Table 5.2. Main E.ON deals (in chronological order)

Privatized Company	Date(s) of Sale	Main Mergers & Acquisitions
VEBA and VIAG (E. ON)	1965, 1986, 1987 (remains 1.9% state owned)	VEBA and VIAG join forces to form E.ON (2000). Sale of non-core assets including its stakes in Orange Communications, Viag Interkom, and Veba Oel (2001–2). E.ON gains full control of Sydkraft/E.ON Sverige (Sweden, 2000–8); acquires Powergen (UK, 2002, and subsequently other UK assets such as TXU's electricity generation assets in the UK, 2002, and Midlands, 2003); purchases Ruhrgas (Germany, 2003); acquires an 84% stake in Jihoceska Energetika (Czech Republic, 2003); takes full control of Thüga (2004), but sells it in 2009; acquires Edasz (Hungary, 2004); purchases a 67% stake EDC Gorna Oryahovitza and Varna (privatized by Bulgarian government, 2005); acquires a 51% stake in Electrica Moldova (privatization, Romania, 2005); acquires NRE Energie (privatization, the Netherlands, 2005); acquired MOL (Hungary, 2006); purchases Pražská plynárenská (Czech Republic, 2006–10); failed takeover attempt of Spain's Endesa in 2006, but E.ON acquires several Endesa assets when ENEL/Acciona take over Endesa; attains a 69% stake in OGK-4 (Russia, 2007); acquires power plants from Electrabel (Belgium, 2009); sale of Transpower (high voltage network, Germany, 2010); purchases a 10% stake in MPX Energia (Brazil, 2012).

$7.6 billion.[79] E.ON focused on increasing its market presence abroad by starting new wind farms in Posen (Poland) and Kergrist (France); spending over €400 million to develop an efficient power plant in Hungary; and, outside of Europe, investing €6.6 million in Vietnam in order 'to reduce the greenhouse-gas emissions of Nam Son landfill near Hanoi'.[80] By 2012 a first big leap was taken into South America when it entered in an agreement with Brazil's MPX Energia to develop renewable sources based power generation and taking 10 per cent of the firm for an estimated BRL850 million.[81] The year 2011 also saw commissioning of combined cycle gas turbine power plants in Russia. This increased its presence in a state where it had already been present since 2007 when it attained a controlling (69.34 per cent) stake in the Moscow-based generating firm OGK-4 for €4.1 billion.[82] Table 5.2 summarizes the main deals pursued by E.ON.

SSE

Scottish and Southern Energy (SSE) is the product of the merger in 1998 between ex-SOEs Scottish Hydro-Electric and Southern Electric. Both Southern Electric and Scottish Hydro were operating since 1947: the former distributed electricity in the south of England while the latter distributed and generated in Scotland.[83] With the Thatcher government privatization of the twelve regional distribution companies, both were 100 per cent sold in the early 1990s: Southern Electric's flotation was in December 1990 for a value of USD 1.248 million, while Scottish Hydro was sold some months later in June 1991 with a transaction value of USD 741.52 million.[84]

The merger between the two took place in 1998, at which time Scottish and Southern Energy was formed, a firm whose name would be rebranded succinctly to 'SSE' in 2010. The 1998 merger which had an estimated value of over €3.8 billion can best be described as a 'nil premium all share merger', where shareholders of both Scottish Hydro-Electric and Southern Electric received one share of Scottish and Southern Electric for every existing share previously owned.[85] After completion of the merger, Scottish Hydro-Electric shareholders held approximately 45 per cent of SSE, while Southern Electric 55 per cent.

Most of SSE's acquisitions since its formation have, somewhat conservatively, been concentrated in the UK and the Republic of Ireland. This lies in some contrast to EDF and E.ON seen previously, and ENEL and Endesa to be seen later, which expanded well beyond one specific geographic area.

In its first major deals in 2000 SSE acquired the retail supplier of energy and gas, South Wales Electricity Board (SWALEC), from British Energy. The vendor, concerned with concentrating on power generation, sold SWALEC to SSE for an estimated €362 million.[86] In 2004 the Ferrybridge and Fiddlers Ferry power stations (both coal-fired power plant operators) were purchased by SSE from US-based American Electric Power (AEP) for an estimated value of €205 million in order to allow SSE to 'diversify its generation base'.[87] This took place in the wake of the 100 per cent purchase the year before of Medway Power (a combined cycle gas turbine power station on the Isle of Grain in Kent), bought for an estimated €284 million from EDF Energy and AES Medway Electric.[88] Other relatively small purchases throughout the mid to late 2000s included: that of UK-based Atlantic Energy and Gas (for a value of €136 million[89]); a gas-fired power station in Fife (for around €18 million[90]); a 7.5 per cent stake in the London-based solar energy solutions provider Solarcentury (for slightly more than €1.43 million[91]); the coal-fired power plant near Newport Wales, Uksmouth Power Company, sold by Welsh Power (for €31.4 million[92]); and the street lighting operator Seeboard Trading that was acquired from EDF (for €12.4 million[93]).

Since the mid-2000s SSE has diversified its portfolio abroad, particularly in Ireland. For example, in 2006 it pursued a 50:50 Joint Venture with the Irish government-owned Electricity Supply Board (ESB) for the construction of the Marchwood natural gas-fired combined cycle power station in Southampton.[94] Links to Ireland continued throughout the decade when in 2008 it purchased the Dublin-based wind farm operator Airtricity, for an estimated €1.455 billion.[95] Within four years SSE increased its Irish investment by purchasing Endesa Ireland Ltd, sold by ENEL (which had taken it over when Endesa was acquired). Its acquisition and planned future investment in power plants in Wexford totalled €488 million.[96] Continuing its commitment to renewables, in the early 2010s SSE added to its wind farm portfolio in the UK by acquiring Keadby wind farm for an undisclosed amount.[97]

Given its strength in the British market, it is considered 'the second largest big six energy supplier in the UK, with 9.6 million customers and the UK's largest generator from renewable sources'.[98] It is also considered the largest renewable energy firm in the UK.[99] Table 5.3 summarizes the main developments in SSE.

Table 5.3. Main SSE Deals (in chronological order)

Privatized Company	Date(s) of Sale	Main Mergers & Acquisitions
Scottish Hydro Electric & Southern Electric	1991 (Scottish Hydro); 1990 (Southern Electric)	Scottish Hydro merged with Southern Electric to form *Scottish and Southern Energy* (SSE, UK, 1998). SSE acquired SWALEC energy supply (2000); acquired Medway Power (UK, 2003); purchases Ferrybridge and Fiddlers Ferry power stations and Atlantic Energy and Gas (UK, 2004); 50:50 Joint Venture with Ireland's Electricity Supply Board (ESB) to construct Marchwood Power Station (UK, 2006); purchases Irish wind farm business Airtricity Holdings (Ireland, 2008); acquires Uskmouth power station (UK, 2009); purchases Keadby wind farm project (UK, 2011); acquires Endesa Ireland Ltd (2012).

ENEL

ENEL (*Ente Nazionale per l'energia Elettrica*, or, the National Agency for Electric Energy) was established in 1962, and was the country's principal company in terms of generation, transmission, and distribution of electricity.[100] Starting in 1963 the firm had established the 'National Dispatching Centre', where operations were centralized around the firm that subsequently absorbed other electricity companies over the next thirty years, which totalled over 1,250 by 1995. Again, not dissimilar to EDF, the oil crisis resulted in the firm building nuclear power plants in the 1970s in order to reduce reliance on both oil and hydroelectricity. The mid-1980s witnessed a focus on renewable energy (with the wind power plant in Upper Nurra), but further development in nuclear energy was suspended after Italians voted against this in November 1987 in the wake of Chernobyl.

ENEL was sold in several tranches from the late 1990s. First, was the IPO on the Milan Stock exchange of over 32.4 per cent, which generated over USD 17 billion.[101] This was followed by sales in 2003 (6.6 per cent), 2004 (19.6 per cent), and 2005 (9.3 per cent), whose combined transaction value was over USD 16.9 billion. Successive small partial sales coupled with a major capital increase of €8 billion in March 2009 meant that the stakes held by the Ministry of Economy and Finance (Ministero dell'Economia e delle Finanze, or, MEF) were reduced to 13.9 per cent by December 2009.[102] However, MEF's direct ownership eventually increased to slightly over 30 per cent in 2010, a stake it still holds today which is related to the sale of the grid, Terna, as discussed in more detail here and in Section 5.3.

In terms of its first major acquisition in the sector, in 2002 ENEL acquired Endesa's subsidiary, Electrica de Viesgo. By paying an estimated €2.147 billion for the Spanish firm which operated in the generation and distribution of electricity, ENEL became 'the fifth largest operator in the Spain's power market ... [and] the first foreign utility to take full control of a Spanish utility'.[103]

The mid-2000s witnessed a focus on Central and Eastern Europe and Russia, in some cases not dissimilar to EDF and E.ON that targeted firms on the privatization block. Deals of significance include:

- A controlling stake (73 per cent) of the Maritza East III (*Tec Maritsa Iztok 3*) power plant in Bulgaria, a target whose total value was estimated at €350 million.[104] In a deal starting in 2003 and completed in 2006, this was purchased from US-based Entergy Corporation, while the Bulgarian government continued to retain 27 per cent.

- A majority stake in two electricity distributors from Romania that had an approximate 20 per cent of the market share in Romania—Electrica Banat and Electrica Dobrogea—was purchased in April 2005. ENEL did so by paying €111.8 million for 51 per cent of the privatized firms' shares, assuming the companies' debts of around €100 million, and promising to invest over €1 billion in the two firms by 2025.[105]

- A second acquisition completed in 2005 was the electricity generator Slovenské Elektrárne (SE), privatized by the Slovakian government which was the 'largest producer in Slovakia and second-largest in Central and Eastern Europe'.[106] In a deal which took around five years to complete, the government initiated the sale of less than 50 per cent of SE in 2001, only to see its laws change in December 2003 which allowed for majority stakes to be sold in companies operating in monopoly sectors. As a consequence, several companies (including CEZ, which is owned by the Czech state) made bids, with ENEL being eventually chosen. In a deal that saw ENEL agree to pay a total value of €840 million for a 66 per cent stake in SE, the Italian firm also promised to invest around €2 billion between until 2013.[107]

- In 2006 ENEL acquired a 49.5 per cent stake in the Moscow-based electricity distributor Rusenergosbyt, which today has over 200,000 customers in over fifty regions of the Federation.[108] This stake was purchased from the energy investment holding company ESN Group for an estimated €88 million.[109] A complementary acquisition took place a year later in 2007, when ENEL acquired 29.99 per cent of the Russian electricity-generating company OGK-5, a target whose estimated overall value is €4.23 billion.[110]

- A final privatized acquisition in 2008 was seen when the Italians revisited Romania and purchased the electricity distributor Electrica Mutenia Sud (EMS).[111] In the first stage, €395 million was paid for a 50 per cent stake in the company, and this was followed by a further 17.5 per cent stake via a capital increase of €425 million. ENEL also promised further investment of €1 billion in the firm until 2023.

During the same time period it was expanding into Central and Eastern Europe and Russia, ENEL also started the sell-off of Terna (*Rete Elettrica Nazionale*), which operated the country's national electricity grid. The first tranche in 2004 saw 50 per cent of Terna floated on the Milan stock exchange in a transaction valued at €1.7 billion.[112] A second tranche saw 29.99 per cent sold to Cassa Depositi e Prestiti (CDP), the government-controlled body engaged in savings and loans. This stake was sold for €1.315 billion in March 2005, while 13.86 per cent was sold that same month to Italian investors for €568.3 million.[113] The remainder was sold in February 2012 for a consideration of over €280.5 million.[114] As examined in Section 5.3, the sale of Terna to CDP helps us better understand the somewhat complicated transaction in which Italy's Finance Ministry (MEF) eventually attained direct control of over 30 per cent of ENEL in 2010, a somewhat rare case of a state reducing, and then increasing, its direct stake in a firm after privatization.

The end of the 2000s saw not only the Italian giant's takeover of Spain's Endesa, but also a focus on increasing cooperation with EDF. Specifically, in 2009 it signed a JV with EDF called Sviluppo Nucleare Italia, which represented a return to nuclear power generation in Italy.[115] The return was short-lived, however, given the ban placed by the government on nuclear energy after the Japanese tsunami and an eventual 2011 referendum where Italians rejected its further use.[116]

Outside of Europe, ENEL acquired Utah-based geothermal power generation firm AMP Resources. Valued at €67.65 million, the 2007 deal carried out through ENEL North America, which had been operating renewable energy plants since 2000, represented ENEL's 'entry into the US geothermal market'.[117] What would eventually become a global leader in renewable energy, ENEL Green Power saw its IPO on the Borsa Italiana in late 2010, with an overall value of €2.6 billion.[118] Examples of deals ENEL Green Power pursued include that of wind farms in Greece and a Joint Venture with Japan's Sharp Corporation, called 3Sun, where €210 million was invested to build solar farms throughout the 2010s.[119] In the latter, both invested around €320 million to build a photovoltaic factory in Sicily and to make use of the panels manufactured there in solar farms by the end of 2016.

Table 5.4 summarizes ENEL's main deals.

Table 5.4. Main ENEL Deals (in chronological order)

Privatized Company	Date(s) of Sale	Main Mergers & Acquisitions
ENEL	1999, 2003, 2004, 2005 (31.24% remains state owned)	ENEL acquires Slovenské Elektrárne (privatized by Slovakian government, 2001–5); purchases Viesgo (subsidiary of Endesa, Spain, 2002); takeover of Maritza East III plant (Bulgaria, 2003–6); sale of Terna (Italian National Grid, 2004–12); acquires 51% of Electrica Banat and Dobrogea (privatization, Romania, 2005); purchases 49.5% of Rusenergosbyt (Russia, 2006); takeover of AMP Resources (US, 2007); acquires 30% of OGK-5 (Russia, 2007); purchases EMS (privatization, Romania, 2008); takeover of Endesa (Spain, 2007–9, including strong presence in Latin America that followed); Joint Venture with EDF, Sviluppo Nucleare Italia (2009, but abandoned in 2011); IPO, ENEL Green Power (2010); JV with Sharp Corporation, 3Sun (2010).

Endesa

Endesa (*Empresa Nacional de Electricidad*, or, The National Electric Company) is historically Spain's principal electricity generator and distributor, while the transmission grid has been controlled by a separate partly state-owned firm, REE (or, *Red Eléctrica de España*). Endesa was founded in 1944 and housed within Spain's INI, and, before its privatization, the SEPI (Sociedad Estatal de Participaciones Industriales, which the INI was renamed to in the 1990s).[120] Endesa was the leading producer of electricity energy ahead of others such as Union Fenosa, Sevillana de Electricidad, Hidro-Cantabrico, Gesa, and the Basque-based Iberdrola (a product of the merger between Iberduero and Hidrola in 1992). It was also Spain's leading producer of coal, representative of close to half of its production, which was used in its power plants. As part of INI's larger strategy of consolidation of its enterprises in the sector, in 1983 Endesa acquired a number of Spanish firms related to energy production (including ENHER, GESA, UNELCO, and ENCASUR) as well as three nuclear power plants.

Endesa's privatization can be broadly seen in two main phases: the first was the minority sale of more than 36 per cent of the firm, pursued by the Spanish Socialists in 1988, 1994, 1995, and 1996, where overall revenues generated totalled more than USD 2.1 billion.[121] Second, most of the remainder of the firm was sold after the PP government led by Aznar won the 1996 elections, with sales in 1996, 1997, and 1998 for a total estimated value of over USD 11 billion. When the remaining state's 2.95 per cent stake was sold during the 2007 takeover by ENEL/Acciona, the state had divested completely.

Even as a partially privatized firm throughout the early 1990s it acquired several of its main Spanish competitors, including Hidroeléctrica de Cataluña in 1993, as well as Fecsa and Sevillana de Electricidad in 1996. By the end of the decade, the firm had Latin America in its sights, using funds from its privatization to target the Chilean giant Enersis of which it gained a 64 per cent controlling stake in 1999.[122] By becoming a majority shareholder it thus effectively controlled other firms acquired by Enersis between 1992 and 1996, including Edesur in Buenos Aires, Edelnor from Lima, and Cerj from Rio de Janeiro. Through Enersis, Endesa then purchased a 60 per cent controlling stake in Endesa–Chile in May 1999, a target with an estimated value of €5.7 billion.[123] By default, Endesa acquired firms Endesa–Chile bought between 1992 and 1997, which included Argentina's Central Costanera S.A. and Hidroeléctrica El Chocón S.A., Peru's Edegel, Brazil's Centrais Elétricas Cachoeira Dourada, and Colombia's Central Hidroeléctrica de Betania and Emgesa. In so doing, it became the leading EU-based electric company with operations in Latin America.

The 2000s witnessed a re-focus on Europe, but started with a lack of success. In 2000 it had agreed to the takeover of the Netherlands municipality-owned Regionale Energie Maatschappij Utrecht (REMU) and NRE Energie. For a price of €1.15 billion, REMU represented 'the fourth-largest energy distributor in the Netherlands... [which] owns and operates a gas and electricity network in the province of Utrecht, has 490,000 electricity clients and 364,000 gas clients, as well as a heating-distribution network with 38,000 clients'.[124] However, both deals were ultimately called off in 2002. Later, REMU was taken over by Netherlands-based Eneco, while NRE was acquired by E.ON (explained in more detail in Section 5.3).

Yet, M&A success was soon to return, with a revamped focus on the Mediterranean region. In 2001 it led a consortium that acquired Elettrogen, the second most important electricity generator in Italy at the time. The consortium, which included Banco Santander Central Hispano and the Italian utility firm ASM Brescia, took on Elettrogen's €1.06 billion debt and paid the vendor, ENEL, €2.6 billion in cash.[125] This would complement a later purchase in Italy when, with Foster Wheeler Italiana, it acquired joint control of Centro Energia Ferrara and Centro Energia Teverola in 2006. And in 2000 Endesa was also successful in its 30 per cent takeover of electricity generator Société nationale d'électricité et de thermique (SNET), whose stake would rise in 2004 to 65 per cent. This combined stake of SNET was sold by Charbonnages de France for an estimated €592 million.[126] As a measure of its successful acquisition in European space and abroad, by the mid-2000s Endesa was thus ranked as one of the world's leading utilities in the Forbes list 2006.[127]

The sale of Endesa's stake in SNET to E.ON in 2008, however, reflects how the Spanish giant was eventually taken over, a process which can best be denominated as an 'Alpha War', as discussed more fully in Section 5.3.

Table 5.5. Main Endesa Deals (in chronological order)

Privatized Company	Date(s) of Sale	Main Mergers & Acquisitions
Endesa	Several Public Offers between 1988 and 1998	Endesa acquires Hidroeléctrica de Cataluña (Spain, 1993), Fecsa and Sevillana de Electricidad (1996); purchases 64% of Enersis (Chile, 1997–9); through Enersis, Endesa purchased Endesa–Chile (May 1999); acquires Elettrogen (2001, Italy); failed takeover of NRE and REMU (2002, the Netherlands); 65% stake in SNET (France, 2000–4, but in 2008 SNET was acquired by E.ON); with Foster Wheeler Italiana, acquires joint control of Centro Energia Ferrara and Centro Energia Teverola (Italy, 2006); E.ON's proposed acquisition of Endesa fails (2006); Endesa is taken over by ENEL and Spain's Acciona (2007); ENEL buys out Acciona's stake and ENEL becomes the global ultimate owner of Endesa (2009).

Highlighting the political factors at play that help explain the Spanish titan's takeover, Section 5.3 will demonstrate how from the mid-2000s onwards the firm was targeted three times, eventually taken over by ENEL and Spanish renewable energy and construction firm Acciona in 2007, only to have ENEL acquire Acciona's stake in 2009. Ironically, as much as the Spanish state sought to retreat from the economy with full privatization of its crown jewels, Endesa's controlling shareholder today is the Italian state. This is examined in the next section, which considers which firms can be considered Alphas or Betas today.

Table 5.5 summarizes Endesa's main deals, including its eventual takeover.

5.2 Determining Whether a Firm is an Alpha or a Beta

As in the previous empirical chapters, this section is concerned about determining which firms are an Alpha or a Beta based on the Global Movers Test as well as the Independence Test outlined in the opening two chapters of the book. Results for both parts of the Global Movers Test are presented, examining Forbes 2000 data from 2014 (in order to gain an understanding of the firms' strength vis-à-vis international peers) as well as the Bureau van Dijk's Amadeus data on European firms (to see how the firms rank against European peers). Thereafter, the results of the Independence Test are given, where we examine whether or not the privatized firm in question has been taken over by another firm after its privatization. The results will indicate that EDF, E.ON, ENEL, and SSE are Alphas, while Spain's Endesa can be considered a Beta.

Global Movers Test

In the first part of the Global Movers Test, analysis is made of the latest Forbes 2000 list (2014). As discussed earlier, in order for a firm to be considered an Alpha, it must appear on the Forbes 2000 list today, which helps demonstrate that it is a leading global giant. In their analysis of this sector they refer to as 'Electric Utilities', which includes both electricity and gas companies, it is clear that it is home to one of the highest number of firms which are on the Forbes 2000 list—eighty-three firms from around the globe, seventeen of which are from the EU. Table 5.6 highlights which firms discussed in the previous section are found on the Forbes list and their ranking within the sector.

EDF, ENEL, and E.ON are not only on the Forbes 2000 list, but also rank as the top three of all companies in the electric utilities sector in 2014. Highlighting the EU's dominance, Spain's Iberdrola is ranked fourth. Immediately following the four European giants are several US firms: Duke Energy,

Table 5.6. Privatized Electricity Companies Studied on Forbes 2000 List, 2014

Company	Country	Ranking of the Company in the Forbes 2000 List	Sectoral Ranking
EDF	France	50/2000	1/83
ENEL	Italy	71/2000	2/83
E.ON	Germany	113/2000	3/83
SSE	UK	336/2000	10/83
Endesa	Spain	Not Ranked	Not Ranked

Source: Forbes 2000 Index, 2014 <http://www.forbes.com/global2000/list/> [accessed 6 June 2014]

Exelon, Southern Company, NextEra Energy, and Dominion Resources. SSE immediately follows Dominion, ranking a respectable tenth place. While Endesa is absent from the list, other EU firms found within the top twenty-five in the sector include those such as GDF Suez and RWE.

To see how the firms ranked compared to other European giants, BvD's Amadeus data was examined for the second part of the Global Movers Test. In a similar vein to the previous empirical chapters, the cut-off point of 'top 1 per cent' was ascertained by performing a search on all of the active companies in the EU-27, with a primary NACE Rev. 2 code 351 (electric power generation, transmission, and distribution) having accounts available in the latest year where there was complete data, 2012. Given the multitude of M&A between electric and natural gas utilities, the search also included companies with NACE Rev. 2 code 352 (manufacture of gas, and distribution of gaseous fuels through mains). As the number of firms found in the Amadeus search of NACE Rev. 2 coded firms of 351 and 352 yielded 23,022 firms in the sector, in order to be considered an Alpha a firm has to be ranked within the top 230 of all companies when analysing the various metrics.[128]

Table 5.7 presents the results of the comparative analysis of the firms, and shows their ranking (out of the top 100 firms) regarding each respective metric. The results indicate the high ranking of all of the firms that are studied when compared to their European counterparts. The main three—E.ON, ENEL, and EDF—generally hold within the top five rankings of the various dimensions, representative of being the cream of the European crop. SSE, while relatively lower, is still well within the cut-off point. Endesa also ranks highly when compared to its European peers; however, having not passed the first dimension of the Global Movers Test (appearing on the Forbes 2000 index), nor the Independence Test that follows, means that it cannot be considered to have attained the thresholds of being an Alpha.

Table 5.7. The European Power Giants, 2012

Company name	Operating revenue (turnover) mil EUR	Total assets mil EUR		Shareholders funds mil EUR		Number of employees	
2012	Rank (Amongst Top 100 Firms in EU-27)		Rank		Rank		Rank
E.ON (Germany)	143,380	1	140,426	4	41,950	3	74,811	3
GDF SUEZ (France)	99,552	2	205,498	2	59,745	1	236,156	1
ENEL (Italy)	86,021	3	171,656	3	53,158	2	74,610	4
EDF (France)	78,180	4	250,118	1	25,858	6	154,730	2
RWE (Germany)	52,638	5	88,202	6	16,437	9	71,419	5
IBERDROLA (Spain)	34,819	6	96,816	5	34,409	4	31,338	7
ENDESA (Spain)	33,933	7	58,778	8	26,741	5	22,995	9
SSE (UK)	33,441	8	24,324	13	3,970	26	19,795	11
CENTRICA (UK)	29,523	9	25,951	11	7,089	15	38,642	6
VATTENFALL (Sweden)	20,749	10	61,566	7	17,062	8	25,131	8

Source: Amadeus

The Independence Test

With regard to the Independence Test[129], one sees today that 84.00 per cent of EDF and 31.24 per cent of ENEL is still owned by the French and Italian states, respectively. Given the dimensions of the test outlined earlier in the book, 'Exception 1' to the Independence Test will be invoked with both firms, considering that the state owns more than 25 per cent. The phenomenon of energy companies still having important stakes owned by the state is indeed not uncommon in Europe, as seen in the cases of Vattenfall which is 100 per cent owned by the Swedish state while the Norwegian state controls Statkraft.[130] While the state owned 10 per cent of E.ON during the 2000s, by 2014 this was lowered to a 1.9 per cent stake, paling in comparison to that seen in France and Italy. If we consider the net incomes generated by these firms, this effectively translates into large Treasury revenues for both the French and Italian states, in particular, with millions also being generated for the state of Bavaria: in 2012 net income for EDF was €3.136 billion, followed by E.ON at €2.641 billion, and ENEL at €1.550 billion.[131] When turning to SSE, no state ownership remains, meaning that none of its estimated net income of €577 million went back to the state.

With regard to Endesa, in terms of the evolution of its ownership structure after privatization, it was eventually taken over by ENEL in different stages between 2007 and 2009. The Italian firm attained its first 9.99 per cent stake in February 2007, which increased to 24.99 per cent by March 2007. By October that year, its ownership increased to 67.05 per cent and within two years it attained Acciona's shares in June 2009, therefore taking a controlling 92.06 per cent of the firm which it holds today (where the remainder of Endesa is traded on the stock exchange). In none of the cases of the five main firms does a family with historical relationship with the firm own stakes in 2014, according to the Amadeus database.

Although not forming a part of the five firms fully studied in the book, we can apply the tests to other firms seen in Section 5.1 in order to demonstrate the classification scheme's versatility. For example, one could argue that Scottish Power, a firm that had a chance to become an Alpha, can be considered a Beta precisely because it attains, today, a BvD Independence Ranking of D: it lost its shareholder independence when it was acquired in 2007 by Spain's Iberdrola, a firm which thus became Scottish Power's global ultimate owner.[132] It would therefore fail the Independence Test and, on this dimension alone, be considered a Beta. The test can also be applied to Iberdrola: it appears on the 2014 Forbes list, ranks highly amongst its European peers (see Table 5.7), and also attains a BvD Independence ranking of A$^+$ and can, therefore, be considered an Alpha.[133]

Table 5.8. Summary of Independence Test Findings for Electricity Companies

Privatized Company	BvD Independence Ranking	Exception 1: Does the state still own more than 25% of the firm?	Exception 2: Does a family with a historical relationship with the firm own more than 25%?	Has the firm been taken over by another firm during or after its privatization? If so, which firm is the Global Ultimate Owner?	Given exceptions, did the firm pass the test?
E.ON	A$^+$	No (but state still holds 1.9%)	No	No	Yes
EDF	D	Yes—84%	No	No	Yes
ENEL	B$^+$	Yes—31.2%	No	No	Yes
SSE	A$^+$	No	No	No	Yes
Endesa	D	No	No	Yes, Endesa was taken over by ENEL after its privatization between 2007 and 2009	No

Table 5.9. Summary of Empirical Tests to Determine Electricity Alphas and Betas

Firm	Global Movers Test, 1st Dimension: Is the Firm on Forbes List?	Global Movers Test, 2nd Dimension: Is the Firm Ranked as a Leading European Firm Amongst its Peers?	Given Exceptions, Did the Firm Pass the Independence Test (If Not, Which Company is the GUO)?	Alpha or Beta?
E.ON	Yes	Yes	Yes	Alpha
EDF	Yes	Yes	Yes	Alpha
ENEL	Yes	Yes	Yes	Alpha
SSE	Yes	Yes	Yes	Alpha
Endesa	No	Yes	No (Global Ultimate Owner of Endesa is ENEL)	Beta

Table 5.8 summarizes the findings of the Independence Test for the five firms studied in the book.

Taking all the information together, Table 5.9 offers a summary of the empirical tests to determine whether or not a firm is an Alpha or a Beta, concluding that EDF, E.ON, ENEL, and SSE are Alphas, while Endesa is a Beta.

5.3 Explaining Why Firms Become Alphas and Betas

This section considers the factors of value in explaining why the ex-SOEs became Alphas and Betas. It first comparatively analyses all of the Alphas

Initial conditions (X1)   Intervening variables (X2)   Outcome variable (Y)

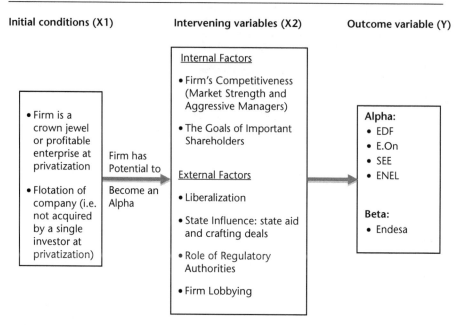

Figure 5.1. The Second Model: How an Electricity Company May Become an Alpha or a Beta (Y) Based on Initial Conditions at Privatization (X1) and Intervening Variables Post-Privatization (X2)

(EDF, E.ON, SSE, and ENEL). It then turns to the only Beta, Endesa, which was the target of two Alphas, E.ON and ENEL.

Because none of the five firms was a loss-making firm taken over by a single investor when privatized, the theoretical conceptualization outlined in the second model in Chapter 2 frames the discussion of the section. As in the other empirical chapters, Figure 5.1 offers the reader a slightly modified version of the second model, highlighting which firms are Alphas and Betas based on Section 5.2's results (Y, the outcome variable).

Explaining the Alphas

Section 5.1 examined that with regard to initial conditions (X1) the Alphas were highly profitable crown jewels that were successfully floated (even though, as seen in Section 5.2, the state maintains significant stakes in both EDF and ENEL). Examining first, internal dynamics with a focus on managers and shareholders, followed by studying developments regarding liberalization, the state, and regulatory authorities, this section discusses the intervening factors at play post-privatization (X2).

INTERNAL FACTORS

Competitiveness (market strength and managers)

In terms of market shares when privatized, the Alphas—particularly those from the continent—were dominant players. As seen in Section 5.1, shortly before and even after privatization the continental Alphas enjoyed a dominant market position. In the 1990s the state-owned EDF—which was a product of the French government nationalizing over a thousand electricity and gas companies—controlled 90 per cent of generation capacity, 100 per cent of the transmission grid, and 95 per cent of the distribution network in France in the 1990s (Chick, 2007, 128). E.ON was a significant player, competing only against other giants such as RWE, while ENEL was the principle company in the sector in Italy. The continental Alphas, in particular, started to decrease national market share only in the 2000s when EU-wide liberalization initiatives were pursued in the 2000s (discussed later). While SSE has faced relatively more competition from other firms even after privatization (as a consequence of UK liberalization initiatives discussed later) it still continues to remain one of the 'big six' energy companies in the UK, as discussed in Section 5.1.

When turning to management teams of the Alphas, the evidence demonstrates three main dimensions. On a first dimension, Alphas are led by CEOs and directors with long-term visions for expansion of the firm. For example, regarding SSE's 2004 acquisition of the Ferrybridge and Fiddlers Ferry power stations, the Chief Executive, Ian Marchant, highlighted that the acquisition:

> ... is consistent with our strategy of acquiring assets which can be successfully integrated into our existing businesses.... It will add to the diversity of our generation portfolio, particularly in the mid-merit sector, and will help us meet peak demand for electricity.[134]

Marchant later stated that the technologically advanced Marchwood power station was a significant, complementary, project for SSE's main market in the UK.[135] This is because 'its development, allied to our other investments in coal-fired power stations and in renewable energy, will help to maintain SSE's position as the electricity generator with the most diverse and flexible portfolio of assets in the UK'.[136]

While managers' long-term vision of SSE largely rested with acquiring within the British Isles, others such as E.ON were led by directors seeking selective investments in certain geographic areas abroad. For example, in the 2005 acquisition of Romania's Electrica Moldova, E.ON was able to successfully negotiate the deal led by the Romanian government over four other contenders: Public Power Corporation (Greece), CEZ (the Czech Republic), Union Fenosa (Spain), and AES (the US). On the one hand, E.ON's eventual success can be explained because CEZ attained another privatized firm, Electrica Oltenia, and therefore dropped out of the race. On the other, the Greek,

Spanish, and German firms were not chosen given that E.ON made the best offer. This was driven by the firm's goal to expand to Central and Eastern Europe, as reflected in the words of E.ON Chairman Wulf Bernotat, who stated that the deal 'further strengthens our position in central and eastern Europe, and wins us great opportunities for leveraging cross-border synergies'.[137] Bernotat similarly highlighted that the 2008 asset swap with Statkraft was clearly linked to managerial desires to consolidate the firm's position in the Nordic region,[138] as was the 2007 OGK-4 deal to buy a technologically up-to-date facility in the growing Russian market.[139]

A second dimension sees an added element of skilled, patient, negotiations coupled with long-terms visions. This is seen in EDF/Edison—taking around a decade to finalize—which is a clear case where (foreign) bosses of companies had to work with (domestic) capital actors in order to set the foundation in order to increase stakes in foreign acquisitions and eventually attain full control. Evidence of working with domestic capital is seen slightly before EDF increased its Edison stake in 2005 through Transalpina: in July 2004 EDF had to hold a series of discussions with original partners in Italenergia. In this regard, in July 2004 'EDF's President, Mr François Roussely, and Fiat's President Mr Luca Cordero di Montezemolo...[met] to decide their future programs for Italenergia and Edison', a fruitful discussion which helped pave the way for EDF's increased stakes.[140] Years later, after nine months of negotiations led by the skilled negotiator Henri Proglio, Chairman and CEO of EDF, in June 2012 the French giant gained full control of Italy's second largest utility.

In a third, related dimension, CEOs have constructively spearheaded some deals by allowing for the target's smooth incorporation. This is achieved by ensuring continuity in the management structures of the acquired firm in the midst of their ownership changes. As seen in the Airtricity deal, whose acquisition set the stage for SSE to become the UK's largest renewables player, part of Marchant's negotiating position was to maintain continuity in the target's management structure, keeping the spirit of goodwill between both firms. In his words:

> Over the past few weeks, the Airtricity and SSE teams have worked very well together, and we've already laid foundations for future success. I am looking forward to working with Paul Dowling (formerly CEO of Airtricity who remained as Chief Executive after the acquisition) on the task of combining SSE's and Airtricity's renewable energy forces and creating an excellent platform for long-term growth that is sustainable in every sense.[141]

Other deals where Alphas either attain a minority stake in another firm, or have pursued Joint Ventures, have also seen a similar type of cooperative spirit brought to the negotiation table. For example, the E.ON/MPX deal also shows how managers of firms with which Alphas cooperate are keen to work with them, as expressed by Mr Eduardo Karrer, CEO of MPX:

> We are excited about our partnership with E.ON, a successful global energy player. By working together, and utilizing E.ON's considerable international experience, we can accelerate the monetization of projects which are already licensed, as well as create new and attractive growth opportunities in Brazil and Latin America.[142]

Similarly, EDF's and ENEL's Joint Venture, Sviluppo Nucleare, though now abandoned, was considered a positive sum game for both parties. On the one hand, the CEO and General Manager of ENEL, Fulvio Conti, highlighted the importance of partnering with EDF in order to help rebuild nuclear energy in Italy and boost the Italian economy. On the other, EDF's Chairman and CEO, Pierre Gadonneix, remarked that the deal would help strengthen its position in Europe while seeking to lead the world in nuclear energy.[143]

Without doubt, given their long-term visions, skilled negotiating abilities, and abilities to work with targeted firms as well as cooperating partners, it seems of little surprise that bosses are rewarded nicely. For example, in the case of Ian Marchant, who was appointed SSE Chief Executive in 2002 and held this position until he quit in 2013, it was reported that along with his GBP 1 million a year salary, he had amassed 'around 240,000 SSE shares according to Reuters data, with a market worth of some GBP 3.3m. SSE's annual report for 2012 showed he also had 350,000 share options, with a paper worth of GBP 4.8m'.[144]

In other cases, Alpha's bosses buy shares in their firm, only to sell them for a quick profit within days. This is seen in a transaction in May 2004 by the then CEO of ENEL, Paolo Scaroni.[145] Based on ENEL management team stock option rights, on 28 May 2004 Scaroni acquired 460,832 shares of ENEL for a price of €6.48 per share. The total consideration was thus €2,986,191.36, which we will call 'x'. Although the Zephyr files do not report the specific date and time that the shares were sold, it does report the sale of the two stakes on 31 May 2004. The first was of 250,000 units sold at €6.70 per share (for a consideration of €1,675,000); the second was the remainder at €6.72 per share (for a consideration of €1,416,791.04). Summing the values, the total consideration for these two transactions is €3,091,791.04, which we will call 'y'. Considering the cost of the total number of shares purchased (x) and the value received when the two stakes were resold (y), suggests that the chairman made gains of around €105,600. Indeed, the buying and selling of shares is not uncommon to other shareholders of Alphas, as well as the firms they acquire, a discussion to which we now turn.

Shareholders (not including the state)

Here I consider the role played by shareholders. I focus exclusively on the role of asset management firms, shareholders of firms targeted by Alphas, and other (non-state) shareholders of Alphas. Later in the chapter, I will offer a more complete analysis of the actions of those states that hold stakes in the Alphas (as well as an analysis of the boards of Alphas and their state ties).

First, taking the world's leading asset management firms examined in other chapters, Figures 5.2–5.5 consider the shares held at the end of the years indicated by BlackRock, State Street, Allianz, Fidelity, Vanguard, AXA, BNP-Paribas, Deutsche Bank, JP Morgan, and Capital Group in the Alphas, namely, EDF, E.ON, SSE, and ENEL.

Taking Figures 5.2–5.5 together, a main observation is that the leading asset management firms generally hold shares in the Alphas throughout the time series. However, ownership is not constant, as shares are bought and sold over

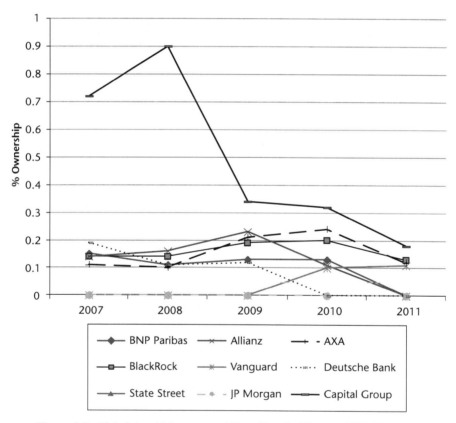

Figure 5.2. Global Asset Management Firm Shareholdings in EDF, 2007–11
Source: Amadeus

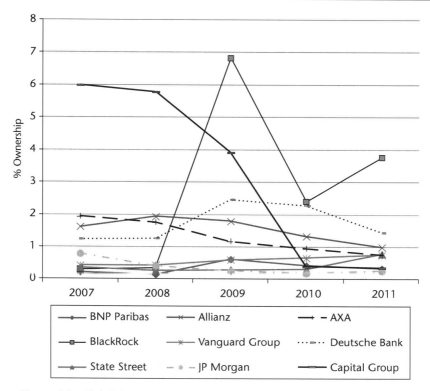

Figure 5.3. Global Asset Management Firm Shareholdings in E.ON, 2007–11
Source: Amadeus

time. The main exceptions to this is Fidelity, which held no shares in any of the Alphas, and specific observations related to State Street (which owned shares in all Alphas except EDF throughout the time series), JP Morgan (in all but EDF), and BNP-Paribas (in all but ENEL). Capital Group has the highest stake in EDF throughout the time series, followed by AXA and BlackRock in 2011. Nevertheless, compared to other Alphas, the overall percentage of EDF in which main asset managers are shareholders is never more than 1 per cent. This relatively lower overall ownership can be explained based on the large percentage of EDF which rests in state hands, and the corresponding small percentage which is traded. In E.ON, Capital Group decreased its ownership over time, while BlackRock's ownership ebbed and flowed in the last three years but was still ahead of Deutsche Bank by 2011. SSE sees significant ownership by both US-based Capital Group and BlackRock especially in the latter years, while ENEL saw one of its most significant shareholders being BlackRock, while no other asset management firm held more than 1 per cent throughout the period. This, similar to EDF, may be explained based on the large percentage of the firm that is still state owned.

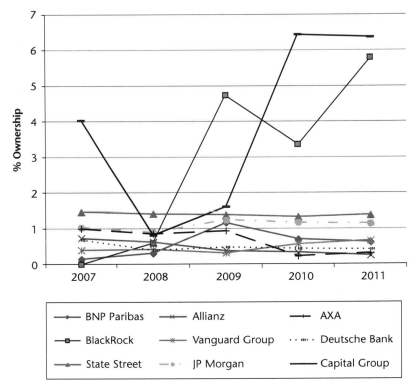

Figure 5.4. Global Asset Management Firm Shareholdings in SSE, 2007–11
Source: Amadeus

To demonstrate how asset managers buy and sell pragmatically, observations from 2010 and 2011 see how BlackRock changed its ownership held in some firms, with a concomitant change in others. For example, by the end of 2010—when the IPO of ENEL Green Power took place—its shareholding in E.ON and SSE dropped from the year before, but its stake in ENEL increased. By 2011, when BlackRock increased its ownership in SSE and E.ON, it decreased its stake in ENEL.

In order to ascertain whether or not leading asset management firms are more likely to invest in Alphas compared to Betas, Table 5.10 considers the ownership in Endesa before and after its takeover by ENEL relying on data from Amadeus of which there are observations since 2003. The year/stake for the 'final observation' in the database will be labelled as such for those for which there are observations in 2007 and 2009. In terms of its takeover, it is useful to recall that ENEL's first stake in Endesa was 9.99 per cent taken in

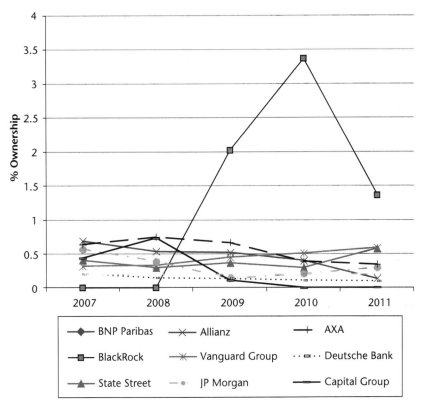

Figure 5.5. Global Asset Management Firm Shareholdings in ENEL, 2007–11
Source: Amadeus

February 2007. It then increased its stake to 24.98 per cent by March 2007, 67.05 per cent by October 2007, and finally, 92.06 per cent by June 2009 when it attained Acciona's shares.

The Table highlights that some of the principal asset managers holding shares in Alphas as seen previously—particularly BlackRock, Capital Group, and BNP-Paribas—*never* invested in Endesa. Part of the explanation for this may be based on the idea that Endesa represented a 'risky' investment given that it was a takeover target since the mid-2000s, as discussed in Section 5.3. The data suggests that many that did buy Endesa shares (such as the JP Morgan, Vanguard Group, AXA, and Deutsche Bank) eventually sold up in 2007 when ENEL/Acciona took over Endesa, while others such as Allianz and State Street maintained ownership for some time thereafter (full details are examined later, where the high price per share offered by ENEL/Acciona is examined, and where relatively smaller actors such as Mediobanca, Caja Madrid, and UBS played key roles).

Table 5.10. Global Asset Management Ownership in Endesa, 2003–11

	BNP Paribas	BlackRock	State Street	Allianz	Vanguard	JP Morgan	AXA	Deutsche Bank	Capital Group
2003	0	0	0	0	0	6.39	0	0	0
2004	0	0	0	0	0	6.39	0	0	0
2005	0	0	0	0	0	6.39	5.35	0	0
2006	0	0	0	0	0	6.39 (last observation)	5.35	5	0
2007	0	0	.11	.16	.26 (first and last observation)	0	.44 (last observation)	4.88 (last observation)	0
2008	0	0	.11	.11	0	0	0	0	0
2009	0	0	.11	.11 (last observation)	0	0	0	0	0
2010	0	0	.11	0	0	0	0	0	0
2011	0	0	.11	0	0	0	0	0	0

Source: Amadeus

Further, if we consider other firms which were taken over, such as Scottish Power which can be considered a Beta given that it was acquired by Iberdrola in 2007, as discussed in Section 5.2, analysis of its data on the Amadeus database also reveals that none of the world's leading asset management firms was a shareholder in the firm between 2003 and 2007, with the exception of Capital Group which owned 2.72 per cent of the company only in 2006. This suggests that the world's main asset managers, particularly those from the US, were less likely to have bought shares in Betas than in Alphas, consistent with previous findings outlined in the airline chapter. But, it is important to note that some did.

Beyond the world's largest asset management firms, evidence of other shareholders is important in terms of understanding some of the M&A that took place. Here there are two main scenarios, where the first relates to the importance of shareholders of target firms in facilitating the transactions—in some cases forcing Alphas to better their offers—and the other considers the gains by Alpha shareholders in some of the deals.

First, with regard to the shareholders of firms that are targeted, the evidence shows that Alphas were paid generously when making acquisitions, resulting in such shareholders not blocking deals. This is seen in the case of Powergen, where its shareholders made a significant amount over their original investment. In the deal, E.ON offered GBP 7.65 in cash for each Powergen share. This offer represented 'a premium of 25.8% over the closing price of Powergen shares of GBP 6.08 on the last business day before the announcement of talks between Powergen and E.ON', subsequently resulting in the directors of Powergen recommending its shareholders accept the offer.[146] This is also seen in EDF's purchase of the remaining 39.09 per cent of Hungarian DÉMÁSZ in 2006, where the offer amounted to 'HUF 20,000 in cash per share, valuing the remaining stake at HUF 28.949 billion. Based on DÉMÁSZ's closing price of HUF 17,300 on August 23, 2006, the last trading day before the offer was announced, the offer represents a premium of 15.61 per cent'.[147]

The case of British Energy also shows that some shareholders were not happy with the initial offer of EDF, potentially blocking the transaction.[148] In early August 2008 EDF originally made an offer at GBP 7.65 per share that was rejected by investors such as Invesco, BE's second largest shareholder holding a reported 14.86 per cent stake (while the state was the largest with 35.2 per cent). EDF eventually made a more attractive offer to those such as Invesco in late September 2008, upping the ante with an offer of GBP 7.74:

> ...which represented a bid premium of 6.91 percent over BE's closing share price of GBP 7.24 on 23/09/08, the last trading day before this offer was announced and a bid premium of 45.76 per cent over British Energy's closing share price of GBP 5.31 on 21/02/08, the last trading day before the acquisition of BE was rumoured.[149]

Second, with regard to Alpha shareholders, the case of EDF's sale of EnBW in 2011 shows the gains made by shareholders (including the state) when divesting, as seen in Section 5.1: by paying a high price, EDF (and its shareholders) was able to attain slightly more than €1 billion in the transaction. A similar case where Alpha shareholders gained on an Alpha divestment is seen when Terna was sold by ENEL: during the 50 per cent IPO of Terna in June 2004 it was agreed that 'up to half the shares are to be issued to existing ENEL shareholders', sold for a price of €1.70 per share.[150] This value would see a general increase over the next years, as Terna shares had a value of €3.28 in March 2012 when the last tranche was sold.[151] Further, it was agreed in the 50 per cent IPO that any cash generated from the Terna sale would be paid out entirely to ENEL shareholders.[152]

Regardless of the driving force of managers and the benefits shareholders gain, the reason EDF stayed in the race in the British Energy acquisition was not so much because of Invesco, but, precisely because the largest shareholder—the British state—was insistent on EDF taking over BE. The case of Terna is also a good illustration that divestment can best be understood in the context of EU liberalization initiatives and the role of the state in using its sale to increase its direct ownership of ENEL. With this in mind, we turn to the external factors to the firm.

EXTERNAL FACTORS

We now consider the importance of the intervening variables (X2) that are related to the external, more political, aspects that can help explain why firms become Alphas. It first considers liberalization, then the role of the state, regulatory authorities, as well as firm lobbying targeting political institutions. Similar to previous arguments developed in the other empirical chapters examining Alphas, the argument is as follows: the liberalization context sets the stage for the different conjunctures when deals could take place; state officials (from home and abroad) not only provided public funds and helped craft deals that ensued in the context of liberalization, but also maintained close ties to firms' boards; and regulators from different levels of governance, with abilities to veto the deals, ensured that the transactions were finalized, which can be explained based on resources that firms earmark towards lobbying.

Liberalization

Of the external, more political variables, it is useful to first consider liberalization dynamics in order to better contextualize the M&A developments in the sector. An important initial observation, from a domestic-level perspective as Mark Thatcher's work neatly explains, is that 'Britain reformed its electricity sector before other European nations' when Margaret Thatcher 'introduced comprehensive reforms, beginning with the 1989 Electricity Act' (Thatcher, 2009, 209). There was subsequent privatization of the twelve regional distribution companies, the three generating companies (National Power, Powergen, and Nuclear Electric), and the transmission company (National Grid). In the UK, privatization was accompanied by liberalization, which thus took place first there, before other member states.

When turning to the continent, as discussed by Cameron (2005) and Thatcher (2009), domestic liberalization in France, Germany, Italy, and Spain was relatively slow to take place. Eventually all pursued reforms, primarily because of EU liberalization initiatives starting from the mid-1990s onwards. The EU's initiatives started with the Council and Parliament's 1996 Directive, which stated that 'between 1999 and 2003, member states must liberalize 25–33 percent of their national markets' (Eising, 2002, 95). As Thatcher explains, 'it also provided access to the monopoly grid for all suppliers so that competition could occur in generation and distribution' (Thatcher, 2009, 207). Greater competition was later prescribed by the Union in 2003, as seen in the EU's Electricity Directive on the creation of an internal market, subsequently allowing for changes in France, Germany, and Italy to have taken place by 2005, ultimately opening markets to competition.[153] Liberalization also helped spur on privatization of companies in these states.

With this in mind, the impact of domestic and supranational level liberalization initiatives help explain three broad, sometimes overlapping, dimensions of the expansionary deals pursued by Alphas. First, firms such as EDF and E.ON initially pursued expansion into the UK, as well as Central and Eastern Europe, in the late 1990s and early 2000s. Second, domestic level transposition of EU liberalization directives, coupled with the Commission's rigorous application of anti-trust policy, meant that firms had to commit to decrease national strength by way of divestments. Third, liberalization simultaneously served as a catalyst for firms to increase (or regain) market shares lost in domestic markets, resulting in their expansion into the rest of Europe (including those countries with firms on the selling block) and globally. I consider each of these dimensions in turn.

First, the first main cross-border M&A pursued by firms such as EDF and E.ON in the late 1990s and early 2000s was reflective of an 'Alpha invasion' into the only liberalized market in the EU, namely the UK. While the UK pioneered liberalization in the sector, it gave an opportunity for other firms to expand, especially from historically less liberalized domestic markets in the continent that were protected, such as France. With this in mind, two complementary scenarios emerged. First, little liberalization domestically (as was the case with France, Italy, Germany, and Spain in the 1990s), coupled with a liberalized market in other EU states (such as the UK), allowed firms enjoying privileged positions at home to also enjoy the ability to expand into the other markets in the community. Second, liberalization at the national level (as was the case in the UK in the 1990s), but not at the EU level (which did not fully come into force until years later), meant that domestic firms in liberalized states would have to compete with rivals from all over the Union (and even the US for that matter) on their home turf, but have little chance to expand into other EU markets.

The evidence presented in Section 5.1 supports both scenarios in understanding developments in the late 1990s and early 2000s, showing why EDF and E.ON were able to gain such a stronghold in the UK, while SSE and other UK firms either stayed at home or sought deals in the US. The French- and German-led Alpha invasion into the UK started in the late 1990s, as seen in EDF's 100 per cent acquisition of London Electricity, a 'renationalization through the back chunnel' (Chick, 2007, 128). EDF's invasion continued with its purchase of SWEB (1999), Cottam Power Station (2001), West Burton Power Station (2001), Eastern Electricity (2001), and Seeboard (2002). In the case of E.ON, its main acquisitions included Powergen in 2001 (which subsequently made other deals in the UK market, including Midlands in 2003).

Section 5.1 also showed that while Powergen's sale was approved by its UK-based shareholders, many of the UK firms sold to EDF were already under foreign ownership: all the vendors of the targets that were acquired by EDF, except for Cottam Power Station that was sold by Powergen, were US-based giants that had previously invested in the UK. This includes Entergy (which sold London Electricity to EDF), PP&L Resources (SWEB), Enron (Sutton Power Bridge), TXU (West Burton Power Station and Eastern), and AEP (Seeboard). With this in mind, foreign ownership of many of these firms in the UK, already established during the time period that the UK had privatized and liberalized, was not something new. This may help explain why there was little domestic opposition during the 'Alpha invasion' and subsequently when Scottish Power and British Energy were later acquired by the Spanish and French, respectively.

Further, even though Alphas initially expanded into the UK in the late 1990s and early 2000s while enjoying relatively protected market positions at home, other UK firms, such as SSE and Scottish Power, were at a competitive disadvantage to enter the closed, continental market. As seen in Section 5.1, those that did make moves outside of the UK in the 1990s (such as BE, Scottish Power, and Powergen) went to North America.

Beyond moving into the UK, in the late 1990s and early 2000s continental Alphas were also catalysed to look at Central and Eastern Europe in anticipation of the impact of EU liberalization. While EU liberalization was being formulated, but still not fully implemented, this 'forced firms' to look abroad, particularly in non-EU countries, in order to make up for market shares that were going to be lost at home. As seen in the evidence presented in Section 5.1, states from Central and Eastern Europe were targeted by Alphas for some time before their accession to the Union in 2004. This may be explained by the absence of full liberalization in the EU market, which meant that Alphas had to move to markets outside the EU. It may also be explained precisely because these markets sought to liberalize before accession to the Union. Evidence of this is seen in the 2005 acquisitions of Electrica Banata and Electrica Dobrogea privatized in Romania, which sought increased liberalization of their home market. This allowed ENEL to acquire 1.4 million consumers that it lost with liberalization in its home market in Italy. It is also reflected in E.ON's acquisition of Electrica Moldova privatized in Romania, as well as EDC Gorna Oryahovitza and Varna privatized in Bulgaria in 2005. These were no different to the case of Russia, whose OGK-4 sale is clearly linked to liberalizing the Russian electricity market.[154] Entering into non-EU states that were privatizing was also seen in EDF's purchase in Slovakia of Stredoslovenská Energetika in 2002, as well as Light in Brazil.

Yet, as EU liberalization was being implemented, this changed the rules of the game, particularly for the continental Alphas: the Union's overall liberalization initiatives meant that players from Italy, Germany, and France could no longer hold a privileged position at home. In this regard, EU liberalization initiatives set the tone for divestments to pursue, in order to open up competition in home markets. For example, ENEL's sale of Italy's second largest generator Elettrogen to Endesa in 2001 was considered 'the first of three power generating companies to be sold by ENEL by the end of 2003 to comply with the EU's liberalization requirements'.[155]

EU liberalization, alongside the European Commission's application of antitrust policy, also forced firms such as E.ON to sell assets throughout the 2000s. In 2006 the European Commission carried out unannounced inspections on premises of electricity companies in Germany, concerned about abuses of dominant position.[156] After a two-year investigation the Commission concluded that E.ON had deterred new competitors in generation and prevented other competitors from the transmission grid. Both parties subsequently agreed to a 'commitment decision' where E.ON would divest around 5,000 MW of generation capacity and sell its transmission system.[157]

In light of this decision, one can better understand the sales of Thüga (2009) and Transpower (2010), where E.ON's CEO Bernotat highlighted that the driving force behind the two sales was motivated by its agreement with the Commission to inject competition into the national market:

> [the sale of Transpower] gives rise to Europe's first cross-border power transmission network. This is another important step towards integration of the European electricity market. By selling our extra high-voltage transmission network and

disposing of 4,800 MW of power generation capacity so far, we have almost completely fulfilled our commitment to the EU Commission as given in 2008. If the sale of Thüga is also taken into account, E.ON has significantly reduced its position in Germany at all stages of the value chain, namely generation, distribution and sales. At the same time this gives fresh impetus to competition on the German energy market.[158]

Marketwatch Energy further suggests that E.ON's anti-trust experience with the Commission had an indirect impact on EDF when it sold its distribution assets in the UK.[159]

The E.ON 'commitment decision' also serves as a good example of the third dimension of the impact of injecting competition: selling assets in this case was also met with an opportunity to enter EU markets previously untapped. This is seen in the asset swap between E.ON and Electrabel, where Bernotat highlights how E.ON was able to kill two birds with one stone:

> The successful swap with Electrabel is another milestone in implementing the commitment with the European Commission to reduce our generation capacity in Germany. It will enrich the competitive landscape in Germany and Belgium, thereby further stimulating competition throughout Europe. For E.ON, the swap with Electrabel *also* marks the successful entry into Belgium's power generation market. With a market share of 9%, we have directly become No. 3 in Belgium. Therefore, we're continuing to rapidly expand our presence in Europe ... (Emphasis added)[160]

In this regard, Thatcher has noted that EU initiatives gave once predominantly domestic-based firms the need to, and the opportunities to, expand into other EU markets beyond the UK (Thatcher, 2009, 215). Or, as Helm and Tindall (2009, 423) explain, mergers and acquisitions across Europe were 'a response to the (EU) liberalization agenda'. In light of this, one can see that after the first British targets, Alphas then made aggressive moves to acquire in two main parts of continental Europe—first, Central and Eastern Europe (before the full impact of EU liberalization kicked in), and then the rest of the EU (once EU liberalization was starting to have more of an impact).

Once EU liberalization initiatives were starting to be fully implemented from the mid-2000s, this 'allowed firms' to do what they were previously unable to do, namely, expand into other EU markets. This is seen not only in E.ON's asset swaps with Electrabel, but also the important case of EDF's expansion into Italy with the Edison deal, where EU initiatives set the stage for EDF acquiring a stake in Edison in the 2000s despite opposition from ENEL. Why? The 1999 Bersani law which transposed early European initiatives envisaged that the 'the new legislation for a progressive liberalization of energy reintroduces competition to the electricity and gas markets', allowing Edison to be 'a key player in this new market, supplying electricity to private clients'.[161] Despite Bersani, however, 'the 2004 electricity law (in) Italy placed limits on ownership of shares by companies from other countries that did not offer reciprocal market access . . . known as the "anti-EdF" law' (Thatcher, 2009, 216). This ultimately prevented EDF, perceived as being a hostile invader, from controlling any Italian electric utility. However, with the European Commission taking the position that the Italian law was illegal in the context of EU liberalization initiatives, coupled with French guarantees to transpose the EU Directives and liberalize their own domestic market by the mid-2000s (Thatcher, 2009, 216), this ultimately served as a basis for EDF to take its controlling stake in 2005, turning to full ownership of Edison by 2012.

Starting around the mid-2000s, one sees other cases where Alphas gained controlling stakes in firms from other EU member states in which they were previously weak or absent players. This includes EDF's expansion into Germany (when it attained a controlling stake in EnBW, although later sold) and Belgium (SPE); E.ON's expansion into Sweden (Sydkraft) and Spain (through assets gained in the Endesa sale, discussed later); and ENEL's expansion into Spain (Endesa). Although relatively less active in terms of M&A in the continent, the movement of SSE into Ireland (with its purchase of Airtricty) can also be understood in this regard. Further, Alphas could expand into Central and Eastern European countries that joined the EU since 2004, such as Poland (EDF's acquisitions of ERSA and Kogeneracja, 2009–12), Hungary (E.ON's purchase of MOL in 2006), and Slovenia (ENEL's purchase of Slovenské Elektrárne, which started in 2001 and was completed in 2005).

Beyond the EU, Alphas also made efforts in the 2000s and 2010s to continue to expand worldwide, including EDF (in North America and Asia), E.ON (in Russia and Brazil), and ENEL (in North America, Russia, and Latin America through its purchase of Endesa).

Ultimately, cross-border purchases had to be negotiated and, in this context, it is necessary to consider the next factor of salience in explaining why firms can become Alphas: both 'home' and 'target' states and their role in shaping Alpha expansion.

State influence: state aid and crafting deals

Similar to airline Alphas seen before, electricity Alphas have not generally received a plethora of European Commission-approved state aid. Of course, there are exceptions, particularly EDF. In one case, the Commission investigated aid given by the French government in the 1990s before EU liberalization was pursued, ultimately concluding that the measures given did not constitute state aid.[162] In another case, however, the Commission deemed that the aid given by France in the late 1990s was illegal and therefore demanded recovery. Of issue was that the French government had waived a tax claim of close to €890 million that was due from EDF and, as such, the unfair tax concession gave EDF a competitive advantage over its rivals.[163] Nevertheless, EDF took the case to the General Court, which in 2009 annulled the Commission's original decision.[164] In turn, the Commission appealed this decision before the ECJ, but this too was dismissed.[165] As one acknowledged expert on the theme noted, the ECJ's decision constituted a 'blow to the Commission's active enforcement of state aid law in the energy industry'.[166]

State aid aside, governments today still earmark state funds to Alphas. This is through various public–private partnerships held, contracts received, or subsidized research projects pursued.

Turning to PPPs and contracts received, SSE's acquisition of Seeboard Trading in 2008 was seen as a means to reinforce its 'position as the UK's leading street lighting contractor', where it believed that the acquisition would result in '(a)dditional street lighting PFI (Private Finance Initiative, or Public–Private Partnership) contracts . . . to build further our presence in this increasingly important sector'.[167] In 2012 ENEL secured millions in public contracts with municipal governments, including the *Comune di Loano* (€411,365), *Comune di Carbonia* (€478,603), and *Comune di Nibionno* (€3,069,318).[168] Perhaps unsurprisingly, in 2012 EDF 'won three calls for tenders issued by the French government for the installation of its first major wind farms off the coast of Saint-Nazaire, Courseulles-sur-Mer and Fécamp with potential new installed capacity totally 1500 MW'.[169]

With regard to research projects, in an initiative that received funding from the federal states of Baden-Württemberg and Bavaria, the latter of which is a minority shareholder in E.ON, the German firm continues to be involved in KW21, 'a public–private initiative that brings together equipment manufacturers, power-plant operators, and universities in Munich and Stuttgart to conduct joint research projects in energy systems and technology'.[170] In another government-funded project, E.ON is involved in a programme with Audi (owned by VW, which shows how Alphas from other chapters work together) 'to test electromobility solutions'.[171]

Table 5.11. EU Funds Received by Electricity Alphas

Company Name	EU Grants Received 2011	EU Grants Received 2012
EDF	€2,000,000	€44,244,431
E.ON	€4,500,000	€1,222,000
ENEL*	€32,129,000	€30,847,804
SSE	€0	€5,488,717

Source: EU Transparency Register (2011) and EU Financial Transparency Register (2012)

*In 2011 there is no evidence that Endesa received grants. In 2012, however, it did receive €10,507,788, which is summed with its global ultimate owner ENEL which received €20,340,016 that year, totalling €30,847,804.

An additional angle to public funds received by Alphas includes not just that provided by home states, but, interestingly, from the European Union which co-finances projects with member states. Table 5.11 outlines grants received from the EU in 2011 (based on data from the Transparency Register) and 2012 (based on data from the Financial Transparency Register).[172]

To what are the millions that the EU gives Alphas related? As E.ON explains in its transparency data registration on its 2011 financing, 'the grants of ca. €4.5 million are mainly based on the EU Energy Programme for Recovery (EEPR), in which E.ON participated alongside a number of other energy companies'.[173] As one Commission official further explains in correspondence with the author, the EEPR:

> provides financial support to selected, highly strategic, projects in three areas of the energy sector: gas and electricity connections, offshore wind energy and carbon capture and storage. By co-financing these projects (where up to 80% of the costs are provided by the Commission while member states can provide up to 20%), the programme helps the European Union to progress towards its energy and climate policy objectives. Almost €4 billion were assigned to co-finance EU energy projects that would boost the economic recovery, increase the security of energy supply and contribute to the reduction of greenhouse gas emissions. The funding is administered by the EU (DG Energy) via grants and tenders allocated to project promoters and comes from the General Budget of the European Union.[174]

Highlighting the lack of transparency in the process, however, when the same Commission official was then asked to clarify the criteria used to select which firms were to receive EEPR funds, and if there was information on other competitors' bids, no response was received.

Beyond state aid and other forms of subsidies/public funds, Alpha home states also play key roles in shaping M&A. E.ON's acquisition of Ruhrgas offers a solid example of this. After E.ON attained an 18 per cent stake in Ruhrgas from the speciality chemicals company Degussa in May 2002, 'the German Cartel office blocked E.ON taking a majority stake in Ruhrgas, but E.ON... appealed to the government to overturn this'.[175] By July 2002 'E.ON announced that it... [had] received ministerial approval (from the Ministry of Economics and Technology) to acquire a majority stake in Ruhrgas'.[176] While the sale was not immediate given that competitors (including the German giant RWE) took the case to court over the next months, it served as the basis for an out-of-court settlement, where the appellants withdrew their opposition and eventually allowed for E.ON's 100 per cent control of Ruhrgas in 2003.

States' involvement in crafting deals is also seen in ENEL's sale of Terna, directly linked to the state increasing its stakes in ENEL even after privatization, as discussed in Section 5.1. When Italy started to transpose EU Directives with the Bersani decree of March 1999, the Italian firm was divided up, and within five years Terna was sold in order to guarantee independence of the national grid and ensure access to all operators. By 2003 ENEL was going to reduce its stake in Terna as prescribed by the decree. As discussed before, 50 per cent was floated in June 2004 (where the deal benefited previous ENEL shareholders who were given preference). During the second tranche sale, 29.99 per cent of Terna was sold to Cassa Depositi e Prestiti (CDP), and 80 per cent owned by the Italian state through the Ministry of Economy and Finance (MEF). At the same time, CDP owned 10.35 per cent of ENEL. As a result, Italian regulators approved CDP's 30 per cent stake in Terna in 2005, but on condition on the sale of its ENEL stake by 2007.[177]

But, this did not happen. CDP was thus given an extension to sell its ENEL stake. It eventually did a few years later, but only after lapping up an extra 7 per cent of ENEL when subscribing to a capital increase in 2009. Owning more than 17.3 per cent of ENEL, a 2010 deal was finally made between CDP and MEF, the latter of which had 13.9 per cent ownership in ENEL since December 2009.[178] CDP swapped its stake in ENEL (with an estimated value of over €6.6 billion), plus its 35 per cent share in Poste Italiane (worth €3.3 billion), plus 50 per cent of STMicroelectronics (worth €810 million) with MEF. In return, MEF gave CDP a 16.4 per cent stake in one of the world's largest petroleum companies, *Ente Nazionale Idrocarburi* (ENI), led since 2005 by ENEL's former boss, Paolo Scaroni. Because this ENI stake was worth an estimated €10.7 billion, the resultant deal was of roughly equivalent value for both parties.

One could effectively argue that because MEF controlled the CDP in the first place this was simply a type of reallocation of resources within different parts of the Ministry. However, one may counter-argue that the move was significant because it positioned itself to allow MEF *direct* control of over 30 per cent of ENEL. Thus, as a consequence of initiatives to liberalize the sector, the Italian state (somewhat ironically) moved from directly owning less than 14 per cent of ENEL by the end of the 2000s, to almost the third by 2010 that it still holds today. In a nutshell, liberalization in Italy had not necessarily resulted in decreased state ownership; in fact, it allowed the state to craft a deal where it attained more direct control over the firm than it had shortly after its privatization. As will be seen when we examine the takeover of Endesa when the chapter closes, the timing of the deal between the CDP and MEF in 2010 was hardly a coincidence.

Finally, EDF's sale in late 2010 of its 45 per cent stake in EnBW also demonstrates the key roles played by state officials. Indeed, because France holds an 84 per cent stake in EDF, it hardly shocks anyone that the French state intervenes in deals. In fact, an earlier illustration of the significance of French state officials, not only in helping engineer deals, but also preventing them, is seen in ENEL's hostile takeover attempt of Suez in 2006 which was blocked by the French state.[179] But the case of EnBW and EDF is slightly different because of the roles played by state officials from Germany (which intervened as acquirer) and those from France (intervening as vendor). As seen in Section 5.1, on 6 December 2010 the state of Baden-Württemberg acquired EDF's stake in EnBW, paying 'a price of €41.50 per share...representing an 18.6% premium on EnBW's closing price on 3 December 2010, valuing the divested stake at €4.7 billion'.[180] It would later emerge that the accountancy firm Warth and Klein Grant Thornton (in Dusseldorf) claimed in a report that the government paid €840 million too much for the EnBW stake.[181]

The EDF/EnBW transaction of 6 December can be best described as one that lacked any transparency, pointing to how officials from both Germany and France crafted a secret deal where the state paid heavily and the vendor benefited nicely.[182] The Prime Minister Stefan Mappus (CDU), who was advised by Morgan Stanley's German head, Dirk Notheis, did not seek permission of the parliament of the state of Baden-Württemberg, despite Mappus' apparent desire to do so. This can partly be explained because the CEO of EDF, Henri Proglio—who was appointed by the French state—demanded an 'unconditional deal' without any involvement of parliament.[183] After the parliament (with a CDU and FDP majority) voted on 15 December in favour of the deal negotiated in secret days before, the SPD and Green opposition announced legal action against the acquisition in January 2011. Both SPD and the Greens later won the election in March 2011, where the EnBW issue played a significant role.

The self-supporting (indeed intertwined) interests of state players from Germany and France, as well as (interestingly) Morgan Stanley, all help explain the secrecy of the deal. First, Mappus believed that regaining control of EnBW would present himself as a 'maker' of important political decisions, which in this case would symbolize Germany regaining some of its energy independence. As such, one may see the deal as a strategic manoeuvre by the government to try to win the upcoming elections given the population's support, even if it meant that standard legislative protocol was not followed.[184] Second, EDF's and the French state's interests lay not only in the financial gains in the deal, but also its desire to dump out of Germany: EDF was not happy with Germany's view on nuclear energy and the increasing costs it placed.[185] As far as the French were concerned, it really was important to take the money and run, quickly: the more the deal went under any parliamentary microscope in Germany, the greater the chances it may fail. Finally, one may argue that EDF's boss, Henri Proglio, and the French state knew that there was some certainty in the Notheis-led offer, precisely because the Chairman and Managing Director of Morgan Stanley France was René Proglio, who is the brother of Henri Proglio.[186] René Proglio, nevertheless, later claimed he did not act in his brother's interests. As far as Notheis was concerned, having the high-priced deal would doubly benefit Morgan Stanley because it would receive a commission of €15 million, thereby allowing the firm to register a profit for the calendar year 2011 which it would not have otherwise been able to do.[187]

Indeed, Alpha home-state intervention in some deals begs the question examined in the other empirical chapters: what percentage of the post-privatized firm's boards of directors (BoDs) have at one time worked for (or presently serve) the state? This may include, for example, being a high-level civil servant, an elected representative, a minister, or even a regulator, where such positions may have been held in either 'Alpha' home states or other countries. To answer this, the biographies of those serving on Alpha BoDs in 2011 found on the Amadeus database were analysed. The composition of the BoDs for firms was verified through analysis of 2011 Annual Reports and, in absence of full information, the webpages of the firms. For comparative purposes, in order to see if the board composition in terms of state links may differ between Alphas and Betas, Endesa's board in 2006 (before it was taken over by ENEL/Acciona) is also summarized. The findings are as follows, where readers will interestingly recognize some of the names from the airline chapter:

- EDF—there are a total of eighteen members in the EDF Group's BoD, of which six Directors are appointed by shareholders, six by the state, and six by employees.[188] Of those appointed by shareholders (a majority of which is effectively the French state), three of the six (Proglio, Jay, and Mariani) have had direct working relationships with the French and UK states, while one (Lafont) has experience having advised officials in China.[189] Unsurprisingly, all of the six appointed by the French state—Comolli, Dubertret, d'Escatha, Lepetit, Loos, and Sellal—all have some state association, many with high-level portfolios in economy, finance, advising the Prime Minister, or representing France at the EU level.[190] Highlighting the continuity between firms after their privatization, one sees that one of the directors appointed by the state, Comolli, is also a member of the board of directors of Air France–KLM, as seen in the airline chapter. This underlines the multiple appointments that officials with state experience may have on firms, given the expertise they may provide. When turning to the employee representatives, unfortunately neither the Amadeus database nor other sources offer much bibliographic information, meaning it is difficult to ascertain such members past association with the state.[191] Excluding these employee representatives, results in ten of the twelve other members—around 83 per cent of the board—have links with the state, proportional to the 84 per cent ownership the French state retains in EDF.

- E.ON—of the twenty members on the E.ON supervisory board, only two have links to the state, or 10 per cent, one with the UK, the other Bavaria.[192] Of particular significance is Baroness Kingsmill, the ex-Deputy Director of the UK's Competition Commission who has also been a Member of the House of Lords since 2006. As seen in the airline chapter, she is also a member of the IAG board. Not dissimilar to Comolli, her case highlights that some directors are sought by many firms and, eventually, chosen to serve on multiple boards. Dissimilar to Comolli, she does not have links to the Alphas 'home state' per se, but, rather, a state into which the Alpha has expanded, in this case starting with E.ON's significant acquisition of Powergen which allowed it to become one of the most important firms in the sector in the UK today. In this regard, Kingsmill's appointment can be seen as based on the firm's expansion into an important market of which she has significant regulatory knowledge. Similar to Kingsmill, another six of E.ON's board members (or, 30 per cent) also served as members of another board, such as Deutsche Telekom, Allianz, and Bayer.[193] This general observation of having a good number of Board members serving on Boards of other significant firms is generally not seen in the other electricity Alphas.

- SSE—of the eleven SSE board members, two have past links with the state, Gillingwater and Beeton.[194] This represents around 18 per cent of the board. Richard Gillingwater held important appointments in the UK such as being the Chief Executive and later Chairman of the Shareholder Executive, whose 'aim is to be an effective shareholder of businesses owned or part-owned by the government and to manage government's interventions in the private sector in order to secure best value for the taxpayer'.[195]

- ENEL—of the nine members, five had previous links with the state, representing slightly more than 55 per cent of the board. This included four which had links with the Italian state –Codogno, Miccio, Napolitano, and Tosi—as well as one with the Spanish state, namely, Pedro Solbes, as discussed more when the targeting of Endesa (the Beta) is examined at the end of the chapter.[196]

- Endesa—before its takeover by ENEL, Endesa's board in 2006 had fifteen BoDs, two of which had former state positions.[197] This is representative of around 13 per cent of the board. It is noteworthy that the type of continuity noted is also manifest: similar to Kingsmill (E.ON/IAG) and Comolli (EDF/AF–KLM), Endesa's board member José Manuel Fernández-Norniella also served as a non-Executive Director of Iberia from 2003, before joining the IAG's board, as seen before.

Taking all the firms together one sees an important relationship with the state, although with varying degrees, highlighting that Alphas ties to states remain strong even after privatization. Similar to the airline and automobile sectors, board members with historical relationships with the state are still the highest in France. This is consistent with a majority of EDF still being owned by the French state. Second to this is ENEL, with members having Italian and Spanish state experience. The other two Alphas which have very little (E.ON) or no (SSE) state ownership, still, nevertheless, see a board composed of some member with important state links. Further, board members in some electricity companies (such as EDF, E.ON, and Endesa before its takeover) also serve(d) double duty as members of boards of some of the airline Alphas, highlighting the concentration of power of some closely affiliated with states. Finally, when compared to the Beta (i.e. Endesa before its takeover), the evidence suggests that, except for E.ON, Alphas generally have a higher percentage of board members with links to the state.

If this highlights the importance of Alpha states in crafting deals and having those with public office experience serving of boards, then a second dimension relates to the role of non-Alpha states in fostering Alpha expansion. This is important when Alphas target firms, especially those being partially or fully privatized. One sees five broad scenarios.

In a first scenario, states that partially own targets play key roles in driving deals, even when other shareholders may have shown signs of reservation. This is seen in EDF's acquisition of BE. As before, Invesco, BE's second largest shareholder, was concerned about the price EDF was offering and EDF ultimately increased the offer, which was accepted. But this was only *after* the British state had intervened: after Invesco rejected the original EDF offer of GBP 7.65 per share on 1 August 2008, it was reported ten days later that 'the government is attempting to revive the BE and EDF talks'.[198] This gave EDF the time it needed to make a better deal, which was agreed to in late September 2008 and officially signed off in January 2009.

Why did the UK government, owning around 35 per cent of BE, favour completing the sale to EDF? There are at least four reasons. First, EDF was chosen because the UK government, frankly, had slim pickings given BE's financial troubles. On the verge of shutting down, BE was rescued by the UK government in 2004 with an aid of around GBP 5 billion, approved by the European Commission.[199] Notwithstanding, years later it was still perceived that BE was performing poorly, coupled with an 'ageing and increasingly unreliable' infrastructure.[200] Other than EDF, European giants such as E.ON, Iberdrola, RWE, and Vattenfall were shying away from BE. Second, the Labour administration knew that EDF was a reliable partner because they, too, were old friends. In this regard, in 2006 Chancellor Gordon Brown had announced plans to develop the Energy Technologies Institute, whose main task was to research and develop low-carbon energy technologies.[201] By September 2007 EDF Energy, E.ON UK, and four other firms (Caterpillar, BP, Rolls-Royce, and Royal Dutch Shell) took part in the public–private partnership with the British Government, signing off a few months before the sale of BE was first rumoured. Third, once it was clear that the reliable French partner with previous relations in the PPP was on board, the government negotiated that it could still play a key role in BE. In particular, the government ensured that its 'special shares in British Energy will remain in place following the completion of the deal [and that] EDF will have to gain special permission in order to sell off its British Energy's plants', thereby ensuring some continuity of the firm and its jobs.[202] Finally, the sale to EDF meant that the interests of another British firm were also served, namely Centrica. Although the 20 per cent stake of BE was not officially acquired by Centrica until later in 2009, EDF indicated in its early bids that Centrica would be a partner in BE's future. Both firms subsequently promised allegiance to governmental policy objectives, agreeing 'to build four nuclear plants on existing sites as part of the government's plans for the country to get more of its electricity from nuclear generation'.[203]

In a second scenario, states may privatize to more than one Alpha, as seen in Romania which was a non-EU member state at the time. When the Romania Ministry of Industry spearheaded the privatization of Electrica Banat and Dobrogea in 2005, other bidders included Greece's Public Power Corporation, Swiss BKW FMB, and Austria's EVN. One may argue that ENEL, from one of the EU's 'Big 5', offered a safe bet for a country that was to join the EU within two years. Similarly, the sale of Electrica Moldova to E.ON in 2005 was also seen by the Romanian government as a strategic transaction with a solid European partner that was keen on expanding into Eastern Europe.[204] Further, ENEL's initial transaction would lead to more opportunities, especially when EMS was being sold in 2008. Despite EMS receiving bids from several competitors (such as the majority state-owned firm CEZ, which is the largest utility in Central and Eastern Europe, EnBW, Iberdrola, RWE, and Spain's Union Fenosa), exclusive talks were entered into only with ENEL. This was because fruitful relations had been previously established since the previous transaction, as highlighted by Mr Teodor Atanasiu who was the President of the Romanian privatization agency, AVAS.[205]

A third scenario sees states potentially reneging on agreements, but Alphas eventually agreeing to extra conditions placed. This is seen in the sale of Slovenské Elektrárne (SE) to ENEL, where the non-Alpha state almost blocked a sale previously agreed. Before it entered the EU, the Slovakian government privatized SE, one of the largest producers in Central and Eastern Europe. With an offer of €840 million, ENEL was able to outbid its rival, CEZ, which offered €690 million. ENEL thus entered into agreement with the state after Economy Minister Pavol Rusko recommended the sale of SE to ENEL in October 2004.

213

Yet, a month later, in November 2004 the government was about to pull out unless ENEL agreed to Slovakia's conditions, which it did. These included making major investments, particularly 'modernization of the Novaky and Vojany coal-fired power plants as well as two of the units of the Mochovce nuclear power plant'.[206]

A fourth scenario sees states reneging on deals originally made with Betas, only to favour either domestic firms or Alphas later on. This is seen in the sale of Netherlands-based NRE Energie and REMU. Even though it appeared in the early 2000s that Endesa was in a strong position to take over both firms, the Dutch Ministry of Economic Affairs decided to block the deal given pressures from parliament.[207] Eventually, Netherlands-based ENECO NV acquired REMU, characterized by some as a process where the country 'protected its own'.[208] Later, E.ON was allowed to take over NRE, at the time the country's fifth largest supplier with 275,000 customers. Interestingly, the evidence suggests that the Germans received a nice discount when compared to what the Spaniards had originally offered: E.ON paid €76.5 million compared to the €404 million previously offered by Endesa,[209] showing how states may facilitate the movement of neighbouring Alphas. The symbiotic relationship between the Germans and the Dutch emerged a few years later when E.ON sold Transpower to TenneT, fully controlled and owned by the Dutch government.

In a final scenario, Alphas make deals in countries where their home state has past historical experiences, seen especially in the case of EDF. This was reflected in early deals in the late 1990s, when it entered the Ivory Coast with Azito Energie. Throughout the 2000s the firm also made headway into states with whom France has historical ties, such as Vietnam and Laos. With regard to the latter, NTPC 'was established in 2002 for the development, construction and 25 years of operation of the 1070 MW capacity Nam Theun 2 hydroelectric power plant ... [where] EDF was the main investor with 40% of the capital, 35% held by EGCO (the Thai electricity generation company), and 25% by the Laotian government'.[210] Another recent transaction in the 2010s has close cooperation with state officials, as seen in La Mitis Community Wind Project in Canada with which the firm worked alongside the Quebec government.[211]

Regulatory authorities
Deals negotiated ultimately needed the approval of regulatory authorities which could have theoretically blocked them. The first level of governance that may have been involved includes national-level regulators. A second level includes decisions made by the European Union. In some cases, national regulators may have also worked closely with the European Commission. Finally, as seen in the automobile chapter, some deals in non-EU countries may have slipped under the regulatory radar, which effectively meant that 'no

decision' was a 'positive decision' in favour of the Alpha. I consider these three dimensions.

First, when turning to national level authorities, some of the deals which did not have a Community dimension were approved by national regulators. A key example of a big SSE purchase, Airtricty, was approved by the Irish Competition Authority, as was the later purchase of Endesa Ireland.[212] When turning to E.ON and EDF, some examples include: the E.ON/NRE deal (as well as ENECO/REMU), which received regulatory approval from the Dutch authority Nederlandse Mededingingsautoriteit (Nma); E.ON's sale of Thüga to the consortium of Integra Energie and Kom9 that was approved by the Bundeskartellamt, which similarly approved EDF's sale of its 45 per cent stake in EnBW; and the sale of Edasz to E.ON, which was approved by Hungary's capital market regulator PSZAF.[213] In Italy, the share swap with CDP and MEF (Italy), whereby MEF gained over 30 per cent control of ENEL, was approved by the *Autorità Garante della Concorrenza e del Mercato*.[214]

Second, the big deals across European space ultimately required the approval of DG Competition. In some of these cases, one sees cooperation between national regulators and the European Commission: in investigating EDF/Seeboard, for example, the Commission worked closely with OFT and Ofgem.[215] In other cases, Commission officials were alerted to potential competition concerns when flagged by national authorities. This is seen in EDF/SPE, where the *Belgian Conseil de la Concurrence* was concerned that the deal would lead to competition concerns in Belgium.[216]

Tables 5.12 (EDF) and 5.13 (E.ON and ENEL)[217] summarize the cases investigated by the Commission, with reference to the major transactions presented earlier, where the Alphas acted as acquirer or vendor. Table 5.12 summarizes those cases related to EDF, while Table 5.13 those related to E.ON and ENEL (save the takeover of Endesa discussed later in the chapter). Both Tables outline the main outcomes and the conditions placed, if any.

Taken together, both Tables highlight that *none* of the transactions investigated by the Commission was ever blocked. A solid majority received Commission approval without any conditions placed. Some of these decisions were almost frighteningly predictable even before the investigation started. This is seen in E.ON's swap with Electrabel as well as E.ON's sale of Transpower to TenneT, both consequences of the Commission's earlier anti-trust investigation, forcing remedies to increase competition in the German market. Exceptions to the general rule of placing no conditions are seen in E.ON/MOL, EDF/EnBW, EDF/BE, and EDF/SPE, even though such remedies did not prove to be deal-breakers. This highlights that, as seen in the other empirical chapters, few barriers were placed by European regulatory authorities when Alphas made acquisitions in order to consolidate their position as global champions.

Table 5.12. Summary of European Commission Decisions: EDF Deals

Deal	Outcome	Decision/Conditions (if any)
EDF/ESTAG (1998)	Approved	Commission found that deal would not significantly impede competition in the single market and no conditions placed (henceforth, simply, 'non-opposition')
EDF/Graninge (1998)	Approved	Non-opposition
EDF/London Electricity (1999)	Approved	Non-opposition
EDF/SWEB (1999)	Approved	Non-opposition
EDF/EnBW (2001)	Approved	Commission concerned deal would strengthen EDF's dominant position in France, given that 'EnBW's supply area is in the south-west of Germany and has a long common border with France'. Remedies pursued include that 'EDF makes available to competitors 6000 Megawatts of generation capacity location in France, equal to 30% of the eligible market', and that EnBW's shareholding in Swiss electricity company WATT is divested
EDF/Cottam Power Station (2001)	Approved	Non-opposition
EDF/West Burton Power Station/ Eastern Electricity/24Seven (2001)	Approved	Non-opposition
EDF/Seeboard (2002)	Approved	Non-opposition
EDF/EnBW/Kogeneracja (2009) & EDF/Kogeneracja (EDF attains full control, 2012)	Approved	Non-opposition
EDF/EnBW/ERSA (2009) & EDF/ERSA (when EDF attains full control, 2012)	Approved	Non-opposition
EDF/British Energy (2009)	Approved	Acquisition conditional upon various commitments, including 'to divest the power generation plant at Sutton Bridge (owned by EDF) and at Eggborough (owned by BE) and to sell certain minimum volumes of electricity in the British wholesale market'.
EDF/SPE (2009)	Approved	Acquisition conditional on EDF divesting assets of one of its companies that was planning power station projects in Belgium
EDF/Edison (2005, EDF joint control; and 2012, full control)	Approved	Non-opposition

Sources: EDF/ESTAG (1998), Case No. COMP M.1107; EDF/Graninge (1998) Case No. M.1169; EDF/London Electricity (1999), Case No. M.1346; EDF/SWEB (1999), Case No. M.1606; EDF/EnBW (2001), Case No. M.1853 (see also European Commission (2001a) from where quote in Table is taken); EDF/Cottam Power Station (2001), Case No. M.2209; EDF/West Burton Power Station/Eastern Electricity/24Seven (2001), Case No. M.2675; EDF/Seeboard (2002); Case No. M.2890; EDF/Kogeneracja (2009 and 2012), Case Nos M.4993 and M.6456; EDF/ERSA (2009 and 2012), Case Nos M.4998 and M.6450; EDF/British Energy (2009), Case No. M. 5224 (see also European Commission (2008c) from where quote is taken); EDF/SPE (Segebel, 2009), Case No. M.5549; EDF/Edison (2005), Case No. M.3729, and (2012) Case No. M.6530.

When turning to dynamics outside of the EU, regulators from the US have been involved in giving the green light in some of the transactions. For example, in the UniStar deal EDF required the approval of the Maryland Public Service Commission.[218] Similarly, in E.ON/Powergen, the state of Virginia approved the deal in 2001, followed by the SEC.[219]

Table 5.13. Summary of European Commission Decisions: E.ON and ENEL Deals

Deal	Outcome	Decision/Conditions (if any)
E.ON/Sydkraft (2001)	Approved	Commission found that deal would not significantly impede competition in the single market and no conditions placed (henceforth, simply, 'non-opposition')
E.ON/Powergen (2001)	Approved	Non-opposition
E.ON/Energie AG Oberösterreich/Jihoceska (2002)	Approved	Non-opposition
E.ON/TXU Europe Group (2002)	Approved	Non-opposition
E.ON/Midlands Electricity (2003)	Approved	Non-opposition
E.ON/MOL (2005)	Approved	Remedies include 'full ownership unbundling of the gas production and transmission activities retained by MOL and the commercial activities acquired by E.ON'.
E.ON/Pražská plynárenská (I) and E.ON PP (II) (2006 and 2010)	Approved	Non-opposition
E.ON/MPE Energia (2009)	Approved	Non-opposition
E.ON/Electrabel (power plants, 2009)	Approved	Non-opposition
E.ON/TenneT (sale of Transpower)	Approved	Non-opposition
Endesa/ENEL–Elettrogen (2001)	Approved	Non-opposition
ENEL/Viesgo (2001)	Approved	Non-opposition
ENEL/Slovenské Elektrárne (2005)	Approved	Non-opposition
ENEL/EMS (2008)	Approved	Non-opposition
Sharp/ENEL Green Power/Joint Venture (2010)	Approved	Non-opposition

Sources: European Commission, E.ON/Sydkraft (2001) Case No. M.2349; E.ON/Powergen (2001) Case No. M.2443; E.ON/Jihoceska (2002), Case No. M.2715; E.ON/TXU Europe Group (2002), Case No. M.3007; E.ON/Midlands Electricity (2003), Case No. M.3306; E.ON/MOL (2005), Case No. 3696 (see also European Commission (2005) from where quote in Table is taken); E.ON/Pražská plynárenská (I) and E.ON PP (II) (2006 and 2010) (Case Nos M.4197 and M.6000); E.ON/MPE Energia (2009), Case No. M.5442; E.ON/Electrabel (2009); Case No. 5512; E.ON/TenneT (sale of Transpower), Case No. 5707; Endesa/ENEL–Elettrogen (2001), Case No. 2553; ENEL/Viesgo (2001), Case No. M.2620; ENEL/Slovenské Elektrárne (2005), Case No. M.3655; ENEL/EMS (2008), Case No. M.4841; Sharp/ENEL Green Power/Joint Venture (2010), Case No. M.5788.

Yet, when turning to privatizations in Central and Eastern Europe before the countries joined the Union, there is little evidence of rigorous regulatory approval. The only exception to this is found in the 2002 sale of the power distributor Stredoslovenská Energetika (sold to EDF), where the Slovak Anti-trust office (PMU) approved the transaction.[220] Other states which privatized before entering the EU—such as Romania, Hungary, Poland, and Bulgaria—did not have approval mechanisms in place. Similar to dynamics in the automobile chapter, this can be explained by these countries privatizing, while being guided by goals to attain reliable partnerships with European giants from established EU countries. Several of such sales took place before accession of their own states into the EU. A similar logic also helps explain why regulators played little role in global deals: those pursued in the Ivory Coast, Brazil, Vietnam, Laos, and China saw firms attain approval by simply working alongside state actors, without any clear, robust regulatory approval process. This was particularly acute in China. For example, the development of the Taishan Nuclear Power Company in 2008 was entered into by EDF along with (state-owned) China's Guangdong Nuclear Power Holding, which may be described as a 'tit-for-tat', where the French were allowed increased global market to do business while the Chinese received nuclear expertise in return.[221] This evidence helps demonstrate that a green light to expand also implicitly occurs when there is no formal approval from regulators.

Lobbying resources

Alpha success in gaining regulatory approval requires direct lobbying of firms in the process, as seen in the other empirical chapters. And such lobbying requires investment by firms, particularly in their Brussels office. By relying on data from the EU's Transparency Register, a joint voluntary registry between the Commission and the EP, we can consider the funding that Alphas earmark towards their lobbying activities. In the absence of an umbrella trade association to which all major utility companies belong, Table 5.14 compiles a list of

Table 5.14. Power Lobbying Costs in Brussels

Company Name	Registered in Joint Transparency Register (2013)	Lobbying Costs Declared in Transparency Register (2013)
E.ON (Germany)	Yes	€2,032,000
GDF Suez (France)	Yes	€3,750,000–4,000,000
ENEL (Italy)*	Yes	€400,000–550,000
EDF (France)	Yes	€2,000,000–2,500,000
RWE (Germany)	Yes	€2,000,000
Iberdrola (Spain)	Yes	€600–700,000
SSE (UK)	Yes	€200–250,000
Centrica (UK)	No	Firm is not registered; data is thus not disclosed
Vattenfall (Sweden)	Yes	€250–300,000
EDP (Portugal)	Yes	€50,000
Electrabel (Belgium)	No	Firm is not registered; data is thus not disclosed
Dong Energy (Denmark)	Yes	€50,000
Fenosa/Gas Natural (Spain)	Yes	€50,000–100,000
National Grid (UK)	Yes	€50,000

Source: European Union, Transparency Register.

* The funds declared by Endesa (€50,000–100,000), which is separately registered, are summed with those of ENEL (€350,000–450,000). The Brussels offices of both are located at the same address, 13/14 Ave. des Arts.

leading European firms previously outlined in Table 5.7 (when the second part of the Global Movers Test was performed), as well as other major players referred to throughout the chapter. It considers whether or not the firm was registered in the Joint Transparency Register in 2013 and, if so, what funds were earmarked when lobbying EU institutions in the previous financial year, 2012.[222]

As a first observation, all of the Alphas studied in the chapter are registered, as well as several other major European players. As the Register is voluntary, however, giants such as Centrica and other players such as Electrabel have chosen to abstain from registration, so it is impossible to know their lobbying costs. A second observation sees that (other than GDF–Suez) the Alphas studied have the highest funds earmarked towards lobbying in Brussels, with EDF between 2 and 2.5 million, and E.ON declaring slightly more than 2 million (roughly on a par with the German giant RWE). That EDF tops the firms studied—indeed, having costs which represented a tenfold increase from its values reported in 2009—may be explained based on lobbying on M&A pursued in 2012. Of particular importance in this regard was the full takeover of Edison. ENEL's declared amount follows, while SSE has the lowest value of all the Alphas. The latter may be explained because the firm has not pursued an aggressive M&A strategy in the continent.

Explaining the Beta: Endesa

As seen in Section 5.1, Endesa had strong potential to become an Alpha after privatization. In terms of initial conditions (X1), it was a profitable firm that was successfully floated. Not dissimilar to EDF and ENEL, it was the main player in Spain: Marcos (2013, 290) estimates that its 'market shares [were] well above 30% in each of the submarkets in the electricity industry'. After privatization of a minority of its stake, it acquired companies in several of its former colonies in South America through its purchase of Enersis and later made significant purchases in France and Italy. By 2004 the company was thus ranked fourth in the world in the utilities sector by Forbes and was one of the most competitive firms in the sector. But it ended up a Beta.

In order to understand this, this section examines how the firm was thrice targeted. The main argument to be developed is that it was eventually taken over not because of those intervening variables (X2) that focus on internal factors, but because of external ones. Of particular salience is the impact of liberalization, the role of the state (including Spain and Italy), and regulators.

The first attempt to take over Endesa was seen in Gas Natural's hostile bid in 2005. But this failed for various reasons, pointing to the importance of shareholders, managers, and state actors. Barcelona-based Gas Natural was one of the main energy companies in Spain, whose main shareholder was the bank (*caja*) controlled by the Catalan regional government, La Caixa. Many in the

Socialist minority government, which had the legislative support of the Catalan regional party CiU, were in favour of the takeover. This was in part based on keeping CiU happy, and, in part, believing that the joining of the two giants could create an even larger Spanish-based global energy giant. But, there was not full consensus and many other private and public actors held reservations. From a managerial and shareholder perspective, the price of €21.30 per share offered by Gas Natural was considered low, valuing the firm at €22.55 billion. This resulted in open opposition to the deal from Endesa's boss, Manuel Pizarro.[223] But, there was also open political opposition, highlighting the regional tensions in Spanish politics. Many in the PP opposition in the Spanish parliament, as well as the PP regional government of Madrid that also controlled one of the largest shareholders in Endesa—Caja Madrid—were wary that a relatively smaller player based out of Catalonia would gain control of Madrid's champion. Further, the state energy regulator that was housed in the Ministry of Industry, the CNE (*Comisión Nacional de Energía*), approved the deal, but imposed various conditions.[224] Later, the Spanish competition authority SDC (*Servicio de Defensa de la Competencia*) stated that the deal would result in a monopoly over gas and electricity distribution. As far as the European Commission was concerned, the transaction did not have a community dimension and it was therefore an issue for national regulators.[225]

Shortly after it became relatively clear that Gas Natural's bid was going to flounder, E.ON's moves in early 2006 marked the start of what can be denominated as an 'Alpha War', where two Alphas target the same firm. The strategic reasons for E.ON seeking 100 per cent control were obvious. First, with EU liberalization initiatives having come into force, E.ON had the opportunity to do so. Buying Endesa strategically meant that the Germans would gain access to the large Spanish market, and gain control of French and Italian assets Endesa owned. More importantly, E.ON would gain a stronghold in Latin America, where at the time Endesa was one of the few European players (other than EDF which had acquired but then sold Brazil's Light). Summing the parts, the transaction would have resulted in 'the world's largest power and gas company with over 50,000,000 customers in more than 30 countries around the world'.[226] As such, the Germans made an initial offer of €27.50 per share that was comparatively attractive to that of Gas Natural. This was significantly bettered over the courtship period, where E.ON upped its final offer to €40.00 per share, thus making a €42.35 billion bid for Endesa.[227] E.ON managers and shareholders were happy, as was the management of Endesa, which recommended its shareholders to accept an offer that represented a bid premium of 115 per cent on Endesa's closing price on the last day of trading prior to Gas Natural's original offer.[228] Everything being equal, if the desires of managers and shareholders were the most important factors, then Endesa would have been sold to the Germans. With the European Commission having approved the deal in April 2006,[229] it appeared set to go through.

That was until the state really exerted its muscle. Clearly, Pedro Solbes, the Vice-Prime Minister and the Minister of Economy and Finance, was openly against any takeover of Endesa by the Germans. Even though Prime Minister Zapatero publicly stated that Endesa could make its own choices as a private firm, Solbes was concerned about the 'national energy future of Spain' and that Spain preferred 'to secure a deal in its national interests in a strategic sector'.[230] So while the E.ON takeover seemed imminent, behind the scenes the government was simultaneously composing three interludes to slow down and then put an end to the German song.

First, the state-apparatus imposed impediments and delayed approval of the proposed sale. Even though the European Commission had approved E.ON/Endesa, in mid-2006 the state argued that it had jurisdiction over the matter. Highlighting what Marcos (2013, 289) describes as a 'good example of the political motivations that can be found behind the pure technical assessments made by the competent authorities and regulatory agencies', the Ministry of Industry's controlled CNE imposed nineteen conditions that E.ON would have to swallow.[231] Angela Merkel criticized the Spanish government, and the European Commission backed her up by stating in September and again in December 2006 that Spain had no jurisdiction to impose such conditions, which were incompatible with the Common Market.[232] From a strategic perspective, however, one may argue that this 'regulatory filibuster' gave the state a smokescreen behind which to concoct its own deal.

Thus, the second composed interlude was to stop E.ON altogether and, then, present a new knight to come to the rescue: Italy's ENEL and the Spanish firm Acciona. Unlike E.ON, they were no strangers to the state. Regarding ENEL, as seen in Section 5.1, through the Viesgo and Elettrogen deals, the Italian firm had previous transactions with Endesa and had been a player since the Spanish market started to open up in the early 2000s. More fascinatingly, to ensure that ENEL was on board, the Spanish and Italian states carved out a symbiotic deal of their own, as reported by the Spanish newspaper *El País*.[233] When Spain's Prime Minister José Luis Zapatero and Italy's Prime Minister Romano Prodi met in Ibiza on 2 February 2007, they agreed that in return for finding an Italian-led solution with ENEL in order to stop E.ON, the Spanish giant Telefónica would take an important stake in Telecom Italia.[234] Such a deal seems unsurprising in retrospect. The ties between Prodi and members of the Socialist administration dated back: Spain's Pedro Solbes, who was championing an end to E.ON's bid, served as European Commissioner for Economic and Monetary Affairs of the Prodi Commission.[235]

Regarding Acciona, the Alcobendas (Madrid)-based firm, with a wide portfolio that primarily worked in construction and renewable energy, had done previous deals with the Spanish state. In 2002 Acciona led a consortium to buy Trasmediterranea, which transports passengers between Spain, the Baleares, Gibraltar, and the Canary Islands.[236] This transport company was housed in the SEPI and privatized by the then PP government. Interestingly, while Acciona was a majority partner in the consortium, a minority partner included the group led by Abel Matutes, the ex-Minister of Foreign Affairs under Aznar's PP administration in the 1990s. By courting a firm that had done deals with the PP, the Socialists were guaranteed little resistance from the opposition, a previous bane in the Gas Natural deal.

In terms of stopping E.ON, and while the Commission and the German government were still fuming with CNE's conditions and raring for a legal fight between Madrid and Brussels, Acciona acquired a 10 per cent stake in Endesa in September 2006 which would raise to 21 per cent by January 2007.[237] Surprising many in the public that were unaware of the Zapatero/Prodi deal, ENEL took a 9.99 per cent shareholding in Endesa. This occurred a day after the Minister of Industry (Joan Clos) had publicly announced on 27 February that a 'Spanish Solution' was being brokered.[238] By 12 March ENEL increased this stake to 24.98 per cent, buying shares from both Italy's Mediobanca and UBS.[239] All of these transactions needed approval of the CNE, which was readily given.[240]

With a combined stake of around 46 per cent between ENEL and Acciona by mid-March, both were thus in a good position as Endesa shareholders to block any proposed sale to E.ON, which required 50.1 per cent. The state's remaining ownership in Endesa, through the SEPI which controlled 2.95 per cent, was also important—but not enough. The last hurdle, therefore, was to get the community of Madrid's controlled Caja Madrid—which owned 9.94 per cent of Endesa—on board, forming the ultimate blocking coalition to the E.ON deal.[241] This was guaranteed by upping the price: the ENEL/Acciona offer was not garnering much political opposition and, as far as Caja Madrid and other shareholders were concerned, the €40.16 per share offer was still better than E.ON's.[242] Other shareholders, as well as management of the firm which owned stock options and would make even more money on the sale, were also on board. Endesa's boss, Manuel Pizarro, alone would make €4.1 million on the sale to ENEL/Acciona, which was still some €16,000 more than if Endesa were bought by E.ON.[243]

The state's third interlude was to then broker a final aspect of the deal on 29 March, putting out kindling fires in Berlin and Brussels. In return for renouncing any future hostile takeover attempts over Endesa, E.ON was allowed to acquire around €11 billion worth of Endesa's assets in France (SNET), Italy (Elettrogen), Poland, and Turkey, as well as the Spanish utility Viesgo that was owned by ENEL.[244] By so doing, E.ON instantly became the fifth largest player in the Italian market, the fourth in Spain, and the third in

France. This final aspect was important because it kept E.ON and ostensibly the German government happy; it also prevented any threats of legal battles (or future tensions) with Brussels based on CNE's previous conditions placed on E.ON.[245] Perhaps as important, divesting key stakes pre-empted any potential remedies that Brussels may have otherwise imposed on the ENEL/Acciona acquisition of Endesa. In April 2007 E.ON officially backed down, but the results show the 'positive sum' nature of the deal in which both Alphas eventually won out. Both of their deals—ENEL and Acciona's takeover of Endesa and the sale of some of Endesa's assets to E.ON—were later approved by the European Commission in the summer of 2007, without conditions.[246]

But the so-called 'Spanish Solution' was not much of one in the end. Both ENEL and Acciona exercised joint control over Endesa starting in October 2007, where Acciona's stake was 25.01 per cent, ENEL's 67.05 per cent, and the rest was traded on the stock market (Marcos, 2013, 310). However, by 2009 Acciona was suffering managerial conflicts with the Italians, coupled with needing cash given its own debts. Acciona subsequently sold its stake in Endesa to ENEL in June 2009 for an estimated €9.627 billion.[247] ENEL's attaining a 92.06 per cent stake in Endesa was approved by the European Commission, without conditions.[248] A year later, as seen earlier, the Italian state then increased its direct control over ENEL to more than 30 per cent, something which can be better understood in light of ENEL taking full control of its former Southern European competitor, forming one of the world's largest energy giants.

Yet, as much as there may not have been a 'Spanish solution', the revolving doors in Endesa's wake simply amaze. First are the revolving doors from the private company to public office, seen in those close to the PP. Endesa's boss during its takeover, Manuel Pizarro, left the firm in October 2007, only to take up a new position on Telefónica's board of directors in December 2007.[249] The next year, however, he left this position and ran for office as a member of the Partido Popular, with the view to take over Solbes' job in Economy and Finance. But having embarrassed himself in a leaders' debate against the calmer and wiser Solbes during the 2008 election campaign, the PP lost and Pizarro eventually had to settle for a seat in the opposition (Chari, 2008). Luck was, however, better for another Endesa board member who eventually did take Solbes' job some years later: Luis de Guindos, who served as the director of the board of Endesa Spain (and Endesa Chile) in 2009, eventually became Minister of the later rebranded Ministry of Economic Affairs and Competitiveness when Rajoy's PP administration was elected in the general election of 2011.[250]

Then there are those revolving doors from public to private office, seen in both the Spanish Socialists and the Partido Popular. Two years after composing the ENEL/Acciona takeover in 2007, and in the same year after ENEL gained full control of Endesa in 2009, Pedro Solbes retired from politics. Two years later he joined ENEL's board of directors, with an estimated basic salary of €85,000.[251] Solbes' important governmental position as Vice-Prime Minister and Minister of Economy and Finance was taken over by Elena Salgado in 2009. Months after the Socialists lost the 2011 general election, Salgado, too, moved on. In 2012 she was named to the board of directors of Chilectra, the Chilean distributor of Enersis that forms part of the Endesa Group, which is now fully owned by ENEL.[252] In their new positions both Socialists could, perhaps unsurprisingly, share some good company with former PP politicians, too: Spain's former Prime Minister, José Maria Aznar, has also served as an advisor to Endesa since 2011.[253]

Conclusions

This chapter started with a brief review of the history, privatization, and key M&A of the five main firms analysed: EDF (France), E.ON (Germany), SSE (the UK), ENEL (Italy), and Endesa (Spain). The second section then performed the Global Movers and Independence Tests, arguing that all firms except Endesa can be considered Alphas today.

In order to understand why firms are Alphas, the third section first paid attention to the internal, more firm-specific, factors. One of the main arguments made was that the strong market positions of the firm before and after privatization, the goals of managers, and the actions of shareholders are important in explaining why these firms have become European and global giants. With long-term visions, in particular, management teams of Alphas have demonstrated to be skilled deal negotiators, cognizant of providing a conducive atmosphere for their acquisitions' smooth incorporation. The roles of shareholders, too, are also important. To this end, attention was given to the world's leading asset management firms, providing evidence of those such as BlackRock that bought and sold shares over time in the Alphas. Further, there is evidence to suggest that such firms were more likely to have invested in Alphas rather than in Endesa (the Beta), which represented more risk. The section also highlighted the importance of those shareholders of companies targeted by Alphas who make significant gains in the deals, as seen in Powergen. Such gains were also enjoyed by Alpha shareholders when divesting, as seen in EDF's sale of EnBW as well as ENEL's sale of Terna.

Yet, as much as internal factors may be important, they are not sufficient in explaining why the firms could expand, successfully pursue global deals, and eventually be considered Alphas today. Rather, similar to the other empirical chapters, the evidence suggests that more external, political, factors are necessary and sufficient, where, again, one can conceptualize an almost sequential relationship that ties the factors together: liberalization (or lack thereof) first defined *what could be done* with regard to expansion (and even protection, in the absence of full liberalization) that would set the foundation for Alphas to pursue deals and become world giants. Both Alpha home states, some with strong vested interests in the firm, as well as other states keen to see the Alphas enter, set the tone for *how it could be done*, intervening and facilitating deals as well as maintaining close firm ties on their boards. And regulators at different levels of governance, lobbied by the firms, ensured *that expansion into different markets could be done*, without blocking or placing conditions on the final deals.

In more detail, liberalization defined where Alphas could make their expansionary deals, or, *what could be done* at certain conjunctures. Having liberalized ahead of other EU states meant that the UK was the first to see an 'Alpha invasion' of continental giants such as EDF and E.ON, which, along with ENEL, also made a dual strategy to target privatized firms in Central and Eastern Europe in the late 1990s and early 2000s. EDF, E.ON, ENEL, and even Endesa were doubly protected in their own domestic markets from invasion by other Alphas (such as SSE) given the lack of full liberalization at home. However, as the 2000s continued, EU liberalization initiatives gained momentum, providing a threat to dominant home market positions, but with an opportunity to more freely expand into parts of European space not hitherto tapped. This set the foundation for the creation of European and world giants.

Second, the evidence highlights the importance of the state, which still maintains sizeable ownership in EDF, an almost third of a stake in ENEL, and a minority in E.ON. With the exception of the EDF case in the 2000s—eventually approved by the ECJ despite the Commission's initial opposition—it was argued that state aid is generally not readily given by the Alphas' home states. Yet, public funds are still earmarked by way of PPPs, contracts, and subsidized research projects to all Alphas, even those such as SSE which sees no state ownership. This supplements the millions that Alphas receive from the European Commission's DG Energy that co-finances the EU Energy Programme for Recovery along with member states. Further, states crucially helped craft deals wherever they could be embarked upon in the context of liberalization dynamics, taking positions on *how expansion could be done*. This is seen in transactions in Central and Eastern Europe, E.ON/Ruhrgas, ENEL/Terna, EDF/EnBW, as well as expansion into ex-colonial areas as seen in EDF. Further, the state's ties to Alphas remain strong after privatization: *all* Alphas still have some directors on their boards which have past (and even present) association, or links, with the state. While Alphas' home states are indeed significant, the evidence also suggests that other states from abroad where Alphas acquire are also keen to facilitate expansion, playing driving roles. This was seen in EDF/British Energy, which saw the active participation of the UK government as well as in several privatizations in Central and Eastern Europe. Such relationships formed between the Alphas and these states set the stage for further deals over time between the newfound partners, as seen in E.ON and the Dutch government.

Finally, regulatory authorities—the ultimate potential veto players—played a key role in ensuring *that it could be done*. Analysis of the several cases at both levels of governance in Europe demonstrates that domestic regulators readily approved the (smaller) Alpha deals and supranational authorities *never* blocked any major M&A (and only in rare cases placed conditions). The latter can be explained in the context of the large amounts of funds that the firms earmark towards lobbying in Brussels. Further, outside of the EU, Alphas could escape the regulatory radar when making some acquisitions, as seen in Central and Eastern European states before joining the EU, as well as Asia and Africa.

When turning to the Beta, the same key variables are at play, as seen in the 'Alpha War' between E.ON and ENEL in the takeover of Endesa, both of whom targeted the Spanish giant as a consequence of EU liberalization that allowed firms to pursue major cross-border acquisitions. Everything being equal, if managers and shareholders of both firms were the driving force, then E.ON would have been successful in its bid. But it was not. This is primarily because of the roles of the Spanish and Italian states, Spanish regulators (which blocked E.ON's attempt), and the European Commission (which approved ENEL's acquisition), ultimately proving key explanatory factors of why Endesa became a Beta eventually fully taken over by ENEL. That said, the evidence also shows that E.ON did not leave empty-handed, which can be explained by the Spanish state's desire to keep both Berlin and Brussels happy, pointing to the positive sum nature of Alpha Wars.

In sum, taking all of the five cases together, a common thread that explains why firms become Alphas or Betas is the impact of liberalization, the influence of states, and the actions, and sometimes inactions, of regulatory authorities.

The final chapter summarizes the main findings, more fully theorizes the relationship between the factors of salience, and considers the larger impact of this work for social scientists, business leaders, and political actors.

Endnotes

1. This is based on information found on the company website: <http://about-us.edf.com/profile/history/1946-1962-43671.html> (accessed 10 March 2014).
2. Quote taken from <http://about-us.edf.com/profile/history/1963-1973-43672.html> (accessed 10 March 2014).
3. Based on information provided in <http://about-us.edf.com/profile/history/1974-1989-43673.html> (accessed 10 March 2014).

4. Quote taken from <http://about-us.edf.com/profile/history/1974-1989-43673. html>.

5. The values for the transaction (in USD) are based on those reported by <www. privatizationbarometer.net> (last accessed 2 January 2014).

6. This was made up of GBP 1.4 million in cash, plus the assumption of GBP 500 million in debt. Data taken from Zephyr Deal ID Number 40566.

7. Based on analysis of Bureau van Dijk's Zephyr database, BvD Deal ID Number 46764.

8. Based on analysis of Bureau van Dijk's Zephyr database, BvD Deal ID Number 58698.

9. Based on analysis of Bureau van Dijk's Zephyr database, BvD Deal ID Number 76444.

10. Based on analysis of Bureau van Dijk's Zephyr database, BvD Deal ID Number 101398.

11. Based on European Commission, Case No. Comp/M.2765, as well as Bureau van Dijk's Zephyr database, BvD Deal ID Number 101639.

12. Five of the twelve nuclear stations placed in Nuclear Electric in 1991—the five newer advanced gas-cooled reactors—were privatized as British Energy (Chick, 2007, 115).

13. Based on analysis of Bureau van Dijk's Zephyr database, BvD Deal ID Number 621873.

14. Quote taken from <http://www.edfenergy.com/energyfuture/edf-energys-approach-about-edf-energy/edf-energys-history>. For further information, see also <http://www.edfenergy.com/about-us/about-edf-energy/our-history.shtml> (both accessed 12 March 2014).

15. This data is based on information provided in UK Power (2012).

16. Based on data found in BvD Zephyr file with ID number 245681.

17. Based on analysis of Bureau van Dijk's Zephyr database, Deal ID Numbers 92957 and 214654.

18. On this history of Centrica between 1997 and 2002, see: <http://www.centrica.co.uk/index.asp?pageid=23&year=2002> and for the press release on Centrica's formation following the demerger in February 1997, see: <http://www.centrica.co.uk/index.asp?pageid=1041&newsid=1127>. In a recent deal, in December 2013 the Centrica-led consortium was chosen by the Irish government to take over the retail unit of the electricity and gas company Bord Gáis. This is part of the country's privatization of remaining crown jewels in order to raise revenues in the wake of the financial and economic crisis. On the Irish financial and economic crisis, including constraints imposed on the state when it agreed to its IMF-led bailout, see Chari and Bernhagen (2011).

19. Based on analysis of Bureau van Dijk's Zephyr database, BvD Deal ID Number 375947.

20. Based on analysis of Bureau van Dijk's Zephyr database, BvD Deal ID Number 1601193222.

21. Based on analysis of Bureau van Dijk's Zephyr database, BvD Deal ID Number 121622.

22. Based on analysis of Bureau van Dijk's Zephyr database, BvD Deal ID Number 201435.
23. Based on analysis of Bureau van Dijk's Zephyr database, BvD Deal ID Number 1601373169.
24. The Zephyr files which discuss the stakes sold during the privatization process have the following ID numbers: 67334 and 53302.
25. The deal where Deutsche Bank and HSBC sell EDF a minority (around 6%) stake can be found on Zephyr deal with ID number 107610.
26. Based on information taken from BvD's Zephyr database, Deal ID Number 36324.
27. Quote taken from BvD's Zephyr database, Deal ID No BvD 545662.
28. Based on analysis of Bureau van Dijk's Zephyr database, BvD Deal ID Number 34360.
29. Based on analysis of Bureau van Dijk's Zephyr database, BvD Deal ID Number 472916. For a history of the firm see: <https://www.edfdemasz.hu/pages/aloldal.jsp?id=6432>.
30. Based on analysis of Bureau van Dijk's Zephyr database, BvD Deal ID Number 38186.
31. Based on analysis of Bureau van Dijk's Zephyr database, BvD Deal ID Number 1601201166.
32. Based on analysis of Bureau van Dijk's Zephyr database, BvD Deal ID Number 94229.
33. See Reuters (2013).
34. Based on analysis of Bureau van Dijk's Zephyr database, BvD Deal ID Number 70860.
35. Based on analysis of Bureau van Dijk's Zephyr database, BvD Deal ID Number 95080.
36. Based on analysis of Bureau van Dijk's Zephyr database, BvD Deal ID Number 147611.
37. On the UniStar deal, see Zephyr file with ID Number 1601022229; on the Exelon/Constellation deal, see BvD ID Number 1601266662.
38. Today, EDF Energies Nouvelles is a fully owned subsidiary of EDF. In 2006 there was an IPO of 28.933% of Energies Nouvelles on Euronext. However, in 2011 the company was delisted and EDF attained full control. Based on information found in the Zephyr database with BvD file Numbers 440610 (on the IPO) and 1601261570 (on EDF's acquisition of 100% of Energies Nouvelles).
39. Based on information found on EDF Canada webpage: <http://www.edf-en.ca/press-display/post/68/EDF-EN-Canada-Obtains-Authorization-from-the-Gover> (accessed 15 March 2014).
40. Based on information found on: <http://asia.edf.com/activities/clean-coal-52204.html> (accessed 1 March 2014).
41. Based on information found on: <http://asia.edf.com/activities/clean-coal-52204.html> (accessed 1 March 2014).
42. Based on information in the Zephyr file with Bvd ID Number 1000011807 as well as information on the EDF Asia webpage, <http://asia.edf.com/activities/nuclear-52202.html> (accessed 1 March 2014).

43. On MECO, see: <http://asia.edf.com/activities/clean-coal-52204.html>. Quote is taken from <http://www.mekong-energy.com/aboutus.html> (accessed 15 March 2014).

44. On NTPC see: <http://asia.edf.com/activities/hydropower-52206.html> (accessed 7 March 2014).

45. On the history of Azito Energie, see: <http://www.ips-wa.com/en/businesses/infra structure/azito-energie.html> (accessed 7 March 2014).

46. On the sale of its stake in 2010, please see Zephyr file with BvD Deal Number 1601227578.

47. As the company webpage where this is explained also notes, eon is the English spelling of the Greek word *aeon*, which means 'a new epoch', 'age', or 'infinity'. See: <http://www.eon.com/en/info-service/faq/about-us.html> (accessed 18 December 2013).

48. All of the information in this paragraph on the history of E.ON is based on the information on E.ON's website: <http://www.eon.com/en/about-us/profile/his tory/1923-99.html>. The information on privatization deal values (where known) is based on information in <www.privatizationbarometer.net>.

49. Except for the ownership in the firm today, information in this paragraph is taken from BvD Zephyr file with Bvd ID Number 70784.

50. Based on shareholder information of E.ON found in the Amadeus database, company ID DE5050056484.

51. Based on analysis of Bureau van Dijk's Zephyr database, BvD Deal ID Number 70020.

52. Based on analysis of Bureau van Dijk's Zephyr database, BvD Deal ID Number 71124.

53. Based on analysis of Bureau van Dijk's Zephyr database, BvD Deal ID Number 54201.

54. Based on analysis of Bureau van Dijk's Zephyr database, BvD Deal ID Number 70332.

55. Based on analysis of Bureau van Dijk's Zephyr database, BvD Deal ID Number 77932.

56. Based on analysis of Bureau van Dijk's Zephyr database, BvD Deal ID Number 72721.

57. Based on analysis of Bureau van Dijk's Zephyr database, BvD Deal ID Numbers 94101 and 117898.

58. As discussed in Zephyr Deal with ID Number 81238, the method of payment in the E.ON/Powergen deal included cash, loan notes, and debt assumed of approximately €6.9 billion.

59. On Powergen's acquisition of Midlands in 2003, see Macallister (2003). A history of Midlands electricity is also found on the company report on Amadeus, with company ID GB02366928. Quote on market share of Central Networks is based on information found on the E.ON website (<www.eon.com>) on its history (under March 2011).

60. Based on analysis of Bureau van Dijk's Zephyr database, BvD Deal ID Number 640331.

61. Quote taken from UK Power (2012).
62. Based on analysis of Bureau van Dijk's Zephyr database, BvD Deal ID Numbers 113538 and 122311.
63. Based on analysis of Bureau van Dijk's Zephyr database, BvD Deal ID Number 194968.
64. Based on analysis of Bureau van Dijk's Zephyr database, BvD Deal ID Number 82490.
65. Based on analysis of Bureau van Dijk's Zephyr database, BvD Deal ID Number 109935.
66. Based on analysis of Bureau van Dijk's Zephyr database, BvD Deal ID Number 170972.
67. Based on analysis of Bureau van Dijk's Zephyr database, BvD Deal ID Numbers 1601004430 and 583451.
68. Based on analysis of Bureau van Dijk's Zephyr database, BvD Deal ID Number 301834; see also <www.eon.com> for E.ON's history (2005) (accessed 18 December 2013).
69. Based on analysis of Bureau van Dijk's Zephyr database, BvD Deal ID Number 1601034150.
70. Based on analysis of Bureau van Dijk's Zephyr database, BvD Deal ID Number 193816.
71. Based on analysis of Bureau van Dijk's Zephyr database, BvD Deal ID Number 242809.
72. Based on BvD Deal ID Number 459983. Information on market share in Bulgaria is also based on the history of E.ON on its webpage <www.eon.com> (2004, when agreement was reached before the deal was signed off in 2005; accessed 18 December 2013).
73. Based on analysis of Bureau van Dijk's Zephyr database, BvD Deal ID Numbers 162603 and 315104.
74. Based on analysis of Bureau van Dijk's Zephyr database, BvD Deal ID Number 424169.
75. Based on analysis of Bureau van Dijk's Zephyr database, BvD Deal ID Number 1601112301.
76. Based on analysis of Bureau van Dijk's Zephyr database, BvD Deal ID Number 620540.
77. Based on analysis of Bureau van Dijk's Zephyr database, BvD Deal ID Number 621907.
78. Based on analysis of Bureau van Dijk's Zephyr database, BvD Deal ID Number 1601226991.
79. Based on information provided in E.ON webpage on its history (<www.eon.com>), under the month of April 2010 (accessed 16 December 2013).
80. Based on information provided in E.ON webpage on its history (<www.eon.com>), under the months of March and October 2010 (accessed 16 December 2013).
81. Based on analysis of Bureau van Dijk's Zephyr database, BvD Deal ID Number 1601331896.

82. Based on analysis of Bureau van Dijk's Zephyr database, BvD Deal ID Number BvD 562283.

83. Based on information found on SSE's website, <http://www.hydro.co.uk/Busi ness/AboutUs/> (last accessed 10 January 2014).

84. Based on information found on <www.privatizationbarometer.net>.

85. Based on analysis of Bureau van Dijk's Zephyr database, BvD Deal ID Number 99356.

86. Based on analysis of Bureau van Dijk's Zephyr database, BvD Deal ID Number 73272.

87. Deal values taken from BvD Zephyr File with Deal ID Number 109782. Quote taken from The Independent (2004).

88. Based on analysis of Bureau van Dijk's Zephyr database, BvD Deal ID Number 194680.

89. Based on analysis of Bureau van Dijk's Zephyr database, BvD Deal ID Number 206029.

90. Based on analysis of Bureau van Dijk's Zephyr database, BvD Deal ID Number 228764

91. Based on analysis of Bureau van Dijk's Zephyr database, BvD Deal ID Number 310945.

92. Based on analysis of Bureau van Dijk's Zephyr database, BvD Deal ID Number 1601097138.

93. Based on analysis of Bureau van Dijk's Zephyr database, BvD Deal ID Number 622808.

94. On the Marchwood JV, see SSE's press release: <http://161.12.6.150/ PressReleases2006/MarchwoodPowerCompletionAgreement/>. In 2013 the Irish government-owned ESB sold its 50% stake in Marchwood to German insurance firm Munich Re (for an estimated €400 million), as part of the Irish state's programme to divest of non-strategic assets which followed the Irish financial and economic crisis. Source: RTE Article entitled 'ESB Sells Stake in Marchwood Power Station to Munich Re'.

95. Based on analysis of Bureau van Dijk's Zephyr database, BvD Deal ID Number 606437.

96. See Keenan (2012).

97. Based on analysis of Bureau van Dijk's Zephyr database, BvD Deal ID Number 1601272132.

98. As reported by UK Power (2012).

99. Based on information provided in The Scotsman (2008).

100. The history of the firm is based on information provided by ENEL on its webpage: <http://www.enel.com/en-GB/group/about_us/history/> (accessed 7 January 2014).

101. All figures on the transactions in 1999, 2003, 2004, and 2005 are based on data taken from <www.privatizationbarometer.net> (accessed February 2013).

102. Based on shareholder data of ENEL found on the Amadeus database. ENEL's company ID Number on the database is: ITRM0756032.

103. Based on analysis of Bureau van Dijk's Zephyr database, BvD Deal ID Number 98311.

104. Based on analysis of Bureau van Dijk's Zephyr database, BvD Deal ID Numbers 155099 and 153459.

105. Based on analysis of Bureau van Dijk's Zephyr database, BvD Deal ID Number 136393.

106. Quote taken from <www.enel.com> (history/year 2005; accessed 7 January 2014).

107. Based on analysis of Bureau van Dijk's Zephyr database, BvD Deal ID Number 10054.

108. More on the company can be found on its webpage: <http://www.ruses.ru/en/about> (accessed 9 January 2014).

109. Based on analysis of Bureau van Dijk's Zephyr database, BvD Deal ID Number 424095.

110. Based on analysis of Bureau van Dijk's Zephyr database, BvD Deal ID Number 550239.

111. Based on analysis of Bureau van Dijk's Zephyr database, BvD Deal ID Number 126412.

112. Based on analysis of Bureau van Dijk's Zephyr database, BvD Deal ID Number 175686.

113. Based on analysis of Bureau van Dijk's Zephyr database, BvD Deal ID Numbers 241707 and 272212.

114. Based on analysis of Bureau van Dijk's Zephyr database, BvD Deal ID Number 1601339425.

115. Based on analysis of Bureau van Dijk's Zephyr database, BvD Deal ID Number 1601056671.

116. On Berlusconi's decision in March 2011, please see Bloomberg Businessweek (2011). For the results on the referendum in June 2011, please see: <http://elezionistorico.interno.it/index.php?tpel=F&dtel=12/06/2011&tpa=Y&tpe=A&lev0=0&levsut0=0&es0=S&ms=S> (accessed 10 January 2014).

117. Based on analysis of Bureau van Dijk's Zephyr database, BvD Deal ID Number 524959.

118. Based on analysis of Bureau van Dijk's Zephyr database, BvD Deal ID Number 1601074968.

119. Based on analysis of Bureau van Dijk's Zephyr database, BvD Deal ID Numbers 16010947 and 1601147435.

120. This brief history of Endesa is based on information found in Endesa's 'INI-file' on the privatization of its first tranche in 1988, which was consulted by the author after SEPI officials allowed access in April 1996.

121. Privatization data based on that found in <on www.privatizationbarometer.net> (last accessed October 2014).

122. Information based on that found in Zephyr file with Deal ID Number 61176.

123. Information based on that found in Zephyr file with Deal ID Number 45031.

124. Based on analysis of Bureau van Dijk's Zephyr database, BvD Deal ID Number 801519.

125. Based on information provided in Zephyr Deal Number 94620.

126. Based on analysis of Bureau van Dijk's Zephyr database, BvD Deal ID Numbers 77902 and 142489.

127. See the Forbes list of 2006, found at: <http://www.forbes.com/lists/2006/18/06f2000_The-Forbes-2000_IndName_19.html> (accessed 28 December 2013).

128. Amadeus searches were performed in April 2013 and verified in August 2013. E.ON, SSE, and ENEL were added to the search given that their NACE Rev. 2 code was not 351, but 7010.

129. The data for the independence test (and the BvD's independence ranking) are taken from the company reports with the following BvD ID Numbers in the Amadeus database: E.ON, DE5050056484; EDF, FR552081317; ENEL, ITRM0756032; SSE, GBSC117119; and Endesa, ESA28023430. The final tests were run between March 2013 and October 2103, and all reports were last accessed in January 2014.

130. In this regard, as of April 2014, BvD's Amadeus gives an Independence ranking of 'D' to Vattenfall and a 'C' to Statkraft. BvD Company IDs are: Vattenfall, SE5560362138; and Statkraft, NO962986277.

131. All net incomes (for 2012) are based on data found on the Amadeus database.

132. BvD Independence Ranking is found on the Amadeus database, where Scottish Power has a BvD ID Number of GBSC193794.

133. The BvD Independence Ranking is found on the Amadeus database, where Iberdrola has a BvD ID Number of ESA48010615.

134. Quote taken from the Zephyr database, file with Deal ID Number 109782.

135. In terms of its technological advancement, the Marchwood 'facility used the latest technology to ensure maximum energy efficiency and minimal impact on the environment. It is currently one of the most efficient power stations in the UK. Impacts on the environment and nearby communities are strictly controlled'. From webpage of Marchwood power, <www.marchwoodpower.com>.

136. Taken from SSE Press Release on the deal, which can be found at: <http://161.12.6.150/PressReleases2006/MarchwoodPowerCompletionAgreement/>.

137. This quote is taken from Zephyr file with ID Number 315104. Another quote to back up this point is seen in comments by E.ON Energie Board of Management Member Dr Walter Hohlefelder, who stated on the deal that, 'We are delighted at getting the go-ahead for Electrica Moldova. It enables us to continue in the systematic pursuit of our strategy of achieving selective growth in Europe, particularly in Eastern Europe.' This quote is taken from Zephyr file with ID Number 162603.

138. In the words of E.ON's CEO, Wulf Bernotat, 'With this agreement, we will gain a strong platform for growth and investment in the Nordic region, and are gaining full freedom of strategic and entrepreneurial action. In line with our ambitious European strategy, we are set to invest around €6 billion in the Nordic market in the period 2006 through to 2013, strengthening energy security and our position in the region. In addition, we will now fully integrate our trading and renewables activities into our new centrally managed European businesses, taking advantage of synergies and bringing together world-wide expertise.' This quote is taken from Zephyr file with ID Number 583451.

139. On the importance of entering the Russian market, Bernotat states that, 'The acquisition of OGK-4 would be another important step into the Russian electricity market, which offers enormous growth potential due to the sharp increase in industrial demand.' He also states on the technological aspects that, 'In addition, OGK-4 has a very attractive generation fleet. Its power plants are relatively new and technologically up to date, have a high utilisation factor and low fuel consumption. They therefore rank among the best and most efficient in Russia.' These quotes are taken from Zephyr file with Bvd ID Number 562283.
140. Quote taken from Zephyr database with ID Number 201435.
141. Quote taken from the SSE Press Release on the Airtricity deal, found at: <http://161.12.6.150/PressReleases2008/AirtricityHoldingsAcquisition/>.
142. Quote taken from Bureau van Dijk's Zephyr database, BvD Deal ID Number 1601331896.
143. The specific quotes from both CEOs, as taken from BvD's Zephyr database, BvD Deal ID Number 1601108102, is as follows: Conti, 'the creation of this joint venture lays the ground for a concrete come back of the nuclear in Italy and represents a unique opportunity for contributing to the recovery of the country's economy, creating specialized jobs and increasing employment. In the past few years ENEL has been able to rebuild the nuclear skills and expertise, thanks to its international operations, and we are now ready to take the lead of the Italian nuclear programme in cooperation with EDF, a world key player in this industry.' Gadonneix: 'EDF is delighted to be able to participate side by side with a major industrial partner such as ENEL in the relaunch of nuclear production in Italy, a secure, competitive and CO2 free source of energy . . . , This partnership is in line with EDF's Group strategy aimed at strengthening its position in Europe and at being the world leader of the revival of nuclear energy.'
144. As reported by Sharp (2013).
145. Analysis is based on Zephyr database files with ID Numbers 251748, 251753, and 251756.
146. Quote is taken from Zephyr Deal with ID Number 81238.
147. Quote taken from Zephyr Deal with ID Number 472916.
148. Based on information from Zephyr Deal with ID Number 621873.
149. Quote taken from Zephy Deal with ID Number 621873.
150. Based on information from Zephyr Deal with ID Number 175686.
151. Based on information from Zephyr Deal with ID Number 1601339425.
152. Based on information from Zephyr Deal with ID Number 175686.
153. For an excellent, more detailed, discussion of reforms pursued at the domestic levels see Thatcher (2009, 209–13).
154. As discussed in BvD, Zephyr database, Deal ID Number 562283 on E.ON/OGK-4, it was argued by E.ON that 'OGK-4 is well positioned for the further liberalisation of Russia's electricity market. . . . '
155. Quote taken from Bureau van Dijk's Zephyr database, Deal ID Number 94620.
156. See European Commission, Memo/06/483, 12 December 2006.
157. See European Commission (2008b).

158. Quote is taken from BvD's Zephyr database, Deal ID Number 621907. On the Thüga sale, he also noted that 'All sides will profit from this transaction. With the sale of Thüga, we are supporting greater competition in the German energy market and in particular the end consumer business. This is good news for energy customers. At the same time, Thüga will benefit from the opening up of better growth opportunities. At E.ON, the further development of Thüga was limited for anti-trust reasons. With the finalising of the Thüga transaction, E.ON has achieved a very good financial result despite the current market conditions. The revenue from the sale has strengthened our power to invest. In the period up to 2011, we want to invest some EUR 30 billion in modern energy supplies with the focus on Europe.' Quote taken from Zephyr file with ID Number 620540.

159. See *Marketwatch Energy* October 2009, Vol. 8, Issue 10, pages 6 and 7. Comparing E.ON's and EDF's divestments at the end of the 2000s, it states that 'although the European energy market often sees M&A activity in which a utility makes a key acquisition of a strategic asset (for example, EDF Energy's purchase of British Energy . . .) recently the trend has been towards more sedate divestments . . . (where) companies strategically trim assets from the balance sheets, for example E.ON's sale of Thüga, and EDF Energy's proposed sale of its UK distribution assets. These sales are motivated by varying degrees by the European Commission's push to mitigate competition concerns, and the desire to free up cash-flow for use with more favored assets . . . '.

160. Quote taken from Bureau van Dijk, Zephyr database, Deal ID Number 1601112301.

161. Quote taken from <http://www.edison.it/en/company/who-we-are/our-history/1999-the-new-market.shtml> (accessed 20 November 2013).

162. On the case where the Commission declares that EDF rebates to firms in the paper industry do not constitute state aid, see European Commission (2000).

163. Please see the Commission Decision C (2003) 4637 final of 16 December 2003.

164. Case T-156/04 EDF v Commission.

165. Judgment in Case C-124/10 P, Commission v EDF, Press Release 70/12.

166. This quote was made by Wim Vandenberghe, an expert based out of Dechert LLP in Brussels as quoted in the *Wall Street Journal* in a report by Torello (2012).

167. Quote taken from Bureau van Dijk's Zephyr database, BvD Deal ID Number 622808.

168. Based on information from the Official Gazette (*Gazzetta Ufficiale*) of the Italian Republic, which can be found on: <http://www.gazzettaufficiale.it/30giorni/contratti;jsessionid=Sz0-f3Dx927FHGjnCA9ugA__.ntc-as1-guri2a>.

169. Quoted in EDF, *Shareholders: The Letter No. 16* (October 2012), page 3.

170. As quoted in E.ON, *Annual Report 2012*, page 21.

171. On this, see: <http://www.eon.com/en/business-areas/sales/mobility/e-mobility/munich-test-region.html> (accessed 1 March 2014).

172. Transparency Register data based on firm registrations accessed in October 2013, which outlined financial data for 2012 plus grants received from the EU in 2011 (<http://ec.europa.eu/transparencyregister/info/homePage.do>). The 2012 data is based on data found in the Financial Transparency System (<http://ec.europa.eu/

budget/fts/index_en.htm>). Financial Transparency System data relates to funding that organizations have directly received from the community budget in 2012, and does *not* include any other potential funding from member states.

173. Quote taken from E.ON's transparency registration, found at: <http://ec.europa.eu/transparencyregister/public/consultation/displaylobbyist.do?id=72760517350-57&isListLobbyistView=true> (last accessed 1 February 2014).

174. Quote taken from email correspondence with an official from the Transparency Register Contact of the Secretariat General, January 2014.

175. Quote is taken from Zephyr file with ID Number 113538. This was eventually allowed with the condition that stakes in Bayerngas and Bremer Stadtwerke had to be disposed of, as discussed in Zephyr file with ID Number 122311.

176. Quote taken from Bureau van Dijk's Zephyr database, Deal ID Number 113538.

177. Based on analysis of Bureau van Dijk's Zephyr database, Deal ID Number 241707.

178. Based on analysis of Bureau van Dijk's Zephyr database, Deal ID Number 1601118109.

179. The later merger between Suez and GDF can be better understood in light of this. Please see: <http://news.bbc.co.uk/2/hi/business/5095746.stm> (accessed 3 February 2014).

180. Taken from EDF's press release on the deal, found at: <http://press.edf.com/fichiers/fckeditor/Commun/Presse/Communiques/EDF/2010/cp_20110217b_va.pdf> (accessed 14 February 2014). Information on the deal can also be found on the Zephyr database, BvD Deal ID Number 1601232490.

181. This is based on information found in: <http://www.stuttgarter-zeitung.de/inhalt.gutachten-zum-enbw-deal-gutachter-mappus-hat-mindestens-840-millionen-euro-zu-viel-bezahlt.cf2d145e-15c1-44de-a00c-92275f99fc47.html> (accessed 7 February 2014). It should be noted, however, that there is some debate as to the precise figure on how 'high' the overpayment was (this idea is based on interviews held between the author and sources from Baden-Württemberg in February 2014).

182. On the chronology of the sale, see Spiegel Online (2012).

183. See: <http://www.stuttgarter-nachrichten.de/inhalt.untersuchungsausschuss-enbw:-ein-codewort-fuer-den-milliardendeal.102159c1-c8aa-4b39-b88b-134d2f49db5f.html > (accessed 28 January 2014).

184. With regard to Mappus conducting the sale in secret and not involving the parliament (which in the end only rubber-stamped a deal previously agreed between German and French officials), his trial for not consulting parliament on the deal is scheduled for 2014. On German public opinion towards nuclear energy, as seen a year later when the Japanese Tsunami took place in March 2011, many in Germany were concerned about the safety of nuclear energy in Europe, and in May 2011 the German state announced its intention to withdraw from nuclear energy altogether.

185. As *World Nuclear News* (2010) reported, 'A presentation by EDF accompanying its announcement (of its sale of 45% of EnBW) identifies a German market with overcapacity characterized by sharply lower prices, and an unfavourable regulatory environment, as background issues to its decision to dispose of its EnBW share. In September 2010 the German government agreed to give operating

nuclear reactors life extensions of 8–14 years, but at a price: a tax on nuclear fuel, which according to EDF will cost EnBW some €440 million ($589 million) per year, plus taxes levied on the additional output from the life-extended reactors to help finance the development of renewable energy, costing EnBW an estimated €298 million ($399 million), or €50 million ($67 million) per year, over the period 2011–2016.'

186. For an excellent overview of the deal and both brothers' role, see *The Economist* (2012).
187. On the commission gained, see Müller (2012).
188. For a discussion of governance bodies and management in EDF, see its Annual Report, 2011, page 91, and the names of the BoD were those taken from the EDF website in September 2012.
189. Biographies on these members are as follows (as taken from the company report of EDF, found in the Amadeus database):

   • Henri Proglio, Chairman and Managing Director of EDF, has served various positions including Deputy Chairman of the Strategic Nuclear Energy Committee and member of the French Atomic Energy Committee. He was appointed to his position, by decree, by the French president in 2009.
   • Michael Jay has served as a diplomat which has various positions, including the British Ambassador in Paris from 1996–2001, Permanent Under-Secretary at the Foreign Office and Head of Diplomatic Service from 2002–6. Since 2006 he has been a Crossbench Member of the House of Lords, later appointed as Chair of the House of Lords Appointment Commission in 2008. In 2012–13 he was a member of the EU Sub-Committee on External Affairs.
   • Pierre Mariani has had a long and distinguished career since he was an Inspector of Finances at the General Inspection of the Ministry of Economy and Finance from 1982–6. In the 1990s he served as a Deputy Director within the Ministry of Economy and Finance.
   • Bruno Lafont has served as a special advisor to the Mayor of the City of Chongqing, a city in China with over 30 million inhabitants.

190. Biographies on these members are as follows (as taken from the company report of EDF, found in the Amadeus database):

   • Jean-Dominique Comolli has served as Commissioner for State Holdings and Director General of French Government Shareholding Agency (APE) since September 2010. Previous experience includes Assistant Director of the Budget Department (1986), and Chairman and CEO of SEITA (1993).
   • Julien Dubertret, having previously worked in economy and finance, with responsibility for the Budget, from 2007 until 2011, he was an advisor to the Prime Minister.
   • Yannick d'Escatha has served as the Chairman of the Centre National d'Etudes Spatiales and Representative of the French government.
   • François Loos was a Technical Advisor to the President of the European Parliament and to the Minister of Research and Technology in the mid-1980s. In the

2000s he held positions such as Deputy Minister for foreign trade and finally Deputy Minister for industry.

- Marie-Christine Lepetit has served as the Head of Inspectorate General of Finance at the Ministry for Economy and Finance.
- Pierre Sellal, formerly a Technical Advisor in the Office of the Minister of Foreign Trade in the early 1980s, held other posts held throughout the 1990s and 2000s including: Head of International Relations at the Ministry of Industrial Redeployment and Foreign Trade; Minister–Counsellor at the French Embassy in Rome; and Secretary General of the Ministry of Foreign and European Affairs.

191. Beyond Amadeus, Internet searches (including searches on <www.linkedin.com>) were performed on the names of the employee representatives—Christine Chabauty, Marie-Hélène Meyling, Alexandre Grillat, Philippe Maïssa, Jean-Paul Rignac, and Maxime Villota—with little success in finding much detailed information on the background of these directors other than that they work for EDF. Searches performed, December 2013–January 2014.

192. This is based on information on the Amadeus database as well as E.ON's Annual Report of 2011, pages 194–5. The twenty members correspond to those who were on the Board at the end of 2011, and does not include those that left during the year, including: Ulrich Hartmann (who was Chairman until 5 May 2011, after which time Werner Wenning took over), Wolf-Rudiger Hinrichsen (who left after 30 September 2011), and Professor Dr Wilhelm Simson (there until 5 May 2011). While Kingsmill is discussed in the text, the second E.ON Board member with links to the state is Dr von Waldenfels, who held various positions in the Bavarian government during the 1980s and 1990s. His appointment can be understood given the firm's historical association with the state of Bavaria, including the small stake the state owns to this day. Dr Waldenfels held several previous positions in Bavarian politics, including the Bavarian Minister of Finance (1990–5) and Head of the Department of Federal and European Affairs (1987–90).

193. E.ON Board members on the Deutsche Telekom Board include: Werner Wenning (the Chairman of E.ON), Ulrich Hocker, Ulrich Lehner, and René Obermann. Henning Schulte-Noelle also simultaneously served on the Board of Allianz, while Hubertus Schmoldt was on the Board of Bayer.

194. This is based on analysis of the Amadeus database as well as SSE's Annual Report, 2011, pages 47–50. While Gillingwater is discussed later, Jeremy Beeton served as Director General of the UK Government Olympic Executive (which oversaw the 2012 Olympic Games.) Although the Chief Executive at the time, Ian Marchant, did not hold a permanent government post at any one time, he had previously worked for Coopers and Lybrand, and his stint there included a two-year secondment to the Department of Energy working on the privatization of Regional Electricity Companies before then joining Southern Electric.

195. On the Shareholder executive, from where the quote is taken, see: <https://www.gov.uk/government/organisations/the-shareholder-executive>. For a biography on Gillingwater, see: <http://www.britishcouncil.org/organisation/people/board-trustees/richard-gillingwater-cbe>. On his move from Chief Executive to Chairman of

the Shareholder executive, see: <http://www.telegraph.co.uk/finance/2941142/Gillingwater-stays-but-new-chief-sought.html> (all accessed 12 January 2014).

196. Based on information on the Amadeus database as well as ENEL's Annual Report 2011, page 8:

- Lorenzo Codogno's experience includes having been a member of the Ministry of Economy and Finance, as Director General in the Treasury Department, and Head of the Economic and Financial Analysis and Planning Directorate in the 2000s.
- Mauro Miccio's experience includes having been a member of the Governing Council of Communications at the Communications Ministry.
- Fernando Napolitano served on the committee for surface digital television of the Ministry of Communications and directed the Italian Center of Aerospace research throughout the 2000s.
- Gianfranco Tosi was mayor of the city of Busto Arsizio between 1993 and 2002.

197. Analysis of the Endesa Board is based on the list of BoDs provided in the firm's Annual Report of 2006, as well as information provided in the Amadeus database.

198. Quote taken from Zephyr file with ID Number 621873.

199. European Commission, Case C(2004) 3474, 22 September 2004.

200. See *The Times* report by Jameson (2008).

201. Based on information provided in the Zephyr database, file with ID Number 1601061790.

202. Quote taken from Zephyr file with ID Number 621873.

203. This quote is taken from a BBC report, <http://news.bbc.co.uk/2/hi/business/8043191.stm> (accessed 14 November 2013). This is consistent with Brown's comments after the deal was finalized, stating: 'New nuclear is becoming a reality. This deal is good value for the taxpayer and a significant step towards the construction of a new generation of nuclear stations to power the country. Nuclear is clean, secure and affordable; its expansion is crucial for Britain's long term energy security, as we reduce our oil dependence and move towards a low carbon future.' Quote taken from the Zephyr database, Deal with ID Number 621873.

204. In its purchase of Romania's Electrica Moldova, the stakes for this firm were being sold alongside those of Electrica Oltenia. After only Czech Republic's CEZ, Spain's Union Fenosa, and Germany's E.ON were left in the running, eventually CEZ was successful in getting Electrica Oltenia, while E.ON was able to attain Electrica Moldova because it made the best offer. E.ON's Board member at the time, Dr Walter Hohlefelder, stated, 'We are delighted at getting the go-ahead for Electrica Moldova. It enables us to continue in the systematic pursuit of our strategy of achieving selective growth in Europe, particularly in Eastern Europe.' Quote taken from the Zephyr database, Deal ID Number 162603.

205. Mr Teodor Atanasiu explains, 'The privatization of Electrica Muntenia Sud (EMS) is a good deal for the Romanian State at least from two perspectives: on the one hand, AVAS has obtained a good price for the transaction: EUR 820 million, and on the other hand AVAS has found a strategic investor in ENEL, who proved its capability and seriousness further to the acquisition of Electrica Banat and

Electrica Dobrogea. The great win is yet in the long run and the beneficiaries will be the end consumers, the Bucharest citizens. We have ensured the energy future of the capital, as regards power distribution and supply, by finding an investor able to carry out a performance management but also the necessary investments, which will lead towards a competitive ratio between price and the quality of the services offered.' Quote taken from the Zephyr Amadeus database, file ID 126412.

206. Quote taken from Bureau van Dijk's Zephyr database, BvD Deal ID Number 100541.

207. The Endesa Press Release of 2002 calling off the deals is reproduced on: <http://www.thefreelibrary.com/Endesa+Will+Not+Acquire+the+Dutch+Distributors+NRE+and+REMU.-a087912631>. On political pressures related to privatization of NRE and REMU see: <http://www.iflr.com/Article/2027410/The-Netherlands.html> (accessed 23 January 2014).

208. On the delay of the Netherlands' privatization, which went against desires of foreign firms seeking to expand and favouring its own domestic actors, see Datamonitor (2002).

209. Based on information found in the Bureau van Dijk's Zephyr database, Deal ID Number 301834.

210. This is quoted from <http://asia.edf.com/activities/hydropower-52206.html> (accessed 2 March 2014).

211. To demonstrate this, it is worth quoting the following from Alex Couture, Director of Project Development for EDF EN Canada, on the Le Mitis deals: 'EDF Energies Nouvelles welcomes with great pride the government decree authorizing the construction and operation of La Mitis Community Wind Project. We sincerely thank the Government of Quebec for its permission to proceed with this innovative project.' See: <http://www.edf-en.ca/press-display/post/68/EDF-EN-Canada-Obtains-Authorization-from-the-Gover> (accessed 2 February 2014).

212. Airtricity's approval by the ICA, signed off by its member Dr Paul Gorecki, can be found on: <http://www.tca.ie/images/uploaded/documents/M08001%20SSE%20Airtricity%20Public%20Determination.pdf>. Similarly, the acquisition of Endesa Ireland can also be found on: <http://www.tca.ie/images/uploaded/documents/M-12-008%20CA%20Clears%20proposed%20Acquisition%20of%20Endesa%20by%20SSE.pdf> (both accessed 3 January 2014).

213. Based on information provided in BvD's Zephyr database, Deal ID Numbers 130528, 620540, 1601232490, and 242809. On the EDF's sale of EnBW, see also <http://www.udo-leuschner.de/energie-chronik/110208.htm> (accessed 10 January 2014).

214. Based on information provided in BvD's Zephyr database, Deal ID Number 1601118109.

215. See European Commission (2002b).

216. This is based on information provided in BvD's Zephyr database, Deal ID Number BvD 1601071325.

217. These Tables outline the main acquisitions made by the Alphas. In the case of E.ON, it does not include its formation when VEBA and VIAG joined, which was approved by the Commission. Other divestments of E.ON not included in the

Table, which were cleared by the Commission, include, for example, the sale of Veba Oel to BP, which was approved in July 2002 (as discussed in Zephyr Deal with ID Number 117898).

218. Based on information provided in Zephyr file with ID Number 160102229.

219. Based on information in Zephyr Deal with ID Number 81238.

220. Based on the information provided in the Zephyr database with Deal ID Number 94299.

221. In the Zephyr file with Bvd ID Number 1000011807, EDF's Pierre Gadonneix stated: 'This agreement is a major step for EDF which, for the first time, will become both investor and operator of nuclear reactors in China. We are delighted to broaden our cooperation with CGNPC, a major player in the Chinese nuclear industry, with whom we have been working in a spirit of trust for more than 20 years, since the construction and commissioning of Daya Bay and Ling Ao. As part of the very fast growing Chinese energy market, EDF will continue to contribute its industrial expertise and experience, acknowledged world-wide, and acquired from the operation of 58 reactors in France, including the experience gained as investor in the EPR technology at Flamanville. EDF will thereby contribute to the safe, dependable and competitive production of electricity, free from greenhouse gases emissions.'

222. Data is based found on the Transparency Register, whose analysis was performed in October 2013. Some firms state exact amounts, while others indicate ranges (as the TR allows in-house corporate lobbyists to do). E.ON data in their registry was based on financial data for 2011.

223. Based on Zephyr file with ID Number 420814. See also Marcos, 2013, 292.

224. Based on Zephyr file with ID Number 420814.

225. For a full discussion on this, see Marcos, 2013, 294–7.

226. As quoted in Zephyr file with ID Number BvD 420814.

227. Based on Zephyr file with ID Number 566197.

228. Based on data found in Zephyr file with ID Number 512885.

229. European Commission, Case No. Comp/M.4110.

230. Quotes taken from Zephyr file with ID Number 420814.

231. One of the conditions, for example, was that 'Endesa's power plants using domestic coal (must) continue to use such an energy source as foreseen in the national mining plans'. See European Commission (2006).

232. Zephyr's file with ID Number 479326 reported that on 25 October 2006 Merkel 'demanded that the Spanish government withdraw its conditions it has imposed on E.ON'.

233. This deal between states was reported by *El País* (2007) weeks after E.ON finally backed down, in May 2007. The academic literature subsequently commented on the 'reciprocal favours' between state leaders, as seen in the work by Goucha Soares (2008, 361–2). The idea was also raised in at least two elite interviews performed by the author in May–June 2013.

234. In April 2007, some weeks after the ENEL/Acciona takeover of Endesa was complete, Telco SpA (of which Telefónica became the controlling shareholder) took over Olimpia's stake in Telecom Italia (TI), thus making Telefónica a main

shareholder in TI. Under the terms of the agreement of the €5.145 billion deal, as discussed in Zephyr file with ID Number 534055, 'Telefónica will hold a 42.3 per cent stake in the new company (Telco), Generali will hold a 28.1 per cent stake, Intesa will hold a 10.6 per cent stake, Mediobanca will hold a 10.6 per cent stake and Sintonia will hold a 8.4 per cent stake.' Readers will note that Mediobanca is also the same firm that sold its shares in Endesa to ENEL, as discussed later. Telefónica's move into Italy is consistent with its desire to slowly take over Southern European competitors, as evidenced in its ownership of approximately 10% of Portugal Telecom, with whom it pursued joint ventures in Brazil (i.e. Vivo). Certainly, as one of the world's giants, it has also gone well beyond Southern Europe, having acquired BellSouth in Latin America (2004), Český Telecom (2004), O_2 (bought in 2006 but later sold), a 5% stake in China Netcom (2007), a 2.8% stake in China Unicom (Hong Kong, 2009), and recent control of E-Plus in Germany, which gained Brussels' regulatory approval in July 2014.

235. For a full list of Commissioners when Prodi was President of the European Commission between 1999 and 2004, see: <http://ec.europa.eu/archives/commis sion_1999_2004/index_en.htm> (accessed 28 February 2007).

236. For details on the sale by SEPI, see its webpage where it discusses the deal in full: <http://www.sepi.es/default.aspx?cmd=0004&IdContent=276&idLanguage=& lang=&idContraste=>.

237. Acciona's stakes in Endesa is taken from the Zephyr's file with ID Number 479326.

238. The term 'Spanish Solution' is found in Zephyr's file with ID Number 518921, but the term *solución española* was readily used by the Spanish Press. See for example an article by *El Mundo* (2007).

239. Based on information provided in Zephyr files with ID Numbers 519608, 519778, 519791, and 522265.

240. 24.98% was the minimum amount which could be acquired before a full takeover bid had to be made. The stock market regulator CNMV had previously indicated that it would not allow any further takeover bids on Endesa until six months after E.ON's presentation of its initial bid. However, it also stated that another bid could be made if E.ON withdrew its offer.

241. Based on information provided in Zephyr file with ID Number 526197.

242. As Marcos rightly notes (2013, 310), a price of €41.30 per share was first offered by ENEL/Acciona, but this later dropped to €40.16 per share. Endesa's Corporate Governance Report (2007), page 15, confirms the figure of €40.16 and it is therefore used.

243. This is based on data from Endesa's Corporate Governance Report (2007), which outlines on page 13 the number of shares of the Board members. Pizarro held 100,004 shares of Endesa, which were sold to ENEL/Acciona at €40.16 per share, resulting in a gain of €4,016,160.64. E.ON's offer (at €40 per share) would have resulted in a gain of €4,000,160, where the difference between the two is €16,000.64. Pizarro was effectively the largest shareholder of all Board members, whose total holdings were 184,108 shares. All together, Endesa Board members made around €7.4 million with ENEL/Acciona's acquisition.

244. As discussed in Zephyr file with ID Number 528180.
245. Based on information supplied in Zephyr file with ID Number 512885.
246. The July 2007 deals were slightly modified and later approved in 2008, again with no conditions. See European ENEL/Acciona/Endesa, Case No. M.4685 (July 2007) and Case No. M.5171 (slightly modified version, June 2008); E.ON/Assets of Endesa/Viesgo Case No. M.5170 (August 2007) and Case M.1570 (June 2008).
247. This is the value reported in Zephyr file with ID Number 626216. This represented a new, reworked amount by both parties, compared to the previous €11.107 billion initially agreed.
248. European Commission, ENEL/Endesa (2009), Case No. M.5494.
249. On this, see Muñoz (2007).
250. On the 2011 general election in Spain, see Chari (2013). For a full (government) biography of De Guidos see: <http://www.lamoncloa.gob.es/gobierno/gabinete/Paginas/mineco.aspx>. On when De Guidos left Endesa Chile, see its 2011 Annual Report, which can be found on <http://phx.corporate-ir.net/phoenix.zhtml?c=106239&p=irol-reportsAnnual> (both accessed 3 March 2014).
251. On Solbes being a member of the Board of Directors of ENEL, see ENEL's Annual Report 2011, page 8. On his reported basic salary as Board member (based on the ENEL statutes), which would of course supplement his pension as having served as a Member of Parliament, see Carcar (2011).
252. On Salgado's being named Chilectra, see Carcar (2012). This is also verified in the Annual Report of Chilectra (2012), page 168: <http://www.chilectra.cl/wps/wcm/connect/142aa8004f1e1b588a75aa39a73230cf/EEFF+Chilectra.pdf?MOD=AJPERES&Tipo=DOC>). While it is generally expected that Spanish officials respect a cooling-off period of two years before entering into the private world, Salgado argued that this only applied to those working in a private firm in Spain, not the rest of the world.
253. On Aznar and Endesa, see Carcar (2011). The article also makes comments about Solbes and other Spanish former politicians in the energy sector, including ex-Prime Minister Felipe González. Reuters (2011) also reported Aznar's role.

6

In the End: The LIFESHAPERS

The Set-Up

The first chapter situated this study within the literatures on privatization and mergers and acquisitions (M&A). It highlighted that countries analysed in this book—the UK, France, Germany, Italy, and Spain—had privatized the most in the EU and witnessed high amounts of M&A over the years. But as much as scholars have written on privatization and M&A pursued in these five states, a significant gap exists because both set of almost disparate literatures have yet to meet eye to eye, a noteworthy omission considering the plethora of mergers and acquisitions pursued by privatized firms.

A two-category ordinal dependent variable (Y, or, outcome variable) was thus constructed to better conceptualize two types of emergent privatized firms that one sees today: Alphas, which are European and global giants that have merged and acquired since privatization, and Betas, which are those that have been taken over by Alphas or other sectoral leaders either when privatized or shortly thereafter. The first central question which therefore guided this book was: which privatized firms can be characterized as Alphas and Betas?

The Alpha–Beta theoretical conceptualization is significant for scholars of privatization because it is based on robust empirical tests which can be applied to any privatized firm that still operates today from any European country, from any sector. Elements of these tests included: that the firm appears in the latest available Forbes 2000 list; that amongst their European peers the firm is within the top 1 per cent of various metrics recorded in the Amadeus database on turnover, assets, shareholders funds, and employees; and that no one shareholder owns more than 25 per cent of the firm as recorded in Amadeus, except in those cases of some state or family ownership. The empirical chapters showed the versatility of this conceptualization by classifying some firms that were not the focus of this book, and which were not necessarily privatized firms, as being either Alphas or Betas.[1]

The second chapter then developed two theoretical models to serve as a guide to better understand the second main question that guided the book, namely, why do privatized firms become Alphas or Betas? The models that were developed were structured on a temporal dimension, examining initial conditions when the firm was privatized (X1) and intervening variables potentially at play post-privatization (X2). The first model conceptualized that initial conditions alone (X1) can explain why a firm became a Beta (Y) at the point of privatization. That is, the firm was a loss-making SOE that the state ensured was taken over by another leading firm when sold. The second model conceptualized that initial conditions (X1) included that the firm was a crown jewel or a profitable enterprise at privatization which was successfully floated. Because the firm thus had theoretical potential to become an Alpha or a Beta, analysis of intervening variables (X2) needed to be theorized. These were subdivided into those factors internal to the firm, and those, more political, factors external to it. Internal factors included the firm's competitiveness (market strength and the role of managers) as well as the role of shareholders, including 'intermediary' financial elites such as asset management firms which may have taken large stakes in the firm after its privatization. External factors included the role of liberalization, the state (including states beyond those from where the firm comes), domestic and supranational regulatory authorities that had to approve M&A, as well as firm lobbying of institutional actors such as regulators. By considering both the internal and external factors to the firm, this holistic approach considered factors not heretofore fully examined in traditional political science literature, namely, those internal to the firm. It also considered those factors oftentimes ignored by business studies' scholars, namely, the more political ones external to the firm.

6.1 The Results: Towards a Theory of 'LIFESHAPERS'

Guided by these ideas, the resultant empirical chapters thus sought to provide evidence to answer the two main questions: which firms can be considered Alphas and Betas, and why? The third chapter examined the airline sector, focusing on firms from the five states of investigation: Air France (which merged with KLM, forming AF–KLM), Lufthansa (Germany), British Airways, Spain's Iberia (where BA and Iberia later merged to form IAG), and Alitalia. The fourth chapter studied the automobile sector, analysing Volkswagen (Germany), Renault (France), Jaguar (the UK), SEAT (Spain), and Alfa Romeo (Italy). And the fifth chapter focused on developments in the electricity sector, studying EDF (France), E.ON (Germany), SSE (the UK), ENEL (Italy), and Endesa (Spain). Each empirical chapter had a similar threefold structure. The first section examined the history, privatization, and M&A of the privatized firms in order to offer the reader essential information referred to throughout the remainder of the chapter, particularly on the multiple deals pursued at home, within Europe and globally. The second section asked which firms are Alphas and Betas, performing the tests established earlier in the study. The third section then examined which of the factors at different times (X1 and X2) help explain why a firm became an Alpha or a Beta (Y), basing the discussion around the two theoretical models developed in the second chapter. The first model was used to examine developments in SEAT and Alfa Romeo (that were taken over at the point of privatization). The second model guided analysis of all other firms, which were crown jewels or profitable enterprises that were successfully (fully or partially) floated and therefore had potential to become either Alphas or Betas.

With this in mind, what does the evidence suggest is the answer to the first main question guiding the book? Table 6.1 summarizes the findings of the main companies studied, while also showing the results of some of the UK's privatized firms in the electricity sector that were referred to in Chapter 5.

In terms of the country where the firms are from, Table 6.1 highlights that:

- All of the French firms studied—AF–KLM, Renault, and EDF—are Alphas.

- Those from Germany—Lufthansa, Volkswagen, and E.ON—are Alphas.

- Considering that IAG is a product of the merger between BA and Iberia, it can be argued that two of the three UK firms studied are Alphas (IAG and SSE) and there is one Beta (Jaguar). The examination of electricity companies in the UK, however, pointed to several having become Betas after privatization. This included Powergen, Scottish Power, and British Energy, some of which were taken over during the 'Alpha invasion' by firms including E.ON and EDF.

- Turning to Italy, ENEL is an Alpha, while Alfa Romeo is a Beta, as is Alitalia in which a controlling stake since 2009 was held by an Alpha, namely, AF–KLM, and in which Etihad is scheduled to take a controlling stake given developments in late 2014.

- In Spain, IAG is an Alpha. The Betas are SEAT (which was taken over by an Alpha, namely, VW) and Endesa (taken over by another Alpha, ENEL, which was engaged in an 'Alpha War' with E.ON over the Spanish giant).

In order to explain *why* the firms become Alphas or Betas, the main argument supported by the evidence is that while a firm's competitiveness (market share and managers) as well as the goals of shareholders are important, they are not sufficient. Rather, factors external to the firm are all necessary and sufficient. These include the impact of liberalization (or lack, thereof); the role of home (and other) states that acted; and the explicit or implicit green light given by regulatory authorities (that were lobbied by firms) across multiple levels of governance. In an integrated discussion, I consider this finding in

Table 6.1. Summary: Alphas and Betas

Sector	Privatized Firm	Alpha or Beta?
Airlines	*Lufthansa* (Germany)	Alpha
	Air France–KLM	Alpha
	IAG (British Airways and Iberia)	Alpha
	Alitalia (Italy)	Beta
Automobiles	*Volkswagen* (Germany)	Alpha
	Renault (France)	Alpha
	Jaguar (UK)	Beta
	SEAT (Spain)	Beta
	Alfa Romeo (Italy)	Beta
Electricity	*EDF* (France)	Alpha
	E.ON (Germany)	Alpha
	ENEL (Italy)	Alpha
	SSE (UK)	Alpha
	*Endesa (*Spain)	Beta
	British Energy	Beta
	Scottish Power	Beta
	Powergen	Beta

more detail by drawing reference to all the Alphas (AF–KLM, Lufthansa, IAG, Volkswagen, Renault, EDF, E.ON, SSE, and ENEL), the firms that had theoretical potential to become Alphas after privatization but ended up Betas (Endesa and Jaguar), and those Betas which became so at the point of privatization (SEAT and Alfa Romeo). In this discussion, the importance of the temporal dimension binding the external, more political, factors will be further conceptualized, where I develop a new theory stemming from the evidence that will be referred to as 'LIFESHAPERS'.

When turning to the internal factors, one saw that all Alphas enjoyed a competitive market position before and after privatization. In terms of market shares, certainly the flag carriers enjoyed an almost equal privileged position in their home markets before liberalization, where they had pursued smaller deals in home markets consolidating their position. Both Volkswagen and Renault of the 1990s were leaders amongst their peers in their sector and continue to be so today. But other sectors saw that even though such firms were 'dominant' in their home markets, they were not all equally so: EDF and ENEL shared almost monopolistic positions compared to other competitors from countries such as the UK. Some of the Betas, such as Jaguar and even SEAT, started to lose market shares throughout the 1980s and subsequently experienced financial difficulties. Yet, the case of Endesa, in particular, helps demonstrate that while having a strong market position before and after privatization was important, it is not a sufficient factor in explaining the fate of a firm. Everything being equal, Endesa was one of the world's giants.

The same can be said about management structures. All of the Alphas' management teams were led by those with strategic, long-term visions, playing skilled negotiating roles in driving deals. Talented managers from the Alphas included, amongst others, Willie Walsh (BA and then IAG), Ferdinand Piëch (VW), Ian Marchant (SSE), and Henri Proglio (EDF). But, that is not to say that firms that ended up Betas were void of talented management teams. Sir John Egan, for example, turned Jaguar around before its sale and led the team after its privatization. And Manuel Pizarro of Endesa was deemed a leader who had the best interests of the firm in mind, as reflected in not succumbing to Gas Natural when it made a hostile bid for the firm in 2005.

The evidence also showed that shareholders of the firms are also important, uncovering novel evidence of specific non-state shareholders of firms in the life of Alphas and Betas. In a first dimension, global asset management firms such as BlackRock, Capital Group, State Street, AXA, Allianz, and Deutsche Bank were examined. The evidence suggested that many of these firms are more likely to invest in Alphas than they are in Betas. In some cases, as seen in BlackRock, they have invested only in Alphas (IAG, Air France, Lufthansa, VW, Renault, EDF, E.ON, ENEL, and SSE), although their shareholding fluctuated over time as they pragmatically bought and sold shares in different Alphas. In the case of BA, it was argued that such an investment by BlackRock was a strategic one, where shareholdings increased before the merger with Iberia, although stakes were subsequently reduced over time as IAG's share price fell. Interestingly, the case of Lufthansa also saw its chief executive, Mr Mayrhuber, later joining the board of directors of UBS, a firm that held shares in the German flag carrier.

In a second dimension, beyond the asset management firms, the chapters examined those smaller shareholders of Alphas who (along with asset management firms in Alphas) saw rewards when certain deals were made, such as EDF's sale of EnBW and ENEL's sale of Terna. It also examined the shareholders of firms that were targeted by Alphas. It was argued that such shareholders (and managers of their firms) may be able to delay (or not agree to) deals until the right price is offered by the Alpha. In this regard, the deals involving Lufthansa/Swiss, Lufthansa/Austrian, E.ON/Powergen, and EDF/BE demonstrated that all shareholders were keen to sell once the price was right. In the case of Jaguar, none of its shareholders (including firm management with various stock-options) contested its sale given the high price offered by Ford, which represented a fivefold increase on its original flotation value.

But while these examples show that shareholders have a significant role in the life of a privatized firm, the actions of shareholders are not sufficient in explaining why a firm will become an Alpha or a Beta. When turning to asset managers, Endesa illustrates that while BlackRock had no stakes in the Spanish firm, other global asset management firms (such as Vanguard, JP Morgan, AXA, and Deutsche Bank) and other smaller ones (such as Mediobanca, UBS, and Caja Madrid) did. Alitalia also saw JP Morgan and BNY Mellon holding stakes before the airline was taken over. Thus, while the overall evidence suggests that global asset management firms are more likely to invest in firms that can be characterized as Alphas, it also shows that asset managers have invested in firms that become Betas. In other words, there does not seem to be a direct causal relationship that firms will become Alphas if asset management companies are shareholders in them. Rather, such investors will pragmatically invest in Alphas because they represent safe investments: shares can be bought and sold, and money can be made over time. Further, everything being equal, E.ON shareholders were keen to acquire Endesa to become the largest electricity company in the world, while Endesa managers recommended to all its shareholders (including small ones) to accept the offer by E.ON. If what shareholders (and their managers) wanted was sufficient, E.ON would have bought Endesa. But it did not. Similarly, as much as shareholders would have wanted the sale of Jaguar to Ford, as recommended by its management team, this was not sufficient because the deal could not have taken place without state intervention.

With this in mind, it is crucial to consider those more external, political, factors at play, including *liberalization, the state* (including those where the firm is from, and those from abroad), and the *role of regulatory authorities* (which are also lobbied by firms) at different levels of governance. When turning to these factors the evidence in the empirical chapters suggested that not only were they necessary and sufficient, but also they were sequentially bound in explaining why a firm becomes an Alpha or a Beta in its life after privatization.

I refer to this as the theory of LIFESHAPERS, whose name can be understood as follows:

L iberalization (or lack thereof)
I mpacts
F irms regarding where, and when, they can
E xpand (or not);
S tates from the firms'
H ome, as well as states from abroad,
A ct accordingly by taking
P ositions that
E nsure protection and/or expansion of some firms, or takeover of others; and
R egulators, investigating the transactions at different levels of governance,
S eal the deals.

LIFESHAPERS is an inductive theory that emerges after consideration of the evidence and patterns observed throughout this investigation. I thus turn to a discussion of the evidence uncovered in the book on firms that expanded and became global giants (Alphas) and firms that were taken over (Betas) that serve as a foundation for the theory.

First, the impact of *liberalization* was a key starting point because it set the tone regarding what could be done in terms of when and where firms could move in the case of Alphas, and subsequently how Betas were targeted. Before liberalization, all three sectors witnessed firms consolidating their position at home and becoming key players well before privatization largely occurred. But, various liberalization initiatives made a big impact by changing the rules of the game. Of significance was the Single European Act signed in 1986 that led to further liberalization initiatives in the three sectors. In the airline sector, for example, various Commission-led initiatives such as the Third Package in the 1990s, which, coupled with the European Court of Justice's ruling in 2002, resulted in the formation of airline alliances, ultimately paving the path for M&A within alliances and the creation of European giants. This started with the 2004 AF–KLM deal, followed by Lufthansa's various acquisitions from various neighbouring states, and the merger between BA and Iberia by the start of the 2010s. While many of the big cross-border deals may have been negotiated by talented CEOs, they could take place precisely because liberalization allowed the firms to expand outside their home country in the first place. Others, such as Alitalia, faced problems in this new competitive environment, thereby setting the stage for its eventual poor performance and eventual takeover.

The SEA itself had an almost immediate impact on the automobile sector and was followed by a later EU-wide agreement in the early 1990s starting to liberalize Japan's car imports into the EU. The same year the SEA was signed, VW targeted its first European firm that would become a Beta, SEAT. The single market also had an impact on foreign firms from Japan seeking to 'transplant' production in the EU. In the case of Nissan, it was able to gain significant market share in the context of the EU-wide liberalization agreement with Japan, becoming a key player whose alliance was eventually sought at the end of the 1990s by Renault. By aligning with the Japanese firm, the French giant could further increase market shares in the EU while being able to tap into the Asian market. Not dissimilar to Japanese firms seeking a stronghold in the single market, US firms such as Ford were keen to enter 'fortress Europe' by acquiring EU firms such as Jaguar: once inside the internal market, goods, services, and capital could move freely within it. Coupled with increasing competition from other European automakers coming into the UK market, adverse exchange rates also helped explain Jaguar's profit reductions as sales fell in one of its key markets to which it exported, the US, resulting in its ultimate takeover by Ford.

The case of the electricity sector saw that there was no symmetrical liberalization, as the UK liberalized well before the continent did. This resulted in both EDF and E.ON being in a position to successfully target UK firms throughout the 1990s and early 2000s in what was referred to as an 'Alpha invasion'. The Germans, French, and Italians also purchased firms outside the EU in Central and Eastern Europe, while being protected in their home markets. Once EU liberalization in the sector started to come into full effect in the 2000s, however, all firms had the opportunity to—and did—compete against each other and seek to expand within EU space. In one case, as seen in Endesa, this resulted in an 'Alpha War' between E.ON and ENEL for the Spanish giant, won by the Italians but nevertheless resulting in a positive sum game for both Alphas. Recuperating markets that were lost with liberalization, particularly in electricity, meant that firms sought global expansion in Europe, Latin America, and Asia.

Second, in the context of liberalization, *states from home and abroad* acted accordingly by taking positions that would ensure expansion of Alphas, or the takeover of Betas. That is, with the creation of the single market and further development of liberalization initiatives, states reacted by either helping their Alphas become strong players and expand globally, or facilitating their Betas' takeover. I first consider Alpha home states, then Beta home states, and finally states from abroad.

Turning to *Alpha home states*, the evidence suggests that they clearly helped direct the future of the firms by adopting positions of continuing with public subsidies, even after privatization. This was most notable in the automobile sector, where states continuously gave state aid to help develop job-generating projects on home soil. In the case of the electricity sector, states also targeted funds to Alphas through public–private partnerships, contracts, and subsidized research projects. Adding to this, the evidence demonstrated that the European Commission itself earmarked millions of euros of grants towards Alphas in the electricity sector, co-financing such projects with member states.

In other cases, states also maintained strategic shares in Alphas, even after privatization, ensuring a key position protecting the firm from takeover. In this regard it is crucial to note that the French state still owns significant stakes in its privatized Alphas (Renault, 15 per cent; Air France–KLM, 16 per cent; and EDF, 84 per cent) and the Germans retain veto power in VW through the Volkswagen Law, protecting the firm from takeover. It was argued that beyond exercising control in the firms, ownership allowed for a key source of Treasury revenues. While Italy owns more than 30 per cent of ENEL, and Spain less than 3 per cent of IAG (through previous shareholdings in Iberia), one may argue that the UK fully privatized all their ex-SOEs studied, something which lies in sharp contrast to the French.

Regardless of state participation in Alphas, the evidence shows that home states played a role by positioning themselves to help drive expansionary deals. Examining the links between privatized firms and the state underlined that *all* Alpha boards of directors had some members with past (and even present) links to the state. In comparative terms, the French scored the highest in this regard, consistent with relatively high ownership percentages in their Alphas. Historically, such links and state intervention were crucial in explaining many of the deals before privatization when firms consolidated their national position in all sectors. But, even after privatization, the evidence shows that various officials with past links to the state were positioned to serve on Alpha boards and help drive M&A. In some cases, these officials were previously involved in the privatization of the firm, highlighting the phenomenon of 'revolving doors' of public officials entering the private world. Examples of deals where the Alpha's home state directly intervened (in some cases exercising their power as shareholder) included: AF/KLM; Lufthansa's joint ventures with Shenzen Airlines and DHL Worldwide Express; BA/British Caledonian; BA/Iberia; IAG/BMI; VW/Porsche; Renault/Nissan; Renault/SOMACA; EDF/EnBW; E.ON/Ruhrgas; ENEL/Terna; and ENEL/Endesa.

Home states of Betas also actively participated in their takeover. This is perhaps not much of a surprise in the cases of SEAT and Alfa Romeo, whose privatizations were led by both the Spanish and Italian states, respectively, that injected significant funds to the firms benefiting the buyers. Perhaps less expected is the active role of states in the sales of the other firms that became Betas after privatization. The firms under investigation of specific relevance were: Jaguar, where the state rescinded its golden share, allowing Ford to buy the company; Endesa, whose takeover by ENEL was a product of a deal between the Spanish and Italian states; and Alitalia, whose takeover by CAI was orchestrated by Berlusconi. This dynamic was also manifest in the case of British Energy, where its takeover by EDF saw the active participation of the British state.

As the case of EDF/BE also highlights, *states from abroad*—that is, states which are not those from which Alphas come, which can also be referred to as 'non-Alpha states'—are also essential in order to understand Alpha expansion. For example, the Austrian state played a decisive role in Lufthansa's purchase of Austrian Airlines. This was also seen in the plethora of privatizations in Central and Eastern Europe, whose state leaders were keen to work with the Alphas from France, Germany, and Italy. In other cases, which were not privatizations per se, states' holding shares in firms would also sell to Alphas, as seen in Lufthansa/BMI. And, finally, states from abroad also gave state aid to Alpha operations in their country. With this in mind, and based on deals summarized from previous chapters, Table 6.2 summarizes where Alphas had to negotiate directly with non-Alpha states, which totals over twenty. As the Table shows, most of the transactions involved privatizations pursued by governments, some outside the EU.

Table 6.2. Non-Alpha States from Abroad Involved in Deals

Deal	Non-Alpha states involved in deals
Air France/KLM	The Netherlands (merger)
Air France/Air Ivoire	Ivory Coast (firm privatized by government; henceforth referred to as simply 'privatization')
Lufthansa/Austrian Airlines	Austria (privatization, linked with aid in the deal)
Lufthansa/BMI	Sweden, Denmark, Norway (sale of stake)
Lufthansa/Brussels Airlines	Belgium (state aid kept the profitable part of Sabena alive, later acquired by Lufthansa)
Lufthansa/Swiss	Switzerland (Swiss Confederation/Canton Zurich), sale of stake
Volkswagen/SEAT	Spain (privatization linked with state aid)
Volkswagen, operations in Bratislava	Slovakia (aid to transform plant)
Volkswagen/FAW	China (Joint Venture)
Volkswagen/Škoda	Czech Republic (privatization)
Renault/Dacia	Romania (privatization)
Renault, operations in Valladolid	Spain (aid towards plant)
Renault/Avtovaz	Russia (controlling stake in firm)
EDF/DÉMÁSZ	Hungary (privatization)
EDF/EC Krakow	Poland (privatization)
EDF/ESTAG	Austria (privatization)
EDF/Light	Brazil (privatization)
EDF/EnBW	Germany (privatization)
EDF/Stredoslovenská Energetika	Slovakia (privatization)
EDF/Taishan Nuclear Power	China (Joint Venture)
EDF/British Energy	UK (sale of 35% state stake)
E.ON/EDC Gorna Oryahovitza and Varna	Bulgaria (privatization)
E.ON/Electrica Moldova	Romania (privatization)
E.ON/NRE Energie	The Netherlands (privatization)
E.ON/Transpower	The Netherlands (sale of Transpower to state-controlled TenneT)
SSE/Marchwood Power Station	Ireland (Joint Venture with state-controlled ESB)
ENEL/Slovenské Elektrárne	Slovakia (privatization)
ENEL/Electrica Banat & Electrica Dobrogea & EMS	Romania (privatization)
ENEL/Endesa	Spain (the government also orchestrated as part of the deal that some Endesa assets go to E.ON)

Third, beyond liberalization and the role of states, *regulatory authorities* at different levels of governance ultimately sealed the deals: they acted in a way that ensured that either expansionary deals could take place for Alphas, or that a Beta's takeover could go through.

In a first scenario, regulatory authorities gave an explicit green light for expansion. This was seen when the Commission approved state aid, some of which went directly to areas where Alphas expanded. More significantly, both domestic regulators and the Commission always approved Alpha M&A: the evidence throughout the empirical chapters highlighted that *no* deal was ever blocked by regulators which had theoretical veto powers. Most striking was the fact that the over fifty major cross-border M&A involving Alphas documented in this study were all approved by the European Commission, mostly without conditions. Some of these deals sealed by the Commission also involved the takeover of Betas, as seen in CAI/Alitalia and, most poignantly, in Endesa, whose takeover attempt by both E.ON and ENEL was closely monitored by the Commission.

This 100 per cent approval rate enjoyed by Alphas at the EU level can be explained, on the one hand, because of the sizeable funds earmarked by firms towards effective lobbying strategies. As data from the EU's Transparency Register shows, some Alphas spend millions towards their lobbying costs in Brussels, which in some cases are high in years when big deals are pursued (as seen in EDF/Edison).

On the other hand, because the European Commission is motivated to create global champions that are trustworthy given previous links to the state, this study argued that the Commission gives preferential treatment to the Alphas when compared to other peers. This was concluded by examining cases that did not involve Alphas, but their competitors in the sector whose proposed M&A were blocked by the Commission. The Commission's apparent favouring of Alphas was demonstrated, perhaps most tellingly, in Volvo's failed acquisition of Scania: Volvo/Scania was blocked by the Commission based on analysis of selective criteria; the negative decision effectively set the stage for VW to eye both Scania and then MAN; and, years later, the Commission subsequently approved VW/Scania/MAN without any conditions. Ryanair, with its three failed attempts to acquire Aer Lingus between 2006 and 2013, has been continuously blocked by the Commission despite various remedies pursued. Blocking Ryanair/Aer Lingus (as well as earlier decisions on Olympic/Aegean) was justified by the Commission in order to prevent a national player from one home state taking a dominant position, even though this reasoning was shelved when it approved IAG's acquisition of UK-based BMI. Coupled with this, the evidence also suggested that the Commission is hesitant to approve deals by 'untrustworthy partners' (deemed so by the Commission itself, or member states) that it is not fully convinced of, simply because once a merger is approved at the EU level it cannot be undone. This has, perhaps, been the bane explaining the failure of Ryanair's attempts to take over Aer Lingus.

In a second scenario, some cases saw the absence of regulatory decisions ever being made, effectively constituting an 'implicit' green light for expansion. This was seen especially in deals outside of the EU where firms were able to fly under the regulatory radar. In this regard, some of the transactions in Central and Eastern Europe, Asia, Africa, and Latin America escaped investigation. In Europe in the 1980s, the absence of regulatory approval was also seen in the case of Jaguar (when the government ensured that the case was not going to be heard by the MMC) and that of SEAT (whose privatization was tightly centred around key members of the Spanish core-executive, almost in secret). It was argued that having these deals never investigated, given the absence of a formal regulatory approval process at the domestic level, meant no barriers were placed against Alpha global roaming or, as in the cases of Jaguar and SEAT, Betas' takeover.

6.2 The Wider Contribution

The theory of LIFESHAPERS stems from detailed evidence found in the evolution of privatized firms from five major EU states in three important sectors. In its entirety, it has synthesized various ideas from scholars writing on liberalization, the role of states, and the decisions of regulatory authorities, showing their key sequential impact on privatized firms. Notwithstanding, more critical scholars may reasonably argue that more evidence needs to be uncovered before the theory can be fully supported. From this perspective, it is hoped that future social science research will test this theory—falsifying or verifying it—by examining developments in other sectors, such as telecoms and petroleum. Such investigation may focus on Europe.

Yet, the strength of the theory for wider social science scholarship lies in the fact that the key factors—liberalization, states, and regulators from various levels of governance—can be analysed when studying the life of any privatized firm in the world. Underscoring the generalizability of the theory, the key factors can *also* be analysed when seeking to better grasp the evolution of *any* firm that has globally expanded with M&A or that has been taken over. With these ideas in mind, it is hoped that the LIFESHAPERS theory offers a basis not only for further scholarly investigation, but also for business leaders as well as political actors to better gauge the political environment in which firms work and even predict firms' future developments. With regard to the latter, LIFESHAPERS suggests that a firm either seeking future global expansion by merging or acquiring, or seeing its ultimate takeover as a possibility, should ask three essential questions that have less to do with business and more to do with politics: do the rules allow for it; will states facilitate it; and will regulators approve it?

Precisely because LIFESHAPERS highlights the importance of these three key factors, its ideas can also offer some fresh insights into both the larger Varieties of Capitalism (VoC) literature and the globalization debates. As discussed in the first chapter, VoC, and the more general scholarship that reflects on the relationship between business and politics, seek to better understand firms' relationship with the state. A main aspect of the globalization debate focuses on how firms globally move given increasing integration of the world economy. In an integrated discussion, I close by considering how this study adds to ideas generated in both sets of literature.

When we turn to the role of 'states' in LIFESHAPERS it is worth recalling the evidence that shows that all firms from France (AF–KLM, Renault, and EDF) and some from Germany (VW, E.ON) maintained significant ownership in life after privatization of some of the Alphas, while Italy still maintains a controlling stake in ENEL. The data demonstrated that, indeed, the French simply privatized differently, as previously indicated in Chapter 1: the state's stakes in the French firms studied ranged between 15 per cent and 84 per cent. This is consistent with how the French have privatized other companies, such as France Télécom (where the state controls 26.95 per cent) and GDF Suez (36 per cent).[2] VW remains 20 per cent state owned (with the state holding a blocking minority via the Volkswagen Law), and the Italian state holds over 30 per cent of ENEL as discussed. Linking this to the VoC debate, one may argue that the state is more likely to maintain direct shareholding in firms after privatization in State Enhanced Economies such as France and Coordinated Market Economies (CMEs) such as Germany. In contrast, the UK (an LME) and Spain (which authors, such as Heywood (1998), argue is closer to an LME than a CME) generally privatized their firms fully. As such, some firms from Spain and the UK that could have become Alphas, but ended up becoming Betas, had little to no state ownership at the time they were taken over. In fact, leaders from both the UK and Spain facilitated the takeover of two 'potential Alphas' after privatization (Jaguar and Endesa). This may be seen as being justified by (and consistent with) the idea that the state should play little long-term role in a liberal economy, and helps explain the positions taken particularly by the UK in both Jaguar and British Energy.

This dynamic points to a lingering *protective function* of the post-privatization state: maintaining significant stakes of state ownership, as seen in especially state-enhanced economies such as France and also coordinated market economies such as Germany, helps explain the evolution of firms from different varieties of capitalism. Not all firms that became Alphas necessarily had state ownership. However, all firms that had significant forms of state ownership are always Alphas, and no firm that has had significant forms of state ownership after privatization ever became a Beta. In essence, the state in a CME and state-enhanced economy helps protect its firms while they operate in the global economy. In contrast, those firms from LMEs that have been privatized do not necessarily enjoy a similar 'protection' by the state and are more likely to end up as Betas as they become the targets of Alphas, some of which are from CMEs and state-enhanced economies. The irony is perhaps self-evident: LMEs sold their assets, only to have some of them eventually lapped up by firms in which non-LME protective states retain ownership. State-ownership did not necessarily end; it was simply transformed.

That said, even though CMEs and state-enhanced economies may hold significant shareholdings and help protect their firms, the evidence also showed that all states, even the LMEs, maintained close links to the Alphas. This was through having former (and even present) public officials holding board positions in the privatized firm and also playing an *expansionist function* by actively helping craft deals at home, in Europe, and overseas. In this regard, and contributing to the *globalization debate*, the evidence has shown that some Alphas have left their global footprints in countries with which states have had historical relationships or former colonies, such as Africa and French Indo-China (in the case of French firms), Latin America (in the case of Spanish firms), Central and Eastern Europe (German and Italian firms), and Ireland and North America (UK firms). This may be explained given the close 'psychic-distance' with such areas of the world, cultivated by pre-established links the state has with these regions. As such, globalization entails not just conquering new global markets, but simply going back to one's roots and re-conquering old ones.

Notwithstanding the protective and expansionary function of states from which firms emanate, the LIFESHAPERS theory proposes that the VoC debate could be enriched by focusing beyond the variety of capitalism found at the domestic level. If we are interested in bringing back the firm into the centre of political economy, then its relationship with, and the role played by, the domestic level really forms only one part of the equation. LIFESHAPERS puts forward the argument that there are three additional dimensions of the *politics of the global environment* in which a firm operates that need to be fully examined by both VoC and globalization scholars. This will allow for a more nuanced understanding of how firms evolve and internationally move.

A first dimension of this politically charged environment for firms includes domestic or regional liberalization initiatives which set the tone for what can or cannot be done, when, and where. Simply put, knowing such rules can help firms to start drawing blueprints for expansion. A second dimension includes firms making new relationships with states beyond their own or even those with past historical relationships. Many of these states abroad, which may be striving to be liberal market economies, are privatizing and liberalizing. They are keen to have global movers enter and acquire. This is regardless of the flag that such firms may wave and, perhaps ironically, regardless of state-owner-ship that may remain in the global mover. From this perspective, what firms can do in global markets depends on what other states, beyond their home one, want and are willing to give. And a third dimension includes having to deal with and effectively lobby domestic and supranational regulators that investigate the deals and are empowered to make or break them. What firms can do in global markets is a function of the actions of regulators, which can potentially veto expansion. Alternatively, easy entry can be made into juris-dictions that do not have much of a role for regulatory authorities, offering an impediment-free path into new markets.

In summary, the life of privatized firms, and perhaps all firms for that matter, is a product of both heredity and environment. In many ways, an ex-state-owned enterprise can be likened to a grown-up child that has left home, where some end up living closer to their parents than others. The grown-up children may be shaped by their heritage and upbringing, and in fact may still rely on their parents for a place to stay and support at times. But, the environment in which they live as adults—and how they adapt to it and deal with others—is equally shaping.

Endnotes

1. In this regard, as seen in the empirical chapters, firms such as Ryanair, easyJet, BMW, and Iberdrola were classified as Alphas, while Betas included Scottish Power, Powergen, and British Energy.

2. In terms of its shareholder structure, as of March 2014 Orange (the rebranded name for France Télécom) has as its main shareholders the French state with a direct stake of 13.45%, and BPIFrance Participations, which is ultimately owned by the French State, owns 13.5%, meaning that the French state controls 26.95%. Orange data is based on the Amadeus company report with Company ID Number FR380129866. GDF Suez data is based on the firm's report in Amadeus with Company ID Number FR542107651.

Bibliography

Abraham, F. (2001) 'Global and Economic Labour Costs', LICOS Center for Transition Economies, *Licos Discussion Paper 102*, available: <http://www.econ.kuleuven.be/licos/publications/dp/dp102.pdf> [accessed 10 July 2014].

Alexandre H. and Charreaux G. (2004) 'Efficiency of French Privatizations: A Dynamic Vision', *Journal of Corporate Finance*, Vol. 10(3), 467–94.

Amyot, G. (2010) 'The Privatisation of Alitalia', in Baldini, G. and Cento Bull, A., eds, *Governing Fear*, New York: Berghahn Books.

Associated Press (1989) 'Jaguar Shareholders Pave Way for Ford Deal', available: <http://www.apnewsarchive.com/1989/Jaguar-Shareholders-Pave-Way-For-Ford-Deal/if-d943fle6fc0954ad61297790021bfe1c> [accessed 2 September 2013].

Auerbach, A., ed. (1988) *Corporate Takeovers: Causes and Consequences*, Chicago: University of Chicago Press.

Auerbach, A. and Reishus, D. (1988) 'The Effects of Taxation on the Merger Decision', in Auerbach, A., ed., *Corporate Takeovers: Causes and Consequences*, Chicago: University of Chicago Press, 157–83.

Avkiran, N. K. (1999) 'The Evidence of Efficiency Gains: The Role of Mergers and the Benefits to the Public', *Journal of Banking and Finance*, 23(7), 991–1013.

Barker, A. (2011) 'Brussels Sues Germany over VW "Golden Share"', *Financial Times*, available: <http://www.ft.com/intl/cms/s/0/7dc5550a-168c-11e1-be1d-00144feabdc0.html#axzz2gZ8dsSd2> [accessed 2 October 2013].

Bauby, P. and Vorone, F. (2007) 'Europeanization of the French Electricity Policy', *Journal of European Public Policy*, 14(7), 1048–60.

Baumgartner, F. R., Berry, J. M., Hojnacki, M., Kimball, D. C., and Leech, B. L. (2009) *Lobbying and Policy Change*, Chicago: University of Chicago Press.

Bekier, M. M., Bogardus, A. J., and Oldham, T. (2001) 'Why Mergers Fail', *The McKinsey Quarterly*, 6–9.

Benz, A. and Goetz, K. H. (1996) *A New German Public Sector? Reform, Adaption, and Stability*, Aldershot: Dartmouth.

Beria, P., Niemeier, H.-M., and Fröhlich, K. (2011) 'Alitalia—The Failure of the National Carrier', *Journal of Air Transport Management*, 17(4), 215–20.

Berne, M. and Pogorel, G. (2004) *Privatization Experiences in France*, CESifo Working Paper No. 1195, May.

Bernhagen, P. and Mitchell, N. J. (2009) 'The Determinants of Direct Corporate Lobbying in the European Union', *European Union Politics*, 10(2), 155–76.

Bhagwati, J. (2004) *In Defense of Globalization*, Oxford: Oxford University Press.

Bishop, M. and Kay, J. A., eds (1993) *European Mergers and Merger Policy*, Oxford: Oxford University Press.

Bjorvatn, K. (2004) 'Economic Integration and the Profitability of Cross-border Mergers and Acquisitions', *European Economic Review*, 48, 1211–26.

Bloomberg Businessweek (2011) 'Italy Puts 1 Year Moratorium on Nuclear', available: <http://www.businessweek.com/ap/financialnews/D9M504RG0.htm> [accessed 10 January 2014].

Boix, C. (1997) 'Privatizing the Public Business Sector in the Eighties: Economic Performance, Partisan Responses, and Divided Governments', *British Journal of Political Science*, 27(4), 473–96.

Börsch, A. (2004) 'What Happens after Privatization? Globalization, Corporate Governance and Adjustment at British Telecom and Deutsche Telecom', *Journal of European Public Policy*, 11(4), 593–612.

Botta, M. (2011) *Merger Control Regimes in Emerging Economies: A Case Study on Brazil and Argentina*, Alphen aan den Rijn, The Netherlands: Kluwer Law International.

Bovis, C. (2006) *Public Procurement: Case Law and Regulation*, Oxford: Oxford University Press.

Braithwaite, J. and Drahos, P. (2000) *Global Business Regulation*, Cambridge: Cambridge University Press.

Brennan, L. and Garvey, D. (2009) 'The Role of Psychic Distance in the Internationalisation of Technology Firms', in Harvey, N., ed., *Irish Academy of Management 12th Annual Conference*, Galway, 31.

Brock, J. W. (2011) 'Economic Concentration and Economic Power: John Flynn and a Quarter-Century of Mergers', *The Antitrust Bulletin*, 56(4), 681–730.

Brown, C. and Medoff, J. (1988) 'The Impact of Firm Acquisitions on Labour', in Auerbach, A., ed., *Corporate Takeovers: Causes and Consequences*, Chicago: University of Chicago Press, 9–25.

Brozen, Y. (1982) *Concentration, Mergers, and Public Policy*, New York: Macmillan Publishers Ltd.

Bruch, H. and Sattelberger, T. (2001) 'The Turnaround at Lufthansa: Learning from the Change Process', *Journal of Change Management*, 1(4), 344–63.

Bryce, R. (2011) *Power Hungry*, Philadelphia: Public Affairs.

Bryman, A. (2008) *Social Research Methods*, 3rd edn, Oxford: Oxford University Press.

Bureau van Dijk (2012) Zephyr Annual M&A Report 2012 (available on BvD's Zephyr).

Cameron, D. (2012) 'China's Jade Cargo Grounds Planes on Weak Demand', *MarketWatch*, available: <http://www.marketwatch.com/story/chinas-jade-cargo-grounds-planes-on-weak-demand-2012-01-01> [accessed 11 November 2013].

Cameron, P. (2005) 'Completing the Internal Market in Energy: An Introduction to the New Legislation', in Cameron, P., ed., *Legal Aspects of EU Energy Regulation*, Oxford: Oxford University Press, 7–39.

Campbell, D., ed. (2011a) *Mergers and Acquisitions in Europe: Selected Issues and Jurisdictions*, Alphen aan den Rijn, The Netherlands: Kluwer Law International.

Campbell, D., ed. (2011b) *Mergers and Acquisitions in North America, Latin America, Asia, and the Pacific*, Alphen aan den Rijn, The Netherlands: Kluwer Law International.

Carcar, S. (2011) 'El exministro Pedro Solbes ficha como consejero del grupo italiano Enel', *El País*, available: <http://elpais.com/diario/2011/04/01/economia/1301608803_850215. html> [accessed 1 March 2014].

Carcar, S. (2012) 'Endesa ficha a Elena Salgado como consejera para su distribuidora en Chile', *El País*, available: <http://economia.elpais.com/economia/2012/03/05/act ualidad/1330940385_562460.html> [accessed 17 February 2014].

Carreras, A., Tafunell, X., and Torres, E. (2000) 'The Rise and Decline of Spanish State-Owned Firms', in Toninelli, P. A., ed., *The Rise and Fall of State-Owned Enterprises in the Western World*, Cambridge: Cambridge University Press.

Carswell, S. (2013) 'Blocking of Ryanair Takeover Bid Was Not Political, Says Competition Commissioner', *The Irish Times*, available: <http://www.irishtimes.com/business/ sectors/transport-and-tourism/blocking-of-ryanair-takeover-bid-was-not-political-says-competition-commissioner-1.1357522> [accessed 31 December 2013].

Chari, R. (1998) 'Spanish Socialists, Privatising the Right Way?', *West European Politics*, 21(4), 163–79.

Chari, R. (2004) *State Aid in the Airline Sector: A Comparative Analysis of Iberia and Aer Lingus*, 13, Dublin: The Policy Institute.

Chari, R. (2008) '2008 Spanish Election: A Balancing Game', *West European Politics*, 31 (5), 1068–76.

Chari, R. (2013) 'The Parliamentary Election in Spain, November 2011', *Electoral Studies*, 32(2), 377–80.

Chari, R. and Bernhagen, P. (2011) 'The Financial and Economic Crisis: Explaining the Sunset over the Celtic Tiger', *Irish Political Studies*, 26(4), 473–88.

Chari, R. and Cavatorta, F. (2002) 'Economic Actors' Political Activity in "Overlap Issue": Privatisations and State Aid Control', *West European Politics*, 25(4), 119–42.

Chari, R. and Heywood, P. (2009) 'Analysing the Policy Process in Democratic Spain', *West European Politics*, 32(1), 26–54.

Chari, R. and Hillebrand O'Donovan, D. (2011) 'Lobbying the European Commission: Open or Secret?', *Socialism and Democracy*, 25(2), 104–24.

Chari, R., Hogan, J., and Murphy, G. (2010) *Regulating Lobbying: A Global Comparison*, Manchester: Manchester University Press.

Chari, R. and Kritzinger, S. (2006) *Understanding EU Policy Making*, London: Pluto.

Chicago Tribune (1989) 'Ford Motor Co.'s $2.5 Billion Bid for Jaguar PLC Won't Be ...', *Chicago Tribune*, available: <http://articles.chicagotribune.com/1989-12-01/busi ness/8903140387_1_jaguar-plc-jaguar-shareholders-billion-bid> [accessed 26 September 2013].

Chick, M. (2007) *Electricity and Energy Policy in Britain, France, and the US since 1945*, Cheltenham: Edward Elgar Publishing.

Chislett, W. (2002) *The Internationalization of the Spanish Economy*, Madrid: Real Instituto Elcano.

Cini, M. (1996) *The European Commission: Leadership, Organisation, and Culture in the EU Administration*, Manchester: Manchester University Press.

Cini, M. and McGowan, L. (2008) *Competition Policy in the European Union*, 2nd edn, Basingstoke: Palgrave Macmillan.

Clausager, A. D. (1990) *Jaguar: A Living Legend*, London: Brian Todd Publishing.

Bibliography

Clift, B. (2001) 'The Jospin Way', *The Political Quarterly*, Vol. 72 (2), 170–9.

Clifton, J., Comín, F., and Díaz-Fuentes, D. (2006) 'Privatizing Public Enterprises in the EU 1960–2002: Ideological, Pragmatic, Inevitable?', *Journal of European Public Policy*, 13(5), 736–56.

CNN News (2000) 'Lauda Quits as Airline CEO', available: <http://cnnfn.cnn.com/2000/11/21/europe/lauda/> [accessed 3 November 2013].

Coen, D. (1997) 'The Evolution of the Large Firm as a Political Actor in the European Union', *Journal of European Public Policy*, 4(1), 91–108.

Coen, D. (1998) 'The European Business Interest and the Nation State: Large-Firm Lobbying in the European Union and Member States', *Journal of Public Policy*, 18(1), 75–100.

Coen, D. (2009) 'Business Lobbying in the European Union', in Coen, D. and Richardson, J., eds, *Lobbying in the European Union: Institutions, Actors, and Issues*, Oxford: Oxford University Press.

Coen, D. and Thatcher, M. (2001) *Utilities Reform in Europe*, New York: Nova Science Publishers.

Coleman, B. (1994) 'Lufthansa's Shift to Privatization Overcomes Hurdle', *Wall Street Journal*, May 5, A11.

Conaghan, C. M. and Malloy, J. (1995) *Unsettling Statecraft: Democracy and Neoliberalism in the Central Andes*, Pittsburgh: University of Pittsburgh Press.

Cuellar Fernández, B., Fuertes Callén, Y., and Laínez Gadea, J. A. (2011) 'Stock Price Reaction to Non-Financial News in European Technology Companies', *European Accounting Review*, 20(1), 81–111.

Dabbah, M. and Lasok, K. P. E. (2012) *Merger Control Worldwide, Cambridge Antitrust and Competition Series*, 2nd edn, Cambridge: Cambridge University Press.

Datamonitor (2002) 'Dutch Energy: Government Protects its Own', available: <http://www.datamonitor.com/store/News/dutch_energy_government_protcts_its_own?productid=E967912D-5CDD-4BE7-8D6C-76624D2C9B06> [accessed 14 March 2014].

Davis, A. (2002) *Public Relations Democracy*, Manchester: Manchester University Press.

Davis, A. (2009) 'Porsche, VW Move Toward Merger', *Mergers and Acquisitions Report*, 22 (19), 6.

Doganis, R. (2006) *The Airline Business*, 2nd edn, London: Routledge.

Done, K. (2004) 'Virgin Express Marriage with SN Brussels Agreed', *Financial Times*, available: <http://www.ft.com/intl/cms/s/0/c4e0aeb2-1734-11d9-bbe8-00000e2511c8.html#axzz2kAoafqrq> [accessed 10 December 2013].

Doytch, N., Mixon, F. G., and Upadhyaya, K. P. (2011) 'Employment Effects of Mergers and Acquisitions in the United States by Sector', *Applied Economic Letters*, 18(10–12), 925–8.

Eising, R. (2002) 'Policy Learning in Embedded Negotiations: Explaining EU Electricity Liberalization', *International Organization*, 56(1), 85–120.

El Mundo (2007) 'Enel asegura entrar "sola" en Endesa, mientras E.ON dice que sigue comprometido con su oferta', *El Mundo*, available: <http://www.elmundo.es/mundodinero/2007/02/28/portada/11772654465.html> [accessed 5 March 2014].

El País (2001) 'La SEPI vende Aerolíneas Argentinas al grupo Marsans', available: <http://economia.elpais.com/economia/2001/10/02/actualidad/1002007974_850215.html> [accessed 5 March 2014].

El País (2007) 'Favores recíprocos', available: <http://elpais.com/diario/2007/05/06/opinion/1178402402_850215.html> [accessed 5 March 2014].

El País (2010) 'Rato es nombrado vicepresidente de Iberia', available: <http://economia.elpais.com/economia/2010/02/12/actualidad/1265963580_850215.html> [accessed 9 December 2013].

Ellwood, W. (2001) *The No-Nonsense Guide to Globalization*, London: Verso.

Enriques, L. and Volpin, P. (2007) 'Corporate Governance Reforms in Continental Europe', *Journal of Economic Perspectives*, 21(1), 117–40.

European Commission (1993) 'Commission Approves Aid to SEAT in Support of an Investment Project', Press Release, IP/93/648, 28/07/1993.

European Commission (1995) 'Commission Approves Aid to Volkswagen and SEAT in Support of the 1994–1997 Restructuring Plan of SEAT', Press Release, IP/95/1188, 31/10/1995.

European Commission (1996) 'Commission Takes a Final Decision on a German Proposal to Provide State Aid to Volkswagen in the New Lander', Press Release, IP/96/562, 26/06/1996.

European Commission (1999) 'Commission Authorises Regional Aid for Fiat Engine Plant at Termoli, Italy', Press Release, IP/99/710, 20/09/1999.

European Commission (2000) 'Commission Declares that EDF Rebates to Firms in the Paper Industry Do Not Constitute State Aid', IP/00/370, 11/04/2000.

European Commission (2001a) 'Commission Clears Purchase by EDF of a stake in German Electricity Firm EnBW Subject to Conditions', IP/01/175, 07/02/2001.

European Commission (2001b) 'Commission Reduces Planned Aid to Volkswagen for New Factory in Dresden (Germany)', Press Release, IP/01/1016, 18/07/2001.

European Commission (2002a) 'Commission Authorises Aid to Renault for Investment in Spain', Press Release, IP/02/819, 05/06/2002.

European Commission (2002b) 'Commission Clears Acquisition of Seeboard by London Electricity Group', IP/02/1166, 26/07/2002.

European Commission (2002c) 'Open Sky Agreements: Commission Welcomes European Court of Justice Ruling', Press Release, IP/02/1609, 05/11/2002.

European Commission (2003a) 'Commission Approves EUR 15 Million Regional Aid for Volkswagen in Navarra', Press Release, IP/03/824, 11/06/2003.

European Commission (2003b) 'Commission Approves Proposed Aid in Favour of VW Mechatronic in Stollberg (Germany)', Press Release, IP/03/1081, 23/07/2003.

European Commission (2004) 'Commission Approves Alliance Between Air France and Alitalia', Press Release, IP/04/469, 07/04/2004.

European Commission (2005) 'Mergers: Commission Approves Acquisition by E.ON of MOL's Gas Business, Subject to Conditions', IP/05/1658, 21/12/2005.

European Commission (2006) 'Mergers: Commission Decides that Spanish Measures in Proposed E.ON/Endesa Takeover Violate EC Law', IP/06/1853, 20/12/2006.

European Commission (2007) 'Towards an Effective Implementation of Commission Decisions Ordering Member States to Recover Unlawful and Incompatible State Aid', *Official Journal of the European Union*, 272(4).

European Commission (2008a) 'Alitalia: The Commission Adopts Two State Aid Decisions', Press Release, IP/08/1692, 12/11/2008.

European Commission (2008b) 'Antitrust: Commission Opens German Electricity Market to Competition', IP/08/1774, 26/11/2008.

European Commission (2008c) 'Mergers: Commission Clears Proposed Acquisition of British Energy by EDF, Subject to Conditions', IP/08/2048, 22/12/2008.

European Commission (2009a) 'State Aid: Commission Approves €46 Million Regional Aid to Fiat For Investment Project in Sicily', Press Release, IP/09/660, 29/04/2009.

European Commission (2009b) 'State aid: Commission endorses €14.3 million aid for Volkswagen in Bratislava, Slovakia,' Press Release, IP/09/1865, 02/12/2009.

European Commission (2011) 'Mergers: Commission Blocks Proposed Merger Between Aegean Airlines and Olympic Air', Press Release, IP/11/68, 26/01/2011.

European Commission (2013a) 'Mergers: Commission Prohibits Ryanair's Proposed Takeover of Aer Lingus', Press Release, IP/13/167, 27/02/2013.

European Commission (2013b) 'Mergers: Commission Approves Acquisition of Greek Airline Olympic Air by Aegean Airlines', Press Release, IP/13/927, 09/10/2013.

European Commission (2014) 'Mergers: Commission approves Etihad's acquisition of joint control over Alitalia, subject to conditions', IP/14/1766, 14/11/204.

Farber, H. S. (1988) 'The Impact of Firm Acquisition on Labor: Comment', in Auerbach, A., ed., *Corporate Takeovers: Causes and Consequences*, Chicago: University of Chicago Press, 28–31.

Faulkner, D., Teerikangas, S., and Joseph, R. J. (2012) *The Handbook of Mergers and Acquisitions*, Oxford: Oxford University Press.

Feigenbaum, H., Henig, J., and Hamnett, C. (1998) *Shrinking the State: The Political Underpinnings of Privatization*, Cambridge: Cambridge University Press.

Felice, E. (2010) 'State Ownership and International Competitiveness: The Italian Finmeccanica from Alfa Romeo to Aerospace and Defense (1947–2007)', *Enterprise and Society*, 11(3), 594–635.

Flynn, J. J. (1988) 'The Reagan Administration's Antitrust Policy, "Original Intent" and the Legislative History of the Sherman Act', *The Antitrust Bulletin*, 33, 259–307.

Folkman, P., Froud, J., Johal, S., and Williams, K. (2007) 'Working for Themselves? Capital Market Intermediaries and Present Day Capitalism', *Business History*, 49(4), 552–72.

Frynas, J. G. and Paulo, M. (2007) 'A New Scramble for African Oil? Historical, Political, and Business Perspectives', *African Affairs*, 106(423), 229–51.

Garrett, J. (2009) 'VW Kills Rabbit Name, Again', *The New York Times*, available: <http://wheels.blogs.nytimes.com/2009/03/27/vw-kills-rabbit-name-again/> [accessed 1 July 2013].

Geradin, D., ed. (2000) *The Liberalization of State Monopolies in European Union and Beyond*, Boston: Kluwer Law International.

Gerber, D. J. (2010) *Global Competition: Law, Markets, and Globalization*, Oxford: Oxford University Press.

Goldstein, A. (2004) *Privatization in Italy 1993–2002: Goals, Institutions, Outcomes, and Outstanding Issues*, CESifo Working Paper Series No. 912, April.

Goutas, L. and Lane, C. (2009) 'The Translation of Shareholder Value in the German Business System: A Comparative Study of DaimlerChrysler and Volkswagen AG', *Competition and Change*, 13(4), 327–46.

Graham, C. (2003) 'Methods of Privatization', in Parker, D. and Saal, D., eds, *International Handbook on Privatization*, Northampton: Edward Elgar Publishing, Inc., 87–101.

Guillén, M. (2005) *The Rise of Spanish Multinationals*, Cambridge: Cambridge University Press.

Hall, B. H. (1988) 'The Effect of Takeover Activity on Corporate Research and Development', in Auerbach, A., ed., *Corporate Takeovers: Causes and Consequences*, Chicago: University of Chicago Press, 69–100.

Hall, P. A. and Soskice, D. (2001) 'An Introduction to Varieties of Capitalism', in Hall, P. A. and Soskice, D., eds, *Varieties of Capitalism: The Institutional Foundations of Comparative Advantage*, Oxford: Oxford University Press, 1–68.

Hancher, L., Ottervanger, T., and Slot, P. J. (2012) *EU State Aids*, 4th edn, London: Sweet and Maxwell.

Hanson, B. T. (1998) 'What Happened to Fortress Europe? External Trade Policy Liberalization in the European Union', *International Organization*, 52(1), 55–85.

Haugh, D., Mourougane, A., and Chatel, O. (2010) *The Automobile Industry in and Beyond the Crisis*, Organisation for Economic Co-operation and Development, Economics Department Working Paper 745.

Hawranek, D. (2009a) 'The Porsche Story: A Fierce Family Feud', *Der Spiegel*, available: <http://www.spiegel.de/international/business/the-porsche-story-a-fierce-family-feud-a-637243.html> [accessed 18 March 2014].

Hawranek, D. (2009b) 'The Porsche Story: The Downfall of a Corporate Upstart', *Der Spiegel*, available: <http://www.spiegel.de/international/business/the-porsche-story-the-downfall-of-a-corporate-upstart-a-637542.html> [accessed 18 March 2014].

Hay, C. (2006) 'Globalization and Public Policy', in Moran, M., Rein, M., and Goodin, R. E., eds, *The Oxford Handbook of Public Policy*, Oxford: Oxford University Press, 587–604.

Hayward, J. (ed) (1995) *Industrial Enterprise and European Integration: From National to International Champions in Western Europe*, Oxford: Oxford University Press.

Held, D. and McGrew, A. (2003) *The Global Transformations Reader*, 2nd edn, London: Polity.

Helm, D. and Tindall, T. (2009) 'The Evolution of Infrastructure and Utility Ownership and its Implications', *Oxford Review of Economic Policy*, 25(3), 411–34.

Heywood, P. (1995) *The Government and Politics of Spain*, London: Palgrave Macmillan.

Heywood, P. (1998) 'Power Diffusion or Concentration? In Search of the Spanish Policy Process', *West European Politics*, 21(4), 103–23.

Ingham, G. (2008) *Capitalism*, Cambridge: Polity.

Jaguar (1984, collected February 2012) *Extract Taken from the 'Offer of Sale' Document of Jaguar Cars*, Jaguar Daimler Heritage Trust.

Jaguar (1990) *The Jaguar Story: A Legend in its Lifetime*, Communications and Public Affairs Department of Jaguar.

James, B. (2002) 'Open Skies Pacts Stifle Competition It Says: EU Court Strikes Down Aviation Accords with the US', *The New York Times*, available: <http://www.nytimes.com/2002/11/06/news/06iht-skies_ed3_.html> [accessed 17 December 2013].

Jameson, A. (2008) 'Centrica joins with EDF in British Energy deal', *The Times; Utilities*, available: <http://www.thetimes.co.uk/tto/business/industries/utilities/article2197475.ece> [accessed 17 February 2014].

Julius, D. (1990) *Global Companies and Public Policy: The Growing Challenge of Foreign Direct Investment*, London: Pinter Publishing.

Kassim, H. (1996) 'Air Transport', in Kassim, H. and Menon, A., eds, *The European Union and National Industrial Policy*, London: Routledge, 106–31.

Kassim, H. and Stevens, H. (2010) *Air Transport and the European Union: Europeanization and its Limits*, Basingstoke: Palgrave Macmillan.

Keenan, M. (2012) 'Airtricity's Owner Buys Irish Arm of Endesa for €320m', *Irish Independent*, available: <http://www.independent.ie/business/irish/airtricitys-owner-buys-irish-arm-of-endesa-for-320m-26865340.html> [accessed 14 February 2014].

Kubo, K. and Saito, T. (2012) 'The Effect of Mergers on Employment and Wages: Evidence from Japan', *Journal of the Japanese and International Economies*, 26(2), 262–84.

Kumar, B. R. (2012) *Mega Mergers and Acquisitions: Case Studies from Key Industries*, Basingstoke: Palgrave Macmillan.

Kurylko, D. T. and Specht, M. (2013) 'BMW Aims to be Technology Leader with i3 Electric Car', *Automative News Europe*, available: <http://europe.autonews.com/article/20130729/ANE/130729899/#axzz2iZ6kuWmk> [accessed 11 July 2013].

Landler, M. (2002) 'Europe's Highest Court Voids Air Treaties with the US', *The New York Times*, available: <http://www.nytimes.com/2002/11/06/business/europe-s-highest-court-voids-air-treaties-with-the-us.html?pagewanted=2> [accessed 26 December 2013].

Macallister, T. (2003) 'Fears for Jobs as Powergen Buys Midlands Electricity', *The Guardian*, available: <http://www.theguardian.com/business/2003/oct/22/utilities> [accessed 20 February 2013].

Macchiati, A. and Siciliano, G. (2007) 'Airlines' Privatisation in Europe: Fully versus Partial Divestiture', *Rivista di Politica Economica*, 97, 123–55.

Maclean, M., Harvey, C., and Press, J. (2006) *Business Elites and Corporate Governance in France and the UK, French Politics, Society and Culture*, Basingstoke: Palgrave Macmillan.

Majone, G. (1994) 'Paradoxes of Privatization and Deregulation', *Journal of European Public Policy*, 1(1), 53–69.

Maloney, W. A. and McLaughlin, A. M. (1999) *The European Automobile Industry: Multi-level Governance, Policy and Politics*, London: Routledge.

Marcos, F. (2013) 'Spain: When Competition is the Last Concern: The Battle for the Control of Endesa', in Rodger, B., ed., *Landmark Cases in Competition Law Around the World in Fourteen Stories*, Alphen aan den Rijn, The Netherlands: Wolters Kluwer Law & Business, 287–318.

Marks, M. L. and Mirvis, P. H. (2011) 'A Framework for the Human Resources Role in Managing Culture in Mergers and Acquisitions', *Human Resource Management*, 50(6), 859–77.

Mason, M. (1994) 'Elements of Consensus: Europe's Response to the Japanese Automotive Challenge', *Journal of Common Market Studies*, 32(4), 433–53.

Maudit L. (2002) 'En France les Privatisations ont Rapporté 70 Milliards d'euros, *Le Monde*, 9 April.

McCarthy, K. J. and Dolfsma, W. (2013) *Understanding Mergers and Acquisitions in the 21st Century: a Multidisciplinary Approach*, Basingstoke: Palgrave Macmillan.

Mcdougall, G. (1995) *The Economic Impact of Mergers and Acquisitions on Corporations*, Working Paper 4, Ottawa: Industry Canada, February.

Megginson, W. L. (2005) *The Financial Economics of Privatization*, Oxford: Oxford University Press.

Megginson, W. L. and Netter, J. M. (2003) 'History and Methods of Privatization', in Parker, D. and Saal, D., eds, *International Handbook on Privatization*, Northampton: Edward Elgar Publishing, 25–40.

Mitchener, B. (1994) 'Privatization Plans Clear German Airline for Takeoff: Lufthansa Sees Profitable Future', *The New York Times*, available: <http://nytimes.com/1994/05/07/news/07iht-luft_0.html>.

Moeller, S. and Brady, C. (2007) *Intelligent M&A: Navigating the Mergers and Acquisitions Minefield*, Chichester: John Wiley & Sons.

Moore, J. (1983) 'Why Privatize?', in Kay, J. A., Mayer, C., and Thompson, D., eds, *Privatization and Regulation: The UK Experience*, Oxford: Clarendon, 78–93.

Moran, M. (2009) *Business, Politics, and Society*, Oxford: Oxford University Press.

Moran, M. and Prosser, T. (eds) (1994) *Privatization and Regulatory Change in Europe*, Buckingham: Open University Press.

Motta, M. (2004) *Competition Policy: Theory and Practice*, Cambridge: Cambridge University Press.

Motta, M. and Ruta, M. (2011) 'Mergers and National Champions', in Falck, O., Gollier, C., and Woessmann, L., eds, *Industrial Policy for National Champions*, Cambridge: Massachusetts Institute of Technology, 91–118.

Müller, A. (2012) 'Deal rettet die Bilanz', *Stuttgarter Zeitung*, available: <http://www.stuttgarter-zeitung.de/inhalt.morgan.stanley-enbw-deal-rettet-die-bilanz.ef587522-c98d-460b-a5c9-10315d69cfa4.html> [accessed 14 February 2014].

Muñóz, R. (2007) 'Manuel Pizarro y Javier de Paz, nuevos consejeros de Telefónica', *El País*, available: <http://economia.elpais.com/economia/2007/12/18/actualidad/1197966781_850215.html> [accessed 5 March 2014].

Neven, D., Nuttall, R., and Seabright, P. (1993) *Merger in Daylight: The Economics and Politics of European Merger Control*, London: Centre for Economic Policy Research.

Nguyen, S. V. and Ollinger, M. (2009) 'Mergers and Acquisitions, Employment, Wages, and Plant Closures in the US Meat Product Industries', *Agribusiness*, 25(1), 70–89.

Nonnenkamp, M. E. (2011) *Volkswagen: A Car for the People*, United States of America: CreateSpace Independent Publishing Platform.

Norman, L. (2013) 'EU Court Opinion: Germany Fully Complied with Volkswagen Law 2007 Ruling', *The Wall Street Journal*, available: <http://online.wsj.com/article/BT-CO-20130529-702001.html> [accessed 1 October 2013].

Park, W. G. and Sonenshine, R. (2012) 'Impact of Horizontal Mergers on Research & Development and Patenting: Evidence from Merger Challenges in the US', *Journal of Industry, Competition, and Trade*, 12(1), 143–67.

Parker, D. (2004) *The UK's Privatisation Experiment: The Passage of Time Permits a Sober Assessment*, CESifo Working Paper No. 1126, February.

Parker, J. and Majumdar, A. (2011) *UK Merger Control*, Oxford: Hart Publishing.

Reuters (2013) 'Deals of the Day—Mergers and Acquisitions', available: <http://www.reuters.com/article/2013/05/24/deals-day-idUSL3N0E51XY20130524> [accessed 3 January 2014].

Reuters (2011) 'Endesa Hire Former Spanish PM Aznar as Advisor', available: <http://www.reuters.com/article/2011/01/11/endesa-aznar-idUSLDE70A1AP20110111> [accessed 3 January 2014].

Ringbeck, J. and Schneiderbauer, D. (2007) *Time for Take-Off: Setting New Strategic Directions for Mid-Sized European Airlines*, Germany: Strategy& (formerly Booz and Company), available: <http://www.strategyand.pwc.com/media/file/Time-for-Take-Off.pdf> [accessed 12 June 2014].

Rizzi, C., Guo, L., and Christian, J. (2012) *Mergers and Acquisitions and Takeovers in China. A Legal and Cultural Guide to New Forms of Investment*, Alphen aan den Rijn, The Netherlands: Kluwer Law International.

Robson, G. (2009) *Jaguar XK8: The Complete Story, Crowood Autoclassics*, Ramsbury, Marlborough: Crowood Press.

Rodger, B. (2009) 'Merger Action Group v. Secretary of State for BERR: External Control of the Scottish Economy, Merger Control and the Scottish 'Ring-fence': the Lloyds TSB/HBOS Merger', *Competition Policy International: The Global Resource for Antitrust and Competition Policy*, available: <https://www.competitionpolicyinternational.com/emmerger-action-group-v-secretary-of-state-for-berremexternal-control-of-the-scottish-economy-merger-control-and-the-scottish-ring-fence-the-lloydstsbhbos-merger> [accessed 5 October 2013].

Sanchez Graells, A. (2012) 'Public Procurement and State Aid: Reopening the Debate?', *Public Procurement Law Review*, 21(6), 205–12.

Santagostino, A. (1993) *Fiat e Alfa Romeo: Una privatizzazione riuscita?*, Milan: Unicopli.

Schäfer, D. (2009) 'Just Another Week at the Office for Piëch', *Financial Times*, available: <http://www.ft.com/intl/cms/s/0/f94c8e7e-787c-11de-bb06-00144feabdc0.html> [accessed 2 April 2014].

Schmidt, V. A. (2003) 'French Capitalism Transformed, yet Still a Third Variety of Capitalism', *Economy and Society*, 32(4), 526–54.

Schütte M. (2013) 'Sector-Specific Litigation and the Rules on State Aid: Future Challenges and Limits of the Automotive Sector', paper delivered at the University of Luxembourg, 20 September.

Segal, J. (2011) 'Game Changer', *Institutional Investor*, December/January, 48–54; 93–94.

Sharp, T. (2013) 'SSE's Marchant to Quit Job in Summer', *Herald Scotland*, available: <http://www.heraldscotland.com/business/company-news/sses-marchant-to-quit-job-in-summer.19998937> [accessed 23 January 2014].

Shea, E. J. and Chari, R. (2006) *Policy Formulation and Feedback in EU Merger*, IIIS Discussion Paper 147, Trinity College Dublin.

Sherman, A. J. and Hart, M. A. (2006) *Merger and Acquisitions for A to Z*, New York: Amacom.

Shipman, A. (2004) *The Globalization Myth*, London: Icon Books.

Shonfield, A. (1965) *Modern Capitalism*, Oxford: Oxford University Press.

Soares, A. G. (2008) ' "National Champions" Rhetoric in European Law', *World Competition*, 31(3), 353–68.

Sparaco, P. (1997) 'Lufthansa Nears Final Step Toward Full Privatization', *Aviation Week & Space Technology*, 147(10), 20–1.

Spiegel Online (2012) 'Chronologie: Die Affäre Mappus', available: <http://www.spiegel.de/politik/deutschland/chronologie-der-affaere-mappus-und-enbw-a-843856.html> [accessed 7 February 2014].

Stacey, S. (2010) 'The EU's Register of Interest Representatives: Why and how a company was "named and famed" ' Presentation given at Policy Institute (TCD) Conference, International Trends in Lobbying Regulation: Lessons Learned for Ireland, December.

Steen, M. (2013) 'Lufthansa Investors Back Mayrhuber as New Chairman', *Financial Times*, available: <http://www.ft.com/intl/cms/s/0/5b0aea7a-b72b-11e2-841e-00144feabdc0.html> [accessed 15 December 2013].

Stephen, R. (2000) *Vehicle of Influence: Building a European Car Market*, Ann Arbour: University of Michigan Press.

Stigler, G. J. (1950) 'Monopoly and Oligopoly by Merger', *The American Economic Review*, 40(2), 23–34.

Stiglitz, J. (2002) *Globalization and its Discontents*, London: Allen Lane.

Tagliabue, J. (2000) 'Business; Renault Pins Its Survival on a Global Gamble', *The New York Times*, available: <http://www.nytimes.com/2000/07/02/business/business-renault-pins-its-survival-on-a-global-gamble.html?pagewanted=all&src=pm> [accessed 1 October 2013].

Tagliabue, J. (2003) 'Air France and KLM to Merge, Europe's No. 1 Airline', *The New York Times*, available: <http://www.nytimes.com/2003/10/01/business/air-france-and-klm-to-merge-europe-s-no-1-airline.html> [accessed 27 December 2013].

Thatcher, M. (2006) 'Europe and the Reform of National Regulatory Institutions: A Comparison of Britain, France, and Germany', in *Council of European Studies Conference*, Chicago.

Thatcher, M. (2009) *Internationalisation and Economic Institutions: Comparing European Experiences*, Oxford: Oxford University Press.

The Economist (2009) 'Volkswagen and Porsche: My Other Car Firm's a Porsche', available: <http://www.economist.com/node/14265041> [accessed 4 June 2013].

The Economist (2012) 'A Rush of Power', available: <http://www.economist.com/node/21557602> [accessed 28 June 2014].

The Guardian (2011) 'British Airways Trades for Last Time Ahead of Iberia Merger', available: <http://www.theguardian.com/business/2011/jan/20/british-airways-trades-last-time-merger> [accessed 3 January 2014].

The Independent (2004) 'Scottish & Southern buys Fiddlers Ferry', available: <http://www.independent.co.uk/news/business/news/scottish-amp-southern-buys-fiddlers-ferry-6164449.html> [accessed 11 February 2014].

The New York Times (1988) 'German Enthusiasm Builds for Volkswagen Stock Sale', available: <http://www.nytimes.com/1988/03/24/business/german-enthusiasm-builds-for-volkswagen-stock-sale.html> [accessed 15 July 2013].

The New York Times (1994) 'A Privatizing of Lufthansa', available: <http://www.nytimes.com/1994/03/07/business/a-privatizing-of-lufthansa.html> [accessed 10 December 2013].

The New York Times (2001) 'World Business Briefing: Europe; Iberia Offering Price is Lowered', available: <http://www.nytimes.com/2001/04/03/business/world-business-briefing-europe-iberia-offering-price-is-lowered.html> [accessed 20 November 2013].

The New York Times (2012) 'Renault–Nissan to Take Control of Russian Automaker', available: <http://www.nytimes.com/2012/05/04/business/global/renault-nissan-to-take-control-of-avtovaz.html?_r=0> [accessed 12 March 2014].

The New York Times (2013) 'Volkswagen Expanding Production in China', available: <http://www.nytimes.com/2013/09/26/business/global/volkswagen-expanding-production-in-china.html?_r=0> [accessed 17 March 2014].

The Scotsman (2008) 'Ian Marchant Interview: Power behind Scotland's Biggest Firm', available: <http://www.scotsman.com/business/ian-marchant-interview-power-behind-scotland-s-biggest-firm-1-1146889> [accessed 1 March 2014].

Torello, A. (2012) 'Top EU Court Backs EDF on State Aid', *The Wall Street Journal*, available: <http://online.wsj.com/news/articles/SB10001424052702303830204577448281008385736> [accessed 22 February 2014].

Towers Watson (2010) *The World's 500 Largest Asset Managers*, available: <http://www.towerswatson.com/en-HK/Insights/IC-Types/Survey-Research-Results/2010/10/The-Worlds-500-Largest-Asset-Managers-Year-End-2009> [accessed 10 July 2012].

Tran, M. (2004) 'BA to Sell Qantas Stake', *The Guardian*, available: <http://www.theguardian.com/business/2004/sep/08/theairlineindustry.britishairways> [accessed 17 December 2013].

UK Power (2012) 'The Big Six Energy Companies', available: <http://www.ukpower.co.uk/the-big-six-energy-companies> [accessed 12 March 2014].

Ulijn, J., Duysters, G., and Meijer, E. eds (2010) *Strategic Alliances, Mergers, and Acquisitions: The Influence of Culture on Successful Cooperation*, Cheltenham: Edward Elgar Publishing.

Van Gerven, D. (2010) *Cross-Border Mergers in Europe*, Cambridge: Cambridge University Press.

Van Houtte, B. (2000) 'Air Transport', in Geradin, D., ed., *The Liberalization of State Monopolies in the European Union and Beyond*, London: Kluwer Law International, 67–98.

Veljanovski, C. G. and Bentley, M. (1987) *Selling the State: Privatisation in Britain*, London: Weidenfeld and Nicolson.

Vermeylen, J. and Vande Velde, I., eds (2012) *European Cross-Border Mergers and Reorganisations*, Oxford: Oxford University Press.

Vickers, J. (2001) 'International Mergers: The View from a National Authority', Speech to the *Annual Conference on International Antitrust Law and Policy*, Fordham University School of Law, New York.

Vickers, J. and Wright, V. (1989) 'The Politics of Industrial Privatisation in Western Europe: an Overview', in Vickers, J. and Wright, V. (eds), *The Politics of Privatization in Western Europe*, London: Frank Cass and Company Limited.

Vickers J. and Yarrow G. (1988) *Privatization an Economic Analysis*, Cambridge: MIT Press.

Vickers, J. and Yarrow, G. (1991) 'Economic Perspectives on Privatization', *Journal of Economic Perspectives*, 5(2), 111–32.

Villalonga, B. (2000) 'Privatization and Efficiency: Differentiating Ownership Effects from Political, Organizational, and Dynamic Effects', *Journal of Economic Behaviour and Organization*, 42(1), 43–74.

Volkswagen (2013a) '1904–1936 The Dream of the Volkswagen', available: <http://www.chronik.volkswagenag.com> [accessed 2 September 2013].

Volkswagen (2013b) '1937–1945 The Foundation of the Volkwagen Plant', available. <http://www.chronik.volkswagenag.com> [accessed 2 September 2013].

Volkswagen (2013c) '1945–1949 The British and Their Works', available: <http://www.chronik.volkswagenag.com> [accessed 2 September 2013].

Volkswagen (2013d) '1950–60 Internationalization and Mass Production in Germany's Economic Miracle', available: <http://www.chronik.volkswagenag.com> [accessed 2 September 2013].

Webb, T. and Wearden, G. (2010) 'British Airways Name Will Disappear from FTSE if Iberia Merger Goes Ahead', *The Guardian*, available: <http://www.theguardian.com/business/2010/apr/08/british-airways-name-to-disappear> [accessed 10 December 2013].

Weiss, R. (2013) 'Lufthansa Board Stares Down Investors in Chairman Dispute', *Bloomberg*, available: <http://www.bloomberg.com/news/2013-05-06/lufthansa-s-mayrhuber-said-to-renew-supervisory-board-candidacy.html> [accessed 15 December 2013].

Welch, J. R. and Fremond, O. (1998) *The Case-by-Case Approach to Privatization: Techniques and Examples, World Bank Technical Papers, Book 403*, Washington: World Bank Publications.

Woll, C. (2008) *Firm Interests: How Governments Shape Business Lobbying on Global Trade*, Ithaca, New York: Cornell University Press.

World Nuclear News (2010) 'EDF sells EnBW stake to state', available: <http://www.world-nuclear-news.org/C-EdF_sells_EnBW_stake_to_state-0712107.html> [accessed 14 February 2014].

Wright, V. (1994) 'Industrial privatisation in Western Europe: pressures, problems and paradoxes,' in Wright, V, ed, *Privatization in Western Europe: Pressures, Problems and Paradoxes*, London: Pinter Publishers.

Wright, V. (1998) *Coordinating the Privatization Process in France*, Nuffield College, unpublished.

Xiaoyang, L. (2012) 'Workers, Unions, and Takeovers', *Journal of Labour Research*, 33(4), 443–60.

Young, S. (1986) 'The Nature of Privatisation in Britain, 1979–85', *West European Politics*, 9(2), 235–52.

Zademach, H.-M. and Rodríguez-Pose, A. (2009) 'Cross-border M&As and the Changing Economic Geography of Europe', *European Planning Series*, 17(5), 765–89.

Index

Index

Index

Printed and bound by CPI Group (UK) Ltd, Croydon, CR0 4YY